Data and Research on Human Trafficking: A Global Survey

Offprint of the Special Issue of
International Migration Vol. 43 (1/2) 2005

edited by
Frank Laczko and Elzbieta Gozdziak

IOM International Organization for Migration

ACKNOWLEDGEMENTS

This publication has benefited from the cooperation of many individuals from within IOM and outside. The generous support of the Government of Italy in supporting this study is gratefully acknowledged. The Government of Italy also hosted a conference in Rome in May 2004 where the papers in this volume were first presented. Thanks are due also to Mr. Luca Dall'oligio at IOM's mission in New York who helped to initiate this study when he was IOM's Chief of Mission in Rome. We should also like to thank Mr. Peter Schatzer and all the IOM Rome staff who contributed to the preparation of the 2004 Rome conference, in particular Teresa Albano. Finally, a special thanks to Ilse Pinto-Dobernig for contributing to the meticulous proofreading and editing of all the texts in this volume, and Niusca Magalhaes, and the IOM Research and Publications staff in Geneva for their inputs.

It has been a pleasure working with the authors whose papers are included in this volume. All submissions to this publication were peer-reviewed by an international panel of anonymous reviewers who offered thoughtful and detailed comments. Although they remain unnamed, the editors warmly thank each of them.

Frank Laczko and Elzbieta Gozdziak

Data and Research on Human Trafficking: A Global Survey

TABLE OF CONTENTS

Introduction

Data and Research on Human Trafficking

Earlier versions of the papers in this volume were initially prepared for a conference held in Rome on 27-28 May 2004, organized by the International Organization for Migration's (IOM) Research Division and hosted by the Government of Italy. One of the aims of this conference was to take stock of current research on trafficking after a decade of substantial growth in the number of publications on the subject. The Rome conference discussed a number of key issues related to trafficking research, including questions such as, what are the strengths and weaknesses of current research on trafficking? How can research and data on trafficking be improved?

Most of the papers in this volume present a broad overview of current research and data on trafficking in particular regions of the world. Nine of the articles focus on specific regions and three of the articles explore issues relating to research methods. The nine regional papers do not provide a detailed summary of the results of studies on trafficking, but rather try to assess the type and quality of research that has been conducted and discuss priorities for further research. The availability and quality of data on trafficking are also discussed in each of these papers. The papers by Tydlum and Brunovskis, Andrees and van der Linden, and Brennan examine in more detail questions related to research methodologies and data collection techniques.

As pointed out by Tydlum and Brunovskis, one of the most challenging problems facing researchers is the fact that most of the populations relevant to the study of human trafficking, such as victims/survivors of trafficking for sexual exploitation, traffickers, or illegal migrants are part of a "hidden population", i.e. it is almost impossible to establish a sampling frame and draw a representative sample of the population. The papers dealing with research methods highlight some of the key problems encountered when conducting trafficking research. They have been placed at the beginning of this volume as trafficking research has been criticized in the past for saying little about the methods used to collect and analyse data (see, in particular, the chapter by Kelly). One of the aims of this publication is to suggest ways in which the research methods used to study trafficking could be made more robust. The volume also includes a human trafficking bibliography organized by region and the Notes and Commentary Section includes a meeting summary on "Identifying and serving child victims of trafficking".

MORE RESEARCH
AND PUBLICATIONS ON TRAFFICKING

Combating human trafficking has become an increasingly important political priority for many governments around the world. At the national level, greater efforts and resources are being devoted to combating this problem, and there is also widespread agreement in the international community on the need for a multilateral response, as reflected in the UN Protocols on trafficking and smuggling signed in Palermo, Italy, in 2000.

The organization of the largest European Union (EU) conference on Preventing and Combating Trafficking in Human Beings, held in Brussels from 18 to 20 September 2002, is but one example of the political priority being accorded to combating human trafficking. The conference brought together more than 1,000 representatives of European institutions, EU Member States, candidate countries, and relevant developing countries drawn from governments, international organizations, and non-governmental organizations (NGOs). The conference issued the Brussels Declaration, which outlines a set of policy recommendations for the EU in the area of human trafficking, adopted by the EU Council on 8 May 2003. The Commission subsequently appointed an Experts Group on Trafficking in Human Beings (see EC, 2004) and is currently preparing a new Communication on Trafficking in Human Beings, which will set out the Commission's approach to tackling trafficking in human beings.

In the United States, trafficking has also become a high-profile issue. In October 2001, the US State Department created the Office to Monitor and Combat Trafficking in Persons, which publishes an annual report assessing global efforts to combat trafficking. In its June 2004 report, the State Department reviews the efforts made by 140 governments to combat trafficking around the world. Funding for counter-trafficking programmes has also increased substantially in recent years. For example, in 2003 the US Government alone supported 190 anti-trafficking programmes in 92 countries, totalling US$ 72 million, an increase from 118 programmes in 55 countries in FY 2001 (US Government, 2004).

Although the origins of the trafficking debate date back to the end of the nine-teenth century (Derks, 2000), the rapid rise in the number of publications on the subject of trafficking reflects the mounting national and international concern with human trafficking and the available means to combat it. While not all of the publications present new research, there is little doubt that research on the sub-ject of trafficking has become increasingly urgent and widespread, spanning historical, political, humanitarian, legal, and socio-economic dimensions. IOM alone has published more than 40 studies on the subject since 1995. Figure 1, based on a review of titles in a bibliography on trafficking prepared by IOM, gives another indication of this growth. More than 260 titles are found in the bibliography, even though it contains only the main titles that could easily be found in English. As can be seen, most of the titles were published after 2000. Studies on trafficking have been conducted in nearly every major region of the world over the last decade, though the bulk of publications and research can be found in Europe and Asia (see Figure 2). This is confirmed in the many papers in this volume, which show that relatively little research on trafficking has been conducted in the Americas, in Africa, and the Middle East.

FIGURE 1

INCREASE IN RESEARCH ON TRAFFICKING

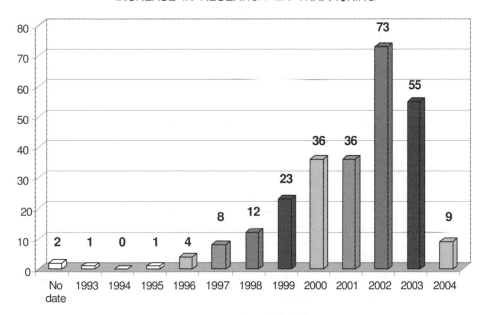

Note: N=260 titles

Source: "Human trafficking bibliography", IOM, Geneva.

FIGURE 2

REGIONAL DISTRIBUTION OF STUDIES ON TRAFFICKING

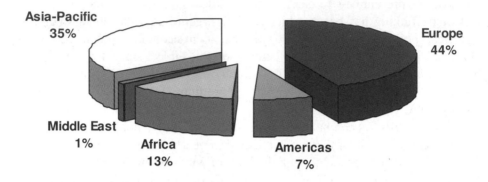

Note: N=260 titles

Source: "Human trafficking bibliography", IOM, Geneva.

ACTION-ORIENTED, SMALL-SCALE NATIONAL STUDIES

One of the strengths of trafficking research is its action-oriented approach, with studies often designed to prepare the ground for counter-trafficking interventions. Since the mid-1990s, a great number of reports covering individual countries and regions have been produced. These studies have usually sought to examine the whole process of human trafficking, investigating the causes and describing the process of recruitment, transport, and exploitation of the victims/survivors. A presentation of existing legal and policy frameworks has regularly been part of these national case studies. A set of recommendations for further action usually completes such reports, most of which aim to inform and contribute to the development of counter-trafficking projects and strategies.

Given that many trafficking cases remain undiscovered, or that victims/survivors of trafficking are often afraid to talk about their experiences, it is very difficult to obtain first-hand information from those who have been exploited. A great deal of research on trafficking is, therefore, based on relatively small samples of survivors, usually identified by law enforcement agencies or persons assisted by NGOs or international organizations. The actual ratio of assisted survivors to the total number of victims is unknown, meaning that studies based only on assisted cases may not be representative of the total number of trafficked persons which may remain undiscovered.

The focus on action-oriented and applied research has meant that studies are often conducted within a fairly short time frame, usually six to nine months, and with limited resources. There has been less funding for long-term research to investigate in more detail the causes of trafficking and the best ways to prevent and combat it, or to make a detailed assessment of the impacts of different interventions and policy responses. There are very few comparative studies of trafficking based on extensive fieldwork in either country of origin or of destination. Most studies are also based on research conducted at one point in time, with little longitudinal research investigating the circumstances of individuals before, during, and after trafficking, including research to assess the extent to which survivors can achieve long-term self-sufficiency. To really understand the long-term impact of trafficking there is a need for more investigation into the experiences of survivors and the extent to which they are able to integrate or reintegrate into their communities and recover both physically and mentally from their ordeal.

There has been a tendency in these "baseline studies" to focus on supply-side questions, such as the factors that contribute to trafficking in countries of origin and the profile of those most at risk of being trafficked, and less on demand-side questions, such as the factors in destination countries that contribute to the existence of, and a market for, trafficking.

Several authors in this volume also make the point that research on trafficking has tended to focus a great deal on the trafficking of women and children for sexual exploitation, neglecting other forms of trafficking. In order to partly redress this imbalance, one of the papers in this volume, prepared by researchers at the International Labour Organization (ILO), specifically discusses the problems of researching trafficking for forced labour.

Another criticism made by a number of authors in this volume is that there has been relatively little independent evaluation of counter-trafficking policies and programmes to assess the real impact and effectiveness of different interventions. Without such research it is difficult to identify best practices and assess which countries have been most successful in their efforts to combat trafficking.

This volume also shows that most research on trafficking has been concerned with international trafficking, and less with internal trafficking inside particular countries. Internal and international trafficking tend to be studied as though they were completely distinct and separate phenomena, and few studies have tried to investigate the linkages between the two. Is internal trafficking a stepping stone to international trafficking? Does international trafficking have a detrimental effect on those left behind, and does this lead to more internal trafficking?

LACK OF AGREEMENT ON WHAT SHOULD BE STUDIED

In October 1994, IOM organized a global conference in Geneva, entitled International Responses to Trafficking in Migrants and the Safeguarding of Migrants' Rights. A quick review of the papers presented at this meeting indicates how much the definition of trafficking has changed over the last decade.

In 1994, trafficking was defined very differently and without specific reference to exploitation (IOM, 1994: 2):

> International migratory movements will be considered "trafficking" if the following conditions are met:
>
> - Money (or another form of payment) changes hands.
> - A facilitator – the trafficker – is involved.
> - An international border is crossed.
> - Entry is illegal.
> - The movement is voluntary.

The above definition is more akin to the current international definition of smuggling in human beings. According to the 2000 UN Convention against Transnational Organized Crime, the "'smuggling of migrants' shall mean the procurement, in order to obtain, directly or indirectly, a financial or other material benefit, of the illegal entry of a person into a State Party of which the person is not a national or a permanent resident".

By the end of the 1990s, a wider and more inclusive approach was developed, resulting in a broader definition of trafficking, which was included in the "United Nations Protocol to Prevent, Suppress and Punish Trafficking in Persons, supplementing the UN Convention against Transnational Organized Crime", adopted by the UN General Assembly in late 2000:

> "Trafficking in persons" shall mean the recruitment, transportation, transfer, harbouring or receipt of persons, by means of the threat or use of force or other forms of coercion, of abduction, of fraud, of deception, of the abuse of power or of a position of vulnerability, or of the giving of payments or benefits to achieve the consent of a person having control over another person, for the purpose of exploitation.

Even if there is agreement at the international level on the legal definition of trafficking, researchers disagree on how trafficking should be defined and studied. This new definition has not resolved the problem of what precisely is meant by the term "trafficking", and what should be the focus of studies on the subject. Many of the papers in this volume discuss the problems involved in defin-

ing trafficking and developing an operational definition for the purpose of research and data gathering. For example, Gozdziak and Collett, in a paper about
trafficking research in North America, point out that the existence of a new legal
definition of trafficking does not mean that the term is used in a uniform way by
researchers. A review of the North American literature indicates that trafficking
can be defined in quite different ways. Some researchers, for example, label all
sex workers as trafficked persons, believing that no one would willingly submit
to such an activity, whilst others make a distinction between voluntary and
forced prostitution. Others argue that it is not always easy to differentiate between smuggling and trafficking, and that this has to be kept in mind when
conducting research on trafficking (see Kelly, this volume).

MORE DATA, BUT POOR INDICATORS OF TRAFFICKING

Another change that has occurred since 1994 is that greater efforts have been
made to estimate the scale of trafficking and to produce more and better statistics
on the phenomenon (Laczko and Gramegna, 2003). It is important to point this
out, because commentators frequently complain about the dearth of reliable
data on trafficking, without acknowledging that there have been some positive
developments in this field. Whilst it is certainly true, as many authors in this
volume argue, that current national statistics and global figures are often no
more than "guesstimates", several new initiatives have been launched during the
last decade to try to improve our understanding of trafficking data and to generate more and more reliable data. These efforts are discussed in more detail
below.

Many of the contributors to this volume highlight the current lack of reliable
data on trafficking and argue that the collection of better data is essential to
combat trafficking more effectively. Most of the regional articles highlight
the lack of comparable regional data, and the lack of sharing of existing data
between states, partly because states are reticent to share what is sometimes
confidential information.

At the national level the situation is not much better. Given the fairly recent
acceptance of the new international definition of trafficking, relatively few governments collect trafficking data systematically. In many countries it is still
common to mingle data relating to trafficking, smuggling, and irregular migration.

Only a few countries are currently able to provide official statistics on trends in
trafficking over several years, making it difficult to accurately establish the
extent to which trafficking may be increasing, as is so often suggested. In

Europe, the German Federal Office of Criminal Investigation (Bundeskriminalamt, BKA) and the Dutch National Rapporteur on Trafficking in Human Beings are among the few providers of national data. The Netherlands, by establishing a national focal point, has been able to map out relevant data collected by different agencies in the country, which has served as a basis for the Dutch National Rapporteur's reports (IOM, 2003).

However, even in Germany and the Netherlands the data have their limitations. The data from both countries refer primarily to cases of trafficking in women for the purpose of prostitution and do not include trafficking in relation to other activities, nor do they include trafficked men. It is also unclear to what extent fluctuations in the statistics are due to a genuine rise in cases of trafficking, or to better police enforcement efforts and improved assistance from NGOs (Laczko and Gramegna, 2003: 183).

Some of the sharpest criticism of trafficking data has been directed against current global estimates of trafficking. Gozdziak and Collett, and Kelly question the merits of producing global estimates of trafficking without a good explanation of how the figures were arrived at. The US State Department, for example, has produced the oft-quoted estimates of the size of the trafficked population world-wide: 800,000 to 900,000 annually. Information provided by the US State Department at the IOM conference in Rome, where the papers in this volume were first presented, includes a brief description of the statistical methods employed to calculate the estimates, but does not explain the methodology used to arrive at the baseline data sources.

There are many reasons why data on trafficking are so poor (Laczko and Gramegna, 2003). Trafficking is a clandestine activity, and most cases probably go unreported because victims are reluctant to go to the authorities, or are unable to do so because of intimidation and fear of reprisals. Most law enforcement agencies give low priority to combating trafficking. If countries have no specific trafficking laws, trafficking crimes may be reported under other headings. In developing countries the capacity to collect data may be very weak.

NEW EFFORTS TO IMPROVE DATA COLLECTION

Despite all these difficulties, a number of new projects have been launched in recent years to promote the better collection, sharing, and analysis of trafficking data. For example, UNESCO with its "Trafficking Statistics Project", based in Bangkok, produced a practical Internet tool to provide worldwide data on trafficking (www.unescobkk.org). It not only aims to assemble trafficking statistics from a variety of sources, but also discusses the methodology used to obtain them.

Since 1999, IOM has been collecting data from persons assisted under the Organization's counter-trafficking programmes. The Counter-Trafficking Module Database (CTM) was created to facilitate the management of assistance and voluntary return/reintegration activities for the victims. It also aims to increase understanding about the causes, processes, trends, and consequences of trafficking, thereby assisting IOM in its policy and project development, research, monitoring, and evaluation.

Because the data collection first began with the assistance programmes in the Balkans, its content is still weighted towards that region. In July 2004, the database contained data on 2,791 victims, representing some 35 nationalities (for 44 victims, or 1.6% of the total, the nationality was unknown (IOM, 2005)).

A global database on trafficking trends was established under the Global Programme Against Trafficking in Human Beings (GPAT) of the United Nations Office on Drugs and Crime (UNODC). This database aims to systematically collect and collate open-source information that can be compared between different countries and regions. The sources used were research reports and statistics compiled and published by authorities, intergovernmental organizations, NGOs, academic institutions, and the media. By June 2004, information from 500 sources had been entered, most originating from industrialized countries. The collected data are divided into country reports, profiles (characteristics of victims of trafficking or traffickers), and trafficking routes.

Various regional initiatives have also been taken. In the Balkans, the Stability Pact Task Force on Trafficking in Human Beings has operated a Regional Clearing Point (RCP) since 2002, responsible for the creation of a regional database on human trafficking. The first annual report on victims of trafficking in southeastern Europe provides verified figures on the number of victims of trafficking identified and assisted in the seven countries and two areas (Kosovo and Montenegro) covered by the Clearing Point, and describes assistance and protection mechanisms for victims of trafficking. The report also outlines gaps and recognizes good practices and measures created to assist victims of trafficking in the region.

CONCLUSIONS

In recent years, progress has been made towards the development of a common understanding of human trafficking and the establishment of international legal norms regarding trafficking in persons. The amount of research on the subject has grown significantly and it is difficult to find regions of the world that have not been included in a trafficking study. We also have more data about trafficking. Global estimates have been prepared and several initiatives have been taken, mainly by international organizations, to collate trafficking data from a wide range of sources. All of this represents progress, but this introduction and the later papers in this volume also highlight many weaknesses in current research and data collection on trafficking.

Much research on trafficking sets out basically to show that trafficking is a problem and tends to be limited to mapping routes and identifying the main countries of origin and destination. To move beyond the "snapshot", short-term approach typical of much existing research, and studies that only focus on one type of exploitation, we need longer-term research, using more comprehensive approaches, and involving both countries of origin and countries of destination.

Trafficking crosses so many disciplinary and mandate boundaries that there is a need for both more interdisciplinary research and research which looks at trafficking issues from a range of different perspectives, including migration, human rights, health, law enforcement, and the like.

There has also been a tendency to focus on studying the "victims", and less attention has been given to studying the traffickers, the clients, and law enforcement agencies who may be involved in different ways in creating the conditions under which trafficking can flourish. Nor have there been many systematic studies of the role of actors involved in the fight against trafficking, such as service providers, law enforcement agencies, and NGOs.

We also need to move beyond stating that trafficking is a problem to assessing in more detail how well we are dealing with this problem. In short, policy approaches should become more evidence-based, drawing on the results of relevant research and evaluations. We need to know much more about the impact of trafficking, not only on the survivors but also their families and communities and all those affected by it. There is a need for donors to give much greater priority to evaluation research, which can help to determine the effectiveness of different programmes and policy approaches.

If our understanding of trafficking is to improve, we also need to find ways to generate much better data and indicators of the problem.

The existing data are most often either general estimates created on the basis of unclear methodologies, or administrative data kept by the various involved authorities or organizations on the victims they assist. The latter, fragmentary datasets cannot be collated into national figures nor compared at international level.

Even without investing substantial new resources, much more could be done to fully exploit the existing information and make it more widely available (e.g. by promoting the sharing of information among agencies working to combat trafficking both within and between states).

In addition, agencies combating trafficking should be encouraged to collect data systematically. As illustrated earlier, IOM's counter-trafficking database provides one example of what agencies could do to collect data on trafficking in a more systematic fashion. The recent Report of the European Experts Group on Trafficking in Human Beings suggests a number of other areas where action could be taken in Europe and which might also be applied elsewhere. For example, the Experts Group recommends the establishment in each EU country of a National Rapporteur or national focal point to pool existing data from a wide range of sources, and to promote the sharing of information between different agencies involved in combating trafficking. Furthermore, in order to make national data comparable, common guidelines for the collection of data should be developed, both with regard to the type of data and to the methods used (EC, 2004: 78).

Frank Laczko
Research and Publications Division
International Organization for Migration, Geneva, Switzerland.

REFERENCES

Derks, A.
  2000   "Combating trafficking in South-East Asia: a review of policy and programme responses", *Migration Research Series*, no.2, IOM, Geneva.
European Commission
  2004   *Report of the Experts Group on Trafficking in Human Beings*, Brussels, 22 December, European Commission, Directorate-General Justice, Freedom and Security.
International Organization for Migration (IOM)
  1994   "Eleventh seminar international response to trafficking in migrants and the safeguarding of migrant rights", October, IOM, Geneva.

2003   "Challenges and approaches in international migration data management",
          Bali Conference Ad Hoc Expert Group 1, Colombo.

Laczko, F., and M. Gramegna
2003   "Developing better indicators of human trafficking", *Brown Journal of
          World Affairs*, X(1).

US State Department
2004   *Trafficking in Persons Report*, Office to Monitor and Combat Trafficking
          in Persons, 5 June, www.state/gov/g/tiprpt/2004.

Describing the Unobserved: Methodological Challenges in Empirical Studies on Human Trafficking

Guri Tyldum and Anette Brunovskis*

INTRODUCTION

As the international awareness to the problem of trafficking in persons has increased, the number of studies and publications on the topic has escalated. A substantial number of these publications set out to describe the various elements associated with human trafficking, including estimates of the scope of the phenomenon, descriptions of trends, and characteristics of victims (Kelly, 2002). However, the methodologies applied are not always well suited for these purposes, and inferences are often made based on very limited data. This has lead to an urgent call for the improvement of research methods to study human trafficking (see for instance Kelly, 2002; Laczko and Gramegna, 2003; EU, 2004).

The concern is not only one of academic pedantry; inadequate data collection methods might result in descriptions that have little to do with reality. Consequently, there is a danger that policies and interventions developed based on these findings will be ineffective (Kelly, 2002). In regard to the use of numbers in the human rights field, Mike Dottridge (2003: 82) argues:

> Some human rights activists argue that exaggeration is not a major problem, as long as attention ends up being given to whatever abuses are occurring. This seems to be a rather idealistic, not to say naïve approach, which ignores the damage that can be done by misrepresenting the scale of a problem. [...] an inaccurate estimate of the problem is likely to result in a remedy being proposed that is equally inappropriate.

---

* Fafo Institute for Applied International Studies, Oslo, Norway.

The action needed to deal with human trafficking from Hungary, for example, is different if the annual number of estimated victims is 200, as opposed to 1,000 victims. Overestimating the extent of a phenomenon can have equally negative consequences as underestimating it. Uncritically using or publishing findings not based on sound methodologies may result in misinformation and hinder the creation of relevant policies and appropriate programmes.

Research in the field of human trafficking is difficult for many reasons. Perhaps the most challenging factor is that most of the populations relevant to the study of human trafficking, such as prostitutes, traffickers, victims/survivors, or illegal immigrants constitute so-called *hidden populations*. A hidden population is a group of individuals for whom the size and boundaries are unknown, and for whom no sampling frame exists. Furthermore, membership in hidden populations often involves stigmatized or illegal behaviour, leading individuals to refuse to cooperate, or give unreliable answers to protect their privacy (Heckathorn, 1997). For empirical studies, this brings other challenges, and requires approaches different from those commonly used for more easily observable populations.

Many policy areas related to human trafficking, such as prostitution, labour market protection, and immigration laws, are highly politicized, and this further complicates the situation. Key actors with access to relevant information can have political agendas that may influence how they choose to use the information they have at their disposal (Vandekerckhove, 2003). A substantial number of publications on trafficking for sexual exploitation are influenced by political debates surrounding these topics. While the importance of a continuous social debate on ideological and moral issues should not be downplayed, there is now a need for more systematic empirical knowledge on the mechanisms of human trafficking, who it influences, and how it can be countered.

In this paper we will discuss the production of *various types of data* on human trafficking, analyse existing data and research, and suggest methods for improving enhanced data collection techniques and developing new methodologies. We will focus both on the development of estimates of victims of trafficking, as well as the production of data that describes the characteristics of this group. The discussion will be based on a review of publications on trafficking for sexual exploitation in Europe (Tyldum et al., forthcoming), as well as our own experiences from the study "Crossing Borders", on transnational prostitution and trafficking in Oslo (Brunovskis and Tyldum, 2004). During our research we found some answers, but also met with several questions and challenges relating to obtaining the best possible quality of data. We hope that our experience in this field may be of use to others working on the same topic, a research field that indeed holds great challenges, but through its urgency and importance also great rewards.

A STUDY OF HUMAN TRAFFICKING
AND TRANSNATIONAL PROSTITUTION IN OSLO

The study "Crossing Borders" was financed by the Norwegian Plan of Action for Combating Trafficking in Women and Children. The aim of the study was two-fold: (1) to gain a better understanding of the prostitution arenas in Oslo in order to estimate the number of women selling sexual services and identify their basic characteristics, including ethnic and national origin; and (2) to explore and develop a better understanding of the mechanisms that make trafficking for sexual exploitation possible.

In order to acquire the broadest possible picture of the phenomenon, several different data collection methods were used, including qualitative and quantitative methodologies, rapid assessment methods (i.e. Capture-Recapture estimations of women in street prostitution), and a telephone survey of women in prostitution who operate through individual advertisements. The latter methodology was somewhat unorthodox, but highly successful. During a four-month period we systematically collected telephone numbers from different advertisements (print and electronic) for escort and massage services. These numbers were called during October 2004 to establish if they were still in use. Much to our surprise, we discovered that it was possible to obtain substantial information from these telephone conversations in order to develop a survey of the basic characteristics of women in prostitution who operate through advertisements. The survey had a response rate of more than 50 per cent, a response rate higher than many surveys in the overall population in Norway.[1] For women who refused to participate, language proficiency (Russian, English, or Norwegian) as well as type of accent were recorded, and used to adjust for non-response for the various national groups. An estimate of the total number of women working in this arena and their characteristics were developed based on the response rates in the various rounds of the survey, information given in the interviews on the number of telephones used per woman, and the number of women per telephone number.

While the telephone survey elicited interesting information, it did not allow us to determine the number of trafficking victims or provide taxonomy of the forms of exploitation they experienced. For reasons of data quality, as well as security for the respondents and interviewers, sensitive information on organizers and pimps was only recorded if the women volunteered this information. The aim of this part of the study was *not* to estimate the number of women trafficked, but to get a better understanding of this arena where human trafficking is known to take place, and to get information on basic background characteristics of a population of which victims of trafficking constitute a subpopulation.

In order to obtain a better understanding of the elements of force and exploitation in the Norwegian prostitution arena we conducted in-depth interviews with a wide variety of respondents, including women in prostitution, emancipated victims of trafficking, and various key respondents in Norway and abroad (for a more thorough presentation of methods and findings, see Brunovskis and Tyldum, 2004).

DETERMINING WHO TO COUNT

The question of numbers of victims of trafficking is in many ways fundamental. This is not because of quantitative idolatry, but because counting something presupposes two basic operations of key concern for researchers and policy makers alike: (1) conceptual identification, and (2) practical identification, i.e. being able to say "this is a victim of trafficking". From that information much else flows: targeting, identifying characteristics, rights and protection under international law, etc. (Pedersen and Sommerfelt, 2001).

In order to count the number of victims, or generally develop our understanding of trafficking in persons, we need to, first of all, define what constitutes trafficking, and what does not. An important step toward developing more coherent research on trafficking arrived with the establishment of a definition of trafficking in the United Nations Protocol to Prevent, Suppress, and Punish Trafficking in Persons (UN, 2000).[2] However, there are still some ambiguities inherent in this definition, and perhaps even more so, in the way it is commonly operationalized. Identification of trafficking victims demands clarification of the interpretation of the UN Protocol, in particular on aspects such as exploitation of the prostitution of others, and exploitation of a position of vulnerability.

Still, independent of the definition used, it is difficult to distinguish traits of victims of trafficking that are externally observable, that is, elements by which we can determine if a person is a victim of trafficking simply through observation. In order to determine if a person has been manipulated or lured, and the extent to which she has been exploited, the person has to give up this information herself. We will, therefore, argue that unambiguous classifications are most easily obtained through survey data.

Determining the stages of trafficking

A basic distinction should be drawn between the stages that a victim of trafficking can occupy in relation to the trafficking process. According to current knowledge, it is reasonable to distinguish between three main stages:

- Persons at risk of being trafficked,
- Current victims of trafficking, and
- Former victims of trafficking.

For each stage we generally want to know the number of people, their characteristics, and their probability of entering the next stage. Those are mainly quantitative concerns, but we are also interested in the much more qualitative question of *process*; how do they enter into one stage from another? And, when in a particular stage, how can their situation and freedom of action be described (Pedersen and Sommerfelt, 2001)?

In order to describe and understand these stages, we need to be comparative. Both in comparing the various stages in themselves, and in comparing with those that are outside. That is, in order to understand who is at risk of being trafficked, we need to compare the population of victims of trafficking with those who have not been subjected to this form of exploitation. Furthermore, we need to understand how variation in one stage influences the probability for entering the next, as well as the challenges and actions that victims face in the next stage of trafficking. Victims of trafficking may be exposed to conditions with large variation in forms of exploitation, coercion, and manipulation. These conditions are likely to influence his/her probability of getting out of the coerced situation, as well as his/her future actions and problems in the course of rehabilitation. While the first comparison (i.e. comparison of groups in different stages) is best facilitated with quantitative data, the second type of comparison is best facilitated through qualitative assessments, for instance, what anthropologists often refer to as life stories.

Time periods and estimates

If we wish to estimate the number of men and women who are current trafficking victims, it is necessary to specify for what time period the estimation is valid. The number of persons living under conditions that can be classified as trafficking at any given time may be significantly different from the number of persons trafficked for i.e. labour exploitation, organ removals, or prostitution every year. We need to know how long people in various groups stay in a particular stage, and how and when people move between stages, in order to understand and correctly interpret any number estimating the total amount of victims of trafficking.

For instance, in the prostitution arena in Oslo, we were able to establish that some 600 women worked in prostitution during the month of October 2003. Of these, one-third were of Norwegian origin, one-third were migrants with permanent residence or citizenship in Norway, and one-third were in Norway on short-term stays. Based on information on length of stay, and number of months worked in prostitution each year, we were able to estimate that a total of 1,100 different women work in prostitution in Oslo every year, and that among these, about 80 per cent are of non-Norwegian origin (Brunovskis and Tyldum, 2004).

ESTIMATION METHODS AND TARGET POPULATIONS

When making inferences from studies of small groups of individuals, it is necessary to consider whether these data are generalizable to larger populations. To our knowledge, there are no studies to date that can claim to be representative of all victims of trafficking within a region. Most current studies of victims of trafficking for sexual exploitation are based on studies of former victims described by, or discovered through, organizations or law enforcement bodies in connection with law enforcement intervention, involvement with a support agency, or within some form of return programme to their country of origin (Kelly, 2002). Another group of studies focus on arenas where systematic exploitation of migrants is known to take place (i.e. prostitution) (see for instance IOM, 1996a, 1996b; Kelly and Regan, 2000), while the final group of studies are based on data on migrants (IOM, 2001). As illustrated in Figure 1, these are populations where victims of trafficking make up a subpopulation (i.e. persons migrating or crossing borders), or populations that in themselves are subpopulations of victims of trafficking (i.e. victims of trafficking registered by law enforcement agencies). The ratio of assisted victims to the number of victims at large is unknown, as is the biases associated with the subpopulation. Furthermore, both the ratios and the biases are likely to vary strongly between regions and over time, making it very difficult to make inferences to the overall population.

Data of subpopulations of victims of trafficking

Data on trafficking cases registered by law enforcement or organizations administrating rehabilitation programmes in the countries of origin are commonly presented in analyses on human trafficking. While some studies mainly use these data to present minimum estimates of numbers of victims, and do not attempt to infer the overall population of victims of trafficking (see for instance Kelly and Regan, 2000; IOM, 1996b; Regional Clearing Point, 2003), these data are too often referred to as describing victims of trafficking as such, as well as differences between countries or regions (IOM, 2001; IOM Armenia, 2001; IOM Kosovo, 2002). While data on these subpopulations holds the advantage that they refer to a concrete population and are based on positive identification of victims, several problems associated with these data require great attention if they should be used for purposes such as developing victim profiles, cross national comparisons, or even for analysing trends.

FIGURE 1

TARGETING VICTIMS OF TRAFFICKING: SUBPOPULATIONS
AND POPULATIONS WHERE VICTIMS OF TRAFFICKING CONSTITUTE
SUBPOPULATIONS (relative sizes of populations
are hypothetical and likely to vary between regions)

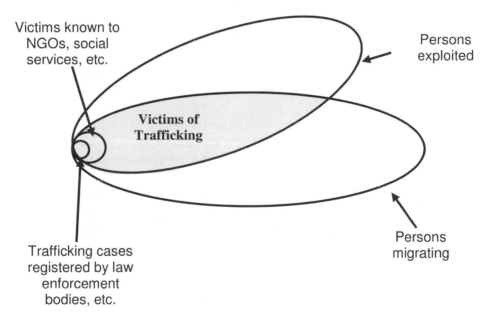

The number of cases registered by law enforcement might be an indicator of the functionality of the law enforcement apparatus in a given country, but is unlikely to be a good estimate of the number of trafficking victims. Recent developments in official trafficking statistics in Norway may serve to illustrate this; human trafficking was until recently believed to be a minor problem in Norway, and up until 2004 only a handful cases with suspicion of trafficking had been registered by law enforcement bodies. With the introduction of the

Plan of Action for Combating Trafficking in Women and Children in 2003, law enforcement bodies were instructed to give higher priority to trafficking for sexual exploitation, and increased resources were given to this field. As a result, there was an exponential increase in the number of cases identified; while only a few cases were identified in 2003, the police became involved in 42 cases[3] where trafficking for sexual exploitation was expected in the first ten months of 2004 (statements made by the Minister of Justice and the Police, Stortingets Spørretime, 2004). There is little that indicates that these numbers reflect an exponential increase in trafficking in persons as such, from 2003 to 2004, but is generally believed to be related to the shift in attention and the increased resources. Clearly, these numbers cannot be used to illustrate any trend in the development of trafficking in Norway over the last years. Similarly, comparisons with other countries will be misleading, unless it can be assumed that a similar approach, amount of resources, as well as legal framework is used for the given year of comparison.

In spite of the strong increase in identified cases of trafficking it remains difficult to determine if the identified cases represent a tip of an iceberg, or if all or close to all incidents of trafficking for sexual exploitation are usually identified. This leads us to the second problem in analysing data from law enforcement or rehabilitation organizations involved – the problem of representativity and bias.

Since the ratio of cases identified by law enforcement or non-governmental organizations (NGOs) to the total number of trafficking cases in an area is seldom known, it is difficult to determine to what extent the identified cases are representative of the universe of trafficking cases, and which biases they introduce to our data. Focusing a study on these groups will not only be problematic in terms of developing estimates and analysing trends, but perhaps even more so in terms of producing data for description of basic characteristics of victims of trafficking.

Cases that are registered by law enforcement are different from all other cases of trafficking because they actually were discovered, and taken seriously, by the police. The cases identified are likely to be influenced by two factors. First, the ability of police and law enforcement agents to recognize trafficking when confronted with it. For instance, in the prostitution arena, some national groups may be identified as being at higher risk of being victims of trafficking, leading law enforcement agencies to increase their attention to segments of the prostitution arena where these national groups are observed. This may again lead to a higher detection rate of these groups. Similarly, since under-aged prostitutes may be possible to identify based on external characteristics, we can expect them to have different detection rates from adult victims, either because they are more often identified by community workers, clients, and others (giving them higher detection rates), or because traffickers are more careful when selling child victims, which consequently makes children more difficult to detect. To date we have too few systematic analyses of these biases, and consequently, any reporting on characteristics such as age distribution or nationality of victims identified by law enforcement is not likely to be representative for the victims at large.

Second, the probability of being identified by the police will depend on how the victims themselves behave in contact with representatives of law enforcement. It is interesting to note that even among trafficking victims who are subjected to severe physical and mental abuse, very few seem to ask for help when they have the possibility, and many go to great lengths to avoid contact with the police (Brunovskis and Tyldum, 2004). Consequently, we may assume that the victims identified by the police may be different in regard to personal resources, in particular in regard to important aspects such as trust and access to information. Since we do not have systematic knowledge about the cases that are *not* disclosed by the police, we cannot know if victims registered by law enforcement were just lucky, or if they were discovered and assisted because they were different.

The same problem of institutional bias can be argued to be valid for the sub-population of victims who come in contact with the rehabilitation apparatus. It is generally believed that this group constitutes a small proportion of those who fall victim to trafficking. According to the International Organization for Migration (IOM) Ukraine, the majority of the women who come in contact with their rehabilitation apparatus contact them on their own initiative, often many months or even years after they have returned to their home country (Personal communication, October 2003). We may assume that having access to resources like education and social networks makes it easier to contact rehabilitation services and ask for help. We can thus expect that the victims who contact NGOs for assistance and rehabilitation are systematically different from those who do not. And perhaps most importantly – seeking help is a realistic option only for those who have and are aware of an active organization in their community. Thus, areas with many NGOs (or where information about rehabilitation services is well known) are more likely to register victims of trafficking.

We do not wish to argue that studies of victims identified by law enforcement bodies or NGOs cannot give valuable information. However, we should be aware of the limitations that are inherent in these data; generalizations in terms of mechanisms are likely to bear greater interest than generalizations in terms of basic characteristics such as age or educational level. For instance, most of the women assisted in rehabilitation programmes in the countries of origin contact the organization on their own initiative. We believe it is reasonable to assume that women similar to the "typical" trafficking victims presented in campaigns and in media in general will find it easier to seek assistance, compared with women with different experiences. In particular, victims of trafficking who knew they were going to work in the sex industry, or had prior prostitution experience (the "unworthy" or "guilty" victims) are likely to be underrepresented. Data on victims identified through NGOs or rehabilitation programmes should consequently not be used to infer about, for example, the share of victims who knew they were going to work in prostitution before they left their country of origin (see for instance, IOM Kosovo, 2001; IOM Tajikistan, 2001; IOM Armenia, 2001). However, such data may hold great opportunities for improving our understanding of *trafficking mechanisms* through comparative analyses, i.e. methods of recruitment, acceptance of coercion, or success in social re-integration comparing women with and without prior prostitution experiences.

Estimations and data on populations where victims constitute a subpopulation

A possible solution to the selection biases discussed above would be to study populations where victims of trafficking make up a subpopulation, such as areas where trafficking is known to take place (areas with prostitution or migrant workers) or among returned migrants in known countries of origin.

If survey data on returned migrants were able to distinguish victims of trafficking from non-victims, this information could serve to evaluate the quality of data obtained through other sources, and possibly provide guidelines about how official migration data could be used for monitoring purposes. Furthermore, such data would enable us to identify groups that are particularly vulnerable to traffickers. The majority of known victims of trafficking seem to have chosen to travel abroad, either to find a job, a husband, seek asylum, or even to earn money in prostitution. And while many migrants do fall victim to trafficking, it is probable that the majority of migrants who cross borders every day are not manipulated and exploited to the extent that it can be classified as trafficking. Obtaining a better understanding of the experiences of returned migrants would thus help us better understand what constitutes successful migration, and which factors increase vulnerability to traffickers.

In addition, knowledge about the operation of, and changes in, prostitution arenas could provide invaluable information. Women operating in known areas for prostitution can relatively easily be observed and counted. Even women in situations of serious exploitation and abuse can never be totally invisible in the prostitution arena, as their organizers need to sell the women to clients.

While it is possible to obtain information about general background character-istics and behaviour of migrants in prostitution, we do not believe it is possible to collect reliable information about forms of exploitation and abuse among victims *currently* experiencing this abuse. In other words, it is difficult to develop reliable, direct measures that can enable us to distinguish victims of trafficking from other women in prostitution because women and men in the most serious forms of slavery and exploitation may be less likely to be reached, and because the victims will be reluctant to provide information that may put them in jeop-ardy (either due to fear of organizers, or due to fear of being sent out of the country). Still, indirect indicators of social integration, freedom of movement, or even coercion may be obtained through, for instance, information about con-tact with and knowledge about health care or legal institutions in the country where they work, language proficiency, or even the number of respondents stopped from participating in interviews by a third party.

Prostitution arenas, and other arenas for migrant workers, should be monitored, not only in order to obtain statistics on victims of trafficking in destination countries, but also in order to increase our understanding of the mechanism that enables trafficking to take place. This relates to other aspects of the role of destination countries, such as the issues of demand of migrant labour/prostitution, the effect of regulation or deregulation of use of migrant labour/prostitution, and the general framework that may discourage trafficking or make it profit-able. Stories of recruitment and exit of women and men in less serious situations of force and exploitation may also serve to enhance our understanding of how trafficking takes place. By supplementing studies based on data on persons detected by law enforcement or NGOs, with data on persons who experienced less severe forms of exploitation, one could obtain a wider description of the field and counteract probable biases in the current body of research. Our data from Oslo indicate that most prostitutes of non-Norwegian origin operate with some form of "assistance" or dependence of organizers and pimps. Only by studying this group can we determine where the line should be drawn between trafficking and non-coerced prostitution

SECONDARY DATA SOURCES

The key respondent approach to arriving at estimates and describing popula-tions is commonly used in empirical studies on human trafficking today (see for instance UNICEF, 2003; IOM, 1996a). This approach is, however, associated with several sources of bias (Heckathorn, 1997). First of all, because numbers and estimates arrived at by expert opinions or involved NGOs cannot be subject to methodological scrutiny or evaluations of external actors, numbers are given weight not based on the methods used to arrive at them (i.e. registration methods, update frequency, or coverage), but based on the authority of the person or organization that provided the estimate.

Secondly, key informants do not interact with a random group of potential clients, and, in particular for hidden populations, key respondents cannot be expected to have an overview of the total population. Few outreach organizations or community workers have adequate systems for keeping registers, and where methodologically trained researchers fail in producing estimates, it should not be expected that community workers do better, even if they have excellent knowledge of the arenas in which they work.

Even if several independent actors present similar numbers to estimate the number of trafficking victims, this should not be taken to indicate that the number is correct, as key respondents in the same field may be influenced by each other, or the same sources of information, media coverage, or general perception in the society. As mentioned above, the introduction of the Plan of Action for Combating Trafficking in Women and Children in Norway had a significant impact in changing the perceptions of many involved actors. In the two years since the plan was introduced, police, researchers, and community workers have changed their description of human trafficking in Norway from a minor problem to one of growing proportions. This perception has been strengthened by the strong increase in detected trafficking cases, and several ongoing court cases. We would expect that most involved actors would estimate the number of trafficking victims to be much higher today than only a few years ago, although there is little indication of an equally strong increase in the actual occurrences of human trafficking in this time period. We will, therefore, argue that in order to obtain good data it is necessary to limit the use of secondary data sources, and instead conduct systematic collection and analysis of primary data.

Estimation and data collection approaches for hidden and difficult to reach populations

In other fields where necessary statistics have been difficult to obtain, methods for developing process indicators of various phenomena based on more easily available data have been developed. For instance, Garfield (2000) estimates child mortality in Iraq from measures of adult literacy, immunization coverage, and percentage of households with potable water, among other indicators. Such an estimation was made possible by decades of thorough research on child mortality conducted in regions where data are more readily available. Since the main causes of child mortality are known, and tend to be consistent across regions and cultures, process indicators could be used to estimate the extent of child mortality in Iraq.

Is it possible to develop methods for using process indicators on the extent and forms of trafficking? Probably, but the current knowledge base is still far from the point where this is possible, as proper production and analysis of statistical data on human trafficking is still rare. Process indicators can be used for estimating the number of victims of trafficking only after the subject has been systematically researched to the extent that causes and related phenomena are well established, and the effects of these phenomena can be calculated and used across regions and political systems.

While compiling data about hidden populations such as victims of trafficking is both technically challenging and potentially costly, a number of methods have been developed to study such populations. One estimation method that has been getting increased attention in more recent studies of hidden populations is the Capture-Recapture methodology, which was, like many other methods for estimating hidden or difficult to reach populations, developed within the field of biology. With the Capture-Recapture methodology, size and basic characteristics of a population can be estimated based on systematic observations and relatively simple calculations (Jensen and Meredith, 2002). The method is still most commonly used within the fields of biology and epidemiology, however, there has been an increasing amount of studies making use of capture-recapture methodology within the social sciences on subjects such as the homeless (Williams and Cheal, 2002), drug misuse prevalence (Hay and McKeganey, 1996), street children (Gurgel et al., 2004; Hatløy and Huser, forthcoming), and women in street prostitution (Brunovskis and Tyldum, 2004).

Another set of data collection methods commonly used for hidden populations are various types of network approaches. In a study conducted by IOM in Azerbaijan, victims of trafficking and persons assumed to be potential victims were recruited through "snowball recruitment" in seven regions with high international migration (IOM, 2002). It is interesting to note that this study presented findings with victim profiles that sometimes differ significantly from findings presented in studies based on interviews with women recruited from rehabilitation centres. However, despite the innovative recruitment method, it is difficult to determine to what extent the characteristics found are representatative for the population of victims/survivors at large, as the recruitment, or snowballing, was not carried out in a way that gives all respondents equal inclusion probabilities, nor allows calculation of such probabilities (at least, such methods are not described in the report). Estimation methods based on snowball sampling generally demand a systematic recruitment system (i.e. that each respondent can recruit a fixed number of respondents, and that a fixed number of waves are carried out), and ideally the initial contacts should be based on a random sample, or at least some form of targeted sampling.

Another network approach that has received increased attention for studies of hidden populations is Respondent-Driven Sampling (RDS), developed by Douglas Heckathorn (1997). Through a double incentive system in recruitment, and estimation methods that take into account the size and characteristics of the individuals network (based on Markov-chain theory and the theory of biased networks) RDS is argued to reduce the biases associated with other network approaches.[4]

CONCLUSIONS

Current data sources where victims of trafficking can be unambiguously identified (i.e. data from law enforcement and rehabilitation centres) do not cover more than a small proportion of the total population of victims of trafficking. The populations that are covered are most likely marked by strong selection bias, and are not representative of the total population of victims. Due to a lack of empirical knowledge about causes and mechanisms tied to trafficking, proxy (or process) indicators such as poverty, migration patterns, or missing persons have limited application for estimating size of the population of trafficking victims.

Any production of data or estimates of victims of trafficking should be based on clear conceptual, but also practical, identification of who the target group is, and who the inferences are valid for. Furthermore, any estimate should clearly state which stage of trafficking is being focused on – whether the target groups are persons at risk of being trafficked, persons recently recruited, persons currently trafficked, or former victims of trafficking.

It is impossible to distinguish victims of trafficking based on external observations, thus, unambiguous classification of victims of trafficking is most easily facilitated if the victims are willing to give up information about exploitation and abuse themselves. For classification in statistics production, this is most easily done through survey data. Survey data of evasive or difficult to reach populations may be difficult and costly to produce. However, halfway solutions will seldom work: the only thing worse than no data is wrong and misleading data.

While the production of reliable statistics and estimations of numbers and characteristics of victims is important for the further development of policies and research on trafficking, the importance of other research topics should not be ignored. In this paper we have considered mainly the statistical aspects of data gathering on victims of trafficking. Although statistical data can be instructive and useful, as we pointed out initially, there is also a need to understand the processes by which men and women experience trafficking; how they are recruited; how they relate to clients, social services, and law enforcement while in countries of destination; how they get away from a situation of exploitation; and how they are rehabilitated. Furthermore, we need a better understanding of the social field that constitutes trafficking, as well as it its bordering fields; i.e. is trafficking best understood as a phenomenon within the field of labour migration, international prostitution, or migration in general, or does trafficking constitute a distinct and separate phenomenon with its separate causes and mechanisms? These questions call for data production and analysis in anthropological and social psychological veins.

Research on trafficking is still in its early stages, and the potential gains from systematic empirical research are large. It should be a goal to move beyond static descriptions of "typical" or "extreme" cases of trafficking, and rather seek to understand the great variation in forms of exploitation, recruitment, and rehabilitation. Comparisons of nationalities and regions as well as social groups should be given priority. High quality data representative for the total population of victims of trafficking are rare, and as they are difficult and costly to produce, will probably continue to be rare in the future. However, minor adjustments toward systematic collection of data (for instance by using probability sampling), and making potential and known biases to the data explicit in the data analysis, could significantly improve the current research base, and as such, our understanding of human trafficking.

NOTES

1. It is also worth noting that Norwegian and other Scandinavian women had the highest refusal rates, while Asian women had the highest participation rate, followed by women from Central and Eastern Europe.
2. "'Trafficking in persons' shall mean the recruitment, transportation, transfer, harbouring or receipt of persons, by means of the threat or use of force or other forms of coercion, of abduction, of fraud, of deception, of the abuse of power or of a position of vulnerability or of the giving or receiving of payments or benefits to achieve the consent of a person having control over another person, for the purpose of exploitation. Exploitation shall include, at a minimum, the exploitation of the prostitution of others or other forms of sexual exploitation, forced labor or services, slavery or practices similar to slavery, servitude or the removal of organs" (UN, 2000).
3. One case can have several involved persons – of the above mentioned 42 cases, the largest case involves 124 persons.
4. For more information on sampling methods for hidden and rare populations, see Heckathorn, 1997; Thompson, 1992; Jensen and Pearson, 2002; Levy and Lemenshow, 1999; Pedersen and Sommerfelt, 2001.

REFERENCES

Brunovskis, A., and G. Tyldum
2004 "Crossing borders: an empirical study of transnational prostitution and trafficking in human beings", Fafo report 426, Oslo.

Dottridge, M.
2003 *Deserving Trust: Issues of Accountability for Human Right NGOs*, International Council on Human Rights Policy, Switzerland.

European Union (EU)
2004 "Draft report of the European Experts Group on trafficking in human beings", presented at the Consultative Workshop in the framework of the EU Forum for the Prevention of Organized Crime, Brussels, 26 October.

Garfield, R.
2000 "A multivariate method for estimating mortality rates among under five year olds from health and social indicators in Iraq", paper presented at the Conference on Statistics, Development and Human Rights, Montreal, 4-8 September.

Gurgel, R.Q., et al.
2004 "Capture-recapture to estimate the number of street children in a city in Brazil", *Archives of Disease in Childhood*, 89: 222-224.

Hatløy, A., and A. Huser
"Identification of street children: characteristics of street children in Bamako and Accra", Fafo report, Oslo (forthcoming).

Hay, G., and N. McKeganey
1996 "Estimating the prevalence of drug misuse in Dundee, Scotland: an application of capture-recapture methods", in *Journal of Epidemiology and Community Health*, 50: 469-472.

Heckathorn, D.D.
1997 "Respondent-driven sampling: a new approach to the study of hidden populations", in *Social Problems*, 44(2): 174-198.

International Organization for Migration (IOM)
1996a *Trafficking in Women to Italy for Sexual Exploitation*, International Organization for Migration, Geneva.
1996b *Trafficking in Women to Austria for Sexual Exploitation*, International Organization for Migration, Geneva.
2001 *Victims of Trafficking in the Balkans: A Study of Trafficking in Women and Children for Sexual Exploitation to, through and from the Balkans*, International Organization for Migration, Geneva.
2002 *Shattered Dreams: Report on Trafficking in Persons in Azerbaijan*, International Organization for Migration, Geneva.

International Organization for Migration (IOM) Armenia
2001 *Trafficking in Women and Children from the Republic of Armenia: A Study*, International Organization for Migration, Yerevan.

International Organization for Migration (IOM) Kosovo
2002 *Return and Reintegration Project: Situation Report, February 2000-September 2002*, International Organization for Migration, Kosovo.

International Organization for Migration (IOM) Tajikistan
    2001   *Deceived Migrants from Tajikistan: A Study of Trafficking in Women and Children*, International Organization for Migration, Dushanbe.
Jensen, R., and M. Pearson
    2002   *Rapid Assessment/Capture – Recapture: A Field Guide*, Cambridge.
Kelly, L.
    2002   *Journeys of Jeopardy: A Review of Research on Trafficking in Women and Children in Europe*, Child and Woman Abuse Studies Unit, University of North London.
Kelly, L., and L. Regan
    2000   "Stopping traffic: exploring the extent of, and responses to, trafficking in women for sexual exploitation in the UK", Police Research Series Paper 125, UK Home Office, London.
Laczko, F., and M.A. Gramegna
    2003   "Developing better indicators of human trafficking", *Brown Journal of World Affairs*, Brown University, Rhode Island.
Levy, P.S., and S. Lemenshow
    1999   *Sampling of Populations*, third edition, John Wiley, New York.
LaPorte, R.E.
    1994   "Assessing the human condition: capture-recapture techniques", *British Medical Journal*, 308(5), 1 January.
Pedersen, J., and T. Sommerfelt
    2001   "What should we know about children in armed conflict and how should we go about knowing it?", paper presented at the conference Filling the Knowledge Gaps: A Research Agenda on the Impact of Armed Conflict on Children, Florence, Italy, 2-4 July,
Regional Clearing Point
    2003   *First Annual Report on Victims of Trafficking in South Eastern Europe*, Regional Clearing Point/Stability Pact Task Force on Trafficking in Human Beings, Vienna.
Tyldum, G., et al.
            "Taking stock: a review of the current research on trafficking in women for sexual exploitation", Fafo report, Oslo (forthcoming).
Thompson, S.K.
    1992   *Sampling*, John Wiley, New York.
United Nations (UN)
    2000   *Protocol to Prevent, Suppress and Punish Trafficking in Persons, especially Women and Children, supplementing the United Nations Convention against Transnational Organized Crime*, United Nations.
UNICEF
    2003   *Trafficking in Human Beings, Especially Women and Children in Africa*, UNICEF Innocenti Research Centre, Florence.
Vandekerckhove, W.
    2003   "Ethische problemen van en voor NGO's in de strijd tegen mensenhandel", in W. Vandekerckhove (Ed.), *NGO's in de strijd tegen mensenhandel: Humanitaire motieven, repressieve middelen?* EPO, Antwerpen (English

translation: http://www.flwi.ugent.be/cevi/docwebi/EP%20for%20NGO.
pdf).

Williams, M., and B. Cheal

2002　　"Can we measure homelessness? A critical evaluation of the method of
'capture-recapture'", *International Journal of Social Research Methodology*, 5(4): 313-331.

Methodological Challenges in Research with Trafficked Persons: Tales from the Field

Denise Brennan*

INTRODUCTION

This article is intended to discuss methodological challenges to conducting research with trafficked persons in the United States. It draws from my experiences as an anthropologist involved in an ongoing book project on life after trafficking.[1] By exploring the methodological difficulties and ethical concerns that I have faced as an anthropologist, I hope to lay bare some of the methodological challenges that researchers across disciplines, particularly social scientists who rely on ethnographic research, are likely to confront when examining this issue. The central focus of this article is on the possibilities of collaboration between academic researchers, trafficked persons, and social service providers on advocacy, research and writing projects, as well as on the possibilities of trafficked persons speaking and writing for themselves. It also considers the role trafficked persons can play in building what the media and activists loosely term the "anti-trafficking movement" and asks what would have to happen for them to move beyond their "victim" status where they are called upon to provide "testimony" about trafficking, to participating in the decision making of the direction of the movement. Since it identifies obstacles to trafficked persons (to whom I refer to in this article as ex-captives)[2] taking the podium and picking up a pen, it explores ways to mitigate potential problems when researchers "speak for" ex-captives.

While much media attention and dialogues among nations have focused on the origins and prevention of trafficking, my own ongoing research project picks up where these discussions leave off. It explores what happens once women

* Department of Sociology and Anthropology, Georgetown University, Washington, DC, USA.

and men are trafficked, and seeks to explain – through ethnography – how they begin to rebuild their lives and regain agency in the wake of being trafficked. By not focusing on the origins of trafficking, but on its effects, this research contributes to ongoing debates among front-line social service providers, labour advocates, and attorneys on how best to protect the rights and facilitate the well-being of ex-captives. Although there has been a great interest in trafficking in the media and by the Bush Administration at a national policy level, attention seems to fizzle out once trafficked persons have escaped or have been rescued and their stories *in* trafficking have been told. Perhaps this is so because their story after their emancipation is one similar to so many immigrants, one about the challenges of the daily, mundane struggles to build a new life in a new place. It is an ongoing story, less finite and flashy than the story of their escape or rescue.

ANTHROPOLOGY'S CONTRIBUTION

Researchers on trafficking find themselves writing on an issue that has been sensationalized, misrepresented, and politicized. With the bulk of media treatment only sensationalizing trafficking – especially in stories of sexual exploitation[3] – social scientists must, in contrast, provide carefully researched on-the-ground accounts of life in and after trafficking. While the issue of trafficking for sexual exploitation has been over-explored in the media – including their use of images that exemplify what Kleinman and Kleinman refer to as the "commercialization of suffering", the raw spectacle-making of violence, abuse, and suffering – other forms of slavery have gone ignored (1997: 19). The Bush Administration, too, not only has focused on trafficking for sexual exploitation, but also has conflated voluntary prostitution with sex trafficking.[4] And, perhaps nothing is more disputed than the numbers of persons who are trafficked world-wide and to the United States.[5]

Anthropologists can make critical contributions based on first-hand interviews to this environment where ideology passes as knowledge. To date, there is a scarcity of research on trafficking to the United States. Outside of legal scholarship, reports in the media, and organizations' documents, there exists little academic writing on trafficking to the United States.[6] Notably absent is writing by trafficked persons themselves, with one exception, the powerful account written by ex-child slave Jean-Robert Cadet (1998). Nor is there much scholarship on their experiences after trafficking. While making his case for the usefulness of anthropologists' writing, Jeremy MacClancy writes that "transmitting words of the marginalized, the poor, and the ignored can bring high-flying approaches back down to the ground and reintroduce the concerns of ordinary people into the equations of policymakers" (2002: 13). In the case of trafficking, legislation already has been passed to protect trafficked persons (the Trafficking Victims Protection Act (TVPA) passed in October 2000) and a new visa has been created that allows them to stay in the United States (a T visa). Anthropologists, with their ground-up perspective, have much to contribute to this issue that most often has been discussed from the top-down.[7] Since "trafficked persons" are spoken of as one entity, anthropologists' focus on "the particular" can help begin to document the many differences among each trafficking case.

Discussions about "public anthropology", along with work in critical medical anthropology, are areas of scholarship from which researchers working on trafficking could draw and contribute (Scheper-Hughes, 1995: 410). Medical doctor and anthropologist Paul Farmer's writings are among the best examples of research labelled "public anthropology", in which he not only analyses the workings and consequences of structural violence,[8] but is also, in Scheper-Hughes' language, "politically committed and morally engaged" (Farmer et al., 1996; Farmer, 1999, 2003).[9] Building on these discussions of structural violence and public anthropology, as well as liberation theology, medical anthropologist Jennifer Hirsch calls for critical medical anthropologists to conduct research on migrant health within a framework of "liberation anthropology". Such an approach would not just involve a "sensitive form of ethnographic storytelling" in which the ethnographer-writer gives "voice, as best she can, to those who have been silenced", but also, much like liberation theology, would involve "a commitment to social analysis which reveals the underlying causes of suffering and ill health" (Hirsch, 2003: 231). Similarly, I argue that trafficking researchers not only are tasked with telling ex-captives' stories until ex-captives are ready and safe enough to do so for themselves, but also with laying bare and analysing the structures through which modern-day slavery – and less-severe forms of exploitation – thrive.

THE "GOLDEN MIDDLE"

The central issues of this article emerge from the challenges to doing research with ex-captives who are both an extremely vulnerable population, as well as one that is extraordinarily diverse and geographically dispersed. Since research with ex-captives in the United States is in the initial stages, researchers, social service providers, and attorneys are still working through the difficulty of balancing ex-captives' safety and well-being with the political need to bring attention to the conditions of trafficked persons.[10] I believe the sustainability of an anti-trafficking movement in the United States hinges not only on ex-captives telling their own stories but also on their taking an active leadership role in its direction, agenda-setting, and policy formulation. As Kleinman and Kleinman observe, bringing "local participants (not merely national experts) into the process of developing and assessing programs" not only facilitates "policy making from the ground-up" but also underscores "what is at stake for participants in local worlds" (1997: 18). Ex-captives' participation in the struggle to end trafficking also could wrest the anti-trafficking message away from a sensationalistic media. This reorientation could help frame the issue as a labour issue that involves a spectrum of abuse, with trafficking at one end of the spectrum.

Researchers and social service providers currently are working through how best to reach what anthropologist Elzbieta Gozdziak refers to as a "golden middle", a kind of middle research ground in which researchers have access to ex-captives (and vice versa), while ex-captives' safety and privacy are assured (Personal Communication, 2004). Decades of research with women who have experienced domestic violence – as well as activism by them – offers one model of how best to secure ex-captives' safety and how to collaborate with "victim" advocates.[11] Social service providers and attorneys need to protect ex-captives not just from their traffickers, but also from exploitation in the media. Since trafficking became a favourite topic in the media, ex-captives' case managers and attorneys have had to handle a barrage of media requests to "present victims". Case managers and attorneys have been understandably reluctant to parade their clients in front of the media. Considering their clients already might have had to tell their stories not only to them, but also to the police and the Federal Bureau of Investigation (FBI), it is no surprise they seek to protect clients from re-telling their story to journalists – or to researchers. Trauma counsellors, in particular, warn of the risk of "secondary trauma" that may occur with multiple recounting of painful memories.

METHODOLOGICAL CHALLENGES

The methodological challenges are daunting when studying trafficking to the United States. The first challenge is the diversity of trafficking contexts: trafficked persons come from a variety of source countries, end up scattered throughout sites in the United States, and are forced into different forms of labour and servitude. They speak different languages, have different socio-economic backgrounds, varying education and work histories, as well as differences in age, sex, and race/ethnicity. They also have different experiences entering and exiting their trafficking experiences, including experiences of transit. The length of time they were held in servitude varies from weeks to years, and while some experience psychological coercion others also undergo physical brutality. As Sue Shriner, the Victim-Witness Coordinator for the United States Immigration and Customs Enforcement describes, "Agents ask me for profiles of traffickers and their victims. I tell them there is no one m.o. of a typical trafficker, there is no typical victim, and the paths that lead them here are varied. I've never seen anything like this before." In sum, a researcher who works in one site, or on one kind of forced labour, or with trafficked persons from one source country, can not easily extrapolate to speak of experiences in other sites, other forms of forced labour, or trafficked persons from other source countries. General portraits can be drawn, and below I discuss some characteristics that cases sometimes share, but for researchers these generalizations can be frustratingly imprecise. Indeed, some trafficking cases are so vastly different from one another that it may not be instructive to draw many connections among them.

To conduct research on trafficking to the United States that highlights the perspective of trafficked persons themselves means working closely with social service providers. Because the fight against trafficking to the United States is relatively young, and persons designated as "trafficked" only have been under the care of social service organizations for the past few years, researchers often can make only preliminary analyses. Three large trafficking cases led to the development of trafficking programmes at three service providers, all of which have emerged as national leaders in assisting trafficked persons: the El Monte sweatshop case in Los Angeles gave rise to the Coalition to Abolish Slavery and Trafficking (CAST); the "deaf Mexican" panhandling case was handled by Safe Horizon, New York City's largest non-profit victim assistance, advocacy, and violence prevention organization; and the American Samoa sweatshop case has been handled by Boat People SOS. Although other organizations have handled trafficking cases over the years (even before the US Government labelled them as such), such as the Break the Chain Campaign in Washington, DC; Heartland Alliance (Midwest Immigrant and Human Rights Center) in Chicago; the Coalition of Immokalee Workers' Anti-Slavery Campaign in Immokalee, Florida; and the Florida Immigrant Advocacy Center's LUCHA programme in Miami, few other service providers have had much direct, hands-on experience with trafficked persons. Indeed, some service providers only came into existence over the past couple of years, in the wake of the passage in 2000 of the TVPA.

Participant observation   a possibility?

Since, to date, there are no communities of resettled trafficked persons in the United States, my ongoing research project is not based on participant observation of a usual kind, the hallmark of which is staying in one place and talking to the same people over time (Peacock, 1986). Even those who were resettled after the largest case in the United States – the American Samoa case – are not living together in any one place in the United States.[12] I have chosen to conduct interviews in different cities where ex-captives have come forward to their case managers requesting to be put in touch with researchers and journalists,[13] or their case managers have identified them as psychologically and emotionally ready to – and interested in – speaking with researchers. At any given time, service providers may have only a couple of clients who have "graduated" from their case management (CAST in Los Angeles has an actual graduation ceremony), let alone interested in speaking with researchers.

The dilemma for the researcher (who inevitably has limited time and resources) is whether to focus on one resettlement site – one city – or to conduct multi-site interviews. The former means the interviews with trafficked persons in one site could be so specific that they would not necessarily clarify a bigger picture of life in or after trafficking in the United States. The latter means the researcher could risk forgoing the ethnographic richness that accompanies conducting research in one place over time (participant observation). And, without conducting informal interviews over time, the researcher is left to rely on the vicissitudes of the scheduled "interview moment". The researcher might miss out on what can be learned by what MacClancy describes as "serendipity", those "chance events" and "accidental encounters" that "may be surprising and at first incomprehensible" (MacClancy, 2002: 6). When possible, I keep in touch with ex-captives I meet in scheduled interviews through social service agencies. In this way, I engage in participant observation in the traditional anthropological sense, by following how they have been settling into their new communities, jobs, and housing, as well as how they create and maintain new social networks of friends, neighbours, and co-workers.

Research that focuses on particular cities, such as ECPAT's "International Trafficking of Children to New York City for Sexual Purposes" by Mia Spangenberg (2002), or on trafficking to a particular state or region, such as Florida State University's Center for the Advancement of Human Rights' "Florida Responds to Human Trafficking" (2004), is one other approach to research design that could maximize both breadth and depth of studies. Given the logistical challenges of conducting fieldwork in multiple sites, trafficking researchers also could work collaboratively to produce comparative research across sites within the United States, particularly since trafficked persons show up in large cities and small towns.[14]

Early stage of trafficking activities

The learning curve about trafficked persons' needs is steep, even for organizations that have experience assisting trafficked persons, since as service providers and trauma counsellors report, each case of trafficking has distinct characteristics. Joy Zarembka, the Director of the Break the Chain Campaign, an advocacy and direct service organization that works with domestic workers in the Washington, DC area explains, "Every case is a little bit different, even cases that look similar, there is always some twist, some difference that makes each case unlike the others". Maria José Fletcher, an attorney in Miami at the Florida Immigrant Advocacy Center who directs the LUCHA Program, observes that these differences demand that social service agencies treat their clients "as individuals" and not lump them together as "trafficking victims". She suggests that this can happen in ways similar to the "individual safety plans" that domestic violence counsellors craft for their clients. Nor is it easy to discern the kinds of trauma suffered by trafficked persons. Dr. Judy Okawa, a licensed clinical psychologist who is the former Director of the Program for Survivors of Torture and Severe Trauma at the Center for Multicultural Human Services in Falls Church, Virginia, and Farinaz Amireshi, the Trafficking Project Coordinator at the Center, assert that few are looking at the mental health implications of trafficking. "We are all in on the ground floor," Okawa explains, since, unlike victims of torture who are a "pure sample" because they must meet the United Nations definitions of torture, "we are seeing a more diverse group of trafficking victims and the symptom response is not as homogenous".

Locating trafficked persons continues to stymie the "protection" part of the trafficking equation (the US Government has developed a three-pronged approach to fighting trafficking: prevention, protection, and prosecution, which keeps service providers concerned about their future grant success. It remains to be seen whether the Bush Administration's new public awareness campaign, "Rescue and Restore" will significantly increase the identification and rescue of persons held in slavery. Even when trafficked persons enter emergency rooms, police stations, or call service providers, they usually do not describe themselves as trafficked, but rather seek help for other issues such as for immigration or domestic violence issues. Since trafficking can be part of what Maria José Fletcher of LUCHA describes as "a continuum of violence" and exploitation in trafficked persons' lives, they may not see themselves as "victims of trafficking". Fletcher explains, "None of the women tell me 'I'm a victim of trafficking', rather they say 'I need help to not get deported'". Nadra Qadeer, Director of the Anti-Trafficking Program at Safe Horizon in New York City, echoed this observation: "People do not talk about trafficking ever. They talk about abuse, things like 'My boyfriend beat me.'"

OVERVIEW OF RESEARCH PROJECT

I now turn to the methodological challenges in my own research on life after trafficking. One question central to my research project asks how severely exploited persons begin to trust others again. It also considers the role community support plays in this process. The issue of trust emerges not only as critical to ex-captives' recovery and resettlement, but also to the role ex-captives can play in trafficking research – and in building an "anti-trafficking movement". I use the term "trust" in ways similar to E. Valentine Daniel and John Chr. Knudsen who analyse how refugees both "mistrust" and are "mistrusted" (1995). How ex-captives trust and are trusted in their new communities are key to rebuilding their lives after trafficking. Trafficked persons who were freed following raids of brothels, factories, or private homes (in the case of domestic servitude) by law enforcement, almost immediately are asked to trust their liberators. Soon after they might find themselves interviewed not only by the local police, but also by the FBI, immigration officials, state and federal prosecutors, and then, their own lawyers. Julie, an Indonesian woman who was in domestic slavery in California worried that the police and other "authority" figures would traffic her again: "You do not know any one. It's hard to trust other people. After I got out, everyone was asking me questions. I thought what if they do the same thing to me again?"

In the process, social service organizations which tend to the multiple needs of trafficked persons, see themselves as trustworthy, yet there is no self-evident reason ex-captives would automatically regard them as such. One community-based educator on trafficking who does outreach to ethnic-based community organizations in New York City reports that there are many disincentives for trafficked persons to come forward. They might be reluctant to come forward out of worry that their "work places" might be raided and their friends (some of whom might not be working in slave conditions) would lose their jobs. Often they do not trust the police and believe the police would not trust them nor believe their stories of servitude. Given that traffickers can be well-known and even respected members in their communities of co-ethnics, trafficked persons also might not believe that they would be safe if they came forward – even to the most well-meaning and well-run community-based organizations. Florrie Burke, Senior Director of the Anti-Trafficking Program at Safe Horizon in New York City, describes the "tentacles" of some rings as so far-reaching – including back to trafficked persons' home countries – that some of her clients are deeply fearful for their and their families' safety.

There are many pressures on trafficked persons to maintain silences about their status.[15] Although similarities emerge between refugees and trafficked persons, especially on issues related to what Gina Buijs calls the "remaking of self", the groups often diverge on the issue of community support (1993). Trauma counsellors who work with trafficked persons in the United States report that the larger community of immigrants where trafficked persons settle (usually composed of co-ethnics) often stigmatizes and rejects trafficked persons. Consider the following experience of an ex-captive who chose not to remain quiet about her experience. At a Haitian community-based organization meeting in New York City, a woman spoke about her experiences being trafficked. The crowd was unsympathetic, questioned her judgement, and criticized her ruthlessly. Since then, the organization has not heard from her again. By all accounts, much more outreach and education needs to reach community-based organizations that work with immigrant groups, the staffs of which might hold misconceptions or stereotypes about trafficked persons. Maria José Fletcher, of LUCHA in Miami, describes conducting a workshop in a southern state with a community-based organization where the staff referred to the co-ethnic women in the town's brothels as *putas* (whores) and was unaware that some of these women might be held against their will.

EX-CAPTIVES' ROLE IN RESEARCH AND ADVOCACY

On many occasions throughout this research I have heard social service providers and human rights attorneys liken this "anti-trafficking movement" to that of the domestic violence movement. However, whereas domestic violence victim-advocates took an active leadership role in that fight, trafficked persons were not a significant part of the fight for anti-trafficking legislation, nor are they now – with the exception of members of the Coalition of Immokalee Workers[16] – shaping the direction of the anti-trafficking "movement". Unlike the research and advocacy environment in Australia that Veronica Strang describes, where there is a "small but growing number of Aboriginal academics, lawyers and political activists" who speak for themselves (2003: 180), the anti-trafficking movement is still so new in the United States that most often non-ex-captives must "speak for" most ex-captives if their story is to be told at this time.[17] The movement activists, at this early stage of the fight against trafficking, are generally elites, often human rights attorneys. In Margaret Keck and Kathryn Sikkink's now-classic book on transnational advocacy networks, they argue that "in a world where the voices of states have predominated", transnational advocacy networks have opened channels to bring "alternative visions and information into international debate" (1998: x). In the case of trafficked persons to the United States, they have been voiceless for different reasons: because of fear of reprisals from their traffickers, their stage in the recovery process, and concern that their community of co-ethnics will stigmatize them. Given these obstacles, it is possible that few ex-captives will ever step out from the anonymity of their case managers' offices, to give interviews to researchers, let alone public presentations or press conferences as part of "anti-trafficking movement" activities.

However, while speaking in public about one's experiences in trafficking is out of the question for some ex-captives, for others it can be therapeutic and empowering. One courageous young woman, Maria, who was in domestic servitude, has chosen to speak publicly both to the mainstream press as well as to audiences at events sponsored by the Philippine Forum in New York City (a non-profit organization that provides services and advocacy for Filipinos, particularly domestic workers). Maria explains that she speaks about her experiences in trafficking since she knows that she is "not the only who was in a bad situation", but, rather, "many others have scary situations". She hopes that by speaking out that she will help other Filipina women either leave an exploitative situation or help prevent them from being trafficked in the future. The demand for "trafficking victims" to speak at events and in the press far outpaces the number of ex-captives who are ready to do so. In some ways, this creates an environment in which the same stories get retold while many go untold, since even when ex-captives do take the podium, they can not possibly give voice to the myriad experiences and viewpoints of all ex-captives. And, Ileana Fohr, the Intensive Case Manager at Safe Horizon's Anti-Trafficking Program in New York City cautions, "For those who are ready to tell their story, it is still draining. It takes so much out of you. Telling the story too many times also can be terrifying and even re-traumatize."

Public speaking which demands a focus on the "trauma story" also can perpetuate the tellers of the stories as victims. Kleinman and Kleinman have written about "victims'" stories as a kind of "currency" and warn that the tellers risk not shaking off their expected role of victimhood (1997: 10). An example is Veronica Strang's description of Aboriginal involvement in the fight for their land claims in Australia. The legal process requires that they "display themselves as victims of colonial violence and subsequent subjugation" which is often "a lengthy account of massacres, murders, poisoning, abductions, rape, the separation of families, dispersal and dispossession" (Strang, 2003: 184). Yet, in other contexts, Beatriz Manz has observed that giving voice to trauma can allow individuals and their larger community "to come to terms with the past, not simply to remain a victim of it" (Manz, 2002: 298). Residents of Santa María Tzejá, a Guatemalan village that was a site of a massacre in 1982, have attended human rights workshops in which, writes Manz, they have been "speaking about the past, and engaging with it" (2002: 301). Quite remarkably, residents also have written and performed a play that documents the massacre, *There is Nothing Concealed That Will Not Be Discovered*. However, Manz acknowledges that "the act of remembering, let alone of retelling, is a highly charged, politicized event, fraught with danger" (2002: 299).

Manz also poses thorny questions on what methodology to use when conducting research on grief since she finds that in the aftermath of violence that a "respondent's perception of the researcher influences, at times determines what is said" (2002: 300). What is left unsaid is perhaps out of reach for most researchers who, as Manz notes, "face a particular challenge in doing research among populations subjected to fear and terror" (2002: 299). Indeed, I do not ask many questions while ex-captives talk about their experiences in slavery. Rather, I simply listen to what they choose to tell and not to tell. My experience speaking with Carmen, an Ecuadorian young woman who had been in domestic servitude in New York, bears out Manz's conviction that speaking about the past can be empowering. Even though her case manager at a social service agency and I had explained to her that I was researching life after trafficking and would not ask her about her experiences in trafficking, Carmen spoke up: "Please ask me questions, it's O.K. It's not a problem with me to talk about the past." Carmen elaborated, "It is like therapy for me, I feel comfortable talking about the past; it helps me. You can ask me any questions, I have no problem." Of course anthropologists are not therapists, a point I not only pressed upon Carmen, but explain to other ex-captives I interview. I have found that having a case manager in the room during an interview not only creates a safe environment, but it is also helpful in drawing clear lines between what case managers (and other counsellors) do, and what researchers do.

Researchers who follow their university Institutional Review Board (IRB) guidelines, which demand that researchers explain what they do and secure written consent to interviews, may not go far enough in the case of research with trafficked persons.[18] Rather, it is also incumbent upon researchers to explain what we do *not* do. After all, ex-captives are a population that has been asked to tell their stories to two general groups of "authority" figures: those who work in the criminal justice system (attorneys and law enforcement) and those who provide social services. These professionals offer them a variety of "deliverables": immigration documents, job contacts, medical attention, housing, and, in some cases, financial remuneration (such as back wages and awards from civil law suits). As a kind of third group, researchers must emphasize that there are no similar set of tangible benefits to speaking with us. We also must make clear how we undertake our work as scholars (and possibly as advocates), what kinds of writing we create, how long it takes the different forms of our writing to be published, and what audiences are likely to read our writing.[19] And, of course, we must consider how our writing can be used, particularly since the issue of trafficking has been so politicized.[20]

COLLABORATIONS

If ex-captives take the podium and tell their stories, the next step might be their participation in an anti-trafficking movement as advocates. In Guatemalan refugee camps in Mexico, anthropologist Patricia Pessar found indigenous women who moved beyond the initial stage of giving testimony in their struggle for women's rights, to participating in the more "'objective' phases of analysis and policy formulation" (Pessar, 2001: 476).[21] I am interested in how ex-captives can move beyond their "victim" status where they are called upon to provide "testimony" about trafficking, to participating – much like the members of the Coalition of Immokalee Workers – in the decision making of the direction of an anti-trafficking movement.

Modern-day slavery exists because a range of other exploitative labour conditions exist. The current legislation that protects trafficked persons and offers them the possibility of staying in the United States with a new visa, is based on a binary conceptualization of labour. One is either trafficked or not; suffered under "severe forms of exploitation" or not; and thus, eligible for benefits or not. The current system of identifying trafficking victims sorts exploited workers into trafficked and non-trafficked categories. It does not allow for a more nuanced understanding of the kinds of work sites where there is a spectrum of abuse and where slavery can flourish. Often, in these sites, those held in servitude labour side by side with contract employees who have a marginal ability to leave. Indeed, in many of the cases that have been prosecuted in the United States, T Visas have been issued to tomato pickers and women working in brothels who worked alongside friends who might make a different wage – though not a liveable one – and therefore do not qualify as "trafficked". I am interested in this liminal space, a kind of grey zone that is not written about in the media's anti-trafficking frenzy. Critical to more ex-captives' participation in the anti-trafficking movement is the inclusion of these individuals who do not qualify for T visas. The Coalition of Immokalee Workers' membership, for example, draws from this liminal group. Since CIW's members who are ex-captives speak publicly about labour exploitation, they are a model organization for how to incorporate exploited workers and ex-captives in the decision making and leadership of an anti-trafficking organization. Their efforts aim to illuminate how the conditions of work create a potential for a spectrum of abuse.

Collaborative research with indigenous intellectuals, such as anthropologist Joanne Rappaport's collaborative research with Nasa intellectuals in Columbia, offers a model for collaborative research projects between ex-captives, labour activists, service providers, and researchers (2005). Rappaport, for example, taught history workshops in Nasa communities to indigenous university students, as well as collaborated on an oral history of the education programme itself. She also participated in a collaborative research team with Columbian academic scholars based in the Columbian Institute of Anthropology in Bogatá. One starting point for ex-captives who already participate in group "empowerment"-

oriented meetings at their service providers, is to create workshops led by ex-captives, possibly in collaboration with researchers and activists. In such settings, much like Rappaport's collaborative workshops in Columbia, ex-captives and their collaborators can identify "pressing issues" to be "reflected upon by groups" which generate "not only data but interpretation" (2005: 125). Setting research agendas according to what marginalized groups identify harkens back to Sandra Harding's feminist call to arms that feminist scholars must "provide for women explanations of social phenomena that they want and need" (1987: 8). Although anthropologists have long been involved in research to promote social justice, a shift toward what Rappaport terms "ethnography as politically motivated dialogue", this kind of collaboration also raises many questions (2005: 125). For example, how compatible are the agendas and methodologies between "internal researchers" and academics? And, we must consider the difference in "consequences" of a research commitment for an academic and an internal researcher (2005: 127). A starting point for research (collaborative or otherwise) with ex-captives would be well-served by following a premise that undergirds the World Health Organization's (WHO) recommendations on interviewing trafficked women: "The degree and duration of the physical danger and psychological trauma to an individual is not always evident. In some cases risks may not be obvious to the interviewer. In other cases, the dangers may not be apparent to the woman" (Zimmerman and Watts, 2003: 5).

CONCLUSION

Researchers on human trafficking face multiple methodological challenges and ethical concerns. With a current media environment of sensationalistic stories about trafficking, carefully conducted research projects can make significant contributions to trafficking discussions among service providers, attorneys, and policy makers. Given the extreme vulnerability of this population, and how they are geographically dispersed throughout the United States, collaboration among researchers could yield research that both involves a wide range of trafficked persons as well as ethnographic richness. And, as a corrective to the absence of voices from trafficked persons, we await more writing by ex-captives such as Jean-Robert Cadet's (1998). In the meanwhile, collaborations between researchers and ex-captives is one way to incorporate trafficked persons' insights into both research design and analysis. These kinds of collaborations, at the nexus of research and advocacy, not only could play a meaningful role in an "anti-trafficking movement", but also contribute to an engaged anthropology.

FUNDING OF RESEARCH

I am grateful to the American Association of University Women for providing me with a Postdoctoral Fellowship during the 2003 to 2004 academic year to conduct field research full-time. Also, two Georgetown University Summer Academic Grants, in 2003 and 2004, have supported field research on trafficking in the Dominican Republic (2003) and in the United States (2004).

NOTES

1. I also have interviewed Dominican women in the Dominican Republic who were designated by the IOM as "trafficked" to Argentina and returned by the IOM to the Dominican Republic. The book, *Life After Trafficking: Creating Home/Returning Home*, will be based on field research with trafficked persons both in the United States and in the Dominican Republic.

2. I use the term ex-captive since it emphasizes that life in trafficking is slavery. Those who have been trafficked usually do not use the terms "trafficking" or "slavery" when they enter into dialogues with law enforcement or social service providers. Nor, do they necessarily use them once they learn about the concept of trafficking and that they have been trafficked. For example, Maria, whom I write about in this article, often refers to "what happened to me" and "her situation" when referring back to her time in domestic servitude.

3. Peter Landesman's article "Sex slaves on Main Street", in the *New York Times Magazine* has been criticized for making unfounded claims (2004). For example, see Jack Schafer's series of critical articles on Landesman's writing on www. slate.msn.com (Schafer, 2004a, 2004b, 2004c, 2004d, 2004e).

4. Elsewhere I write about the clear differences between voluntary and forced prostitution, along with the debates over how to conceive of women's sexual labour, see Brennan (2004).

5. The latest State Department Trafficking in Persons (TIP) Report puts the number of people annually trafficked into the United States within a range of 14,500 to 17,500 (2004: 23). This revised estimate is down from the 2003 TIP Report's figure of 18,000 to 20,000 (2003: 7). And, prior to these revised estimates, the figure circulating in many government documents was 50,000 (O'Neill Richard, 2000).

6. For legal scholarship see Hyland, 2001 and Young, 1998; for research by organizations see Anti-Slavery International, 2003; and for articles in the media see Bowe, 2003 and Browning, 2003 on agricultural servitude, and see Yeung, 2004 on domestic servitude. Also see Joy Zarembka's chapter on trafficking into domestic servitude in the United States in *Global Women* (2002). One notable recent report about trafficking in Florida was produced by a collaborative research team comprised of social service providers and academics, see Florida State University (2003). And, the latest collaborative effort is a report "Hidden

slaves: forced labor in the United States" by the non-profit Free The Slaves and The Human Rights Center at the University of California, Berkeley (2004).

7.   An example is the Department of Justice's press conferences where prosecutions of traffickers are announced, thus situating attorneys and law enforcement at the centre of fighting trafficking.

8.   Farmer describes structural violence as a "broad rubric that includes a host of offensives against human dignity: extreme and relative poverty, social inequalities ranging from racism to gender inequalities, and the more spectacular forms of violence that are uncontestedly human rights abuses" (2003: 8).

9.   Farmer writes: "I could never serve as a dispassionate reporter or chronicler of misery. I am openly on the side of the destitute sick and have never sought to represent myself as some sort of neutral party" (2003: 26).

10. The importance of safety cannot be emphasized enough. Psychiatrist Judith Herman situates safety as the first stage in her three "stages of recovery" from psychological trauma, with "remembrance and mourning" and "reconnection" as the next two stages (Herman, 1992: 155-156). And, a WHO report of recommendations for interviewing trafficked women suggests that interviews should not be conducted "if there is a risk that making a request for an interview or the interview itself will cause harm or compromise a woman's safety or her mental health" (Zimmerman and Watts, 2003: 5).

11. For example, see WHO (2001) and Schwartz (1997).

12. The "American Samoa" case involves Kil Soo Lee (a Korean national) who was sentenced on 29 January 2004 for involuntary servitude in a factory he owned in the territory of American Samoa. From 1999 through November 2000, Lee "used threats, arrest, deportations, starvation, confinement, and beatings to hold over 200 Vietnamese and Chinese garment workers in servitude" (Department of Justice, 2004). The conviction of Lee and his co-conspirators is the largest human trafficking case prosecuted by the Department of Justice.

13. To date, researchers have been put in touch with trafficked persons through social service providers. For example, in a European study on health risks associated with trafficking researchers "sought to interview participants through relevant support organizations both in EU partner countries and in three countries of origin" (Zimmerman et al., 2003: 16). The same kind of collaboration between researchers and social service providers also occurred in the Florida State University Study (2003) and in the report by Free the Slaves and the Human Rights Center at Berkeley (2004).

14. Hirsch notes the benefits for migration research from "cross-fertilization and collaboration between migration researchers and anthropologists" who conduct long-term fieldwork (2003: 252). In fact, there are a number of large migration studies in which scholars have joined forces. For example see two studies on the second-generation (Kasinitz et al., 2004; Levitt and Waters, 2002).

15. Because of a kind of "learned" silence as a survival strategy during civil war or genocide, refugees also are known to not speak about their past experiences. Aiwha Ong writes about Cambodian refugees who, while living under the terror of the Pol Pot regime "in the midst of life-and-death choices and the extremity of daily survival", depended on "subterfuge, disguise, lying, and silence" (Ong,

2003: 47). Once resettled in Oakland and San Francisco, they tried "to disappear into the local old people among who they were settled" (2003: 47).

16. While, the absence of "victim"-advocates is a striking dimension of this stage of fighting trafficking, the Coalition of Immokalee Workers is one exception. The CIW, located in Immokalee, Florida, has members who had been held in agricultural slavery and now are worker-advocates.

17. The problems of anthropologists "speaking for" marginalized individuals have been well documented, including anthropologist Pat Caplan's discussion of "exactly for whom one is speaking" and the pressures for minority groups to speak with one voice (2003: 17).

18. For more on ethical guidelines for conducting anthropological field research see the American Anthropological Association's website (at www.aaanet.org) for the following documents: "Statements on ethics: principles of professional responsibility" (adopted by the Council of the American Anthropological Association, May 1971) and "American Anthropological Association Statement on Ethnography and Institutional Review Board" (adopted by AAA Executive Board, 4 June 2004). And, see recommendations on conducting interviews specifically with trafficked persons in a WHO report (Zimmerman and Watts, 2003: 5). The report includes sample standard informed-consent questions "to help the researcher assess security", such as: "Do you have any concerns about carrying out this interview with me?" and "Do you feel this is a good time and place to discuss your experience? If not, is there a better time and place?" (2003: 5). It also includes questions that are based on the premise to "Treat each woman and the situation as if the potential for harm is extreme until there is evidence to the contrary" (2003: 5). An example is: "Do you think that talking to me could pose any problems for you, for example, with those who trafficked you, your family, friends, or anyone who is assisting you?" (2003: 5).

19. The WHO report I write about in the previous endnote also suggests asking: "Have you ever spoken with someone in (interviewer's profession) before? How was that experience?" which underscores the work process of researchers and journalists (Zimmerman and Watts, 2003: 5).

20. See recent news articles on how organizations – both on the right and the left – have claimed human trafficking as one of their major issues (Shapiro, 2004; Jones, 2003; Bumiller, 2003).

21. For example, Pessar recounts the story of an indigenous woman who was part of a delegation visiting New York but was told that she would not accompany the larger group because "this time it was not about giving testimony". A 23-year-old Ixil woman, Elena, commented on this delegate's exclusion: "Presenting women as 'victims' goes hand-in-hand with discrimination....We can continue to give testimony, but we can also provide analysis and even write a book. We must become the protagonists in our own struggle" (Pessar, 2001: 476).

REFERENCES

American Anthropological Association
  1971   "Statements on ethics: principles of professional responsibility", adopted by the Council of the American Anthropological Association, www. aaanet.org/stmts/ethstmnt.htm.

Anti-Slavery International
  2003   *The Migration-Trafficking Nexus: Combating Trafficking through the Protection of Migrants' Human Rights*, www.antislavery.org.

Bowe, J.
  2003   "Nobodies: does slavery exist in America?", *New Yorker*, 21 April and 28 April.

Brennan, D.
  2004   *What's Love Got to Do With It? Transnational Desires and Sex Tourism in the Dominican Republic*, Duke University Press, Durham.

Browning, M.
  2003   "Still harvesting shame", *Palm Beach Post*, 7 December.

Buijs, G.
  1993   "Introduction", in G. Buijs (Ed.), *Migrant Women: Crossing Boundaries and Changing Identities*, Berg Publishers Ltd., Oxford: 1-19.

Bumiller, E.
  2003   "Evangelicals sway White House on human rights issues abroad: liberals join effort on AIDS and sex trafficking", *The New York Times*, 26 October: A1 and A4.

Cadet, J-R
  1998   *Restavec: From Haitian Slave Child to Middle-Class American*, University of Texas Press, Austin.

Caplan, P.
  2003   "Introduction: anthropology and ethics", in P. Caplan (Ed.), *The Ethics of Anthropology: Debates and Dilemmas*, Routledge, London and New York: 1-27.

Daniel, E.V., and J.C. Knudsen
  1995   "Introduction", in E.V. Valentine and J.C. Knudsen (Eds), *Mistrusting Refugees*, University of California Press, Berkeley: 1-12.

Department of Justice
  2004   *Anti-Trafficking News Bulletin*, US Department of Justice Civil Rights Division, February, 1(2), www.usdoj.gov/trafficking.htm.

Farmer, P.
  1999   *Infections and Inequalities: The Modern Plagues*, University of California Press, Berkeley.
  2003   *Pathologies of Power: Health, Human Rights, and the New War on the Poor*, University of California Press, Berkeley.

Farmer, P., et al. (Eds)
  1996   *Women, Poverty and AIDS: Sex, Drugs and Structural Violence,* Common Courage Press, Maine.

Florida State University
    2003   "Florida responds to human trafficking", Center for the Advancement of
            Human Rights, Florida State University.
Free the Slaves and Human Rights Center
    2004   "Hidden slaves: forced labour in the United States", Free the Slaves,
            Washington, DC and Human Rights Center, University of California,
            Berkeley.
Harding, S.
    1987   "Introduction: is there a feminist method?", in S. Harding (Ed.), *Feminism
            and Methodology: Social Science Issues*, Indiana University Press,
            Bloomington and Indianapolis: 2-14.
Herman, J.
    1992   *Trauma and Recovery: The Aftermath of Violence – from Domestic Abuse
            to Political Terror*, Basic Books, New York.
Hirsch, J.
    2003   "Anthropologists, migrants, and health research: confronting cultural
            appropriateness", in N. Foner (Ed.), *American Arrivals: Anthropology
            Engages the New Immigration*, American Research Press, Santa Fe:
            229-258.
Hyland, K.
    2001   "Protecting human victims of trafficking: an American framework", *Ber-
            keley Women's Law Journal*, 16: 29-71.
Jones, M.
    2003   "Thailand's brothel busters", *Mother Jones*, November/December.
Kasinitz, P., et al.
    2004   *Becoming New Yorkers: Ethnographies of the New Second Generation*,
            Russell Sage Foundation Publications, New York.
Keck, M.E., and K. Sikkink
    1998   *Activists Beyond Borders*, Cornell University Press, Ithaca.
Kleinman, A., and J. Kleinman
    1997   "The appeal of experience; the dismay of images: cultural appropriations
            of suffering in our times", in A. Kleinman, et al. (Eds), *Social Suffering*,
            University of California Press, Berkeley: 1-23.
Landesman, P.
    2004   "Sex slaves on Main Street", *New York Times Magazine*, 25 January.
Levitt, P., and M.C. Waters
    2002   *The Changing Face of Home: The Transnational Lives of the Second
            Generation,* Russell Sage Foundation Publications, New York.
MacClancy, J.
    2002   "Introduction: taking people seriously", in J. MacClancy (Ed.), *Exotic No
            More: Anthropology on the Front Lines*, University of Chicago Press,
            Chicago: 1-14.
Manz, B.
    2002   "Terror, grief, and recovery: genocidal trauma in a Mayan village in Gua-
            temala", in A. Laban Hinton (Ed.), *Annihilating Difference: The Anthro-
            pology of Genocide*, University of California Press, Berkeley: 292-309.

O'Neill Richard, A.
2000 "International trafficking in women to the to the United States: a contemporary manifestation of slavery and organized crime", Center for the Study of Intelligence Monograph, April.

Ong, A.
2003 *Buddha is Hiding: Refugees, Citizenship, the New America*, University of California Press, Berkeley.

Peacock, J.L.
1986 *The Anthropological Lens: Harsh Light, Soft Focus*, Cambridge University Press, Cambridge and New York.

Pessar, P.
2001 "Women's political consciousness and empowerment in local, national, and transnational contexts: Guatemalan refugees and returnees", *Identities*, 7(4): 461-500.

Rappaport, J.
2005 *Intercultural Utopias: Public Intellectuals, Cultural Experimentation, and Ethnic Pluralism in Columbia*, Duke University Press, Durham (manuscript from author).

Schafer, J.
2004a "Sex slaves of West 43rd Street", *Slate*, 26 January, www.slate.com.
2004b "Doubting Landesman", *Slate*, 27 January, www.slate.com.
2004c "The *Times Magazine* strikes back", *Slate*, 28 January, www.slate.com.
2004d "How *not* to handle press critics", *Slate*, 29 January, www.slate.com.
2004e "Enslaved by his sources", *Slate*, 3 February, www.slate.com.

Scheper-Hughes, N.
1995 "The primacy of the ethical: propositions for a militant anthropology", *Current Anthropology*, 36(3): 409-440.

Schwartz, M.D. (Ed.)
1997 *Researching Sexual Violence Against Women: Methodological and Personal Perspectives*, Sage Publications, California and London.

Shapiro, N.
2004 "The new abolitionists", *Seattle Weekly*, 25-31 August.

Spangenburg, M.
2002 "International trafficking of children to New York City for sexual purposes", ECPAT-USA, www.ecpatusa.org/trafficking.asp.

Strang, V.
2003 "An appropriate question?: The propriety of anthropological analysis in the Australian political arena", in P. Caplan (Ed.), *The Ethics of Anthropology: Debates and Dilemmas*, Routledge, London and New York: 172-194.

US Department of State
2003 "Trafficking in persons report", US Department of State, Washington, DC, June, www.state.gov/documents/organization/21555.pdf.
2004 "Trafficking in persons report", US Department of State, Washington, DC, June, www.state.gov/documents/organization/21555.pdf.

Yeung, B.
  2004   "Enslaved in Palo Alto: a domestic worker from Kenya has accused her
          employer – a prominent African journalist – of human trafficking",
          SFWeekly, 18 February, www.sfweekly.com.
Young, B.
  1998   "Trafficking of humans across United States borders: United States laws
          can be used to punish traffickers and protect victims", *Georgetown
          Immigration Law Journal*, Fall(13): 73-104.
World Health Organization (WHO)
  2001   "Putting women first: ethical and safety recommendations for research
          on domestic violence against women", WHO, Geneva.
Zarembka, J.M.
  2002   "America's dirty work: migrant maids and modern-day slavery", in
          B. Ehrenreich and A. Hochschild (Eds), *Global Woman: Nannies, Maids,
          and Sex Workers in the New Economy*, Metropolitan Books, New York:
          142-153.
Zimmerman, C., and C. Watts
  2003   "WHO ethical and safety recommendations for interviewing trafficked
          women", World Health Organization, Geneva.
Zimmerman, C., et al.
  2003   "The health risks and consequences of trafficking in women and
          adolescents: findings from a European study", London School of Hygiene
          and Tropical Medicine, London.

Designing Trafficking Research from a Labour Market Perspective: The ILO Experience[1]

Beate Andrees and Mariska N.J. van der Linden*

INTRODUCTION

Until recently, the International Labour Organization's (ILO) knowledge base on trafficking in human beings consisted mainly of reports reviewing the implementation of relevant Conventions in member states. Trafficking-related information was also obtained through numerous studies of the ILO International Migration Branch,[2] though often not framed explicitly as research on human trafficking. The growing international interest in the illegal movement and exploitation of human beings has led to new and innovative research within the ILO, covering various issues such as child trafficking,[3] irregular migration, and forced labour.[4] However, the ILO's new research programme initiated under the ILO Special Action Programme to Combat Forced Labour (SAP-FL) has commissioned a dozen studies on trafficking and other forced labour outcomes of migration, and has also published training, legal, and other information material in this field.[5]

The ILO is particularly well placed to develop a better understanding of the labour dimensions of human trafficking. The bulk of the existing literature focuses on trafficking for sexual exploitation of women and children. While this has helped develop clearer definitions and uncover the mechanisms of trafficking, it only presents a partial picture. The starting point of ILO/SAP-FL was that trafficking for labour exploitation is significant and under-researched. The following article aims to critically discuss methodologies used for the purpose of this research as well as "lessons learned" and preliminary results.[6] Our main argument is that the trafficking paradigm presents a useful entry point to better

---

* International Labour Organization, Geneva, Switzerland.

understand some of the worst forms of exploitation existing in the world today. If too narrowly defined, however, it limits rather than enlarges our knowledge base on exploitation linked to the movement of people. This also has consequences for taking action to eliminate human trafficking.

The following article starts with a brief discussion on the "state-of-the-art" in trafficking research. It then goes into more detail explaining the research design, some preliminary results and recommendations. Given the overall purpose of this publication the main focus is on methodological aspects.

A BRIEF REVIEW OF CURRENT RESEARCH
ON HUMAN TRAFFICKING

Research on trafficking is in its early stages and though much has been done, even more must be done. Trafficking of women and children for sexual exploitation has been the focus of most anti-trafficking actions and it is the main target of research on trafficking. Research looks chiefly at the most blatant cases, often driven by abhorrent media reports and political discourses. Additionally, it tends to focus on the supply side of trafficking, whereas demand factors have received less attention (for a pioneering study confined to trafficking for sex work and domestic service, see Anderson, 2003). Research using secondary sources prevails over primary studies.

Primary research on trafficking, considering it involves a rare and elusive population, does not usually involve attempts at random sampling. Instead, studies tend to target a particular population. For example, the Regional Clearing Point obtained a comprehensive dataset based on identified and assisted victims in south-eastern Europe (Regional Clearing Point, 2003). However, the report acknowledges that this approach reflects most of all the institutional view of trafficking. The result is that the overwhelming majority of victims interviewed were female and trafficked for sexual exploitation. This type of bias can also be found in other studies as victims are often contacted through assistance organizations, shelters, and detention centres.

There are only a few studies that take into account trafficking for forced labour exploitation. Anti-Slavery International has recently launched a study of laws and policies on the treatment of victims of trafficking thereby compiling a number of cases that have come to light through the activities of service providers, law enforcement agencies, and the judicial system (Anti-Slavery International, 2002). Another study on forced labour which also takes migration and trafficking into consideration is "Disposable people: new slavery in the global economy" by Kevin Bales (1999). It contains some rough estimates and descriptions of forced labour in different parts of the world, obtained by discussions with key informants and relevant secondary sources.

As such, the research pool on trafficking is small. However, within this pool there are very few studies on forced labour outcomes of trafficking. Those that do exist are either based on secondary research such as policy analysis, reflecting the institutional perception of a victim, or on primary research, which also presents bias in terms of a myopic view of the identity of the victim, which is propagated via selection bias.

Based on this, ILO/SAP-FL identified two main lacunae in current trafficking research where its expertise could be of use. ILO/SAP-FL aimed, first of all, to focus research on all types of trafficking as well as other forced labour outcomes of migration, thereby broadening the scope of research on trafficking. Of course this does not mean that trafficking for sexual exploitation should receive less consideration, yet it will be placed in a larger framework by taking into account trafficking for labour exploitation, other forced labour outcomes of migration, men as well as women, and a variety of economic sectors. Second, our aim is to expand our knowledge on the demand side, in particular economic factors that are the driving force behind trafficking for labour exploitation.

DESIGNING THE RESEARCH: DEFINITIONS AND METHODOLOGIES

Definitions of forced labour and human trafficking

Developing a definition of trafficking that is based on current legal understanding but at the same time not too legalistic is an important first step. Our qualitative studies have helped to obtain more clarity on the definition, which in turn has informed the framework for our quantitative research.

Though recent international instruments have helped to clarify definitions, there are still serious inconsistencies between different instruments as well as between terminologies used by individual researchers. To begin with, the 2000 *Palermo Protocol to Prevent, Suppress and Punish Trafficking in Persons, Especially Women and Children*, provides a comprehensive definition describing three key elements:

(1)   The *activities* that constitute human trafficking (recruitment, transportation, harbouring, receipt of persons);

(2)   The *means* being used (force, coercion, abduction, fraud, deception, abuse of power or of a position of vulnerability);

(3)   The *purpose*, which is exploitation (prostitution of others, sexual exploitation, forced labour or services, slavery or practices similar to slavery).

The key of the Palermo definition is the purpose of the activity, which relates to the *intention* of the perpetrator. However, with trafficking, as well with other crimes, intention, or *mens rea*, is highly subjective and difficult to prove in court proceedings. Though determining intention is perhaps an avoidable problem, the Palermo definition of trafficking is further complicated by the fact that there is no standard definition of exploitation. In our research, we have therefore relied on the ILO definition of forced labour, which limits the range of cases to the most severe forms of exploitation.

Forced labour has been defined in the ILO Convention No. 29 (1930). According to this definition forced labour is: "all work or service that is exacted from any person under the menace of any penalty and for which the said person has offered himself voluntarily" (Art. 2). There are two main elements in this definition: (1) menace of penalty, and (2) the notion of consent. Again, these elements pose some challenges: What should be the nature of the penalty to qualify as forced labour? And how is consent being viewed when workers are actually not in the position to make an informed, consensual decision?

The ILO supervisory bodies have responded to these questions by stating that (a) penalty does not have to take on the form of a penal sanction, it might as well be linked to the loss of rights or privileges; and that (b) consent is rendered meaningless if a worker has been induced into employment by deceit, false promises, the retention of identity documents, or force (ILO, 2003, see also the provisions of the Palermo Protocol). More importantly, the ILO supervisory bodies have concluded that the worker's right to free choice of employment remains inalienable, hence a worker must always have the possibility to revoke a previously made consensual agreement. In order to determine whether a case could be classified as forced labour in our research, interviews with migrant workers included the following key question: *Have you been free to change or leave your employment at any given time?* This question was also central in the assessment of cases based on secondary material such as court proceedings.

In a second step, cases were classified according to the trafficking dimension of forced labour, using the following two variables: (1) deceptive and/or coercive recruitment, and (2) forced labour exploitation. This is independent of whether the movement took place across international or within national borders.

In fact, it was only during the research process that we have begun to understand recruitment mechanisms into forced labour that are linked to the labour market in the destination country. This means that a migrant who has initially been smuggled across the border and was then recruited into forced labour would be counted as a trafficked victim. Where there was no connection between movement, recruitment, and final employment we referred to "non-trafficked victims of forced labour" as opposed to "trafficked victims of forced labour". It should be noted that this was a sociological, not a legal, distinction.

In the first scenario, there are generally two or more actors who benefit from the exploitation, including the smuggler, the recruiter, and the employer. A trafficker can take on either one or all of these roles, provided he/she has the intention to exploit the migrant. The perpetrators can be part of an organized crime network, but they can also act independently while still playing into each other's hands. For example, the smuggler can be an individual (i.e. taxi driver) transporting irregular migrants for a fee across the border; the recruiter can be a perfectly legal recruitment agency that procures workers to an employer (i.e. a subcontractor in the construction industry). If the recruiter is based in the origin country, she/he can also arrange the border crossing. Again, this could be a seemingly legal agency, such as a travel or recruitment agency. What is important, however, is that *all* profit from the vulnerability and exploitation of irregular migrant workers, their isolation in the destination country, and their lack of viable alternatives. All these actors could, therefore, be qualified as traffickers.

In the second scenario, we find migrant workers who, for example, have been legal in the destination country for a certain period of time, and do not depend on an intermediary (either for the transportation, contacts to the employer, credit, etc.). For several reasons, forced labour may not only be the outcome of trafficking as perceived by the Palermo Protocol. For example, we found contract workers in forced labour situations who have been employed by a company from their country, which in turn was subcontracted by a company based in a western European country. Others have first been recruited through their own social networks, and then moved into a different employment relationship where they became victims of forced labour.

Whether all these different cases should be defined as trafficking or not is more than an academic question. It has indeed serious political consequences, as the emphasis on forced labour and other forms of exploitation would require looking at migration as a whole. It would also require an analysis of the restructuring of economic sectors that goes well beyond an analysis of the demand for sexual services. Since the ILO is primarily concerned with the exploitation of migrant workers we have focused on victims of forced labour regardless of how they have organized their journey or where they came from.

Main methodological challenges

Any trafficking-related research, whether it focuses on trafficking for sexual or labour exploitation, faces methodological challenges that have to be considered in the research design. The most challenging issue is probably related to sampling. While there seems to be consensus that trafficking affects rare and elusive populations and that random sampling is nearly impossible, there are, however, differences in the nature of samples. As mentioned above, many samples have a clear selection bias, reflecting more the institutional activity than the actual distribution of trafficked victims. This bias is difficult to avoid because of the hidden nature of the phenomena – it is mainly through service providers and intensified action of public authorities that trafficking cases come to light. Trafficking for labour exploitation is no exception in this regard. One solution to counter balance this institutional bias is to select a specific subpopulation, such as foreign sex workers in a given country or a specific migrant community.

Given these constraints, samples of trafficked victims are usually not representative. Therefore, it is impossible to arrive at credible estimates of actual numbers based on interviews with victims of trafficking. Estimates have to rely on proxy indicators or on secondary information of actual reported cases (Laczko and Gramegna, 2003). Samples can at best help to produce "guesstimates", using a mix of additional sources and indicators. Even though not representative, samples are useful to understand trends and characteristics within a subpopulation, for example, returned migrants in a specific country.

Whether sampling or a more anthropological approach is being used, ethical issues should always be considered when designing the research (Kelly, 2001). General ethical principles in research, such as consent of the interviewee, confidentiality, and truthfulness do not need further explanation. But there are some ethical considerations that apply particularly to trafficking research: (1) the safety of the interviewee, the interviewer, and third persons has to be guaranteed to the extent possible; and (2) it is important to respect the subjectivity of the "victim" instead of trying to find the "ideal victim". As we know from numerous accounts of exploited/trafficked sex workers, they may not perceive their situation in the same way as the researcher. The same applies to "victims" of forced labour, maybe more so because exploitation is less frequently imposed by means of physical violence, hence less blatant. The design of structured and semi-structured interviews should, therefore, integrate the subjectivity of the respondent.

Research methodology

ILO/SAP-FL research methodologies varied in particular between origin and destination countries. Taking into account the covert nature of trafficking and forced labour as well as the fact that research on these topics still finds itself in a more or less exploratory stage, a quantitative approach was complemented by a more qualitative one in order to better understand these phenomena from a real life perspective. The political, legal, and economic situation of the locality where the research is carried out poses additional constraints, for example the degree of freedom of expression influences the number of media reports and legal frameworks define recorded cases. Therefore, almost all the studies were multi-method.

Origin countries

The methodology applied in the four origin countries (Albania, Romania, Moldova, and Ukraine) consisted of three parts: (1) a standardized questionnaire for 160 returned migrants in each country,[7] (2) semi-structured interviews with key informants, and (3) focus group discussions (ILO/SAP-FL 2002).

The main sampling method used was snowballing[8] though returned migrants were also selected more randomly, for example through directly approaching persons in public spaces. The research teams were asked to select an equal number of women and men to the extent possible. In addition, information from a more or less equal number of trafficked/forced labour victims and "successful migrants" was sought in order to understand specific vulnerability factors.

The questionnaire investigated the following topics: demographic characteristics, the pre-migration situation of the migrant, how they obtained their job abroad (recruitment), and how the travel to the destination country was organized. In addition, the survey looked at conditions of employment/exploitation abroad, forms of coercion used by employers/exploiters, the awareness of assistance, and how the migrant managed to exit the forced labour situation.

Destination countries

The research in destination countries covers France, Germany, Hungary, Japan, Russia, Turkey, and the United Kingdom. Researchers were asked to document at least 15 cases of forced labour per country, sometimes focusing exclusively on one ethnic group, for example Chinese immigrants in France. The case studies represent the situation in various economic sectors such as agriculture, construction, catering, domestic service, entertainment, transportation, and small sweatshop production in the textile and leather industries.

Respondents were found through key informants (mainly NGOs or trade unions) or "gatekeepers" to a specific migrant community. The interviewers used open-ended questions and were asked to reproduce the narrative as closely as possible where tape recording was impossible. In the study on irregular migration and forced labour in Russia, the qualitative case studies were complemented by a random sample of 360 migrant workers in three different regions of the country. The intention was to develop a better understanding of working and living conditions of migrant workers in Russia from which the cases of forced labour differed.

The primary research was partially based on interviews. Cases were also constructed based on interviews with key informants, media reports, and court proceedings. In countries where anti-trafficking legislation covers forced labour, court material proved to be a valuable source. The topics of the semi-structured interviews with migrants in destination countries were the same as those investigated in origin countries. In all cases interviews were either recorded, or, where that was impossible, they were written down as faithfully as possible after the interview.

PRELIMINARY RESULTS

Though the main focus of this paper is on research methodologies, some preliminary results will be discussed in this section in order to indicate directions for further research.

Countries of origin

At the beginning of the research the focus was on two main categories: victims of trafficking versus successful migrants. Yet, as more and more data flowed in, it became apparent that it was useful to enlarge this distinction. The initial distinction, using the Palermo Protocol definition as a starting point, was based on two main groups of questions, the first pertaining to different forms of coercion experienced at work, the second to deception by a recruiter in terms of the destination country and/or working conditions. Though those that were deceived always experienced coercion in the country of destination, yet another group that was not deceived/coerced by the recruiter also experienced exploitation amounting to forced labour. This group was dissimilar from the successful migrants, which had been neither deceived nor coerced in any significant way. After careful consideration of all the data, three categories were elaborated: Trafficked victims of forced labour, non-trafficked victims of forced labour, and successful migrants. This distinction allowed us to investigate varying degrees to which migrants can become victim of exploitation, routes that lead into forced labour, and individual strategies to escape from coercion and control.

Based on the number of valid interviews from the sample, ILO/SAP-FL created a database containing only information from respondents classified as victims of forced labour (trafficked and non-trafficked). Up to now, that database contains 298 entries of forced labour victims: 186 (62.4%) were trafficked whereas 112 (37.6%) were not. Among the trafficked victims for forced labour the majority are women (64%), but men make up an important share (26%). The reasoning is similar though less pronounced for non-trafficked victims of forced labour: a small majority were men (53.8%), though almost half were women (46.2%). Hence, women constitute the majority of cases.

The studies have also provided insight into the recruitment of victims. Trafficked victims of forced labour mostly found a job abroad via an intermediary[9] (43%) though social networks were also important (39.1%). Non-trafficked victims of forced labour mostly obtained work abroad through their social connections (54.7%). Agencies also played a role in trafficking (11.9%) as well and other forced labour outcomes of migration (15.1%). These results probably indicate that the lack of social connections abroad is a vulnerability factor when considering trafficking, though this is not always the case. No recruitment method currently used eliminates the possibility of forced labour, which shows the need for migration management, particularly the monitoring of recruitment of migrant workers.

Once arrived in the destination country, trafficked and non-trafficked victims of forced labour often work in the same sectors, though the proportions present in each sector vary. In a hierarchical order, trafficked victims of forced labour are mostly present in sex work (32.4%), construction (16.8%), entertainment/dancing/bartending (12.8%), and agriculture (12.3%). The majority of trafficked women were forced to provide sexual services (sometimes in conjunction with other work). Non-trafficked victims of forced labour are mainly present, in a decreasing order, in construction (31.5%), agriculture (14.8%), and sex work (11.1%). Therefore, working sectors do not allow a clear differentiation between trafficked and non-trafficked victims of forced labour and a focus on sex work as the main activity of trafficked victims of forced labour seems somewhat restrictive.

The studies also considered forms of coercion, leading to a better understanding of coercive factors that create and maintain the forced labour situation. The research considered different forms of coercion used: use of violence against the migrant, the use of violence against others close to the migrant, debts to employer/intermediary, lack of freedom of movement, withholding wages, threats of violence against the migrant, threats of violence against others close to the migrant, threats of being reported to the police, and threats of deportation. The most serious form of coercion for all victims was the lack of freedom of movement (trafficked victims 65.1%, non-trafficked victims 60.7%). In general, all other forms of coercion were considered more serious by trafficked victims of forced labour in preventing them from leaving employment, except for the lack of ID documents, which was equally important for both groups, and threats of deportation, which were considered slightly more serious by non-trafficked victims of forced labour.

The investigation of these forms of coercion has demonstrated a *forced labour continuum*, where trafficked victims of forced labour (most of them forced sex workers) are in the most abusive situations, followed by non-trafficked victims of forced labour. Trafficked victims of forced labour are subjected to the worst abuses because there are several actors who have vested interests in keeping them vulnerable. These victims suffer the most direct restraint and tend to have the least freedom of movement. The most common forms of exploitation among non-trafficked victims of forced labour are non-payment of wages and/or retention of identity documents. Moreover, on the forced labour continuum, women are generally worse off than men in their category (i.e. trafficked victims or non-trafficked victims). More successful migrants also suffered exploitation in the shape of working significantly more than five-day, 40-hour workweeks under unacceptable conditions at the workplace.

Thus, since both those who are subject to coercion at the outset of the migration project as well as those subject to coercion at a later stage are victims of severe exploitation, the academically interesting distinction between trafficked versus non-trafficking victims of forced labour becomes obsolete at a policy and legislation level. The conception of trafficking as a cross-border phenomenon, maintained by many actors in the field of trafficking, is not conducive to concerted action that encompasses all victims. Indeed, it should not matter when or where the coercion started, but that a person was subjected to it.

The consideration of the different ways in which victims exited forced labour gave a deeper understanding of the "victim" as such. The main ways of exiting forced labour were slightly different according to category of victim, though both reflect a certain amount of initiative. Trafficked victims of forced labour mostly exited forced labour situations by fleeing (30.5%), whereas most non-trafficked victims of forced labour exited because they "decided to go" (31.5%). The second main method of exiting forced labour for trafficked victims was through a police raid (25.6%), whereas for non-trafficked victims it was fleeing

(19.8%). Thus, the second main mechanism of exiting forced labour for non-trafficked victims was again based on initiative.

These results point to a certain amount of agency that the victim maintains in a forced labour situation. Non-trafficked victims exercise more agency in exiting forced labour than trafficked victims. This implies first of all that trafficked victims are probably even worse off than non-trafficked victims, which corroborates the hypothesis of a forced labour continuum. Secondly, it suggests that forced labour should be seen as a process rather than a state: a migrant is not a victim of forced labour from one moment to the other, but he/she becomes one over a period of time. Indeed, those who were deceived at the outset of the labour migration project, i.e. the trafficked victims, suffered more abuse in forced labour and were able to exercise less agency during exit. This implies that there are degrees of victimization associated with the time spent in forced labour and/or the route into it. The forced labour process is perhaps best seen as an ever-narrowing labyrinth where one's perceived alternatives become less and less viable, though, perhaps victims have some agency up to a certain point.

Destination countries

Research in destination countries helped to shed light on the structural factors influencing forced labour and forms of coercion in the final employment stage. In each country, we found a range of structural factors that contribute to the extreme dependence of migrant workers on the mercy of their employer regardless of how they entered into employment/exploitation, including the inability to obtain a regular status, work permits that bound migrants to one specific employer, and the lack of worksite inspections and monitoring of private employment agencies, as well as corruption of officials. The isolation of the victim, the lack of language skills, and general knowledge about working conditions in the host country also play into the hands of abusive employers and traffickers.

The studies also exposed the interrelationship between recruitment mechanisms and the channels that migrant workers use to enter a country legally or illegally. This, in a complementary fashion to the more quantitative studies in origin countries, demonstrated how difficult it is to draw the line between trafficking and other forced labour outcomes of migration.

For instance, Chinese migrants travel to France using various routes. They pay a lot of money for the trip to a person belonging to a large network of "facilitators". Once they arrive in France, they must work many years to pay off their debt. Often the last "facilitator" does not deliver them into the hands of an abusive and exploitative employer though many end up in exploitative informal work that is not always forced labour, often in sweatshops of the garment industry, restaurants, or domestic service. There are other cases, which could be clearly defined as trafficking, in the sense that recruiter and employer are one and the same person or part of the same network. This is, however, often based on family connections, which makes it more unlikely that the victim will denounce these abusive practices (Gao and Poisson, forthcoming).

Yet, the network of "facilitators" profits from the migrant's labour for many years in the form of a high interest on an exorbitant debt. In this type of case it is very hard to determine whether the migrant has been trafficked or smuggled. Indeed, each case must be studied in minute detail in order to categorize the migrant either as a victim of trafficking or an irregular migrant suffering exploitative working conditions that do not constitute forced labour.

Flagrant examples of forced labour can be found among migrant workers in the Russian Federation. Whereas in previous years workers, for example men from Tajikistan, were recruited by "gangmasters" in the origin country and taken to Russia, most leave independently today. Intermediaries still play a role in the destination country, but many find employment through their own social networks. The working conditions, however, are such that many of them have experienced forced labour or at least elements of it (Tyuryukanova, 2004).

The studies in the countries of origin and destination confirm the hypothesis that trafficking for forced labour as well as other forced labour outcomes of migration are an important issue. Though the numbers above are not representative, they still indicate that trafficking of women for sexual exploitation may only be the tip of the iceberg. And whereas it may be easy to distinguish between the sectors in which migrants are exploited, the route into this sector can be difficult to define. Trafficking appears to be part of the larger occurrence of forced labour, which in turn is a subgroup of forced labour outcomes of migration, which, finally, belongs to the encompassing category of abuses and exploitation related to labour migration.

PROBLEMS ENCOUNTERED

Though a tentative attempt was made to sample randomly, the interviewees in the countries of origin were largely returned migrants contacted through snowball sampling. This implies a certain bias in the sample. Yet, large samples using

ITEM ON HOLD

Title: Data and research on human trafficking : a global survey / edited by Frank Laczko and Elzbieta Gozdziak ; International Organization for Migration.

Author:

Call Number: JV6035 .D38 2005

Enumeration:

Chronology:

Copy:

Item Barcode:

Item Being Held

Patron: Mario Keaton Thomas

Patron Barcode:

Patron Phone: 8159289422

Hold Expires: 5/11/2007

Pickup At: Circulation Desk

the general population as a framework would most likely not contain enough returned migrants. Therefore, though the method used is probably the best way to approach the sampling difficulties involved in a study on a covert and underground topic, it nonetheless implies that the results are not representative. A good example of this is the time spent in forced labour abroad. Basing the period of forced labour on those who have exited it means that those remaining in forced labour, and who are perhaps not able to exit it, are excluded. Thus, the time spent in forced labour is likely to be grossly underestimated.

Other problems during the research were encountered while interviewing migrants. It is highly likely that social desirability influenced the answers given to the interviewers. When taking into account that forced labour and trafficking constitute highly sensitive topics, it should not be forgotten that pride, honour, and shame may bias the way interviewees answer questions. It is generally known and accepted that returning migrants tend to exaggerate the good sides and underplay the more negative ones about their experience abroad. In the case of forced labour and trafficking – particularly for sexual exploitation – there is the risk of social stigma if the matter became public. However, merely the acknowledgment of having been tricked into working without (adequate) payment can stigmatize a returned migrant worker (see Tyldum and Brunovskis, 2005).

Social desirability issues may have lead to an underestimation of the numbers of victims in this research, as well as the severity of the conditions under which they were made to work. Data are often missing because respondents have been reluctant to talk about sensitive issues such as illegal border crossings, salaries, deception, and experienced violence. Furthermore, even though interviews took place upon return of the migrants, they are still distrustful of the actual intention of the researcher. The rather formal setting of an interview based on a standardized questionnaire prevents the interviewer to really engage with the respondent and vice versa. Focus-group discussions have yielded more intimate information though they sometimes also had a negative effect on the willingness of respondents to share their experiences.

Identifying cases of forced labour in destination countries proved to be very difficult for several reasons. First, migrants with an irregular status are reluctant to share their experience as they risk being discovered and deported or cause trouble for their boss, who can in turn often cause trouble for them. Many of them cannot see an immediate value of this research and do not want to share very personal and often humiliating experiences. Again ethical problems arose when migrants requested the interviewers' help.

Second, when relying on official sources, such as police reports or court proceedings, the findings are limited due to narrow legal and institutional frameworks. Only some countries have already approved of anti-trafficking legislation that is not restricted to trafficking for sexual exploitation. The following example taken from ILO/SAP-FL research in Germany (Cyrus, forthcoming) illustrates this point: Between 2000 and 2002, a German couple recruited eight young women from Poland and Lithuania to work as *au pairs* in Germany. The women were recruited under false pretences, smuggled into the country, and severely exploited. Some escaped, but one woman committed suicide in 2003, which brought the case to the public's attention. Since the German anti-trafficking law at the time was restricted to trafficking for sexual exploitation, the couple was punished for other offences such as deceit and smuggling. Apart from the fact that this implied lower sanctions, the case was not counted in the German court and police statistics as a trafficking case. Many of the national experts who have been interviewed for the purpose of this research had a clear bias in their perception of trafficking being closely related to women in prostitution. The same can be said for the media that primarily reports about trafficking cases for sexual exploitation.

As such, the same term can reflect different practices and perceptions. This means that cases on forced labour and trafficking as defined by international conventions may not reflect cases in the media or other reports using the same term. An example of the results of contextual variations of the interpretation of the term "trafficking" is the tragic death of 20 Chinese cockle pickers at Morecambe Bay in Great Britain in 2004. Though it received much media coverage, the deaths were not linked to trafficking. The general perception is still that women are trafficked (mostly for the purpose of commercial sexual exploitation) while men are smuggled for labour exploitation.

RECOMMENDATIONS FOR FUTURE RESEARCH

Considering the difficulty of establishing a sample frame and using it to sample randomly, the best approach to sample selection remains a selective one, such as snowballing from key informants, for instance. However, a way around this could be to have a standardized survey at borders, where all passing migrants could be interviewed on their return. In addition, the more quantitative material can be complemented by in-depth interviews and focus groups, as was done in the ILO/SAP-FL studies on Albania, Moldova, Romania, and the Ukraine.

The definitional problems of the studies are hard to counter. Indeed, the difficulty related to the distinction between forced labour and other forms of severe exploitation seems inevitable. Further exploration of this concept should help establish more concrete criteria of forced labour exploitation. Though the ILO/SAP-FL studies have contributed to this, more research into this area needs to be done.

Another major problem is the rapport between the interviewees and the interviewer. It is difficult to eliminate bias due to social stigma and fear. It is hard to circumvent this problem, which is surely aggravated by using a standardized questionnaire. Training interviewers on interviewing about sensitive topics and developing an adequate rapport with interviewees, even in more quantitative research, is important. Researchers should understand the process of trafficking with all its different degrees and nuances. They should avoid trying to look for the "ideal victim". This ideal type, often thought of as the young women/girl trafficked for sexual exploitation, can prevent a researcher from identifying other victims. This can be particularly difficult since many victims do not see themselves as such and may not like being framed as a "victim". In this respect, researchers should also be careful in the usage of language that denies interviewees any form of agency.

Therefore, the understanding of who the victim is should be deepened. Taking into account that most victims of trafficking and forced labour are not held in chains but suffer more indirect coercion and restraint, even the choice of the victim to stay in an exploitative situation must be understood as well as how he/she managed to break out. This can be done by considering forced labour from the point of view of a lack of viable alternatives. The process of trafficking and forced labour diminishes the amount of viable alternatives perceived by the victim, as the latter sinks deeper into forced labour. Not only structural factors should be taken into account, the psychology of forced labour should be given equal attention. It must not be forgotten that the purpose of research, in the long run, is to broaden the scope of viable alternatives for victims so that they may break out of forced labour or, even better, broaden the scope of choices for migrants so that they do not become victims in the first place.

Possible ways around the problems related to the rapport between the interviewer and the interviewee may perhaps be found in anthropology (Hsiao-Hung, 2004). Still, this demands a specific profile of the researcher in terms of ethnicity, language skills, and so on. More importantly, this type of research can seriously endanger the researcher who is operating in a crime-ridden environment. However, it is precisely this kind of research that can help gain a better understanding of the victim.

Yet, this still leaves problems of a more ethical nature. The researcher should be aware of available assistance and support, and relevant laws and regulations. In fact, it would be advisable that the research be embedded in a support network. For instance, research in Germany and France was done in collaboration with support organizations, also for the purposes of snowballing. Though this may cause a bias in the sampling, ethical considerations should be put first.

Secondary sources can be used to supplement primary research. However, if the institutional framework views trafficking mainly as the trafficking of women for sexual exploitation or if cultural-historical factors significantly influence the meaning of the term, then care must be taken with media and official sources. These are undoubtedly biased, though they may give a good overview of the position of a country on trafficking. In order to obtain the desired information from these sources on forced labour, abuse, and exploitation linked to labour migration as understood by international conventions, the scope of the search must be widened to include migrant workers, irregular migration, exploitation, informal economy, and so on.

In terms of the thematic selection of future research on human trafficking, there are several proposals that emerged from ILO research. For example, the linkages between "recruitment, harbouring, and receipt" as well as the exploitative elements of the three trafficking-related activities are not yet sufficiently understood across the migration/trafficking cycle. To what extent do intermediaries (including legal job employment and other agencies) play into the hands of abusive employers? Furthermore, we found strong indicators that the accumulation of debt at point of departure or at a later stage increases vulnerability. But at which point does debt turn into bondage? Is the lack of financial resources in origin countries systematically exploited by traffickers or is the offer of credit to pay for a particular service (such as help in crossing a border) a "legitimate" business? Finally, what are the incentives of employers to coerce workers into labour? Are profits high enough to pay off possible risks in terms of punishment? Are there differences in the demand for coerced sex workers and other types of forced labour?

CONCLUSION

Though the paper ends with a series of questions, our main intent was to clarify issues of definitions and methodologies that have informed the design of the ILO/SAP-FL research programme on the forced labour outcomes of human trafficking. We have started with the hypothesis that previous trafficking research has focused, maybe rightly so, on the most blatant cases of exploitation that affect mainly women and children trafficked for sexual exploitation. The main focus of our research programme was, however, on trafficked forced labour in other economic sectors, such as agriculture, construction, and the textile industry. Every research method comprises its own problems, whether it is more quantitative or qualitative, whether it uses secondary sources or primary ones. The lacunae in one research method can at times be compensated by the merits of another method in order to provide the most complete and comprehensive picture. This makes it imperative to approach research on trafficking and other forced labour outcomes of migration from a multi-method perspective, using triangulation and trying out innovative research methods. By broadening the focus of our research, we have been able to show that trafficking in human beings is part of wider phenomena that needs deeper analysis: the vulnerability and exploitation of today's migrant workers.

NOTES

1. The responsibility for opinions expressed in this publication, which are not necessarily endorsement by the International Labour Office, rests solely with the authors.
2. See, for example, Taran and Moreno-Fontes Chammartin (2003) and Taran and Geronimi (2002). For more information on migration, see http://www.ilo.org/protection/migrant/.
3. The International Programme for the Elimination of Child Labour has also commissioned a range of studies on child trafficking, which can be found at http://mirror/intranet/english/standards/ipec/.
4. The term "forced labour" in this paper is understood to mean "forced labour and services", as such it includes forced sexual services (sexual exploitation).
5. Research includes Gao (2004) and Tiuoriuokanova (2004). Legal material includes ILO (2005). The guidelines discuss the relevance of ILO Conventions in the context of new international standards regarding human trafficking. Training material includes ILO/SAP-FL (forthcoming). Other material includes, for example, Van Liemt (2004). For more information on trafficking and forced labour issues in general, see http://www.ilo.org/forcedlabour.
6. Research was first initiated in Europe and Central Asia covering ten different countries of origin and destination.
7. The results of the studies are presented in a report for each country in the form of graphs, percentages, and averages. Considering convenience sampling was used and thus the results are not representative, some may oppose reporting actual figures as some readers might interpret these figures as being representative. However, because of the length of the reports, the large amount of data, as well as the risk of idiosyncratic description of the results in future papers, it was decided that actual figures would be used.

8. Snowballing is a sampling method leading to non-probability samples and is, among other situations, used when there is no pre-existing sample frame, as is the case of research on trafficking. A researcher will start by contacting key informants, who will then refer the researcher to other potential participants, which can then refer the researcher to other participants, and so on.

9. An intermediary is understood to be a non-legal person, working on his/her own or as part of a network, with the aim of recruiting potential migrants for work/ forced labour abroad. Agencies, on the other hand, are considered as legal, semi-legal or pretending to be legal entities seeking to recruit potential migrants for employment/forced labour abroad.

REFERENCES

Anderson, B.
    2003   "Is trafficking in human beings demand driven? A multi-country pilot study", IOM, Geneva.
Anti-Slavery International
    2002   "Human traffic, human rights: redefining victim protection", Anti-Slavery International, www.antislavery.org/homepage/resources/humantraffic humanrights.htm.
Bales, K.
    1999   *Disposable People: New Slavery in the Global Economy*, University of California Press, Berkeley.
Cyrus, N.
            "Report on forced labour and human trafficking in Germany", ILO/SAP-FL, Geneva (forthcoming).
Gao, Y.
    2004   "Chinese migrants and forced labour in Europe", ILO, Geneva.
Gao, Y., and V. Poisson
            "Rapport final de l'enquête de terrain sur le travail forcé et la traite en France: la situation des Chinois clandestins", ILO/SAP-FL, Geneva (forth-coming).
Hsiao-Hung, P.
    2004   "Inside the grim world of the gangmasters", *The Guardian*, 27 March.
International Labour Organization (ILO)
    2003   *Fundamental Rights and Work and International Labour Standards*, ILO, Geneva.
    2005   *Human Trafficking and Forced Labour Exploitation: Guidance for Legislation and Law Enforcement*, ILO, Geneva.
ILO/SAP-FL
    2002   *Human Trafficking from Albania, Moldova, Romania and Ukraine for Labour and Sexual Exploitation: Methodology Guidelines for the Rapid Assessment Survey*, ILO/SAP-FL, Geneva (unpublished).

Trafficking for Forced Labour: How to Monitor the Recruitment of Migrant Workers, ILO/SAP-FL, Geneva (forthcoming).

Kelly, L.
2001 *Conducting Research on Trafficking: Guidelines and Suggestions for Further Research*, IOM, Geneva (unpublished).

Laczko, F., and M.A. Gramegna
2003 "Developing better indicators of human trafficking", *Brown Journal of World Affairs*, X(1).

Regional Clearing Point
2003 *First Annual Report on Victims of Trafficking in South Eastern Europe*, IOM, ICMC, and the Stability Pact for South Eastern Europe, http://www.icmc.net/docs/en/publications/rcp00.

Taran, A., and E. Geronimi
2002 "Globalization, labour and migration: protection is paramount", *MIGRANT* (ILO), Geneva.

Taran, A., and G. Moreno-Fontes Chammartin
2003 "Stopping exploitation of migrant workers by organised crime", *MIGRANT* (ILO), Geneva.

Tyldum, G., and A. Brunovskis
2005 "Current practices and challenges in empirical studies on trafficking: a Northern European perspective", *International Migration*, 43(1-2).

Tyuryukanova, E.
2004 "The new forced labour in Russia", ILO/SAP-FL, Geneva.

Van Liemt, G.
2004 "Human trafficking in Europe: an economic perspective", ILO, Geneva.

Review of Research and Data on Human Trafficking in sub-Saharan Africa

Aderanti Adepoju*[1]

INTRODUCTION

Sub-Saharan Africa (SSA) is a region characterized by a variety of migration configurations, including cross-border movements; contract workers; labour migrants; and the migration of skilled professionals, refugees, and displaced persons. Human trafficking is the latest addition to this list. Insight into the phenomenon came not from statistical data but from the alarm raised by activists, the media, and non-governmental organizations (NGOs) in Nigeria, Togo, and Benin in the late 1990s. For instance, the Constitutional Rights Project, a Nigerian NGO, in one of its reports in September 1996, focused attention on child trafficking within, into, and out of Nigeria. At about the same time, WAO-Afrique, a Togolese NGO assisting children brought from rural areas to work as domestic servants in Lome, investigated reports of Togolese girls being trafficked abroad, especially to Gabon. In 1997, a representative of the NGO brought the problems of trafficking children in West and Central Africa to the attention of the United Nations Commission on Human Rights Working Group (UN, 1999). Unlike ongoing migration configurations that are male dominated and, in many cases, confined largely to the region, trafficking in human beings takes place within, outside, and into the region; involves intermediaries or third parties, especially scams and criminal gangs; and infringes on the victims' human rights. Indeed, in recent years, trafficking of women and children, as commercial sex workers or as exploited domestic servants, has assumed such an alarming proportion that African leaders, especially in Nigeria, are breaking the normal culture of silence to address the issue with the urgency it deserves. For example, the Nigeria Television Authority routinely carries prime news items, special features, and plays on human trafficking to educate the public and raise awareness of the plight of trafficked victims.

---

* Human Resources Development Centre, Lagos, Nigeria.

The focus of the paper is four-fold: (1) to present an overview of the main features of trafficking, its dynamics, and its root causes in SSA; (2) to review current research on trafficking in the region, focusing in particular on the methodology used and the extent to which findings of these studies can be generalized nationally; (3) to identify the ways in which governments have responded to human trafficking; and (4) to outline gaps in knowledge and suggest a range of research themes that could help enhance understanding of the dynamics of trafficking in the region.

OVERVIEW OF MAIN FEATURES AND DYNAMICS OF TRAFFICKING IN SSA

Recent years have witnessed a gradual increase in the smuggling of migrants and trafficking in human beings to and from Africa, as well as within the continent. The exploitative nature of the treatment of the victims of trafficking often amounts to new forms of slavery. Many countries find it difficult to control and prevent the smuggling of human beings partly because they do not have effective policies designed to combat trafficking in human beings. Plus, they lack the capacity to respond adequately, as there are no national legislations with regulations to deal with the problem. The general public is insufficiently aware of trafficking in human beings in all its aspects, the extent to which organized criminal groups are involved in trafficking in human beings, and the fate of the victims. Parents or guardians of trafficked children are under false illusions and are unaware of the severe exploitation to which their wards are often subjected. A survey conducted by the United Nations Children's Fund (UNICEF) indicates, for instance, that about half of African countries recognized trafficking as a problem, and that child trafficking is usually perceived as more severe than trafficking in women (UNICEF, 2003). There are, however, notable exceptions among the subregions. In West and Central Africa where trafficking is perhaps more widespread and recognized, more than 70 per cent of the countries identified trafficking as a problem, compared to one-third (33%) of countries in East and southern Africa (UNICEF, 2003).

Until a few years ago, little was known, and even less had been written on human trafficking in SSA. Three main types of trafficking have since been identified in the region, namely trafficking in children primarily for farm labour and domestic work within and across countries; trafficking in women and young persons for sexual exploitation, mainly outside the region; and trafficking in women from outside the region for the sex industry of South Africa (Sita, 2003; IOM, 2003). Trafficking takes place at different levels, including exploitative labour and domestic work and sexual exploitation of women and girls within, outside, and into countries of the region. Trafficking in the region is defined as the "recruitment, transportation, transfer, harbouring or receipt of persons by means of threat or use of force or other forms of coercion...deception...for the purpose of exploitation" (ILO, 2002).

The geography of trafficking in West Africa is as complex as the trafficking routes. Ghana, Nigeria, and Senegal are source, transit, and destination countries for trafficked women and children. The trafficking in young children from rural areas to capital cities, especially from Mali, Benin, Burkina Faso, Togo, and Ghana to Côte d'Ivoire's commercial farms, from and through eastern Nigeria to Gabon has increased in recent years (Dottridge, 2002). UNICEF estimates – though this is highly contestable – that up to 200,000 children are trafficked annually in West and Central Africa.

Veil (1999) identified six types of child trafficking in West and Central Africa: abduction of children, payment of sums of money to poor parents who hand over their children on the promise that they will be treated well, bonded placement of children as reimbursement for debt, placement for a token sum for specified duration or for gift items, and enrolment for a fee by an agent for domestic work at the request of the children's parents. In the sixth form, parents of the domestic workers are deceived into enlisting their children under the guise that they would be enrolled in school, trade, or training.

The main suppliers of child labour in the subregion include Benin, Ghana, Nigeria, Mali, Burkina Faso, Mauritania, and Togo for domestic work in Gabon, Equatorial Guinea, Côte d'Ivoire, Congo, and Nigeria. Togolese girls are being trafficked into domestic and labour markets in Gabon, Benin, Nigeria, and Niger, and locally within the country while boys are trafficked into agricultural work in Côte d'Ivoire, Nigeria, and Benin. Most of these children are recruited through the network of agents to work as domestic servants in informal sectors or on plantations (UNICEF, 1998, 2000). Parents are often forced by poverty and ignorance to enlist their children, hoping to benefit from their wages and sustain the deteriorating family economic situation. In many circumstances, however, some of these children are indentured into "slave" labour, as in Sudan and Mauritania, and are exploited and paid pittance, below living wages. The traffickers have recently extended the destination of child trafficking to the European Union (EU), especially the Netherlands, the United Kingdom (UK), and so on.

Some Ghanaian women and children are trafficked to neighbouring countries for labour and prostitution (Anarfi, 1998), while other women are trafficked to Europe and forced into prostitution (ILO, 2003). Ghana is a transit route for

Nigerian women trafficked to Italy, Germany, and the Netherlands for commercial sex. Togolese young women are being trafficked as prostitutes to Ghana, Gabon, Côte d'Ivoire, and Lebanon (Taylor, 2002). Children are trafficked from Nigeria to Europe, the Gulf States, and some African countries for domestic labour and for sexual exploitation to France, Spain, the Netherlands, and South Africa (Human Rights Watch, 2003). Women are trafficked particularly to Italy, France, Spain, the Netherlands, Sweden, Germany, Switzerland, the UK, Saudi Arabia, and the United Arab Emirates (UAE) for prostitution and pornography; they are also trafficked to Côte d'Ivoire and South Africa. Senegal is both a source and transit country for women trafficked to Europe, South Africa, and the Gulf States for commercial sex, and is also a destination country for children trafficked from Mali and Guinea Conakry.

Women from war-torn Liberia and Sierra Leone are forced to prostitute in Mali, just as local women are trafficked to Burkina Faso, Côte d'Ivoire, and France. Mali also serves as a transit country for trafficking women from Anglophone countries to Europe. Trafficking is done by syndicates who obtain travel documents and visas for the women and link them with brothels abroad. Hundreds of illegal immigrants and trafficked persons, especially those from West African countries en route to Spain, get stranded in Morocco for upwards of four or more years.

In East Africa, Ugandan women working as prostitutes in the Gulf States lure young girls from their country because they are usually preferred by male clients. More traumatic is the situation of young girls and women abducted from conflict zones in the north of the country who are forced to serve as sex slaves to rebel commanders or are literally "sold" as slaves to affluent men in Sudan and the Gulf States. In Kenya, trafficking of young girls to Europe by syndicates run by Japanese businessmen, and of girls from India and parts of South Asia to Kenya, is essential for the local sex industry. Kenya also serves as a transit route for trafficked Ethiopian women to Europe and the Gulf States (Butegwa, 1997). In Uganda and Kenya some orphaned girls in the care of relatives are reportedly "sold" to traffickers under the guise of securing them a better education, scholarship, or marriage. There are reports of Ethiopian migrant women recruited to work as domestics in Lebanon and the Gulf States who have been abused and sexually assaulted (UNICEF, 2003). Traffickers transport Ethiopian women via Tanzania and Kenya to avoid the Ethiopian Government's employment recruitment regulations, especially the Private Employment Agency Proclamation of 1998 which sought to protect the rights, safety, and dignity of Ethiopians employed and sent abroad, and imposed penalties for abuses of the human rights and physical integrity of workers (IOM, 2001).

Trafficking in women and children for sexual exploitation is a simmering problem in southern Africa, especially in Lesotho, Mozambique, Malawi, South Africa, and Zambia. South Africa is the destination for regional and extra-regional trafficking activities. The trafficking map is complicated, involving diverse origins within and outside the region. Women are trafficked from refugee-producing countries through the network of refugees resident in South Africa. Children are trafficked to South Africa from Lesotho's border towns; women and girls trafficked from Mozambique are destined for South Africa's Gauteng and Kwa-Zulu Natal provinces. In Malawi, women and girls are trafficked to northern Europe and South Africa. In addition to these configurations, women are also trafficked from Thailand, China, and Eastern Europe (IOM, 2003).

Ethnically based criminal syndicates in South Africa's refugee camps recruit and transport their victims, usually married women from their home countries. In Lesotho, traffickers recruit male and female street children, victims of physical and sexual abuse at home, or children orphaned by AIDS. Such children normally migrate from rural areas and border towns to Maseru, the capital, from where they are trafficked by mostly South African white Afrikaans who use force and/or promise of employment in Eastern Free State, asparagus farms in the border region, and Bloemfontein. At the destination, victims are locked up in private homes and starved of food while being sexually, physically, and verbally exploited (IOM, 2003). Sexually exploited, humiliated, and penniless, these young victims are later dumped at border towns to make their way back to Maseru. Long-distance truck drivers also traffic their victims from Lesotho to Cape Town, Zambia, and Zimbabwe, with the help of corrupt immigration officials at the border posts.

Mozambican traffickers are mainly local women in partnership with their compatriots and South African men who transport trafficked victims from Maputo to Johannesburg or Durban. After impounding the victims' documents and personal properties, they are sexually exploited and abused. Victims are sold as sex workers to brothels in Johannesburg or as wives to mine workers on the West Rand. With some 1,000 victims recruited and transported every year, the trade is lucrative for traffickers (IOM, 2003).

In Malawi, victims are trafficked to Europe and South Africa. Victims trafficked to Europe are recruited by Malawian businesswomen or are married to Nigerians living in Malawi who employ deception and job offers in restaurants and hotels to lure the unsuspecting young Malawian and Zambian girls through Johannesburg to Germany, Belgium, or Italy to be enlisted as prostitutes. Before departure, rituals are performed to frighten the victims from escaping. A study by the International Organization for Migration (IOM) noted that the Nigerian "madam" who receives the trafficked women and girls at the destination would threaten death by magic if the victims refused to cooperate (IOM, 2003b). Malawian businesswomen also collaborate with long-distance truck drivers to recruit young victims locally with offers of marriage, study, or employment in South Africa. The victims are gang raped or killed en route if they resist (Mertens et al., 2003). Tourists from Germany, the Netherlands, and the UK use gifts and cash to lure young boys and girls under age 18 who reside at tourists' spots into pornographic sex acts. They later put the films on the Internet with the victims' names and addresses. The victims' parents are deceived with gifts under the pretence that their wards would be assisted with education and jobs abroad. The unsuspecting children who follow the tourists to Europe end up as sex slaves to the traffickers or are distributed into the paedophile network.

Between 800 and 1,100 women aged 25 to 30 from Bangkok, Hong Kong Special Administrative Region of China, Kuala Lumpur, and Singapore are trafficked into South Africa annually. Traffickers arrange transport for the victims while the Thai *mama-sans* (male agents) in South Africa coordinate their arrival with brothel owners. Trafficked victims from southern China are recruited by Chinese or Taiwanese agents with links to the Triad groups. They then enter South Africa through Johannesburg or land borders from Lesotho or Mozambique using tourist visas, study permits, or false Japanese passports and are forced to work in the sex industry. Trafficked victims from Eastern Europe include Russian and Eastern European women lured to South Africa with offers to be waitresses and dancers. These and other victims recruited for the South Africa-based Russian and Bulgarian mafia end up in Johannesburg and Cape Town brothels (Mertens et al., 2003).

ROOT CAUSES OF TRAFFICKING

A variety of factors, including deepening poverty, deteriorating living conditions, persistent unemployment, conflicts, human deprivation, and hopelessness fostered the environment for human trafficking to flourish in the region (Salah, 2004).

Child trafficking is a serious human rights issue but the problems of child abuse and neglect in SSA are rooted primarily in the deteriorating economic situation. Deepening rural poverty forces poor families to give up their children to traffickers, under the pretext of providing them the opportunity to secure good jobs and better lives (Dottridge, 2002). Poverty, lack of access to education, unemployment, family disintegration as a result of death or divorce, and neglected AIDS-orphaned children, make young persons vulnerable to traffickers (ILO, 2003; Moore, 1994).

countries, poverty is a major factor forcing young children into st evidence of unemployment came not from statistical data but about the appearance in various towns of people who obviously They came in increasing numbers, and lived in shanty towns in nd poverty. Street children as beggars who simply work on the streets or live without families or homes are increasing in number in SSA's major cities – Addis Ababa, Dakar, Lagos, and Nairobi (Moore, 1994). In Senegal, some of these children are forced by religious teachers to beg for food and money in the streets. Their lifestyle makes them vulnerable to exploitation from adults and they are easily drawn into prostitution, drugs, alcohol, and crime (Aderinto, 2003). As the products of famine, armed conflicts, rural-urban migration, unemployment, poverty, and broken families, street children are highly vulnerable to traffickers. Prostitution is often a common way for boys and girls on the street to make money, making them susceptible to sexually transmitted infections (STIs), especially HIV/AIDS. In Nairobi, for example, such girls may be selling sexual services during the day and returning to their "community" at night (Moore, 1994). Girls are particularly vulnerable to sexual violence and exploitation. Thus, for instance, some of the young girls from Benin who work across the border in Nigeria, as are Ghanaian children in north-eastern Côte d'Ivoire, are sexually abused by older members of the host families.

It is alleged that some of the children are "sold" by their parents or contracted to agents for work in exchange for cash. The dramatic changes in Africa's economic fortunes have undermined the abilities of families to meet the basic needs of its members. Driven by desperation, some fall prey to traffickers' rackets in desperate search for survival. Irregular migration as well as trafficking in young boys and girls was stimulated and intensified by worsening youth unemployment and rapidly deteriorating socio-political and economic conditions and poverty. Most of these youths risk everything to fight their way hazardously to rich countries with the assistance of traffickers and bogus agencies, in search of the illusory green pastures. This traumatic development reflects the depth of the deterioration of SSA economies and poverty (ILO, 2003).

Many parents interviewed in a study in Togo had never been to school, were in polygamous unions, and had many children (Human Rights Watch, 2003). In such traditional settings parents often prefer to send girls into domestic service and use the income to finance the education of boys. In an African cultural setting, children are regarded as economic assets, and from around age 6, they are gradually integrated into the family's productive process, performing various services. In a subsistence economy, labour is a critical production asset and children are enlisted into the family labour pool, a situation dubbed child labour in the literature. Despite acceding to the various conventions designed to eliminate child labour, the practice is widespread in SSA as a result of generalized poverty and economic crisis. In many cases, the assistance that children provide – child caring, herding and fetching water or fuel wood – releases the adults, especially women, to undertake more urgent and major tasks. Thus, in seasons when extra hands are needed, families see no contradiction in withdrawing girls from school so that they can help, because all children are considered a family resource at all times (Adepoju, 1997).

Investment in family members is made based on who is perceived to be most likely to bring the highest returns. In most cases this boosts the biased family investment in education in favour of boys. Moreover, domestic work for children not enrolled in school or who have dropped out is an integral part of family upbringing strategies and survival mechanism. Poor parents, especially in rural areas, facing difficult resource constraints enlist their children in domestic work, hoping thereby to diversify family income (Veil, 1998). But in the process, fostered children and domestic workers, mostly young girls, may be unable to learn a trade or attend school even when they want to because of the exploitative heavy work schedule. The inability of parents to pay the fees for their ward's education is exploited by traffickers who lure young girls with offers of education and employment opportunities elsewhere. In Togo, for instance, child trafficking begins with a private arrangement between an intermediary and a family member, with promises for education, employment, or apprenticeship only to be turned to exploitative domestic workers. Sometimes, parents have to pay an intermediary to find work for their children, in a number of cases, parents accepted money from traffickers as inducements for the transaction.

In SSA, traditionally child rearing is a shared communal responsibility, particularly in close-knit rural areas. As children who provide help in the home and on the farm are enrolled in schools, especially in the cities, this resource disappears from the family pool. This is evidenced by the case of Gabon where compulsory schooling and strict labour laws create a huge demand for domestic labour. A survey of 600 working children in Gabon from 1998 to1999 found that only 17 were Gabonese. In 2001, between 10,000 and 15,000 trafficked Togolese girls were working in Gabon, recruited as domestic servants by agents who paid their poor parents and transported them for domestic work (UNICEF, 1998; Veil, 1998).

Child trafficking in SSA is a demand-driven phenomenon – the existence of an international market for children in the labour and sex trade, coupled with an abundant supply of children from poor families with limited or no means for education in a cultural context that favours child fostering (ILO, 2002). Child trafficking has also increased as a result of a growing network of intermediaries, an absence of clear legal framework, a scarcity of trained police to investigate cases of trafficking, ignorance and complicity by parents, corruption of border officials, and the open borders that make transnational movement intractable (Salah, 2004). Child trafficking networks are secretive, informal, and involve rituals and cults. However, normal cross-border migration is equally infiltrated by child trafficking.

With regard to trafficking in women, the literature also indicates that women often fall prey to traffickers as a result of poverty, rural-urban migration, unemployment, broken homes, displacement, and peer influence. Butegwa (1997) insists that in SSA, poverty is also the major reason for trafficking in women. Unemployment, low wages, and poor living standards drive some desperate women into the hands of traffickers. These women then end up offering sexual services in brothels or as domestic servants. Poor women who wish to migrate to rich countries may simply be looking for better job opportunities in order to assist their families. In the process, some fall prey to traffickers. Though some of the trafficked women are willing to participate in prostitution in order to escape the poverty trap, deception is the most common strategy used in procuring them and young girls under the guise of offers for further education, marriage, and remunerative jobs. The trafficked persons who obtain huge loans for procuring their tickets, visas, and accommodations discover on arrival that the promise was bogus, and their passports are seized to prevent their escape. Many are stranded and helpless, but the absence of a judicial framework limits attempts by law enforcement agencies to prosecute and punish perpetrators and accomplices for their trafficking crimes.

Many women assume sole responsibility for family members after their husband's die of AIDS. Saddled with increased responsibilities, some opt for migration in search of employment to improve their families' well-being only to fall prey to traffickers. Sexual exploitation may also expose such women to HIV/AIDS. Trafficked women in the sex trade often work without the use of condoms and may lower their prices for sexual services to pay back their debt bondage. Some may be raped, tortured, and subjected to other forms of inhumane physical abuse by clients and traffickers. Repatriated women arriving back in Nigeria through Lagos are forced to undergo medical tests including tests for HIV/ AIDS as part of the screening process (Pearson, 2002). Afonja (2001) reported that many trafficked Nigerian girls in Italy were battered by their clients and beaten by their employers for failing to cooperate, prompting some of them to seek protection from the Italian Government, NGOs, and the church. When deported, their reintegration is made difficult by the stigma of failure, and the local communities are wary that the repatriated victims may spread diseases they contracted abroad. Many such victims of trafficking end up engulfed in, rather than escape from, the trap of poverty, bringing in its wake personal trauma and dishonour to their families.

HIV/AIDS can in itself be a cause and consequence of trafficking. In southern Africa, for example, the perception that having sexual intercourse with a young girl diminishes the risk of contracting HIV/AIDS has increased demand for young sex workers, and unscrupulous scams are cashing in on this situation by trafficking young girls to the country. In the case of trafficked girls from Benin and Togo, who travelled by sea to Gabon through transit points in southeastern Nigeria, some were raped, a few prostituted themselves, and others sold their belongings in order to survive while awaiting their boats. Many died when their rickety boats capsized. At their destination, many girls suffered physical and emotional abuse and sexual exploitation by boys and men in the hosts' homes, experiences that pushed some to the streets as prostitutes. Despite the risks, few insisted on the use of condoms because clients pay more for unprotected sex, exposing themselves to HIV infection. A study of sex workers in Lome in 1992 showed that nearly 80 per cent of the women tested were HIV positive (Fanou-Ako et al., nd; Nagel, 2000; Human Rights Watch, 2003).

RESEARCH ON HUMAN TRAFFICKING: CONCEPTUAL AND METHODOLOGICAL APPROACHES

Data on international migration in SSA is scanty and information on irregular migration is harder to find. Trafficking, as Kornbluth (1996) noted, lies along a continuum that runs from illegal migration to alien smuggling by criminal groups, including coercion of migrants into drug smuggling or prostitution. Like illegal migration, trafficking has become highly organized and extremely complex. Yet, the data base remains extremely poor and our knowledge of trafficking within or outside the region is incomplete.

Research efforts in West Africa have focused on gathering data on young children recruited and transported across frontiers and later exploited to work in agriculture and domestic service and for women trafficked into the sex industry. Often, researchers have glossed over or completely ignored the broader socio-cultural and economic contexts in which migration, in general, and more strictly trafficking in human beings, takes place. Yet it is obvious that these contexts, in the African situation, define who is selectively sponsored for migration, the nature of networks, the role of intermediaries, and the returns to migration. Child labour and "child" migration for work are engrained aspects of the migratory configuration in many parts of Africa. As some of the studies reviewed below illustrate, a lot of grey areas exist between the concept of female migration for work, the aim being to improve the migrants' conditions and those of her family, and illegal migration, smuggling, and trafficking of women.

A dozen or more studies have been conducted in SSA countries with a focus on child labour, child trafficking, and trafficking in women. Some of these studies are small scale, covering areas considered recruiting grounds for trafficked children and women; a few are based on secondary, archival sources, while others are empirical, based on surveys and interviews with victims and stake-holders, stretching from weeks to months. Some of these studies were funded by organizations mandated to work on trafficking; others were conducted directly by such agencies using primary or secondary sources of data, in collaboration with national research organizations or individual researchers. A selection of these studies from West Africa (Nigeria, Togo, Mali); Central Africa (Gabon, Cameroon); eastern Africa (Tanzania, Zambia), and southern Africa (Lesotho, Malawi, Mozambique, Swaziland, and South Africa) is presented below.

West Africa

Nigeria

The aim of the study on trafficking in women and girls for prostitution in Nigeria's Delta and Edo States is to assist the Government of Nigeria and local partners in identifying measures for the adequate protection of victims of trafficking returning to Nigeria, and the development of appropriate prevention measures to combat trafficking in women and girls. In doing so, it also aims to generate basic data for the development of measures to combat trafficking in women and girls (Afonja, 2001). The study used several approaches: structured question-naires for household heads, women and girls at risk (unemployed, school drop-outs, women of easy virtue, final year senior secondary school girls), and victims and returnees in the state capitals; in-depth interviews with stakeholders, in-cluding medical practitioners, teachers, market women, government officials, international organizations, and NGOs; and five focus group discussions (FGDs) in Edo State, two with market women, one each with female and male adoles-cents in schools and another with male adolescents out of school. In Delta State, FGD were held for female and male adolescents in school and adult males and females. Opinion leaders, government officials, NGOs working on violence against women, and officials from the embassies of Belgium, Italy, Germany, and the Netherlands were also interviewed. A purposive sample selection cap-tured 100 household heads, 400 women and girls at risk, and ten victims and returnees interviews, mostly people willing to be interviewed oblivious of the state's anti-prostitution law passed in September 2000 to prohibit trafficking and prostitution in Edo State. Secondary data from media reports, case studies, and policy statements were also collected from governments, NGOs, and the print media to complement the primary data.

The researchers noted that participation in trafficking involves a third party, which takes the form of an invitation from family members, friends, even strangers, who approach either the household heads or the girls concerned. The actual trafficking involves four processes: the planning phase, the trip to the country of destination, the sojourn, and the return journey, based on the group or the individual model. The group model involves the so-called *Italios*, adolescents aged 10 to 19 years old, their sponsors, and hosts in the country of destination. Before departure from the state, rituals are performed by the parents, *Italios*, and sponsors to "cement" a covenant between them, to protect them from being apprehended, and to incur favour with their employers. Parents involved in initiating the contractual arrangements provide all or part of the funds for the journey and may also be indebted to the sponsors (Afonja, 2001).

Togo

The study of child trafficking in Togo, conducted by the Human Rights Watch (2003), documents the problems of internal and external child trafficking, especially the trafficking of girls into domestic and market work, the trafficking of boys into agricultural work, and the hazards faced by the trafficked children. In the study, carried out between April and May 2002 in Lome and 13 towns and villages in the country, 90 trafficked children who had been released by their traffickers or who had fled and were identified through local authorities familiar with child trafficking cases and NGOs providing services to abused or neglected children, were interviewed. This procedure omitted other trafficked children who were unable to escape. In-depth interviews were also conducted with 32 government, NGO, and foreign embassy officials, judges, parents, teachers, police, social workers, and other stakeholders. Of the 90 children interviewed, 72 (41 girls and 31 boys) were trafficked according to the UN Trafficking Protocol; 13 were trafficked internally within Togo, 24 were trafficked outside Togo to Gabon, Benin, Nigeria, and Niger; and four were trafficked to Togo from Benin, Nigeria, or Ghana. All the 31 boys, mostly illiterates or dropouts, were trafficked from Togo to parts of Nigeria, Benin, or Côte d'Ivoire.

Mali

The research on child trafficking in Mali focused on the causes, context, and consequences of youth migration in four communities at risk, two each in central and south-east Mali; the perception and definition of the phenomenon of trafficking by communities and parents and an assessment of the factors that motivate young people to leave their home villages; identification of the routes that both trafficked and non-trafficked migrants take; and the experiences of the reintegration of trafficked and intercepted children into their home communities (Castle and Diarra, 2003).

The fieldwork, carried out between August and October 2002 in purposively chosen villages to incorporate areas of high migration and especially those where trafficking and repatriated children (so-called trafficked children) had been reported, focused on children aged 10 to 18 years. The researchers assumed that those younger than age 10 were unlikely to migrate and those older than 18 were less likely to experience problems as autonomous migrants (Castle and Diarra, 2003). A range of approaches was used: a random sample of households and screening of 10 to 18 year olds in the villages; a purposive sample of households furnished by village chiefs and elders where migrants had experienced hardship or trafficking and screening of 10 to 18 year olds; a purposive sample of households drawn from a list of names of individual 10- to 18-year-old migrant children ("trafficked children") furnished by NGOs working with the authorities who had repatriated them; and a snowball sample based on names of migrants age 10 to 18 and their households furnished by interviewees who were able to recount hardship stories of their friends and peers in the villages.

Interviewers probed children for descriptions of the role, relationship, financial benefits, and remuneration received by intermediaries. In all, 950 children, 431 aged 10 to 13 and 519 aged 14 to 18, were screened. Of these, only four fulfilled the criteria as having been trafficked. Based on availability and whether their story appeared typical or atypical, 108 were eventually interviewed. In addition, four FGDs were conducted in each region involving 12 mothers and five fathers from the first village and seven and 13, respectively, from the second village. These were purposively selected to ensure a mix from each migration category. In each village, seven community leaders (chiefs and counsellors, imams, leaders of women's groups, and teachers) who had strong social, religious, or political roles were interviewed. FGDs were held with transporters, law enforcement officers, local government officials and NGO representatives, and jurists.

This study is innovative in some respects. The qualitative-quantitative screening procedure identified subjects of study, around which was built a systematic classification of children by migration category, before a final selection of interviewees was made. The study also captures a wide variety of contextual migration, of which trafficking is an important subset, highlights many weaknesses in the conceptualization of international definitions of trafficking and the difficulty of operationalizing these in the field.

West and Central Africa

Veil's (1998) study of child labour and trafficking in young girls as domestic workers in ten West and Central African countries (Senegal, Ghana, Mali, Togo, Benin, Burkina Faso, Gabon, Equatorial Guinea, Côte d'Ivoire, and Nigeria) was based on secondary data, archival documents, and studies by UNICEF, the International Labour Organization (ILO), NGOs, and research institutes. The key objective was to analyse the factors affecting the supply of and demand for domestic labour, the various forms of domestic traffic and its volume, and cross-border networks. The focus was on trafficking in child domestic workers, particularly the situation of girls in domestic service, factors responsible for child domestic labour, as well as policies and measures at the national, regional, and international levels aimed at combating the phenomenon.

West, Central, and eastern Africa

Butegwa's (1997) report is designed to sensitize African women's rights NGOs to the magnitude of trafficking in women in Uganda, Kenya, Mali, Cameroon, Namibia, Tanzania, Zambia, and Nigeria. In-depth interviews were conducted in Kenya, Mali, Uganda, and Nigeria with women who have been involved in trafficking as recruiters, the victims, money lenders, government officials in immigration, justice, police and social welfare departments, and journalists. In Cameroon, Namibia, Tanzania, and Zambia, questionnaires were administered to NGOs actively involved in trafficking matters. The author highlights difficulties in conceptualizing trafficking in women for prostitution, forced labour, and slavery-like practices, particularly from a human rights perspective and provides a descriptive analysis of the situation and the challenges arising from trafficking in Africa. The report documents the various national legislative provisions and international legal standards applicable to trafficking in women, contradictions implicit in the standards and their applicability to the Africa region. Based on country case reviews, the author outlines the efforts of governments and NGOs to control trafficking in women from Africa. Not much is available on the methodology used for the study.

Southern Africa

IOM's (2003) study in southern Africa covered Lesotho, Malawi, Mozambique, Swaziland, and South Africa's four major cities (Johannesburg, Durban, Cape Town and Pretoria). It focuses on the various definitions of trafficking, the legal dimension, and the trafficking of women and children for sexual exploitation. The concentration on women and children, while recognizing the existence of trafficking for other kinds of forced labour, and of men, was due largely to the extreme vulnerability, abusive, and dehumanizing nature of the exploitation (Mertens et al., 2003). The survey, conducted from August 2002 to February 2003, interviewed trafficked victims, sex workers, traffickers, police and government officials, NGOs, and the media. The South African Broadcasting Corporation's Special Assignment programme documented cases and trends of trafficking in Mozambique (IOM, 2003). Researchers spent three months in Johannesburg, Durban, Cape Town, and Pretoria identifying and interviewing victims and other sources whose stories could be traced back along the trafficking routes to the source countries. The second phase, devoted to locating source communities to assess the reasons for, and extent of their vulnerability, was confined to Lesotho, Malawi, Mozambique, and Swaziland, leaving out Botswana, Namibia, Tanzania, Zambia, and Zimbabwe. Of the 232 interviews conducted, 25 trafficked women and children from 11 countries were identified, following which the number multiplied exponentially

While these pioneering studies were conducted on difficult terrains and used painstaking approaches, the samples were small and non-random; hence, their results cannot be generalized in view of variations within countries. Future research on trafficking could also explore the use of quantitative and qualitative rapid assessment data gathering techniques to target girls and women at risk, those trafficked within the country, and others who returned. Tracer studies of trafficked victims at the destination involving collaborative efforts of researchers in the countries of origin and destination of trafficking are most desirable and should be encouraged.

GAPS IN KNOWLEDGE AND PRIORITY RESEARCH THEMES ON TRAFFICKING

A clearer picture of the map, route, causes, and dynamics of trafficking in children and women in, from, and to SSA is emerging. But the knowledge base remains poor and the distinction between trafficking per se, especially with respect to children, and the long standing seasonal migration of young persons for work across borders is blurred.

There is an urgent need to improve data gathering and training and retraining of officials in migration data collection and statistics in order to capture the main trends of trafficking. In the process, data collection on trafficking and other configurations of migration that may include elements of smuggling should be standardized. Because no single research methodology can adequately capture trafficking ramifications, a battery of methods is desirable both to capture the diverse sources, causes, and dynamics of trafficking and to ensure that research findings can be generalized.

While information on the trafficking process and health conditions of the victims of trafficking is essential for the fight against trafficking, there is a general lack of data on the health aspects in SSA countries. Data based on the number of convictions, number of complaints launched, number of victims assisted, and medical data about trafficked victims simply do not exist in the region. Collecting such information would advance our knowledge.

One of the main obstacles in collecting data on trafficking in SSA is ignorance and, in some cases, indifference to the subject matter. Many people do not yet see trafficking as a serious crime, and many countries in the region do not have appropriate legal framework that makes trafficking a punishable offence. Child traffickers apprehended by the police are rarely prosecuted because most penal codes do not have specific provisions against trafficking in women and children, and where they are in force, parents and guardians are ignorant of its provisions. The lack of appropriate anti-trafficking legislation and weak enforcement has to be addressed by strengthening laws and policy framework to enable effective action against trafficking in human beings for labour or sexual exploitation through training and capacity building.

Trafficking is related to general vulnerability, and exacerbated by poor access to or withdrawal from education. Poverty and lack of parental support renders orphans more vulnerable to being trafficked. Governments must address the specific needs of extremely vulnerable groups (exposed to trafficking and forced labour) and make poverty alleviation the cornerstone of people-centred development strategy.

Research is needed on the root causes of trafficking in a broader context especially the traditional practices of child placements, child fostering, and domestic work, which are conducive to trafficking. Such studies should focus on the cultural values and traditional belief systems that push children to traffickers and weaken the protection of children's rights. A more realistic approach is required to encompass the broader issue of children's work, child labour migration (internal and cross-border), and child trafficking.

As Castle and Diarra (2003) suggested, there is a need to reconceptualize definitions of trafficking in view of the difficulties associated with its operational application in respect to child labour, migration of youths for labour, and child trafficking in, especially, West Africa. Violence, deception, and exploitation can and do occur within both regular and irregular systems of migration and employment within and outside national borders, which complicates a meaningful definition of trafficking. We need to broaden our understanding of the mechanisms of border crossing and expand conceptual frameworks to incorporate internal child trafficking on which much less is known.

In West Africa, in particular, the direct involvement of traditional leaders in the identification and implementation of measures against trafficking is essential. In doing so, researchers need to posit trafficking in the broader context of forced and compulsory labour, as well as in local, historical, and socio-cultural contexts. The origin, causes, and manifestations of forced labour in former francophone West African countries require qualitative approaches that examine these issues in an integrated way, especially the cultural attitudes to and the economic imperative for child labour and trafficking.

In-depth gender sensitive studies are needed on the frequency of forced labour and trafficking. The results can help promote greater awareness among traditional and social institutions, as well as in consensus building, on the reality of forced labour and trafficking in the context of traditional social practices.

Incisive participatory research is required on the role of tourism in trafficking young persons for the sex industries in rich countries. The tourism industry in SSA has low entry barriers, is labour intensive, employs women and young boys and girls, and reaches remote rural areas. It is speculated in media reports in Gambia and Senegal that trafficking syndicates from rich countries have infiltrated the industry to recruit unsuspecting young boys and girls, as in Malawi, for the sex industry, including pornography and paedophilia, in Europe. Tourists must also respect the religion, culture, and traditions of local communities.

Leaders of trafficking rings employ intermediaries in source countries who make contact with potential migrants, organize transport for and sometimes accompany the migrants to ensure their arrival, and/or compel compliance with the terms of the agreement between the smugglers and their victims. These syndicated groups should be distinguished from intermediaries to whom parents entrust their children and the role of the latter needs to be re-examined in the context of Africa's complex cultural reality. Trafficking occurs when: a migrant is illicitly engaged (recruited, kidnapped, sold, etc.) and/or moved either within national or across international borders, and intermediaries (traffickers) during any part of this process obtain economic or other profit by means of deception, coercion, and/or other forms of exploitation under conditions that violate the fundamental human rights of migrants. Culturally, social and economic transactions in many SSA societies are conducted in the presence of a third party, an intermediary, who is paid in kind or cash. In Mali, for instance, many of the presumed traffickers were found by Castle and Diarra (2003) to be simple intermediaries operating within a cultural system that demands payment for services.

Cooperation between governments is crucial to combating trafficking, more so because strict immigration policies in receiving countries can actually fuel markets for trafficking and smuggling and irregular migrations. Cooperative research and information sharing between countries of origin and destination, and increased operational contact between law enforcement authorities of recipient countries to share information on numbers and nationalities of trafficked persons, smuggling routes, and methods of interdiction should be encouraged. Cooperation between researchers in origin and destination countries with focus on tracer studies of trafficked victims is desirable. Above all, linkages between countries of destination and origin must be established and reinforced, and information sharing is a major component of cooperation.

OVERVIEW AND CONCLUSION

Africa's human trafficking and smuggling map is complicated, involving diverse origins within and outside the region. Little was known until recently about the dynamics of this trafficking. Today, analysts are looking into trafficking in children (mainly for farm labour and domestic work within and across countries); trafficking in women and young persons for sexual exploitation mainly outside the region, and trafficking in women from outside the region for the sex industry of South Africa.

In West Africa, the main source, transit, and destination countries for trafficked women and children are Ghana, Nigeria, and Senegal. Trafficked children are recruited through networks of agents to work as domestic servants, in informal sectors, or on plantations. Parents are often forced by poverty and ignorance to enlist their children, hoping to benefit from their wages to sustain the family's deteriorating economic situation. Some of these children are indentured into "slave" labour, as in Sudan and Mauritania. In East Africa, young girls and women abducted from conflict zones are forced to become sex slaves to rebel commanders or affluent men in Sudan and the Gulf States. Ethiopia is a source of trafficked women to Lebanon and the Gulf States. South Africa is a destination for regional and extra-regional trafficking activities. Women are trafficked through the network of refugees resident in South Africa, and trafficked from Thailand, China, and Eastern Europe to South Africa. Traffickers have recently extended the destinations of children to the EU, especially the Netherlands, UK, and beyond. Women and children are trafficked to Europe (Italy, Germany, Spain, France, Sweden, UK, the Netherlands) for commercial sex. Children are similarly moved in connection with domestic labour, sexual exploitation, and pornography. Trafficking syndicates obtain travel documents and visas for women and link them up with brothels abroad.

Leaders and politicians at the highest level are increasingly paying attention to human trafficking. This in part derives from the intensive advocacy by NGOs working in the subject area, and the wide media coverage of incidents of trafficking and repatriation of trafficked persons often in inhuman circumstances. The detailed account of human rights abuses and dangers to trafficked persons en route and at destination as chronicled by researchers in the case of Malawi, Lesotho, Togo, and so on provide sufficient evidence that human trafficking in the region has reached a crisis proportion and that national leaders need to take timely action to redress the deteriorating situation.

In the late 1990s, for instance, the adverse publicity on trafficking spearheaded by NGOs, activists, the media, and recently researchers in Côte d'Ivoire prompted the governments of that country and Mali to set up a commission of inquiry which led to the signing of a Memorandum of Understanding in September 2000 to cooperate at borders in combating child trafficking for labour, repatriation of trafficked children, detection and tracking of networks for trafficking in children.

The intensive international media coverage of 45 trafficked girls that travelled to Gabon in a ramshackle boat in 1996 with only eight surviving the hazardous journey probably prompted the Government of Togo to draft a new anti-trafficking legislation, establish committees to raise awareness, and make efforts to repatriate trafficked children. These are encouraging steps but the government also needs to address the root causes that foster child trafficking – poverty; denial of educational opportunities, especially to girls; and sustained commitment to prevention, prosecution, and protection of trafficking (Human Rights Watch, 2003). In 2000, the Government of Mali adopted a National Emergency Action Plan to combat trans-border child trafficking (Castle and Diarra, 2003). Surveillance committees organized information meetings with local communities and Transporters' Unions who would inform their colleagues of the measures taken by the government to end child trafficking. In June 2002, a special legislation was enacted encompassing all measures for Child Protection in the country.

In Nigeria, where 25,000 nationals – 19,000 boys and 6,000 girls including trafficked children and prostitutes – were deported over the last two years from Germany, Turkey, Libya, Italy, and so on, an environment has been created to ensure the full protection and promotion of the rights of the child by the Child Rights Bill signed into law in 2003, thanks to the unrelenting efforts of local and national advocacy groups. This has fully domesticated the UN Convention on the Right of the Child. All segments of the population are being sensitized to the Act, especially with respect to child labour, child trafficking and sexual exploitation of children, and the penalty for offenders. The Nigerian National Trafficking in Persons Law Enforcement and Administration Act approved in

July 2003 criminalizes child trafficking and stipulates harsh punishment for offenders. This outcome is credited largely to the efforts of the NGO headed by the wife of the country's vice president and others. Also, the National Agency for the Prohibition of Traffic in Persons was set up to investigate, prosecute offenders, counsel, reintegrate, and rehabilitate trafficked persons (Salah, 2004). An anti-prostitution law was passed in September 2000 by Edo State Government in Nigeria to prohibit trafficking and prostitution in the State. Opening the Fourth Regional Conference on Child Abuse and Neglect in Enugu, Nigeria in March 2004, President Obasanjo identified child labour, child trafficking, and sexual exploitation with all their attendant abuses as the greatest afflictions confronting humanity today, adding that any situation in which children are subjected to exploitative labour or sexual exploitation, with all forms of abuse and neglect, amounts to a crime against humanity.

At the subregional level, ECOWAS Foreign Affairs Ministers adopted in December, 2001 in Senegal, a Political Declaration and Action Plan against Human Trafficking which commits their respective governments to ratify and fully implement relevant international instruments that strengthen laws against human trafficking and protect trafficked victims, especially women and children. Training of police, immigration officials, prosecutors, and judges are essential components of the Plan, the aim being to combat trafficking of persons, prevent and prosecute traffickers, and protect the rights of victims (Sita, 2003). ECOWAS countries agreed to set up direct communication between their border control agencies and expand effort to gather data on human trafficking. Its Parliament has also prepared an action plan on human trafficking.

Early in 2002 in Libreville, officials from West and Central African countries agreed to a common Platform of Action to enact laws designed to protect child workers, improve the system of custody for child victims of trafficking, strengthen cooperation among governments, and establish transit and reception centres for repatriated children. As a follow-up, Benin, Mali, Gabon, and Nigeria established inter-ministerial committees to address the issue of child trafficking (Salah, 2004). Gabon has also established a National Commission to combat trafficking on children. In Benin, Togo, and Nigeria, the police have strengthened control posts along their common borders to track and repatriate trafficked children.

In eastern Africa, Ethiopia set up a consulate in Beirut to provide support for its female nationals being abused and exploited in that country. In southern Africa, South Africa's Law Reform Commission's investigation of human trafficking is aimed at developing legislation to punish traffickers and protect victims. NGOs, rather than governments, are active in setting up projects for child victims of commercial sexual exploitation. The subdued interests of governments of southern and eastern Africa in problems of human trafficking could also be related to their perception of the subject matter – indeed, less than one-third of countries in these subregions recognized trafficking as a problem compared to 70 per cent of countries of West and Central Africa (UNICEF, 2003). In that sense also, very limited information is available on concrete efforts, if any, by governments in southern and eastern Africa to curb human trafficking through bilateral or related initiatives.

These measures are not limited to the region. In September 2002, for instance, an Africa-Europe Expert Meeting on trafficking in human beings, sponsored by the Governments of Sweden and Italy, called for a number of measures in both origin and destination countries related to: prevention and combating of trafficking and awareness-raising, protection and assistance to victims, legislative framework and law enforcement, and cooperation and coordination within and between states and regions. In Turin, Italy, one of the main destinations for trafficked Nigerian women, an outreach unit has assisted 1,250 victims, 60 per cent of them Nigerians, with practical assistance, including access to health services. Other countries of destination for African trafficked victims – Spain, the Netherlands, and the UK – are implementing a variety of such schemes.

Researchers need to refine their methodologies to ensure that they adequately capture trafficking ramifications, especially its diverse sources, causes, and dynamics. Data on the prevalence of trafficking using the number of convictions, number of complaints launched, number of victims assisted, and medical data about trafficked victims simply do not exist in the region. Collecting information on the cultural context of broader children's work, child labour migration (internal and cross-border), and child trafficking would advance our knowledge. Above all, there is a greater need for information sharing and cooperation between researchers in origin and destination countries with a focus on tracer studies of trafficked victims.

NOTE

1. I acknowledge the untiring efforts of Frank Laczko who encouraged me to write this paper; he and the librarian made available useful documents from the IOM library. My gratitude also goes to the two anonymous reviewers whose comments on the draft have enriched the final version of the paper. I can be contacted at AAderantiadepoju@aol.com.

REFERENCES

Adepoju, A.
1997   "Introduction" in A. Adepoju (Ed.), *Family, Population and Development in Africa*, Zed Books Ltd., London and New Jersey.
Aderinto, A.A.
2003   "Socio-economic profiles, reproductive health behaviour and problems of street children in Ibadan, Nigeria", paper presented at The Fourth African Population Conference: Population and Poverty in Africa – Facing Up to the Challenges of the 21st Century, UAPS, Tunis, 8-12 December.
Afonja, S.
2001   "An assessment of trafficking in women and girls in Nigeria Ile Ife", unpublished mimeo.
Anarfi, J.K.
1998   "Ghanaian women and prostitution in Côte d'Ivoire", in K. Kempadoo and J. Doezema (Eds), *Global Sex Workers: Rights, Resistance and Redefinition*, Routlege, New York.
Anderson, B., and J.O. Davidson
2003   "Is trafficking in human beings demand driven? A multi-country pilot study", *IOM Migration Research Series No. 15*, IOM, Geneva.
Anti-Slavery International
2001   "Is there slavery in Sudan?", Anti-Slavery International, London.
Butegwa, F.
1997   *Trafficking in Women in Africa: a Regional Report*, mimeographed.
Castle, S., and A. Diarra
2003   *The International Migration of Young Malians: Tradition, Necessity or Rites of Passage*, London School of Hygiene and Tropical Medicine, London.
Dottridge, M.
2002   "Trafficking in children in West and Central Africa", *Gender and Development*, 10(1): 38-49.
Fanou-Ako, N., and A.F. Adihou
2002   *Rapport de recherche sur le trafic des enfants entre le Bénin et le Gabon*, Anti-Slavery International and Enfants Solidaires d'Afrique et du Monde.

Fitzgibbon, K.
   2003   "Modern-day slavery? The scope of trafficking in persons in Africa",
           African Security Review, 12(1).
Human Rights Watch
   2003   *Borderline Slavery: Child Trafficking in Togo*, 15(8A), Human Rights
           Watch, New York.
International Labour Organization (ILO)
   2002   *Unbearable to the Human Heart: Child Trafficking and Action to
           Eliminate It*, ILO, Geneva.
   2003a   *Trafficking in Human Beings: New Approaches to Combating the Prob-
           lem: Special Action Programme to Combat Forced Labour*, ILO, Geneva.
   2003b   *The Trafficking of Women and Children in the Southern African Region,
           Presentation of Research Findings*, ILO, Geneva, 24 March.
Kornbluth, D.A.
   1996   "Illegal migration from North Africa: the role of traffickers", in A.P. Schmid
           (Ed.), *Migration and Crime*, ISPAC, Rome: 173-177.
Moore, H.
   1994   "Is there a crisis in the family?", Occasional Paper No.3, World Summit for
           Social Development, UNRISD, Geneva.
Nagel, I.
   2000   *Le traffic d'Enfants en Afrique de l'Ouest*, Rapport d'étude, Osnabrück,
           Terre des hommes, janvier.
Pearson, E.
   2002   *Human Traffic, Human Rights: Redefining Victim Protection*, Anti-
           slavery International, London.
Salah, R.
   2004   "Child trafficking: a challenge to child protection in Africa", paper pre-
           sented at the Fourth African Regional Conference on Child Abuse and
           Neglect, Enugu, March.
Sita, N.M.
   2003   *Trafficking in Women and Children: Situation and Some Trends in African
           Countries*, UNAFRI, May.
Taylor, E.
   2002   "Trafficking in women and girls", paper prepared for Expert Group
           Meeting on Trafficking in Women and Girls, Glen Cove, New York,
           18-22 November.
United Nations
   1999   United Nations Commission on Human Rights, Sub-committee on Pre-
           vention of Discrimination and Protection of Minorities, Working Group
           on Contemporary Forms of Slavery, 24th Session, 23 June to 2 July, Geneva.
UNICEF
   1998   Atelier sous-régional sur le trafic des enfants domestiques en particulier
           les filles domestiques dans la région de l'Afrique de l'Ouest et du Centre,
           Cotonou, Bénin, 6-8 juillet.
   2000   *Child Trafficking in West Africa: Policy Responses*, UNICEF Innocenti
           Research Centre, Florence.

2003   *Trafficking in Human Beings Especially Women and Children in Africa*, UNICEF Innocenti Research Centre, Florence.

Vayrynen, R.
2003   "Illegal immigration, human trafficking and organized crime", Discussion Paper 2003/27, WIDER, Helsinki.

Veil, L.
1998   *The Issue of Child Domestic Labour and Trafficking in West and Central Africa*, report prepared for the UNICEF Subregional Workshop on Trafficking in Child Domestic Workers, particularly girls in domestic service, in West and Central Africa Region, Cotonou, 6-8 July.

Research on Human Trafficking in North America: A Review of Literature

Elzbieta M. Gozdziak and Elizabeth A. Collett*

INTRODUCTION

As the number of traffickers apprehended, and the number of victims offered protection have both increased, an opportunity has been afforded to the research community to make an empirical assessment of the trafficking phenomenon in North America, including collection of baseline data on the prevalence of human trafficking in the region, trafficking trajectories, the characteristics of both victims and traffickers, and the services needed to protect and support victims. However, despite these opportunities there has been little systematic, empirical, and methodologically rigorous research on trafficking in human beings in Canada, the United States, and Mexico. This paper is a modest attempt to survey existing literature on trafficking in human beings in the region. It includes a discussion of a broad spectrum of publications, not all of which relate to human trafficking as defined in the *UN Protocol to Prevent, Suppress, and Punish Trafficking in Persons, Especially Women and Children*. We include them nevertheless because their authors argue that they indeed inform the human trafficking discourse. The examination of existing literature is carried out against a backdrop of the discussion of the antecedents of the contemporary trafficking phenomena as well as existing definitions of trafficking. This paper aims to map out the research that currently exists and make note of the research gaps that need to be filled in order to establish appropriate and effective policies and programmes for trafficked victims. We attempt to answer the following questions:

* Institute for the Study of International Migration, Georgetown University, Washington, DC, USA.

- Who is funding and who is conducting research on trafficking in human beings in North America?
- What methodologies and data sources are used to conduct this research?
- What are the foci of trafficking research in North America?
- What types of studies are conducted?
- What are the research gaps that need to be filled?

OLD PHENOMENON, NEW IMPORTANCE

The subject of human trafficking has received an increased international attention in the past two decades. However, the origins of the trafficking debate date back to the end of the nineteenth century when feminists such as Josephine Butler brought involuntary prostitution into the international discourse under the term "White Slave Trade", a term derived from the French *Traite des Blanches*, which related to *Traite des Noirs*, a term used in the beginning of the nineteenth century to describe the Negro slave trade (Derks, 2000). "White slavery" referred to the abduction and transport of white women for prostitution and in a manner similar to today's campaigns, the issue received wide media coverage, a number of organizations were set up to combat it, and national and international legislation was adopted to stop the "trade" (Doezema, 2002). The movement against "white slavery" grew out of the so-called abolitionist movement, which campaigned in England and other western European countries as well as in the United States against the regulation of prostitution (Bullough and Bullough, 1987).[1]

The first international agreement against "white slavery" was drafted in 1902 in Paris and signed two years later by 16 states (Doezema, 2002). The *International Agreement for the Suppression of the White Slave Trade* did not equate "white slavery" with "prostitution". Initially, the agreement addressed the fraudulent or abusive recruitment of women for prostitution in another country, although later, in 1910, its scope was broadened to include the traffic of women and girls within national borders (Wijers and Lap-Chew, 1997). In 1921, during a meeting held under the auspices of the League of Nations (later the United Nations) the traffic of boys was also incorporated into the agreement.

In 1933 a new convention was signed in Geneva. The *International Convention for the Suppression of the Traffic in Women* condemned all recruitment for prostitution in another country. The abolitionist standards of the 1933 convention were reiterated in the 1949 *UN Convention for the Suppression of Traffic in Persons and the Exploitation of the Prostitution of Others,* which stated that:

Prostitution and the accompanying evil of the traffic in persons for the purpose of prostitution are incompatible with the dignity and worth of a human person and endanger the welfare of the individual, the family, and the community of a person.

In the international arena, a renewed interest in human trafficking was influenced by developments regarding migration flows, the feminist movement, the AIDS pandemic, and child prostitution and child sex tourism in the 1980s (Doezema, 2002; Wijers and Lap-Chew, 1997). In the 1990s trafficking in human beings, particularly women and children, re-appeared on the agenda of the UN General Assembly, the Commission for Human Rights, the World Conference on Human Rights in Vienna in 1993, and the World Conference on Women in Beijing in 1995. By 1996, 70 countries ratified the 1949 Convention (Kelly and Regan, 2000). In November 2000, the UN General Assembly adopted the *UN Protocol to Prevent, Suppress, and Punish Trafficking in Persons, Especially Women and Children*. Other relevant international instruments followed, including the *International Labour Organization Convention Concerning the Prohibition and Immediate Action for the Elimination of the Worst Forms of Child Labour* and the *Protocol to the Convention of the Right of the Child on the Sale of Children, Child Prostitution and Child Pornography*. Many international organizations such as the International Labour Organization (ILO), UNICEF, and the International Organization for Migration (IOM) as well as the European Union (EU) have engaged in anti-trafficking campaigns.

There are, however, some networks that are not too enthusiastic about this increased attention to trafficking. The Network of Sex Work Projects (NSWP), an informal alliance of some 40 international organizations promoting sex workers' health and human rights, is concerned that directing attention to the trafficking issues will detract from a broader agenda of the sex worker rights movement. According to Jo Doezema, one reason for this concern is that most anti-trafficking campaigns focus exclusively on "human rights violations committed by 'pimps' or traffickers against 'innocent women', who are often understood to be non-sex workers" (Murphy and Ringheim, 2002). Sex worker rights organizations, on the other hand, identify the state, particularly the police, as the prime violators of sex workers' rights. The result of shifting the locus of concern from state repression of sex workers to individual acts of violent traffickers (reprehensible as these are) is that anti-trafficking campaigns lack a critical attitude toward the state.

In the United States trafficking became a focus of activities in the late 1990s and culminated in the passage of the Trafficking Victims Protection Act (TVPA) signed into law by President Clinton on 16 October 2000. The TVPA of 2000 (P.L. 106-386) and the Trafficking Victims Protection Re-authorization Act of 2003 (H.R. 2620) are considered the main tools to combat trafficking in persons both worldwide and domestically. The Act authorized the establishment of the Office to Monitor and Combat Trafficking in Persons, headed by Ambassador John R. Miller, and the President's Interagency Task Force to Monitor and Combat Trafficking in Persons to assist in the coordination of anti-trafficking efforts. In passing the TVPA, the US Government set standards for other countries with respect to prevention of human trafficking, prosecution of traffickers, and protection of victims, and designated itself the auditor of these activities.

Canada was heavily involved in the negotiations leading to the adoption of the UN Trafficking and Smuggling Protocols, with participation of representatives from the Department of Foreign Affairs and International Trade (DFAIT) and Status of Women Canada (Department of Justice, Canada). Canada was also among the first nations to sign (December 2000) and ratify (May 2002) the Protocols. At home, an ad hoc Interdepartmental Working Group (IWG) coordinated the Canadian Federal Government's efforts regarding trafficking. The IWG members do not have a homogenous perspective on trafficking. According to Oxman-Martinez et al. (2005), a security lens was helpful in getting human trafficking onto the public agenda, especially post-September 11. However, today many members feel that it is time to frame the issue within a human rights framework. In the spring of 2004, the Federal Minister of Justice formalized the role of the IWG; IWG received an official mandate to develop a comprehensive anti-trafficking strategy. To date, most Canadian anti-trafficking efforts have focused on prosecution of traffickers and interception of "irregular migrants"; Canada still does not have legal guidance for the protection of victims (Oxman-Martinez et al., 2005).

Although Mexico is often described as source, transit, and destination country for persons trafficked for sexual exploitation and labour, information about the Mexican Government's involvement in anti-trafficking activities is scarce. According to the Trafficking in Persons (TIP) report, the Government of Mexico does not fully comply with the minimum standards for the elimination of trafficking. At the moment, Mexico lacks national-level commitment to fight trafficking and a national anti-trafficking law. The country did sign the Mexican-Guatemalan March 2004 Memorandum of Understanding on trafficking. In addition, Mexico participated in recent conferences on trafficking in persons, including a conference organized by the US Department of Labor as part of ongoing cooperative activities between the Governments of Canada, Mexico, and the United States under the North American Agreement of Labour Cooperation (NAALC), and a conference on Strategies for Combating Human Trafficking within the United States, Canada, and Mexico, organized by the Chicago-Kent College of Law, and sponsored by the Canadian Department of Foreign Affairs and International Trade and the Mexican Consulate in Chicago.

The different level of involvement by North American countries in anti-trafficking activities is related to the differences in defining the problem. Or is it the other way around?

NEGOTIATING THE DEFINITION

The international definition of trafficking has emerged only fairly recently, in December 2000, with the signing of the UN *Protocol to Prevent, Suppress, and Punish Trafficking in Persons* in Palermo, Italy. Prior to the crafting of the UN definition, trafficking in persons was often viewed as human smuggling and a type of illegal migration (Laczko, 2002). The Protocol is a result of two years of negotiations at the UN Centre for International Crime Prevention in Vienna. The Protocol was the target of heavy lobbying efforts by religious and feminist organizations. The lobby efforts represented two opposing views of prostitution: the Human Rights Caucus, which saw prostitution as legitimate labour, and the Coalition Against Trafficking in Women (CATW), which saw all prostitution as a violation of women's human rights (Doezema, 2002).

The differences between these two lobby groups became largely apparent in the most controversial part of the negotiations, namely in the crafting of the definition of trafficking in persons. CATW and their supporters argued that trafficking should include all forms of recruitment and transportation for prostitution, regardless of whether force or deception took place (CATW, 1999), while the Human Rights Caucus, who supported the view of prostitution as work, argued that force or deception was a necessary ingredient in the definition of human trafficking. The Caucus also maintained that the term "human trafficking" should include trafficking of women, men, and children for different types of labour, including sweatshop labour, agriculture, and prostitution (Human Rights Caucus, 1999).

The two groups also presented differing views of the notion of "consent". CATW argued that prostitution is never voluntary, because women's consent to sex work is meaningless. The definition CATW championed differed very little from the proposed definition of trafficking in children. The Human Right Caucus, on the other hand, stated that:

> Obviously, by definition, no one consents to abduction or forced labour, but an adult woman is able to consent to engage in an illicit activity (such as prostitution). If no one is forcing her to engage in such activity, then trafficking does not exist (1999: 5).

The Caucus also argued that the Protocol should distinguish between adults, especially women and children, and avoid adopting a patronizing approach reducing women to the level of children in the name of "protecting" women as such a stance historically "protected" women from the ability to exercise their rights (Human Rights Caucus, 1999).

In the end the signatories of the Protocol rejected the broadened definition championed by some feminist organizations and religious groups, arguing that it would impede the capacity of the international community to achieve consensus and act decisively against traffickers (Miko, 2004). As a result of this decision, the Protocol defines trafficking in persons as:

> (..) the recruitment, transportation, transfer, harbouring or receipt of persons, by means of the threat or use of force or other forms of coercion, of abduction, of fraud, of deception, of abuse of power or of a position of vulnerability or of the giving or receiving of payments or benefits to achieve the consent of a person having control over another person, for the purpose of exploitation.

In addition, the Protocol states that:

> Exploitation shall include, at a minimum, the exploitation of the prostitution of others or other forms of sexual exploitation, forced labour or services, slavery or practices similar to slavery, servitude or the removal of organs.

Achieving baseline consensus on the definition has been a landmark achievement; however, there is still a need to create a comprehensive legal definition that will establish trafficking as an international crime and human rights violation (see Hyland, 2001a). The weakness of the Protocol is its excessive focus on criminalizing traffickers to the detriment of making protection of trafficked person the priority. Although the Protocol includes measures to protect trafficking victims, the signatories are not mandated to include them at the top of their priority list. As of this writing 117 countries signed and 79 ratified the Protocol. While all three North American countries signed the Protocol in 2000, only Canada and Mexico ratified it in 2002 and 2003, respectively. The United States is yet to follow suit.[2] There is hope that the signatories will create domestic laws in response to the Protocol, but for now there is only hope.

In North America, only the Unites States has passed a comprehensive legislation that addresses prevention and protection for victims in addition to prosecution of traffickers. Canada and Mexico are yet to do the same. Instead of developing a special legislation, Canada opted to add specific offences against human trafficking to the Immigration and Refugee Protection Act (IRPA) as well as utilize many of the Criminal Code offences that apply to trafficking. The Canadian legislative provisions reflect the traditional association between trafficking and work in the sex trade. Furthermore, although some of these provisions target traffickers, when the legislation is enforced the victims are also charged, generally under section 210 of the Criminal Code (Jimenez and Bell, 2000a, 2000b). Bruckert and Parent (2002) note that while victims may seek asylum based on humanitarian and compassionate considerations, this does not constitute a guarantee of protection to encourage them to testify against traffickers.

Mexico also relies on the Criminal Code that includes penalties for "offences to public morality"; the "corruption of a minor under the age of 16"; for induced or forced prostitution and for maintaining brothels; for employment of minors under age 18 in taverns, bars, and other "centres of vice"; and for the procurement, inducement, and concealment of prostitution (Shirk and Webber, 2004). To our knowledge there is no evidence-based research that would indicate which approach is more effective. The best legislation, without proper enforcement and implementation, may not result in the expected outcomes; four years after the passage of the TVPA of 2000, the outcomes are lacking: only 717 victims have been identified. On the other hand, aggressive enforcement of criminal codes might be very effective in prosecuting traffickers.

Like the international community, the United States has grappled with creating a comprehensive definition of trafficking in human beings. The first US definition of trafficking in persons was created by the President's Interagency Council on Women, a body charged by President Clinton with coordinating US domestic and international policy on human trafficking.[3] The Council crafted the following working definition to guide policy development on trafficking in persons:

> Trafficking is all acts involved in the recruitment, abduction, transport, harbouring, transfer, sale or receipt of person; within national or across international borders; through force, coercion, fraud or deception; to place persons in situation of slavery or slavery-like conditions, forced labour or services, such as prostitution or sexual services, domestic servitude, bonded sweatshop labour or other debt bondage (O'Neill Richard, 1999).

This policy definition was later replaced by a legal definition of trafficking in persons, created under the 2000 TVPA (Division A of Public Law 106-386). The Act defines severe forms of trafficking in persons as:

(a) sex trafficking[4] in which a commercial sex[5] act is induced by force, fraud, and coercion,[6] or in which the person induced to perform such act has not attained 18 years of age; or
(b) the recruitment, harbouring, transportation, provision or obtaining of a person for labour or services, through the use of force, fraud or coercion for the purpose of subjection to involuntary servitude,[7] peonage, debt bondage,[8] or slavery (US Government, 2002).

Implicit in this definition are three key concepts that help frame both the understanding and the potential response to trafficking in persons. First, the definition
identifies two types of trafficking, including sexual and labour exploitation. Second, the definition includes "force, fraud, or coercion", which encompasses
two of the most common trafficking scenarios: (1) a scheme where victims are
falsely promised one job and forced or coerced into another; and (2) a situation
where victims choose or consent to a particular job in an industry or the
commercial sex trade, but are deceived about the working conditions. Third,
the definition distinguishes between human trafficking and human smuggling.
Trafficking is distinguishable from smuggling because it includes slavery-like
conditions and because it may occur within national borders, while smuggling
requires crossing of international borders. The differences between these
separate crimes require separate policy, legislative, and law enforcement
responses. In the United States, a typical response of the law enforcement to
persons smuggled into the country is deportation, but trafficking victims are
accorded protection, including immigration relief (Hyland, 2001a).

According to the 2000 study by the Consulting and Audit Canada, there is no
agreed upon definition of trafficking in persons among the individual member
departments of the Canadian Government's IWGTIP. In addition, there is no
process or criteria in place to identify victims of trafficking, making it virtually
impossible for the Canadian Government to grant victims any level of protection
(Canadian Council for Refugees, 2004). Research sponsored by the Canadian
Government (see Langevin and Belleau, 2000; Bruckert and Parent, 2002) uses
definitions developed by Dutch researchers, Marjan Wijers and Lin Lap-Chew
(1997: 36), who relate human trafficking to:

> All acts involved in the recruitment and/or transportation of a woman within and across
> national borders for work or services by means of violence or threat of violence, abuse
> of authority or dominant position, debt, bondage, deception or other forms of coercion.

Mexico ratified multiple agreements related to human trafficking, but the country's
efforts to combat trafficking in persons have relied mainly on existing laws
pertaining to prostitution or sexual exploitation, threats to public health, "moral
corruption", and pimping (*lenocino*) (Shirk and Webber, 2004). None of these
penal codes includes a comprehensive definition of trafficking.

Paradoxically, the existence of a legal definition of trafficking in persons does
not necessarily mean that the term is uniformly operationalized. Messy interpretations of the term can be found both in the United States, a country with a
legal definition of trafficking as well as in Canada and Mexico, countries which
lack a legal definition. A review of literature indicates that many North American
researchers use the term "trafficking in person" to discuss very different co-

horts of people. As will be discussed in more detail later in this paper, some researchers focus primarily on trafficking in women and girls for sexual exploitation to the detriment of excluding men from the discussion and ignoring trafficking for other forms of labour. Some label all sex workers as trafficked persons, believing that no one would willingly enter or stay in this occupation. Still others do not distinguish between victims trafficked across international borders and those trafficked within a particular country. Some argue that the definition of trafficking in women must be "broadened to encompass the complex problems associated with trafficking and the diverse situations of women" and include in their analysis of trafficking mail-order brides, arranged marriages, sham adoptions, forced labour, and slavery-like practices (Langevin and Belleau, 2000). For example, studies conducted as part of the research programme funded by Status of Women Canada focused on such diverse populations as live-in caregivers, mail-order brides, and migrant sex workers.

Conflations of migrant abuse, trafficking, and sex slavery seems to be a common rhetorical device in anti-trafficking discourse and counter-trafficking campaigns (Chapkis, 2003) as well as in research. Some commentators prefer to avoid the term completely, but debates on the sex industry and on female migration continue to be placed under the heading "Trafficking" or "Trafficking in Women" (Bindman, 1997). In the United States, for example, the writings of Kathleen Barry (1979) and Janice Raymond (1998) are consistently included in bibliographies on human trafficking and discussed in a variety of articles on the subject despite the fact that they studied prostitutes not trafficked victims. Raymond and Hughes, co-directors of a research project titled *Sex Trafficking of Women in the United States*, carried out the study under the auspices of CATW, an organization founded by Barry, also position their study within the trafficking framework; they argue that:

> Trafficking and sexual exploitation are intrinsically connected and should not be separated merely because there are other forms of trafficking; or because some countries have legalized/regulated prostitution and thereby want to censor any discussion of prostitution from regional and international policy agendas (Raymond, 2002).

SLIPPERY STATISTICS

Messy definitions result in slippery statistics ridden with methodological problems. Few governments, including North American governments, systematically collect data on human trafficking and when they do provide statistical information they often mix data related to trafficking, smuggling, and illegal migration (Laczko, 2002). In some accounts all undocumented migrants assisted in crossing, for example, the US border, are counted as having been trafficked

(Gordy, 2000). Other reports reserve the term "trafficking" exclusively to victims of sexual slavery (Chapkis, 2003). In some instances, all transnational or migrant sex workers are defined as trafficking victims regardless of consent and conditions of labour,[9] while other reports emphasize abusive conditions of employment or deceptive recruitment policies used in the sex trade.[10] As a result, available data is confusing and unreliable.

The US State Department, for example, has produced the oft-quoted estimates of the size of the trafficked population worldwide: 800,000 to 900,000 annually, with 14,500 to 17,500 trafficked into the United States alone.[11] These figures are used by a number of international organizations, including the UN and IOM, as authoritative, yet there has been no release of information with respect to the methodology used to obtain the baseline data. Information provided by the US State Department at the conference in Rome where the papers in this volume were first presented includes a brief description of the statistical methods employed to calculate estimates, but does not explain the methodology used to arrive at the baseline data sources either.

Indeed, the number of trafficking victims entering the United States has been revised at least three times: down from 45,000 to 50,000, a figure reached by the Central Intelligence Agency (CIA) in 1999 (O'Neill Richard, 1999), to 18,000 to 20,000 victims reported in 2003, and even further down to 14,500 to 17,500 quoted in the 2004 TIP report. Each time an improved methodology was cited as a reason for these new figures. Charles Keely, Professor of International Migration and Demography at Georgetown University, comments that any estimate of trafficking in the United States (or in any other country) requires a reliable source of data, presumably a partial count, and then a justified basic rule with which to extrapolate and estimate from this basic data. Given that "neither government nor NGOs have a sufficient overview or a data source for extrapolation that allows for a national estimate" in the United States, he believes that the US State Department figures are merely "guesstimates."[12]

That there are a plethora of estimates globally is an acknowledged problem: the United Nations Educational, Scientific and Cultural Organization (UNESCO) has undertaken a trafficking statistics project attempting to trace the origins and methodologies of statistics cited and evaluate their validity.[13] It is likely that little of this data is accurate. The Protection Project at Johns Hopkins University in Washington, DC is also attempting to produce an overview of global trafficking trends. As part of this work, the project has produced maps of commonly used trafficking routes worldwide, yet there is no referencing of how these routes have been determined. It is difficult to assess whether the maps are based on any documented cases in countries of origin and destination and/or whether the maps are based on a handful of cases or on a critical mass of cases. Perhaps the researchers at Johns Hopkins utilize the same threshold of 100 or more cases of victims that the US State Department uses in making a determination about which countries to include in the annual TIP report. Unfortunately, we can only guess because the methodology is not discussed.

Researchers cannot gain an overall picture of the scale and characteristics of the human trafficking trade into North America without a comprehensive analysis of routes and destinations. Without reliable data it is also very difficult to combat human trafficking and design programmes for victims. However, reliable data on trafficking victims are difficult to obtain and many methodological questions remain: How do we quantify clandestine phenomena? Should we look at numbers of victims found in every city? Or should we look at research on the sex industry and prostitution and extrapolate number of victims trafficked into sexual exploitation? And what about victims trafficked for labour? How do we arrive at those numbers? It is impossible to imagine that employers who knowingly hire trafficked persons would provide researchers with the number of victims or allow them access to factories and sweatshops to identify and count victims.

Richard Estes, for example, estimates that as many as 17,000 children are trafficked into the United States every year (Estes and Weiner, 2001), which does not correspond with the most recent numbers provided by the CIA. As indicated above, the CIA's current estimates put the number of trafficking victims (adults and children combined) at 14,500 to 17,500 per annum. Estes' data, however, is problematic in many other ways. When presenting his research at a conference on identifying and serving child victims of trafficking in Houston, Texas, Estes was not able to differentiate between children who have crossed international borders and those who were trafficked within a particular North American country. He also did not collect data on nativity, and therefore was not able to provide information whether the children he studied were foreign-born or native-born. Data on nativity is important for many reasons, including referral and determination of eligibility for particular services. In the United States, foreign-born child victims of trafficking are eligible for a full complement of assistance, including immigration relief, under the provisions of TVPA, while US-born child victims obviously do not need immigration assistance and would be referred to child protective services for appropriate protection and services.

At the moment the only reliable US data relate to the number of trafficking victims officially certified by ORR. As of 18 March 2005, ORR certified 717 survivors of trafficking, including 651 adults and 66 children. The group included 213 males and 504 females.

Canadian data is also problematic; it includes different cohorts of people and often combines trafficking victims with illegal migrants. A 1998 study commissioned by the Solicitor General of Canada concluded that the impact of migrant trafficking in Canada is estimated at between US$120 million to US$400 million per year and accounts for approximately 8,000 to 16,000 people arriving in Canada each year illegally (Porteus Consulting, 1998). The report uses the term "migrant trafficking" rather loosely, without specific reference to accepted definitions of human trafficking.

There are no official government estimates of trafficking into Mexico, but the UN lists Mexico as the number one source of young children trafficked to North America (Hall, 1998). Mexico is the largest source of undocumented migrants and a major transit point for third-country migration to the United States, but these statistics usually refer to illegal and smuggled migrants without making any attempt to even hypothesize whether any of them might be victims of trafficking. Recent reports suggest that Mexico is a major destination for sex tourism from the United States (Shirk and Webber, 2004) and that as many as 16,000 Mexican children are subject to commercial sexual exploitation annually (Correa, 2001). The latter statement seems to be equating sexual exploitation of children with trafficking, while child abuse, an equally horrific and punishable offence, might have been a more accurate classification of the crime.

It is interesting that to any conscientious social scientist, the discrepancies in the most commonly quoted estimates of human trafficking would be a cause for considerable suspicion of the reliability of the research, yet when it comes to data on trafficking, "few eyebrows are raised and the figures are easily bandied about without question" (Kempadoo, 1998). It is noteworthy that despite the difficulties in establishing clear and reliable statistics, the trafficking phenomenon has often been described as mushrooming or being on the raise globally, while in fact these assertions are often based on very few cases. Wendy Chapkis, for example, posits that the TVPA of 2000 "makes a strategic use of anxieties over sexuality, gender, and immigration" and "does so through the use of misleading statistics creating a moral panic around 'sexual slavery'" (Chapkis, 2003).

Jo Doezema (2000) in an article on the re-emergence of the myth of "white slavery" in contemporary discourses of "trafficking in women" points out that contemporary historians, including Walkowitz (1980), Bristow (1982), Corbin (1990), and Guy (1991), are unanimous in their opinion that the actual number of cases of "white slavery" (defined as the procurement by force, deceit, or drug, of a white woman or girl against her will for prostitution) were very few and yet the issue became very prominent both in Europe and in America. The extent of the "white slave panic" in Europe and in the United States has been extensively documented (see, for example, Bristow, 1977, 1982; Connelly, 1980; Grittner, 1990). Doezema argues that the view of "white slavery" as a myth can account for its persistence and power. She invokes Grittner's examination of the American version of the white slavery panic and his argument that "myth does not simply mean that something is 'false', but is rather a collective belief that simplifies reality" (Doezema, 2000).

GATW undertook an 18-month investigation into "trafficking in women" internationally at the request of the UN Special Rapporteur on Violence Against Women and concluded:

> Finding reliable statistics on the extent of trafficking in women is virtually impossible, due to a lack of systematic research, the lack of a precise, consistent, and unambiguous definition of the phenomena and the illegality and criminal nature of prostitution and trafficking (Wijers and Lap-Chew, 1997).

This does not, however, stop various "experts" from quoting huge numbers of victims of trafficking. At this backdrop of messy definitions and slippery statistics, research or what passes for research is being conducted and numerous publications are published.

WHO IS FUNDING AND CONDUCTING THE RESEARCH?

Much of the research conducted within the United States has emanated from, been funded, and conducted by the US Federal Government. The Office to Monitor and Combat Trafficking in Persons (O/TIP) in the State Department was created specifically as the trafficking focal point within the US Government. It produces high profile government publications, including the annual TIP Report mandated by the TVPA of 2000. The usefulness of the TIP Report is often questioned; the report provides no in-depth analysis of the nature of trafficking and the office itself and offers little aside from fact sheets, and commentary on conference proceedings.

The National Institute of Justice (NIJ), the Research, Development, and Evaluation Agency of the US Department of Justice (DOJ), has been a leader in the United States in funding and commissioning research on trafficking issues. Since 1998 NIJ has been funding and participating in a range of human trafficking research projects and initiatives, including a diverse mix of research, demonstration projects, collaboration, and technical assistance programmes that focused on exploitation of children, social consequences of sex trafficking, human smuggling in China, and trafficking in women from Ukraine. To date, six major research projects have been undertaken: (1) Needs Assessment for Service Providers and Trafficking Victims (Caliber Associates, 2001), (2) Evaluation of Services Provided to Victims of Trafficking (a collaborative project with the Office for Victims of Crime), (3) Commercial Sexual Exploitation of Children in the United States, Canada and Mexico (Estes and Weiner, 2001), (4) Trafficking of Women in the United States: International and Domestic Trends (Raymond and Hughes, 2001), (5) Characteristics of Chinese Human Smugglers (Zhang and Chin, 2004), and (6) Trafficking in Persons in the United States (regional studies of two key trafficking hot spots, Chicago and southwest Florida, and one emerging port of entry, Washington, DC). As indicated above, some of these studies, such as the project co-directed by Raymond and Hughes, did not study trafficked victims, but focused on transnational and domestic sex workers. Others focused on human smuggling and still others on commercial sexual exploitation of children in North America, not on trafficking per se. However, one can argue that some of this research informs our knowledge about trafficked persons. For example, the study carried out by Estes and Weiner, which examined the extent, nature, and causes of commercial sexual exploitation of children in the United States, Canada, and Mexico, also attempted to identify networks of adult criminals exploiting children, which might shed light on similar networks of traffickers of children.

A number of in-house reports and studies have been produced by a variety of government agencies, such as the CIA's monograph, *International Trafficking of Women to the United States: A Contemporary Manifestation of Slavery and Organized Crime* (O'Neill Richard, 1999), or the Citizenship and Immigration Services (formerly INS) report to Congress on *International Matchmaking Organizations* (United States Citizenship and Immigration Services, 1999). In fact the CIA study was one of the first monographs to outline the problem of trafficking in persons in the United States. However, the majority of government-sponsored research has been specifically commissioned from experts in the field, either NGOs such as the CATW and the Global Alliance Against Trafficking in Women, or those in the academic community. This has also occurred to a limited extent at the state level, including a study commissioned by the state of Florida and conducted by a research team at Florida State University (FSU).

Some US agencies have pursued research projects related to their own operations. For example, the Office of the Inspector General in the Department of Defense (DOD) carried out investigations into military personnel's use of brothels in Korea and the Balkans. These two studies were conducted at the request of the US Congress primarily in response to accusations in news reports that servicemen were frequenting establishments staffed by trafficked women. Unfortunately, the first report does not detail the investigation into the veracity of the allegations, and merely assesses the adequacy of educational programmes implemented to prevent such occurrences. The Balkans report, on the other hand, noted that a "plethora" of information was available to document human trafficking in the region and detailed the extent of the US forces involvement in the sex industry in the area (United States Office of the Inspector General, 2003a). With respect to armed forces in South Korea, the Inspector General made several on-site visits to military camps and red-light districts, and spoke with high-ranking US and Korean military officers as well as NGO representatives. However, little empirical research was published based on these investigations (United States Office of the Inspector General, 2003b).

Government-funded research has focused a great deal upon an evaluation of services offered to victims of trafficking, with the intention that the research should fuel future policy initiatives. For example, Caliber Associates was commissioned by NIJ to conduct a *Needs Assessment for Service Providers and Victims* (Caliber Associates, 2001). The survey conducted by the consulting firm included interviews with a number of victims, and the characteristics of trafficking victims were detailed. This research into the nature of the crime and victims' characteristics was used to assess the need for appropriate victims' services.

In addition to the US Federal Government, states most affected by the phenomenon have begun to look more closely at ways to approach human trafficking, including legislative responses and service provision. Research initially focused upon services has resulted in the need for a closer empirical examination of trafficking victims, and their pre- and post-trafficking experiences. For instance, the FSU Center for the Advancement of Human Rights expanded their state commissioned project to assess services to include an overview of trafficking cases and victim characteristics. The state of Washington was the first region to enact local legislation to combat trafficking in human beings. As part of this initiative, the Office of Crime Victims produced a Task Force Report looking at both the problem and responses to the trafficking phenomenon and to the service needs of trafficked victims within the state.

Aside from the US Government, there have been some large research projects conducted by the NGO community and funded by non-governmental sources. A prime example of this is the *Comparative Study of Women Trafficked in the Migration Process: Patterns, Processes and Health Consequences in Five Countries (Indonesia, the Philippines, Thailand, Venezuela, and the United States)*, coordinated by Janice Raymond of CATW and funded by the Ford Foundation. Although the study is touted as research on trafficking, it focused primarily on women in prostitution. In the two chapters on the United States, the authors have pieced together a composite picture of the ways immigrant women, women with temporary visas, and undocumented women end up exploited in prostitution in the United States. The researchers consider these women victims of trafficking because they subscribe to the notion that all prostitution includes force and coercion. Gender, children, and human rights advocacy groups such as End Child Prostitution, Child Pornography and Trafficking of Children for Sexual Purposes (ECPAT), the Global Survival Network, and Human Rights Watch have all produced research on particular aspects of trafficking. Finally, there is a notable absence of research in academic circles, aside from pieces drawing on government-funded studies. Most academic pieces focus upon analysis of legislative and policy responses at the national and international level, particularly in response to the passage of the TVPA of 2000 and the UN Protocol on Trafficking (see Gallagher, 2001; Ryf, 2002).

In Canada, Citizenship and Immigration Canada has a strong reputation for research-based policy making. As part of an effort to base major policy decisions related to international migration, Canada has created the Metropolis Network, drawing upon the resources of a number of Canadian universities. However, despite a great deal of research on the nexus of gender and migration, the impact of immigrants on urban settlements, and immigrant integration, the Metropolis Network has not produced any research on human trafficking to Canada. Instead, in 1998, the Policy Research Fund of Status of Women Canada, the department with primary responsibility for gender issues in the country, issued a call for research on the theme of *Trafficking in Women: The Canadian Dimension* which identified the need for research in order to gain a greater insight into the extent of the problem in Canada and possible legal and social approaches to this issue. This research resulted in three reports, which centred upon specific groups of people such as mail-order brides, migrant sex workers, and immigrant live-in caregivers, and on particular source countries or regions such as the Philippines, eastern Europe, and the former Soviet Union. These reports were released between November 2000 and February 2002, and will be discussed later in this paper.

Several Canadian researchers, including Annalee Gölz, Jill Hanley, Cheryl Harrison, Harriet D. Lyons, Andrea Martinez, Jacqueline Oxman-Martinez, Jyoti Sanghera, and Rhonda Williams, are also engaged in research and writing about trafficking in women as well as organizing meetings under the auspices of the Canada chapter of the Global Alliance Against Traffic in Women (GAATW). For example, Oxman-Martinez and colleagues have conducted studies on the Canadian Government's response to trafficking in human beings; Lyons wrote about representation of trafficking in persons in Asia; and Sanghera wrote about the intersection of sex trade, prostitution, and globalization. Lyons and Sanghera argue that the North American perspective on trafficking and prostitution can be best developed in relation to and in conjunction with the understanding of these phenomena in other regions of the world.

Despite the small but growing number of publications on trafficking by Canadian authors, there is a general recognition that greater knowledge of the trafficking phenomenon is necessary in Canada. The Strategic Planning and Policy Unit of Consulting and Audit Canada conducted an *Inventory of Information Needs and Available Information on Trafficking in Women* in 2000. The report concluded that the "scope of the problem has not been well documented and there is little hard data", though "considerable anecdotal evidence" exists. Finally, the Canadian Royal Mounted Police have conducted a literature review linking human trafficking with organized crime, which also noted paucity of available material (Bruckert and Parent, 2002).

In Mexico, however, the government has been less proactive. The National Migration Institute (NIM), part of the Secretariat of Government (Mexico's Ministry for Interior Affairs) has produced just one report. This report concerned the threat posed to national security by organized crime syndicates using Mexico as a transit country for smuggling and trafficking human beings into the United States (Thompson, 2003). Despite an increased focus on trafficking as a human rights issue by the United States, the Mexican Government has made little effort to map the problem.

There are a number of human and children's rights groups in Mexico that have looked at the problem of trafficking, despite insufficient funding for comprehensive research. Casa Alianza, an NGO providing shelter and services to street children conducted a *Regional Investigation on Trafficking, Prostitution, Child Pornography and Sex Tourism with Children in Central America and Mexico* (2001). Partly supported by the Canadian Government, this joint investigation (with ECPAT and others) looked not only at the networks used by traffickers, intermediaries, and clients, but also assessed the effectiveness of current laws to address the problem. The research in Mexico focused upon the state of Chiapas, and interviews were conducted with both victims of sexual exploitation and the owners of businesses where that exploitation took place.

Finally, there are a number of independent Mexican researchers who collaborate with research organizations based in the United States and Canada, offering them access to information in Mexico, and conducting their own research. An example is the support given by the Centre for Advanced Studies in Social Anthropology in Mexico City to the study on the Commercial Exploitation of Children completed by Richard Estes.

WHAT METHODOLOGIES AND DATA SOURCES ARE USED
TO CONDUCT RESEARCH ON TRAFFICKING?

Primary data on trafficking are difficult to obtain. We have already discussed the lack of precision and methodological transparency in providing estimates of the number of trafficked victims in North America. Elsewhere in this volume, Denise Brennan points out methodological challenges to conducting social science research with trafficked persons in the United States. Most researchers draw information from newspaper reports and media investigations to compile a picture of trafficking in North America or base their studies on interviews with intermediaries: social service providers, counsellors, law enforcement, victim advocates, pro bono attorneys, and others working with trafficking victims. This methodological approach offers a different, and not necessarily unimportant, viewpoint. *The Needs Assessment for Service Providers and Trafficking Victims* conducted by Caliber Associates for the National Institute of Justice (NIJ) is based on interviews with 207 service providers, representing shelters, health clinics, and legal assistance groups, as well as focus group discussions with trafficking victims. It is notable that the research, initially limited regionally to New York, Florida, and Atlanta, had to be expanded to other regions, as there emerged only a limited number of service providers in those regions with experience in trafficking. Other research has assessed information from prosecuted cases, often high-profile ones. This methodological approach yields a great deal of information, but can potentially skew the data as only certain types of cases reach the courts. However, as the DOJ increases its numbers of indictments and prosecutions, this information should become more useful.

Researchers often face a choice between conducting an in-depth study of a particular geographic region, perhaps skewing the results toward a certain profile of trafficker and victim, and a more scattered approach, which risks forgoing "ethnographic richness". Some research has taken the former approach and focused upon the problem in a particular geographic area. The Global Survival Network completed an eight-month investigation into forced labour in the garment industry in the Commonwealth of the Northern Mariana Islands, a US territory, concluding that there were approximately 40,000 indentured workers in the province. Due to the difficulties in accessing these workers, the authors used several undercover researchers, one posing as a garment buyer, and the other as a university researcher interested in migrant workers. The result was more than an in-depth look at the characteristics of the problem in the region, but an enlightening window into the lucrative business model presented by trafficking in persons.

WHAT ARE THE FOCI OF RESEARCH
ON TRAFFICKING IN NORTH AMERICA?

A great deal of research has focused on trafficking for sexual exploitation, to the detriment of investigating trafficking for bonded labour and domestic servitude. The emphasis on trafficking for sexual exploitation can be attributed to a variety of reasons. The increased influence of the American religious right on policy decisions in a variety of arenas is one such reason. At the same time, groups with roots in the American feminist movement, such as CATW and GAATW, have been at the forefront of the push to raise awareness about trafficking in human beings, and have thus promoted research into women in the sex industry, not necessarily trafficked women. Despite a number of high profile cases of domestic servitude uncovered recently in the Washington, DC metropolitan area, there is less interest in trafficking for bonded labour than in trafficking for sexual exploitation. The limited focus on trafficking for labour can be attributed to the close ties of the current US administration to the business community. The administration is reluctant to commission studies that would investigate its greatest ally and supporter. This criticism notwithstanding, the US Department of Labor has recently organized a conference on trafficking for labour exploitation and subsequently solicited grant applications for research on the worst forms of child labour. As the review of these grant applications has not been finalized at the time of this writing, it remains to be seen what type of studies will get funded and what the research findings will reveal.

Most studies focus on women. Females have been the focus of research on trafficking for sexual exploitation as well as studies on matchmaking and arranged marriages, supported by both the US and Canadian Governments. This research is closely related to the research on the sex industry, and especially the sexual exploitation of women in prostitution. While studies of the domestic sex industry and transnational sex work do not constitute research on trafficking *sensu stricto*, they can offer insights into the effects of exploitation on individuals. Research on women in the sex industry has a much longer history and better developed methodologies than research on trafficked women. Very little is known about trafficking of men and boys, either for sexual exploitation or bonded labour.

In the United States, virtually all research has focused on individuals who have been officially identified as victims of severe forms of trafficking. Given the large disparity between those rescued and charged (484 and 110 over a three-year period, respectively),[14] and the current annual estimates of those caught up in the industry (14,500-17,500), one has to wonder about the effectiveness of research based solely on known cases.

WHAT TYPES OF STUDIES ARE CONDUCTED?

Researchers representing different disciplines have studied trafficking in human beings in North America. However, despite a growing interest of scholars in studying human trafficking, the body of academic research on trafficking in persons in North America is still very small. Legal research is leading the way among the still scarce academic research on human trafficking. Published in 1998, before the adoption of the UN Protocol on Trafficking and before the passage of the TVPA, Janie Chuang's article (1998) is an early example of legal analysis of the scope and practical efficacy of proposed legal protections applicable to victims of trafficking. Articles by Kara Ryf (2002), Kelly E. Hyland (2001b), and Wendy Chapkis (2003) are examples of a growing body of legal research analysing the provisions of the TVPA of 2000.

Kara Ryf posits that instead of fighting trafficking through immigration policy, the TVPA treats the problem as a human rights issue. In her article "The first modern anti-slavery act," Ryf provides an analysis of the ways in which the Act addresses the world's trafficking crisis as well as arguments that some of the Act's provisions fail short to provide appropriate solutions. She addresses the disparity of the current law, which in her opinion punishes trafficking victims for their immigration violations and prostitution activities more harshly than their captors, thereby making trafficking in persons a low risk and high profit industry despite the fact that the intention of the advocates of this legislation was to turn the trafficking industry into a high risk and low profit enterprise through international cooperation to capture, prosecute, and adequately punish those who traffic in human beings.

While Ryf focuses primarily on the provisions of the Act related to elimination of world trafficking, Hyland evaluates the adequacy of the protections the TVPA affords to victims. She considers the Act landmark legislation:

> Its approach to the crime of trafficking is not centred solely on law enforcement, but instead is a combination of prevention, prosecution and law enforcement, and protection and reintegration. This holistic approach indicates a dedication to combating crime and to protecting and assisting victims.

Hyland asserts that the Act's three-part framework could serve as a model for states that have the desire and ability to implement a comprehensive approach. She also admits that the Act is not perfect and argues for further legislation, primarily to create a private right of action, to make sanctions discretionary, and to permit asset forfeiture in trafficking cases. Indeed, such provisions might provide an increased incentive to testify against traffickers and would contribute to victims' early self-sufficiency. One could, however, argue also that these provisions might inadvertently result in a larger number of illegitimate claims.

Wendy Chapkis (2003) analyses both the TVPA and the debates surrounding its passage and argues that the law makes strategic use of anxieties over sexuality, gender, and immigration to further curtail migration. She argues that the law does so through misleading statistics creating a moral panic around "sexual slavery", through the creation of gendered distinction between "innocent victims" and "guilty migrants", and through the demand that assistance to victims should be tied to their willingness to assist in the prosecution of traffickers. She concludes that the Act does little to strengthen the rights of most migrant workers, both in the sex industry and elsewhere. In her view a truly effective response demands more than symbolic action against gross economic disparities between the rich and the poor countries of the world. Chapkis rightly suggests that feminists should look critically at the legislation, which relies heavily on narratives of female powerlessness and childlike sexual vulnerability. Of course no one should be forced to trade sex or safety to survive, but addressing the abuses of women working in and outside the sex industry necessitates an acknowledgement that women can consent to both economically motivated migration and to sex, which does not mean that the possibility of that consent should be used to excuse violation.

In Canada, Langevin and Belleau (2000) analysed the legal frameworks governing the hiring of immigrant live-in caregivers under the Live-in Caregiver Program (LCP) and the mail-order bride business. Although these populations do not meet the criteria (coercion and deceit) of the UN definition of trafficking, the authors consider these two groups victims of trafficking; they define trafficking in women as:

> (...) Exploitation of a woman, in particular for her labour or services, with or without pay and with or without her consent, by a person or group of persons with whom she is in an unequal power relationship (2000: x).

Indeed, the authors argue that the unequal relationship between an immigrant live-in caregiver and her employers, the obligation to live in their home for a period of two years, as well as the precariousness of her work during this period, lead to situations of abuse. Similarly, they stress the vulnerability of a fiancée who comes to Canada as the so-called mail-order bride to an abusive consumer-husband. They also emphasize the relationship between the phenomenon of mail-order brides and criminal activity, such as domestic violence or procuring for the purposes of prostitution. Furthermore, they argue that the phenomenon of immigrants as live-in caregivers and mail-order brides have antecedents in the enslavement of black and Aboriginal women in Canada and in the *filles du Roy*, brought to New France in the seventeenth century, respectively. Their definition is inspired both by a feminist and intersectional approach, and so are their solutions. Unfortunately, this approach assumes that the women who migrate to Canada to work as live-in caregivers or to marry Canadian citizens have no choice in the matter and do not act in their own name. It also does not take into account the fact that not all live-in caregivers or foreign-born women who marry Canadians end up being abused and exploited. In fact, the authors never provide any statistics to back up their assertion that the majority of the situations they examine result in exploitation.

Jacqueline Oxman-Martinez and colleagues have published several articles assessing the Canadian Government's policy and practice regarding human trafficking as well as a paper on gendered impacts of Canadian immigration policy on trafficked women. Their most recent article provides a four-year analysis of Canadian practice surrounding human trafficking since the adoption of the UN Protocol on Trafficking in 2000 (Oxman-Martinez et al., 2005).

Scholars of criminology have investigated organized trafficking networks as a manifestation of transnational crime; in the United States the work of Louise Shelley (1998, 2003) is an example of this approach, while Bruckert and Parent (2002) follow a similar framework in Canada. Bruckert and Parent's paper was commissioned by the Royal Canadian Mounted Police to provide a global overview of literature on trafficking in human beings and organized crime. Given the limited data on the involvement of organized crime in human trafficking in Canada, the authors provide a content analysis of the English-language press in the country between 1994 and 2002. The sources of data consulted for the analysis included three national magazines, two national dailies, and ten regional dailies. The authors concluded that on the whole, media coverage of human trafficking was rather limited with widely used wire stories and few locally written articles. Until 1999, the presence of criminal groups or networks was reported only occasionally and it was only in 1999 and 2000 that the involvement of organized crime in trafficking in women became more apparent in Canadian media, possibly because several national and international reports on this issue were released in 2000, the same year Canada signed the United Nations Convention Against Transnational Organized Crime.

Human rights and anti-trafficking NGOs have produced perhaps the largest body of literature on this subject (see, for example, Center for the Advancement of Human Rights, 2003; Human Rights Watch, 2001; Pearson, 2001), although many NGOs conduct such research within particular ideological frameworks.

Anne Gallagher (2001) analysed human rights and the UN Protocols on Trafficking and Migrant Smuggling, while Alice Miller (1999) wrote about human rights and sexuality. Works written by trafficked persons themselves are notably absent in North American literature on trafficking; Jean-Robert Cadet's (1998) testimonial about his harrowing youth as a *restavec* is one exception. Journalists have conducted interviews with anti-trafficking activists and trafficked persons (see Bowe, 2003; Cockburn, 2003; Yeung, 2004), while documentaries also present the voices of these individuals (see McMahon, 1999; Zarembka, 2003; Hilton and Woolf, 2003). Finally, activists and advocates working with trafficked persons have published book chapters, conference papers, and magazine articles grounded in their work on trafficking and with trafficked persons.

Yet, little academic research – particularly empirically based – on trafficking to and within North America has been conducted and published in academic outlets. In general, we can point to two approaches to trafficking research. The first, a labour framework, has often been taken up by journalists (Bowe, 2003) as well as by activist researchers (Chang, 2000; Louie, 2001). The second, a migration framework, has been the most frequently employed by academic researchers to date such as Gushulak and MacPherson, though journalists and activist researchers such as Hilton and Woolf and Zarembka have also used the migration framework. Nevertheless, while a few scholars have published academic research on trafficking to and within other parts of the world (see especially Bales, 2000), there is a lack of research on trafficking in general and with respect to North America in particular. Gushulak and MacPherson, for example, specifically note the lack of public health research on trafficked migrants (2000: 76); others note a lack of reliable empirical data, especially data that pertain to individuals trafficked for purposes other than that of sexual exploitation (Laczko, 2002). Creating a more nuanced and complex picture of trafficking to and within North America is a key component of future anti-trafficking work.

WHAT ARE THE RESEARCH GAPS?

Despite the increased public awareness of and concerns for trafficking victims in the federal and state governments in North America as well as among NGOs, the knowledge base is still very weak. Research on trafficking has not moved beyond estimating the scale of the problem; mapping routes and relationships between countries of origin, transit, and destinations; and reviewing legal frameworks and policy responses. There is no reliable data on the number of trafficking cases and the characteristics of the victims and perpetrators. The methodologies used to produce estimates of the scope of trafficking in North America are not very transparent; therefore, it is hard to evaluate the validity and reliability of the data. One element contributing to this limited knowledge is the fact that development of research methods on human trafficking remains in its infancy. Most studies rely on overviews, commentaries, and anecdotal information.

Research fulfils a number of roles, one of which is to offer an independent and critical assessment of current policy and practice. Future research needs to move beyond stating that there is a problem, to more systematic and rigorous data collection and analysis on a wide range of issues, including the organization of trafficking in human beings, its impact on victims, their family and community members, the efficacy of counter-trafficking initiatives, the effectiveness of anti-trafficking legislation, and the success of return and reintegration programmes. Now that the hard work has been done within the international community to create the common conceptual foundations of a trafficking definition, research can begin to build a solid layer of empirical evidence and understanding as to the real nature of the problem in North America.

There is a need for both qualitative and quantitative research that would provide macro- and micro-level understanding of the trafficking phenomenon. Methodologically sound compilation of official statistics on the number of trafficked victims would enable large-scale quantitative analysis and inform appropriation of funds for counter-trafficking efforts and services for victims. Rigorous ethnographic and sociological studies based on in-depth interviews with trafficking survivors would provide baseline data on trafficking victims and their characteristics. Too often victims of trafficking remain one-dimensional figures whose stories are condensed and simplified, which does not bode well for the development of culturally appropriate services. In order to develop appropriate assistance and treatment programmes for trafficking survivors, increased attention needs to be paid also to the expertise and practical knowledge of NGOs and their experience in working with different groups of trafficking survivors, including women, men, and children. Therefore, monitoring and evaluation studies should be an integral part of every assistance programme, public and private. Well-designed monitoring and evaluation studies, particularly external evaluations, can identify effective policies and "best practice" approaches as well as assess the success of different programmes.

There is also a need for effective cooperation and coordination of research within North America and between North America and other regions of the world, particularly source countries. In addition, there is a need to establish a forum where research results can be exchanged between different scholars as well as shared with policy makers and service providers; such a forum can take a form of a specialized publication or an international task force. The need to fill in the gaps in our knowledge and share research results is urgent. Lack of research-based knowledge may inadvertently "deepen, rather than loosen the factors that make trafficking both so profitable and difficult to address" (Kelly, 2002: 60).

NOTES

1. In this context, abolition meant not necessarily the abolition of prostitution, but the elimination of reglementation and tolerated houses for prostitution.
2. See http://www.unodc.org/unodc/en/crime_cicp_signatures_trafficking.html.
3. *See Memorandum on Steps to Combat Violence Against Women and Trafficking in Women and Girls*, Pub Papers 358-360 (11 March 1998 directing the President's Council on Women to coordinate domestic and international policy on "trafficking in women and girls".
4. "Sex trafficking" means the recruitment, harbouring, transportation, provision, or obtaining of a person for the purpose of a commercial sex act.
5. "Commercial sex act" means any sex act on account of which anything of value is given or received by any person.
6. "Coercion" means (a) threats of serious harm to or physical restraint against any person; (b) any scheme, plan or pattern intended to cause a person to believe that failure to perform an act would result in serious harm to or physical restraint against any person; or (c) the abuse or threatened abuse of the legal process.
7. "Involuntary servitude" includes a condition of servitude induced by means of (a) any scheme, plan, or pattern intended to cause a person to believe that, if that person did not enter into or continue in such condition that that person or any other person would suffer serious harm or physical restraint; or (b) the abuse or a threatened abuse of the legal process.
8. "Debt bondage" means the status or condition of a debtor arising from a pledge by the debtor of his or her personal services or those of a person under his or her control as a security for debt, if the value of those services as reasonably assessed is not applied toward the liquidation of the debt or the length and nature of those services are not respectively limited and defined.
9. See, for example, the report prepared by CATW at www.uri.edu/artsci/wms/hughes/catw.
10. See, for example, reports prepared by the GAATW.
11. See US State Department Office to Monitor and Combat Trafficking in Persons website at http://www.state.gov/g/tip/.
12. Email exchange and interview, 22 April 2004.
13. See http://www.unescobkk.org/culture/trafficking/trafficing.htm for details and database.
14. Based upon those given T-visas since implementation of 2000 TVPA Act as stated in *Recent Developments in US Government Efforts to End Trafficking in Persons*, Fact Sheet, Office to Monitor and Combat Trafficking in Persons, State

Department, 18 March 2004, and Prepared Remarks of Attorney General John Ashcroft, National Conference on Human Trafficking, Tampa, Florida, 16 July 2004.

REFERENCES

Barry, K.
1979   *Female Sexual Slavery*, Avon, New York.
Bindman, J.
1997   "Redefining prostitution as sex work on the international agenda", www.walnet.org/csis/papers/redefining.html
Bowe, J.
2003   "Nobodies: does slavery exist in America?", *The New Yorker*, 21 April: 106-133.
Bristow, E.J.
1977   *Vice and Vigilance: Purity Movements in Britain since 1700*, Gill and Macmillan, Dublin.
1982   *Prostitution and Prejudice: The Jewish Fight against White Slavery 1870-1938*, Clarendon Press, Oxford.
Bruckert, C., and C. Parent
2002   "Trafficking in human beings and organized crime: a literature review", Royal Canadian Mounted Police, www.rcmp-grc.gc.ca.
Bullough, V., and B. Bullough
1987   "Women and prostitution: a social history", in A. Derks, *From White Slaves to Trafficking Survivors*, Prometheus Books, New York: 262.
Cadet, J-R
1998   *Restavec: From Haitian Slave Child to Middle-Class American*, University of Texas Press, Austin.
Caliber Associates
2001   *Needs Assessment for Service Providers and Trafficking Victims*, Caliber Associates, Virgina.
Canadian Council for Refugees
2004   *Trafficking in Women and Girls*, Canadian Council for Refugees, www.web. net/~ccr/trafficking.htm.
Center for the Advancement of Human Rights
2003   *Florida Responds to Human Trafficking*, Center for the Advancement of Human Rights, Florida State University, Tallahassee, http://www.cahr.fsu. edu/the%20report.pdf.
Chang, G.
2000   *Disposable Domestics: Immigrant Women Workers in the Global Economy*, South End Press, Cambridge.
Chapkis, W.
2003   "Trafficking, migration and the law", *Gender and Society*, 17(6): 926.

Chuang, J.
  1998   "Redirecting the debate over trafficking in women: definitions, paradigms, and context", *Harvard Human Rights Journal*, 11.
Coalition Against Trafficking in Women (CATW)
  1999   "Prostitutes work, but do they consent?", CATW, www.uri.edu/artsci/wms/hpughes/catw.
Cockburn, A.
  2003   "21st century slaves", *National Geographic*, 204(3): 2-26.
Connelly, M.T.
  1980   *The Response to Prostitution in the Progressive Era*, University of North Carolina Press, Chapel Hill.
Corbin, A.
  1990   *Women for Hire: Prostitution and Sexuality in France after 1850*, Harvard University Press, Cambridge.
Correa, Y.
  2001   "Mexico: 16,000 children sexually exploited UNICEF says", *La Cronica de Hoy*, 19 March.
Derks, A.
  2000   "From white slaves to trafficking survivors: notes on the trafficking debate", working paper 00-02m, The Center for Migration and Development, Princeton University, Princeton.
Doezema, J.
  2000   "Loose women or lost women? The re-emergence of the myth of 'white slavery' in contemporary discourses of 'trafficking in women'", *Gender Issues*, 18(1): 23-50.
  2002   "Who gets to choose? Coercion, consent and the UN Trafficking Protocol", *Gender and Development*, 10(1).
Estes, R., and N. Weiner
  2001   *Commercial Exploitation of Children in the US, Canada and Mexico*, University of Pennsylvania (amended April 2002), http://caster.ssw.upenn.edu/~restes/CSEC_Files/Abstract_010918.pdf.
Gallagher, A.
  2001   "Human rights and the new UN protocols on trafficking and migrant smuggling: a preliminary analysis", *Human Rights Quarterly*, 23: 975-1004.
Gordy, M.
  2000   "A call to fight forced labour", *Parade Magazine*, 20 February.
Grittner, F.K.
  1990   *White Slavery: Myth, Ideology and American Law*, Garland, New York.
Gushulak, B., and D. MacPherson
  2000   "Health issues associated with the smuggling and trafficking of migrants", *Journal of Immigrant Health*, 2(2): 67-78.
Guy, D.J.
  1991   *Sex and Danger in Buenos Aires: Prostitution, Family and Nation in Argentina*, University of Nebraska Press, Lincoln.
Hall, A.
  1998   *The Scotsman*, 25 August.

Hilton, C., and A. Woolf
    2003   "Dying to leave", Wide Angle Documentary Series, PBS, 25 September.
Human Rights Caucus
    1999   Recommendations and commentary on the draft protocol to combat inter-
            national trafficking in women and children supplementary to the draft
            convention on transnational organized crime, www.hrlawgroup.org/site/
            program/traffic.
Human Rights Watch
    2001   "Hidden in the home: abuse of domestic workers with special visas in the
            United States", Human Rights Watch Reports, 13(2), http://www.hrw.org/
            reports/2001/usadom/.
Hyland, K.F.
    2001a   The Impact of the Protocol to Prevent Suppress and Punish Trafficking
            in Persons, Especially Women and Children, Human Rights Brief,
            www.wcl.american.edu/pub/humanright/brief/index.htm.
    2001b   "Protecting human victims of trafficking: an American framework", Ber-
            keley Women's Law Journal, 16: 29-71.
Jimenez, M., and S. Bell
    2000a   "650 charges in Canadian sex-slave trade", The National Post, 14 May:
            A1.
    2000b   "Police charge 80 in strip club raids", The National Post, 16 June: A23.
Kelly, L.
    2002   Journeys of Jeopardy: A Review of Research on Trafficking in Women
            and Children in Europe, IOM, Geneva.
Kelly, L., and L. Regan
    2000   "Stopping trafficking, exploring the extent of, and responses to, traffick-
            ing in women for sexual exploitation in the UK", Police Research Series,
            paper 125, Home Office, UK.
Kempadoo, K.
    1998   "Introduction: globalising sex workers' rights", in K. Kempadoo and
            J. Doezema (Eds), Global Sex Workers: Rights, Resistance, and Redefini-
            tion, Routledge, New York.
Laczko, F.
    2002   "Human trafficking: the need for better data", Migration Information
            Source, Migration Policy Institute, Washington, DC.
Langevin, L., and M-C Belleau
    2000   Trafficking in Women in Canada: A Critical Analysis of the Legal Frame-
            work Governing Immigrant Live-in Caregivers and Mail-Order Brides,
            Status of Women Canada, Ottawa.
Louie, M.C.Y.
    2001   Sweatshop Warriors: Immigrant Women Workers Take On the Global
            Factory, South End Press, Cambridge.
McMahon, K.
    1999   "Trafficking of women: a report from Los Angeles", paper presented
            to the Traffic in Women Revisited: Women Speak Out from World War II
            to the Present Workshop, Berkshire Conference on the History of

Women, University of Rochester, 3-6 June, www.trafficked-women.org/ berkshire. html.

Miko, F.T.
2004   "Trafficking in women and children: the US and international response", CRS Report to Congress, The Library of Congress, Washington, DC.

Miller, A.
1999   "Human rights and sexuality: first steps toward articulating a rights frame-work for claims to sexual rights and freedoms", *American Society of International Law, 1999 Proceedings*: 288-303.

Murphy, E., and K. Ringheim
2002   "Interview with Jo Doezema of the Network of Sex Work Projects: does attention to trafficking adversely affect sex workers' rights?", *Reproductive Health and Rights: Reaching the Hardly Reached*, PATH, Washington, DC.

Pearson, E.
2001   "Slavery/Trafficking", New Internationalist, August, http://www.newint. org/issue337/trapped.htm.

Porteus Consulting
1998   *Organized Crime Impact Study: Highlights*, Solicitor-General Canada, www.psepc-sppcc.gc.ca/publications/policing/pdf/1998orgcrim _e.pdf.

Raymond, J.G.
1998   "Prostitution as violence against women: NGO stonewalling in Beijing and elsewhere", *Women's Studies International Forum*, 21(1): 1-9.
2002   "The new UN Trafficking Protocol", *Women's Studies International Forum*, 25(5): 491-502.

Raymond, J., and D. Hughes
2001   *International and Domestic Trends in Sex Trafficking of Women in the United States, 1999-2000*, US National Institute of Justice, Maryland.

Shirk, D., and A. Webber
2004   "Slavery without borders: human trafficking in the US-Mexican context", *Hemisphere Focus*, 12(5).

O'Neil Richard, A.
1999   *International Trafficking in Women to the United States: A Contemporary Manifestation of Slavery and Organized Crime*, www.odci.gov/mono-graph/women/trafficking.pdf.

Oxman-Martinez, J., et al.
2005   "Canadian policy on human trafficking: a four-year analysis", *International Migration*, not yet published.

Ryf, K.
2002   "The first modern anti-slavery law: the Trafficking Victims Protection Act of 2000", *Case Western Reserve Journal of International Law*, 34: 45-71.

Shelly, L.
1998   "Transnational organized crime in the United States: defining the prob-lem", *Kobe University Law Review*, 32(1).
2003   "Trafficking in women: the business model approach", *The Brown Journal of World Affairs*, 10(1): 119-131.

Thompson, B.R.
2003 "People trafficking, a national security risk in Mexico", *Mexidata*, www. mexidata.info/id93.html.
US Office of the Inspector General
2003a *Assessment of Department of Defense Efforts to Combat Trafficking in Persons, Phase I, United States Forces in Korea*, US Department of Defense, http://www.dodig.osd.mil/AIM/alsd/H03L88433128PhaseI.PDF.
2003b *Assessment of Department of Defense Efforts to Combat Trafficking in Persons, Phase II, Bosnia, Hercegovina and Kosovo*, US Department of Defense, http://www.dodig.osd.mil/AIM/alsd/HT-Phase II.pdf.
US State Department
2002 *Trafficking in Persons Report*, Office to Monitor and Combat Trafficking in Persons, 5 June, www.state/gov/g/tip/tiprpt/2002/10678.htm.
Walkowitz, J.
1980 *Prostitution and Victorian Society: Women, Class and the State*, Cambridge University Press, Cambridge.
Wijers, M., and L. Lap-Chew
1997 *Trafficking in Women: Forced Labour and Slavery-like Practices in Marriage, Domestic Labour and Prostitution*, Foundation Against Trafficking, the Netherlands: 20.
Yeung, B.
2004 "Enslaved in Palo Alto: a domestic worker from Kenya has accused her employer – a prominent African journalist – of human trafficking", *San Francisco Weekly*, 18 February.
Zarembka, J.M.
2003 "America's dirty work: migrant maids and modern-day slavery", in B. Ehrenreich and A.R. Hochschild (Eds), *Global Woman: Nannies, Maids, and Sex Workers in the New Economy*, Metropolitan Books, New York: 142-153.
Zhang, S., and K-L Chin
2004 *Characteristics of Chinese Human Smugglers*, NIJ Research Brief, Washington, DC, August.

A Review of Recent OAS Research on Human Trafficking in the Latin American and Caribbean Region

Laura Langberg*

INTRODUCTION

No review of research on human trafficking worldwide would be complete without an examination of the situation in Latin America and the Caribbean. In the past few years, the Latin American and Caribbean regions have witnessed increased activities by the US Government, international organizations, and civil society alerting governments and migrants on the continually evolving nature of human trafficking, both domestically and across international boundaries. Effective policy responses to the scourge of human trafficking require reliable data based on solid empirical research. The clandestine nature of this criminal activity makes it only possible to rely on estimates, primarily from the non-governmental organization (NGO) community. As in most parts of the world, before the year 2000 the problem had been overlooked and understudied in Latin America and the Caribbean. In an effort to ameliorate this problem and provide governments information that more fully addressed the scope and nature of the problem, the Inter-American Commission of Women (CIM) and the Inter-American Children's Institute (IACI), both of the Organization of American States (OAS), collaborated with the International Human Rights Law Institute (IHRLI) of DePaul University to study human trafficking in Latin America and the Caribbean.

As indicated in the project title – *The Trafficking of Women and Children for Sexual Exploitation in the Americas* (Trafficking in the Americas) – the OAS/ DePaul research focused on the trafficking of women and children for sexual

---

* Inter-American Commission of Women (CIM), Organization of American States (OAS), Washington, DC, USA.

exploitation. From the beginning of the study and during the interviewing process, the general confusion between migrant smuggling and trafficking in human beings became clear and, in many cases, was even quite explicit. The same lack of distinction was encountered in government institutions and civil society organizations. Two main factors account for this confusion. The first point of confusion is the translation from English into Spanish of the word "trafficking". The word generally used in Spanish countries is *tráfico* (in reference to drug trafficking, arms trafficking). In the case of trafficking in persons, the United Nations (UN) official documents translated "trafficking in persons" not as *tráfico de personas*, but as *trata de personas*. It is the only situation where the word "trafficking" does not translate as *tráfico* but as *trata*. The second point of confusion is the absence of a clear understanding of the difference between "trafficking" and "smuggling", which is also a problem in other regions of the world.

While trafficking for forced labour other than sex work is definitely a pressing problem in Latin America and the Caribbean, trafficking for sexual exploitation was perceived as more widespread and oppressive for women, adolescents, and children. The project aimed to provide an understanding of the sex trafficking practice in seven countries in Latin America and the Caribbean: Belize, Costa Rica, El Salvador, Guatemala, Honduras Nicaragua, Panama, the Dominican Republic, and Brazil.

A large number of local NGOs conducted the field research in each of the target countries. Most of them had expertise assisting abused women and children. The study focused on adolescents and women. Representatives from IHRLI/ DePaul and the CIM verified and complemented the research with interviews in the field, at the governmental and non-governmental levels. Despite the underground nature of the phenomenon, the multitude of factors that encourage silence and impunity, and the lack of trafficking-specific indicators which make the quantification of trafficked persons impossible, the project's research data provides governments and international organizations a factual base to draft and implement adequate policy responses to combat trafficking and protect victims. The results of the research are compiled in a series of publications (see IHRLI, 2002; Leal and Leal, 2003).

Since 2004, CIM, and the OAS Anti-Trafficking Coordinator's Unit, in partnership with the International Organization for Migration (IOM), have been implementing a one-year capacity building and applied research project to study, train, and raise awareness on the importance and need for coordinated mechanisms to address trafficking. This effort is being carried out in Bolivia, Mexico, and Belize, with funding from USAID and a contribution from the Government of Mexico for its country project. The project is coordinated by the CIM/OAS, using the resources and expertise of IOM field staff in the countries. In 2004, IOM received funding from the office of Population, Refugee and Migration (PRM/DOS) to implement a similar project in partnership with CIM/OAS in the following countries: Bahamas, Barbados, Guyana, Jamaica, the Netherlands Antilles, Suriname, and Saint Lucia.

This paper reflects the findings of the first research project (IHRLI/ CIM/IACI-OAS).

METHODOLOGY OF THE STUDY

A first step in the project was to convene a meeting of experts held at the OAS headquarters on 11 April 2000, in Washington, DC. More than 60 persons, including representatives of UNICEF, IOM, UNIFEM, OAS, as well as US Government officials, attended the meeting to discuss methodology and strategy for accomplishing the trafficking research. Most of the major US and Latin American NGOs working in the field participated at the meeting, including: the Women's Caucus, National Organization for Women (NOW), Amnesty International, Human Rights Watch, Lawyers Committee for Human Rights, experts from several universities in the United States, International Human Rights Law Group, and several Latin American groups from Argentina, Brazil, Uruguay, and Costa Rica. The discussions and results were crucial in outlining the methodology of the Trafficking in the Americas project.

The research design that developed from the meeting included four key elements:

1. IHRLI guidance and collaboration with NGOs as counterpart organizations in each participating country;
2. Initiation of public debate on the issue of trafficking through a national consultation meeting in each country;
3. Field investigation on the trafficking of women and children for sexual exploitation; and
4. Use of the study's findings and conclusions to draft effective regional and national recommendations for trafficking.

The fieldwork research included the following components:

1. Interviews with relevant government officials to contribute to a diagnosis of each state's recognition and reaction to the problem;
2. Interviews with non-governmental actors and other key informants regarding the incidence of trafficking and the effectiveness of the government's response;

3. A study and evaluation of national legislation, including policies and laws, related to trafficking, and its enforcement;
4. A study and evaluation of international protections and mechanisms applicable and/or available to combat trafficking and its effects; and
5. The compilation and analysis of data from all available sources of the patterns and practices of trafficking and exploitation.

Interviews were conducted first by the NGOs and local consultants, and later by experts from IHRLI and OAS. Meetings and interviews included represent-atives of government institutions, women's affairs, youth and children, health and AIDS commissions, labour, immigration offices, foreign affairs, national and local authorities, and tourism offices. Consulates played an essential role, particularly those consulates with a large number of smuggled and potentially trafficked victims (Dominican Republic, El Salvador, Honduras, Guatemala, Nica-ragua) and Central American consulates in countries of transit and destination (Costa Rica, Panama, Mexico).

In addition, interviews were held with representatives of international organ-izations (ILO/IPEC, IOM, UNICEF), civil society organizations such as aca-demic institutions, research institutes, churches, NGOs active in the fields of human rights, women and children, individuals involved in or affected by traf-ficking practices, family members of disappeared adolescents and women, and media representatives (see IHRLI, 2002: 91, 127-142).

The research was conducted in two phases. A structured questionnaire was discussed among the main partners and used by NGOs as a basis during the first phase of the preliminary research. The second phase was conducted by representatives of IACW and DePaul University. This phase aimed at validating the first phase and to expand or deepen the questionnaire, according to the information gathered during the first phase.

DIFFICULTIES IN DATA COLLECTION

The study in Central America, the Dominican Republic, and Brazil had the objective of assessing trafficking based on reliable information and data. However, the collection of accurate data posed great difficulties, owing to cir-cumstances such as violence, abuse, coercion, trauma, and stigma associated with sexual exploitation. Victims were very reluctant to denounce their recruit-ers and preferred to remain silent, in many cases because of the existence of institutional disincentives, such as policies that criminalize rather than protect victims, the absence of witness protection programmes, and judicial proceed-ings that tend to re-victimize the victims of trafficking.[1]

Political leaders recognized publicly the existence of smuggling but did not have enough information on trafficking for sexual exploitation. Trafficking is considered to be related to prostitution, rather than to slavery. Gender and age discrimination foster an acceptance regarding the sexual exploitation of trafficking. These aspects ensure that knowledge of trafficking activities remains anecdotal (IHRLI, 2002: 80). As is the case with most black market and clandestine activities, essential information is guarded and corruption is fed by the traffickers. Traffickers have good networks and more resources than law enforcement officers, whose investigative capacities are extremely limited by human, technical, and financial resources. Finally, the already scarce collected data in government offices is often lost in inadequate management and coordination systems.[2]

In general, consulates recognize only those individuals who have escaped from their trafficking experience; in some cases consulates realized that women were involved in the sex industry, but did not discover their exploitative conditions. Health officers, for their part, attend to only the most visible populations who work in streets, parks, markets, relatively open bars, and other establishments.[3] This research initiative was a first step to bringing to light the realities of sex trafficking in Central America, the Caribbean, and Brazil. A more targeted research remains necessary to complete the understanding of this exploitative situation of migrants, particularly regarding other trafficking purposes, such as domestic servitude and forced labour.

RESEARCH FINDINGS/GAPS

Trafficking in Latin America is fuelled by several factors: poverty, political and social violence, gender attitudes leading to inequalities, and a general indifference toward women, adolescents, and children. Globalization, liberalized borders policies, and ease of movement of people have exacerbated the problem by creating what some call market opportunities for traffickers in human beings (IHRLI, 2002: 40 and 46). There is a lack of adequate anti-trafficking legislation and training at all levels, whether national, regional, or municipal. The crime of trafficking as such is not explicitly defined in the legislation. Moreover, the enforcement of existing laws against pimps and facilitators is practically non-existent.

Many of the focus population, young adult women (aged 18 to 25) and children (aged 12 to 17) fell victim to traffickers because of economic necessity, responsibility as single heads of households, illiteracy or minimal education, lack of technical skills, and a history of physical and sexual abuse. Other external factors contributing to an environment conducive to trafficking are widespread gender discrimination, unemployment and poverty, attitudes of disdain, lack of respect for women and children, weak migration controls, corruption, as well as the impact of globalization. The sex market, sex tourism, and other forms of demand for sexual services are also fundamental components in the existence of trafficking networks (IHRLI, 2002: 47).

Traffickers act as businessmen and are savvy in their tactics. They are well aware of migration policies, legislation, and practices and frequently operate through legal means for illegal purposes. Traffickers have a network with private and public agents including shippers, taxi drivers, cyclists (rickshaws), and truckers who participate in the recruitment and transportation process. They make use of the media to recruit through classified ads with false jobs and radio announcements. In addition, internet service stimulates demand through web pages that offer sex tourism and arranged marriages with foreigners. Attorneys are intermediaries in the forgery of documents, or prepare fraudulent marriage documents. Owners of nightclubs, brothels, cabarets, bars, massage parlours, and hotels participate in the process of recruiting and exploiting, receiving and gaining control over the victims' earnings, and withholding their documents to ensure a position of power over them. Most frequently, they operate with impunity. Public officials, including immigration and police officers, assist traffickers together with other public officials.

The demand in the region is mainly for prostitution and pornography. It is concentrated in areas where there is tolerance of trafficking, such as border areas, tourist areas, ports, locations along international routes, and certain agricultural areas where migrant workers are primarily men. The increase in organized sex tourism and the massive establishment of casinos in the region have opened up a growing international market.

The study also identified source countries, such as the Dominican Republic, El Salvador, Guatemala, Honduras, and Nicaragua, and transit and/or destination countries, such as Mexico, Belize, Costa Rica, and Panama. The source countries are characterized by the lowest GDP figures and the highest youth illiteracy rates together with the lowest female primary school entrance rates (IHRLI, 2002: 27-30). Other relevant reports and studies in Central America and Panama have been taken into account and their findings mentioned in the report.[4] In 1995, a study on adult prostitution in Panama concluded that lack of housing, unemployment, and economic reasons were the most common causes among those interviewed, representing 42.5 per cent of the total. Another indicator is that the sex worker was victimized by friends, neighbours, or familiar persons; family disintegration and abandonment were also part of the principal causes, registering 22 per cent and 16 per cent respectively (Villareal, 1995).

Researchers, NGOs, and service providers emphasize that providing employment alternatives could significantly reduce the risk for women to fall prey to human trafficking. Where female labour training programmes exist, they have focused on beautician skills, sewing, and cooking. These programmes are thus far ineffective. Some businesswomen associations expressed concern over the growing problem of sex trafficking, but little has been done so far to offer alternatives to poor women, such as training in sustainable micro-enterprises or commercial skills.

Combinations of political, legal, cultural, and socio-economic factors, which create a deep level of desperation in vulnerable communities, provide ground for traffickers. Taking into consideration particularities in each country, similar problems and obstacles were detected in all of them. It is important to remember that trafficking in persons is a recent issue for the governments, and that the UN Protocol has had a very short life since it was signed in 2000. A first analysis detected the following: absence of public policies against trafficking and smuggling; legal gaps or inadequacy of existing legislation and corruption affecting particularly police, border migration, and consulates. All of these lead to the impunity of the traffickers (recruiters, intermediaries, owners of establishments). The lack of adequate services for the victims (health and legal assistance, economic alternatives, etc.), are push factors to becoming re-trafficked. The chain in the process of deportation-smuggled-trafficked continues without adequate intervention, particularly in the routes from Central America to Mexico.

Other challenges are the lack of specialization in the investigative police, including the police gender unit; and prejudicing the appropriate handling of victims, resulting in the absence of charges due to a fear of authorities and lack of confidence in the judicial system. The scarcity of human, technical, and financial resources is alarming. It is difficult to quantify trafficking cases owing to the absence of registration systems. Governments and NGOs do not maintain regular data on specific or potential trafficking cases. Social tolerance to sexual abuse, discriminatory stereotypes of women and children victims of sexual exploitation, and a culture that discourages reporting those suspected of trafficking make the crime less visible. Few court proceedings are initiated. Practically no one is convicted on charges of trafficking or as promoting the entry of women for prostitution. Health and welfare services for women and children rarely offer assistance to the victims.

POLICY RESULTS

The research study was designed to assess the existence of sex trafficking in Latin America and the Caribbean, to survey existing programmes and policy responses to the problem, and to identify local as well as regional needs to formulate effective strategies to combat the problem. The fieldwork and the research study created some awareness of the need to adopt policies at the General Assembly of the OAS.

The results of the study by itself cannot be measured without considering the debates that have emerged in numerous meetings at the OAS. The institutional responses from different areas of the government produced slow but steady changes in the attitude toward trafficking victims. The fieldwork by the NGOs, CIM/OAS, and IHRLI, visits to border areas, and interviews conducted with some 40 public offices in each country during several months contributed to promoting awareness and creating interest in understanding how to conduct prevention and information campaigns. In addition, the meetings and discussions held at OAS headquarters on the subject had a positive impact within the OAS agencies and in the member states.

The outcome of the efforts to promote policies within the OAS can be summarized as follows:

- Recognition of trafficking in persons as a human rights violation, a criminal activity and the responsibility of governments to take immediate actions;[5]
- Inclusion of civil society and the private sector in partnership with the government, in any plan of action;[6]
- Adoption of the two General Assembly Resolutions on the subject and instructing the appointment of an OAS Coordinator on the Issue of Trafficking in Persons;[7]
- Prevention of trafficking in women and children in the tourism sector, at the meeting of Ministers of Tourism in the Americas;[8] and
- The Fifth Meeting of the Ministers of Justice and Attorneys General of the Americas (REMJA-V).[9]

RECOMMENDATIONS/FUTURE RESEARCH NEEDS

The Latin American and Caribbean regions are two of the most under-researched and under-funded regions in the world on trafficking in persons. The official data is extremely insufficient, and the available information on smuggling cases is scarce and does not provide much help to the researchers. Until very recently, governments have been reluctant to acknowledge the existence of trafficking, and in most cases the focus never moves beyond sexual exploitation. While this type of exploitation is extremely damaging to the mental and physical health of victims, and violates a number of human rights, there are other forms of trafficking for exploitation less visible but also severe: domestic servitude and labour exploitation.

Governments and civil society must recognize the existence of trafficking in persons as a form of labour exploitation, more than just as the movement of migrants. More attention should be given to internal trafficking. Countries like Argentina, Brazil, Mexico and Costa Rica are already concerned about sex tourism and are in the process of designing policies on the prevention of internal trafficking of children to satisfy the demand in tourist areas. Officials working on anti-trafficking cases might include and give more emphasis to situations of forced labour, domestic servitude, begging, and other forms of exploitation in their national agendas. Thus, officials from labour ministries, particularly labour inspectors, who have access to much of the workforce, play an essential role and have specific responsibility in identifying situations of exploitation in a variety of workplaces. They should do more than giving a warning and/or fine to the employer. They could help timely interventions, during the rescue and the referral of victims to existing protection networks, and assist the authorities during the investigation. Ministries of labour are engaged in some countries in a practice of authorizing work permits for "entertainment visas".[10] These regulations should be reviewed in light of the cases that emerged from abusing this visa category to facilitate the trafficking for purposes of sexual exploitation.

The following are the areas in need of further research:

- The demand-supply dynamic and the sex industry.
- The trafficking for other purposes of exploitation and the demand for cheap labour (forced labour, domestic servitude) and removal of organs.
- Little attention has been given to those who economically benefit from the trafficking business, either individuals or associations.
- More data is needed to study the connections between corruption and trafficking networks.
- A better understanding of the sociological root causes of massive migration and of good practices to favour orderly migration. Changing the focus of future research could complement what has been done so far and contribute to making substantial and positive policy decisions at the national and regional levels.

NOTES

1. National Reports, especially Nicaragua, Honduras, Dominican Republic and Brazil, unpublished and on files at the IHRLI-DePaul University and Inter-American Commission of Women.
2. National reports on Nicaragua and Belize (unpublished).
3. National report of Belize (unpublished).
4. Special recognition to Casa Alianza for facilitating its report "Investigación regional sobre tráfico : prostitución, pornografía infantil y turismo sexual infantil en México y Centroamérica", Costa Rica, 2002 (Spanish).
5. CIM Assembly of Delegates resolution "Fighting the crime of trafficking in persons, especially women, adolescents and children" (CIM/RES.225 (XXXI-O/02), expresses that trafficking in persons is a "flagrant violation of human rights of women, adolescents and children who are victims of trafficking, who live in dangerous and inhumane conditions during their transfer, reclusion and exploitation in the countries of origin, transit and ultimate destination, and the impunity of the criminal networks (recruiters, carriers and owners of establishments) that thrive on this criminal activity".
6. CIM Assembly of Delegates resolution "Fighting the crime of trafficking in persons, especially women, adolescents and children" (CIM/RES.225 (XXXI-O/02) states: "to engage the private sector, especially the travel and tourism industry and the media, in strategies designed to eradicate trafficking in persons…".
7. "Fighting the crime of trafficking in persons, especially women, adolescents and children" (GA/RES.1948 (XXXIII-O/03) and GA/RES.2019 (XXXIV-O04), in which the General Assembly reaffirms that "trafficking in persons, especially in women, adolescents, boys and girls is a modern form of slavery…", and resolves "…to instruct the Secretary General to appoint an OAS Coordinator on the Issue of Trafficking in Persons, Especially Women, Adolescents and Children…".
8. "Declaration and Plan of Action adopted by the Inter-American Tourism Congress, (XVIII Inter-American Travel Congress, 18-20 June 2003, Guatemala): The Ministers of Tourism of the Americas agreed to include in the Declaration "that the trafficking and exploitation of women, adolescents and children for sex tourism is a serious scourge on our societies, which negatively impacts the structure of families and the image of our countries as tourism destinations…".
9. Held in Washington DC, 28-30 April 2004, included in its agenda the discussion of trafficking in persons, organized crime and the adoption of specific recommendations to prevent and combat trafficking in persons, especially women and children. The recommendations (OEA/Ser.K/XXXIV.5, REMJA-V/doc.7/04 rev. 4, 30 April 2004) are expressed in Section VI.
10. In Spanish *Visa de Alternadora*, which means working in bars in prostitution, illegal in itself but misguided under these special permits or visas.

REFERENCES

International Human Rights Law Institute (IHRLI)
2002 "In modern bondage: sex trafficking in the Americas, Central America and the Caribbean", IHRLI, DePaul University College of Law, in Association with the Inter-American Commission of Women and the Inter-American Children's Institute of the Organization of American States, October.

Leal, M.L., and M. de Fatima Leal (Eds)
2003 "Study on trafficking in women, children and adolescents for commercial sexual exploitation in Brazil", National Report, Pestraf Brazil, International Human Rights Law Institute, in association with the Inter-American Commission of Women and the Inter-American Children's Institute of the Organization of American States, July.

Organization of American States
2002 "Fighting the crime of trafficking in persons, especially women, adolescents and children", resolution adopted by the Assembly of Delegates of the Inter-American Commission of Women, OAS (CIM/RES.225(XXXI-O-02), 31 October, Dominican Republic.

2003 "Fighting the crime of trafficking in persons, especially women, adolescents and children", resolution adopted by the General Assembly of OAS (AG/RES.1948 (XXXIII-O-03), 10 June, Chile.

2004 "Fifth meeting of Ministers of Justice or Attorneys General of the Americas: conclusions and recommendations", (OAS/Ser.K/XXXIV.5, REMJA-V/doc.7/04 rev.4), 30 April, Washington, DC.

Villareal, G.V.
1995 *Análisis Socio-Jurídico y Criminológico de la Prostitución*, originally in Spanish, translation by IHRLI.

Treading along a Treacherous Trail: Research on Trafficking in Persons in South Asia

A.K.M. Masud Ali*

INTRODUCTION

This paper presents an overview of research on trafficking in persons in South Asia. The trend of trafficking is on the rise, but the existing knowledge base is inadequate for a full understanding of the phenomenon at the regional level. The paper is based on secondary data and analysis of existing literature on trafficking in South Asia.

TRAFFICKING IN PERSONS: AN OVERVIEW OF THE SITUATION IN SOUTH ASIA

India and Pakistan are the major destination countries for trafficked women and girls in South Asia (IOM, 2002). India and Pakistan are also transit countries from Bangladesh to Middle Eastern countries, where boys are exploited as camel jockeys and girls and women are trafficked for sexual exploitation. For Bangladeshi women and girls, India is also a transit point en route to the Middle East and Pakistan.

Research suggests that low employment prospects and lack of opportunities are the main reasons for women and men to venture out in search of better living conditions (IOM, 2002). The economic motives are compounded by other social and political factors. The importance of economic factors in deciding to migrate is, in all probability, due to a lack or low level of education among women and men resulting in poor job prospects in their native countries. Apart from the

* Integrated Community and Industrial Development in Bangladesh (INCIDIN), Dhaka.

economic reason, discrimination against women that can lead to desertion, divorce, or a husband's second marriage; dowry issues; and early marriage also play an important role in pushing women to look for independent lives inside or outside the country. This makes them easy targets for traffickers. A number of external factors have also been identified:

- Impacts of globalization have included the spread of modernization with greater access to transport, media, etc. However, it also led to the loss of traditional sources of income and rural employment, pushing the poor and unskilled to migrate to survive. Competition among countries in South Asia has driven the cost of labour down further, encouraging some employers to use illegal practices, such as bonded labour, to access cheaper labour sources.
- Conflicts and natural disasters force communities to move, often en masse, to survive. When such individuals have no marketable skills or education, and are exposed to health risks, their capacity to secure sustainable livelihoods is limited and their risk of being trafficking is heightened.
- Migration policies frequently exclude the unskilled, particularly women, from legal migration and force them to seek alternative livelihood options through illegal means.

The source countries

In South Asia, Bangladesh and Nepal are the major source countries. Sri Lanka is also a source country for women and girls trafficked to Middle Eastern countries. This section presents the major features of trafficking in the source countries.

Trafficking in persons: Bangladesh

Existing reports suggest that trafficking in children is increasing at an alarming rate (INCIDIN, 2002). Ironically, because of its elusive nature, reliable statistics regarding the magnitude of the problem widely vary (see Table 1) and are unreliable. Estimates of the spread of the problem are further complicated by the fact that the crime often goes unreported. Missing children are often not taken into account when dealing with trafficking, although some might have been victims of trafficking. It is also difficult to estimate the reach of criminal networks working in and outside the country.

In Bangladesh, women and children become victims of trafficking mainly for the purpose of sexual exploitation, forced labour, camel jockeying (exclusively boys), cheap or bonded labour, domestic servitude, sale of organs,[1] and marriage. While there are reports of men being trafficked, the literature is silent on this issue. Men are predominantly seen as "migrants", while women and children are typically seen as "victims of trafficking", reflecting a strong gender bias in mainstream literature on trafficking. Though more recent thinking on trafficking has recognized the phenomenon of trafficking in men, the discussion is only just beginning (Bangladesh Counter Trafficking Thematic Group, 2003). Men in Bangladesh are exposed to the risks of trafficking to Middle Eastern countries and Asian neighbouring countries (such as Malaysia) where they may end up in slavery-like working conditions.

TABLE 1

DATA ON THE NUMBER OF WOMEN TRAFFICKED FROM BANGLADESH

No. of Women	Frequency/ Time Frame	Destination	Source
200-400	Monthly	-	BNWLA, 2000
24,000-48,000	Annually	-	BNWLA, 2000
200,000	Over 10 years	-	Rape of Minors; Worry Parents, 1998
200,000	-	Pakistan, India, Middle East	Rape of Minors; Worry Parents, 1998
500	Daily	Pakistan, via India (press statement)	BNWLA, 1998
200,000	1990-1997	-	Centre for Women and Children Report, 1998
1 per cent of 500,000 foreign commercial sex workers (CSWs)	-	India	Central Social Welfare Board, 1997; BNWLA, 1997
13	Daily	-	The Daily Ittefak, 1990; UBINIG, 1995
4,000 or more	Annually	-	The Daily Ittefak, 1990; UBINIG, 1995
50	Daily	-	UBINIG, 1995 (approximately 6,000 annually)
27,000	-	Indian brothels	Centre for Women and Children Report, 1998
10,000-15,000	-	India	UN Special Rapporteur, 2001

Source: ADB, 2003.

In terms of major studies, a report prepared jointly by the Ministries of Home, Social Welfare and Women and Children Affairs, is one of the most frequently cited documents on the magnitude of the problem of trafficking in children in the country. The report indicates that, over the last five years, at least 13,220 children have been smuggled out of the country; of those only 4,700 have been rescued. The study used media reports and police records as data sources. The report does not clarify how the authors arrived at these estimates. At the same time, the study has not made any distinction between trafficking and irregular migration or smuggling in persons.

Between 1990 and 1999 the International Organization for Migration (IOM) carried out a mapping study (IOM, 2002) of missing, kidnapped, and trafficked children and women from print media reports (Shamim, n.d.). The IOM report shows that 3,397 children up to 16 years of age were trafficked during that time period, among them 1,683 boys and 1,714 girls (Shamim, n.d.: 33). Being solely based on reports of different agencies with varied understanding on the issues, the study had to deal with the varied nature of data labelled trafficking, kidnapping, and missing children. The news was often not followed up so in many cases no clear conclusion on the status of the missing children could be drawn. Furthermore, the study suspects the number of missing children to be higher than reported in the media, as most cases of missing children were not reported to law enforcement authorities.

Within these limitations, the study indicated that the number of kidnapped children is one-third less than that of missing children (Shamim, n.d.: 22). According to another study (INCIDIN, 2002), on average 13 per cent of households in the study areas have had at least one incident of missing children within the last five years. Only in half of the missing cases were the children found again. Experience of missing children is important as it indicates that a large portion of the missing cases can very well be trafficking incidents. However, no study exclusively focusing on missing children has been conducted.

A nationwide survey on child and women trafficking by the Bangladesh National Women Lawyers Association (BNWLA) in 1997 presented the magnitude of the problem by citing some statistics of the number of children being trafficked outside the country:

- 13,220 children trafficked out of Bangladesh in the past five years
- 300,000 Bangladeshi children work in brothels in India
- 200,000 Bangladeshi children work in brothels in Pakistan
- 4,700 children were rescued from traffickers in the past five years
- 4,500 women and children trafficked to Pakistan yearly

- 1,000 child trafficking cases were documented in the Bangladeshi press during the period 1990 to 1992
- 69 children were reported rescued at the border during a three-month study in 1995.

These figures came from several sources but none involve any baseline. Interestingly the figure of 13,222 children trafficked out of Bangladesh over the last "five years" reappeared in the Nationwide Survey of BNWLA from the government report mentioned earlier. The figure on Indian brothels was estimated by the documentation cell of BNWLA; no cross reference of this figure could be traced. Nothing on how figures were estimated has been mentioned in the report. The figure regarding Pakistan was first produced by the Lawyers for Human Rights and Legal Aid, Pakistan. It was cited first in Bangladesh in 1995 by UBINIG, and then kept reappearing. The primary sources of these data are almost always "estimations" based on sample surveys or news paper reports with vague reference to official sources. Another aspect is that these data have been around for more than a decade and have been outdated in the absence of updates.

Trafficking in children and women from Nepal

It is important to note that there is almost no evidence of trafficking in men from Nepal in the existing literature on trafficking. All research reports conclude that the 1,740-mile open border between Nepal and India facilitates the clandestine trade and trafficking exclusively in girls and women. Under the 1950 treaty with India, there is no immigration control or documentation procedure for Nepalese travelling or migrating to India. In such conditions, the data on mobility in general and trafficking in particular are very difficult to collect at exit points.

Several studies suggest that every year thousands of Nepalese girls born in poverty and hardship end up in commercial sex. In Nepal, some micro studies have been carried out with a small geographical span within the source areas. In 1998, the Centre for Legal Research and Resource Development carried out a field study that compared the number of girls younger than 18 years old who were out of the district at known and unknown destinations (Community Action Centre, 2001). However, there are no studies, even at the village level, that examine trends in Nepal. It is also misleading to project estimates of the volume of trafficking in other areas of Nepal based on micro studies, such as the one cited above. The prevention programmes currently underway in Nepal do not monitor such trends systematically, so even project reports and evaluations do not reveal additional useful information (ADB, 2002c).

A study notes (ADB, 2002c) that in case of Nepal, there are three possible points at which estimates can be made: (1) from the number of missing persons reported at the community level, from which a proportion can be assumed to have been trafficked; (2) from data collected at border crossings for estimates of those moving out of Nepal into India, where they may remain or be moved on to another destination; or (3) from the point of exploitation, for example studies carried out in brothels in India or Kathmandu, factories,[2] or estimates of domestic workers. It needs to be noted that comparisons between these kinds of data are not possible. Another data limitation comes from the clandestine nature of trafficking which keeps the perpetrators hidden from most of the monitoring activities. At the same time, incidence of prosecutions being rare, the crime statistics present a low estimate of the incidence of human trafficking. At this backdrop, in case of Nepal, most data of human trafficking are estimated and tend to be quoted and cross-quoted in all literature (see Table 2).

TABLE 2

THE NUMBER OF WOMEN TRAFFICKED FROM NEPAL

No. of Women	Frequency/ Time Frame	Destination	Source
5,000-11,000	Annually	-	STOP/Maiti, 2001
300,000 "globally"	-	-	CAC Nepal, 2001
200,000 (10% 14-18 years)	-	-	CWIN, 1994
5,000	Annually	-	Ghimire, 2002
5,000-7,000	Annually	-	Population Council, 2001
50,000	-	-	STOP 2002
100,000-200,000	-	-	Asian Development Bank (ADB), Nepal Country Report, 2002
200,000	-	Sex industry	Population Council, 2001

Source: ADB, 2003: 28.

The Nepalese Government estimated in 1992 that 200,000 Nepalese women and girls worked in Indian brothels. In fact, the most common figure found in various documents, without however citing a source or being cross-referenced, is 200,000. The ADB study concludes that variations and inconsistencies in data collection make it impossible to derive trends with any accuracy (ADB, 2002c).

The ADB study goes on to conclude that the lack of concrete data has led to a dependency of organizations upon anecdotal information to plan where activities should be focused. It also makes it difficult to lobby with the government. This has also established many myths regarding the magnitude and nature of trafficking. The study stresses on the need to re-examine those myths as the migration and trafficking trends shift and respond to changed economic and social concerns (ADB, 2002c).

Traditional cultural practices, such as the *Deuki* system, in which the rich families without daughters are increasingly buying young daughters from impoverished rural families and offering them to temples as their own, also increased the vulnerability of girls to trafficking in Nepal. These girls are prohibited from marrying and often end up as "kept wives" or commercial sex workers. In 1992, 17,000 girls were reportedly endowed as *Deuki* (CEDPA, 1997).

Along with economic hardship, studies indicate that in many parts of Nepal family members, village leaders, and neighbours may not perceive that the removal of a child or a young woman from a family as a criminal act. This may be seen as a viable survival strategy for poor families. These attitudes are especially prevalent in areas where the social practice of dowry payment is followed.[3] Within the backdrop of gender disparities, payment of dowry portrays a girl as a liability in a family. Traffickers often succeed in persuading parents to hand their daughters over to their control, with the false prospects of "dowry-less" marriage (ADB, 2002c).

While most of the girls end up in brothels in India, the majority of boys are trafficked to India and the main areas of work are embroidery, wage labour, hotel work, and driving (WOREC, 2002). Various cases have been noted where Nepalese girls have been trafficked either directly or after spending time in India to places such as Hong Kong, Thailand, and the Gulf countries (ADB, 2002c).

In terms of patterns, the ADB (2003) study illustrates that most of the brokers in Nepal travel by local buses to New Delhi, then travel by bus or train to Mumbai. Actual routes change frequently for fear of being intercepted.

Trafficking in persons: the Sri Lankan scenario

Discussions on trafficking in South Asia seldom include Sri Lanka, and few studies at the regional level include the Sri Lankan trafficking scenario. However, Shamim (2001) presents a brief overview of trafficking in girls and women in Sri Lanka. It shows that in Sri Lanka girls and women in general are more literate and socially mobile than in other countries in South Asia, although their status varies widely according to class, ethnic group, and religion. The current ethnic conflict has displaced populations and exposed many girls and women to acts of violence.

The best known figures on trafficking in Sri Lanka are:

- 10,000 to 12,000 children from rural areas are trafficked into prostitution by organized crime groups (West, 1997).
- 80 per cent of labour migrants in 1994 were women. Job trainees in Korea and Japan have disappeared into underground exploitation, such as prostitution (CATW-Asia Pacific, n.d.). It may not be that all of these women are trafficked, but there is a big demand for "prostitutes" around the military bases in Korea, where there are 18,000 registered and 9,000 unregistered prostitutes, reports the same source (CATW-Asia Pacific, n.d.).

Once again these figures are mostly estimations and spread through news media and cross citations. Another case of cross-citation without validation of the original figures is revealed when the figure of 10,000 to 12,000 children cited by the first news source is taken into consideration. Initially it was the ILO report (Goonesekara and Wanasundare, 1998) that popularized the figure globally. It reported that that during the period from 1988 to 1990, PEACE found that there were approximately 10,000 children in prostitution younger than age 18 (PEACE, 1996). However, later most of the reports cited these figures as provided by ILO's rapid assessment. Importantly, the initial figure provided by PEACE is a sample-based estimation. More interestingly, the Department of National Planning estimates that figure to have increased exponentially to around 30,000 by 1991 (Goonesekara and Wanasundare, 1998). Another such study by End Child Prostitution in Asian Tourism informs that almost 30,000 boys are engaged in prostitution in Sri Lanka (Deutsche Presse Agentur, 1996). This study is also providing estimated figures.

Nevertheless, the presence of child prostitution and illegal immigration indicates a high probability of trafficking. The same sample-based studies also draw the same conclusions (West, 1997). The women are increasingly being drawn in, as migration for employment is a rising phenomenon in the Sri Lanka economy where 80 per cent of migrants are female. The review of existing literature reveals that the true extent of this vulnerability has not been the clear focus of the existing body of research. The attempted estimations on the magnitude of the incidence of trafficking in persons show the anecdotal nature of available information.

Destination countries

In South Asia, India and Pakistan are the major destination countries. However, both countries are also transit for other international destinations, such as the Middle East.

India as transit and destination

India is both a destination and transit area for the trafficking of women and children for South Asia. No data or discussions regarding India as a sending country are available. This is an area that needs additional attention, as it seems implausible that Indians are never trafficked out of India (ADB, 2003). However, it is estimated that cross-border trafficking represents about 10 per cent of the coerced migrants. This indicates that interstate trafficking could make up as much as 89 per cent of trafficking victims (ADB, 2003). Of the 10 per cent of victims of cross-border trafficking, approximately 2.17 per cent are from Bangladesh and 2.6 per cent are from Nepal (Mukerjee and Mukerjee, 1991). Once again these are anecdotal conclusions drawn from a sample with no clear indication how it was scaled up to measure the national magnitude. However, these data indicate the prevalence of both internal and cross-border trafficking in India. Table 3 shows the various data available on trafficked women in Indian brothels.

TABLE 3

NUMBER OF TRAFFICKED WOMEN IN INDIAN BROTHELS

No. of Women	Nationality	Location/ Time Frame	Source
70% of 1,000 to 10,000	Bangladeshi	Kolkata/ over last 5 years	Sanlaap, 2002
800 (140 flying commercial sex workers (CSWs)	Bangladeshi	Kolkata/ 1990–1992	Sanlaap, 2002
30,000	Bangladeshi	Kolkata	Trafficking Watch – Bangladesh, Reuters, 1997
2,000	Bangladeshi	various cities	Coalition Against Trafficking in Women (CATW), Asia Pacific
10,000	Bangladeshi	Mumbai, Goa	Trafficking Watch – Bangladesh, Reuters, 1997
200,000	Nepalese	-	Ghimire, 1996
27,000	Bangladeshi	-	Shamim, 2001
2.7 per cent of women	Bangladeshi	Kolkata	Central Social Welfare Board, India, 1991

Source: ADB, 2003: 28.

The constraints towards developing a comprehensive database on trafficking in persons are numerous. To begin with the trafficked individuals in India (i.e. at a destination country) are not interested in revealing their national identity. They fear both the traffickers and the law enforcers. Second, lingual and physical similarities (such as between the Bangladeshis and Bengalis of West Bengal) may work to make the trafficked persons invisible both to authorities and re-searchers. Third, at present there are only a few border checkpoints available to monitor the flow of migrants and trafficked persons. Moreover, the categories of the crime data collection system in India do not clearly reflect the frequency of trafficking.

The ADB study leads one to conclude that future research in India can focus more on ethnographic approaches in order to learn more about the origins of trafficking, and the returnees that set up networks or recruit or initiate *dhabas* (kiosks) around which trafficking networks are centred. It further stresses that studying trafficked labour and reviewing the categories in national crime data collection systems would provide expansive and accurate data in relation to cross-border flows (ADB, 2002b).

Trafficking in women and children in Pakistan

The body of research and data on trafficking in women and children in Pakistan are also anecdotal, and outdated data are recycled without clarification. As cited earlier, there are several figures on Bangladeshi trafficked women in Pakistan, all of which are anecdotal and outdated (1991 to 1997). Most of the figures originate from studies conducted by Lawyers for Human Rights and Legal Aid (LHRLA). The reported 200,000 Bangladeshi trafficked women to Pakistan were also derived by LHRLA. Based on official records, LHRLA further reports that there were about 1,500 Bengali women in jails (UBINIG, 1995). Once again, these figures have been found to be cited over and over without any clear indication of their validity (UBINIG, 1995; BNWLA, 1997).

A media review was initiated by the Karachi-based non-governmental organ-ization (NGO) Lawyers for Human Rights and Legal Aid (LHRLA), which con-ducted a study of all the trafficking cases reported in Pakistan's newspapers during 2002. The report documented 29 cases of child trafficking for camel racing in the United Arab Emirates. This is an increase from the 20 cases re-ported during 2001 (Anti-Slavery International, 2003). For obvious reasons, this is a partial picture, and the increase in reported cases does not necessarily reflect an increase in trafficking. The increased media reporting can also be a result of increased awareness about trafficking in women and children.

RESEARCH ON TRAFFICKING: THE SOUTH ASIAN EXPERIENCE

The data at the regional level have so far been collected by human rights organizations or development agencies. Throughout South Asia, therefore, research initiatives on trafficking in persons have been undertaken from the perspective of either human rights violations or development interventions. This has led to reports focusing on the phenomenon from particular perspectives. More importantly, the issue of human trafficking has been often narrowed down to trafficking in women and children.

Major features of the existing research

The research on human trafficking in Bangladesh and South Asia in general reveals four points of data collection within the trafficking process. The nature of data also varies at each point. Table 4 illustrates all four points and their nature.[4] The data collection typically occurred through sample-based surveys, while others were studies done in pocket areas or based on media coverage of incidents reported to the police or found during investigative work. Table 5 provides an overview of the different types of problems that have been taken up and their implications.

Identifying gaps

In most cases, researchers find it extremely difficult to estimate the number of women and children being trafficked. Aside from the illegal nature of the activity, which motivates the actors who control the women and children to hide them and maintain secrecy, if a child is trafficked at a very early age she/he may forget her/his real identity and address. Moreover, sometimes the family members themselves are involved with the traffickers and develop vested interests. In other cases, families and community members withhold information to protect their reputation and to avoid legal consequences. It has been further found that the available data on crime suffers from unclear categorization and underreporting. In the absence of birth registration and baseline data the sample surveys have led to anecdotal estimations which are highly confusing and outdated.

As discussed earlier, in South Asia men are seldom viewed as "victims of trafficking" but rather in the context of irregular migration. This has limited the availability of knowledge and data on trafficking in men in South Asia and around the world. It should be noted that the gender of victims of trafficking is systematically recorded only by a minority of European Union governments that contribute data on trafficking to the Intergovernmental Consultations, and that trafficking statistics are rarely disaggregated by age (O'Connell Davidson and Anderson, 2002).

TABLE 4

DATA COLLECTION WITHIN THE TRAFFICKING PROCESS

Source of Data	Nature of Data	Use of Data
Origin or source areas	The number of missing persons reported, of cases filed, of persons abducted, of returnees; people's perception of migration and trafficking, mobility of people in general; causes to embark on risky movements, etc.	Estimating probable number of trafficked persons and trends, designing prevention programmes, designing Behavioural Change and Communication (BCC) materials, planning community-based interception and integration programmes, etc.
During the process of movement	Data collected at border exits on number of persons, the nature of the trafficking network, actors and their roles, linkage with irregular migration network, role of border communities, role of NGOs and law enforcement agencies, etc.	Estimating probable number of trafficked persons and designing awareness-raising programmes and BCC material, identifying local allies, strategies of interception, creating access to information for prospective migrants.
Destinations	Location and number of trafficked individuals, nature of human rights violation, role of actors of trafficking network in exploitation, perception of the trafficked individuals regarding better future, different interventions of NGOs and role of law enforcement agencies, etc.	Estimating probable number of trafficked persons and designing programme for their rescue, rehabilitation/recovery and re/integration, facilitating policy and legal reform, measuring span of the problem, etc.
Institutional rehabilitation process both at source and destination	Number of rescued individuals, nature of existing services, assessment of existing rescue, rehabilitation/recovery and re/integration services, causes of trafficking, means and processes of trafficking, roles of different actors and factors, experience of abuse and human rights violation in trafficking process and trafficked state, etc.	Estimating probable number of trafficked persons and designing programme for their rescue, rehabilitation/recovery and re/integration, facilitating policy and legal and institutional reform, identifying indicators and standards, assessing the scale of the problem, etc.

TABLE 5

RESEARCH PROBLEMS AND LESSONS LEARNED

Research Problem	Lesson Learned
Estimate of the scale of trafficking	Sample surveys of the study area cannot lead to authentic figures on the scale of the problem. A baseline survey is essential. However, the available database provides adequate indications of the wide spread of the problem. The knowledge base is also helpful in programme design.
Consequence: violation of human rights	Concentration so far has been on the issues of human rights violations of women and children. Trafficking in men has not received much attention. Moreover, the focus has largely been on prostitution. In this respect HIV/AIDS has also emerged as an important item on the development agenda. In Bangladesh this has also led to tension between the activist groups who try to "rescue" trafficking survivors from brothels, and the AIDS activist who would like to extend services to them in the brothel setting. However, the paradigm of Bangladesh Counter Trafficking Thematic Group attempts to resolve the conflict by introducing the issue of "agency" as an integral part of recovery of trafficked individual. This is the ability of a trafficked survivor to choose to remain in the brothel setting and there move towards recovery, while others may choose to leave it as a precondition to recovery.
Cause analysis	The causes are no longer treated solely as "criminal". Trafficking is treated as a social phenomenon and complex interplay of socio-economic, cultural and political factors and actors. However, concentration so far has been on the supply side. Demand side analysis still has to receive the attention it deserves.
Mapping	Mapping is still in its infancy. The database used for mapping is most often built on sample groups of studies or on media reporting. The absence of an electronically accessible, upgradeable and authentic database hampers the quality and scope of mapping initiatives. Moreover, only recently has the mapping process been directed towards understanding the nexus between migration and trafficking. While these are far from accurate trends, they do help to build indicative maps based on these data.
Stock taking	Stocktaking on service providers and knowledge sources lead to quality and coordinated programming. However, triangulation of data is a very complex process, especially regarding field-level reality and documents (e.g. on NGO activities).

Trafficking is driven by both supply and demand. Most studies concentrate on the supply side and demand is normally neglected. In South Asia, most research initiatives have also dealt with the supply-side dynamics in trafficking in persons. There are only a few studies on the demand dynamics of human trafficking (O'Connell Davidson and Anderson, 2002). However, these studies do not provide adequate information regarding the factors influencing demand, nor the effect on the parties involved (primarily the employers and consumers of the product of trafficked labour).

Studies that have looked into the quality of data on trafficking reveal that:

- The existing body of data and analysis on trafficking is unsatisfactory because it is an amalgam of information from different sources, collected in different ways, at different times, using different definitions of trafficking, by different agencies for very different reasons (O'Connell Davidson and Anderson, 2002). The experience in Bangladesh has been the same. INCIDIN (2002) noted that different studies have applied different methodologies, which further complicates their use in developing a national overview.
- No national baseline database is available. This makes it difficult to measure trends in trafficking. It also makes it difficult to measure the impact of different interventions by government agencies and NGOs.
- Some of the figures (such as the number of Bangladeshi children engaged in prostitution in India and Pakistan) have not been verified by any national agency or upgraded over the years (INCIDIN, 2002).
- In the absence of a standard definition of trafficking, the findings of individual studies are rarely comparable, and this further undermines the reliability of global claims and estimates based on several different single country and/or regional studies (O'Connell Davidson and Anderson, 2002).
- In South Asia, trafficking-related studies focus more on women and children and have almost always linked trafficking to prostitution.

Community knowledge and institutional research

For the community at grassroots level, there is no authentic source of information and institutional setup to raise awareness of trafficking. The information available to the community is based on their own experiences, stories, myths, and the experiences of interventions by NGOs, government agencies, and the media. Nevertheless, the major sources still remain informal, and the role of NGOs (engaged in research, development, or humanitarian services) has been found to be minimal (INCIDIN, 2002). According to research findings, the major source of information for people at the grassroots level appears to be informal human networking (around 80% have gathered information on trafficking from their neighbours, while one-third of the respondents were informed by relatives). Among the institutional sources, radio (almost one-third), television (12 to 16%) and newspaper (up to 9%) were mentioned. A negligible portion of respondents (less than 4%) received their information on trafficking through NGOs (INCIDIN, 2002).

Thus, the findings of the studies on trafficking and the knowledge gathered in the process have largely not reached the people who are exposed to the risks of being trafficked. Nevertheless, the research process of the Bangladesh Counter-Trafficking Thematic Group has produced heightened conceptual understanding of trafficking.

Innovative research methods and thematic framework: the case of Bangladesh

Some of the studies have adopted innovative approaches, leading to a greater understanding of the issues and opening new ways of approaching old problems.

Participatory learning workshop

In an attempt to overcome a subjective bias of the individual researchers concerning qualitative data, a participatory learning workshop process was introduced at the end of the field data collection (INCIDIN, 2002). This has been adopted during the Rapid Assessment on Trafficking in Children for Exploitative Employment in Bangladesh. Through this approach: (1) the entire research team had the opportunity of participating in the data analysis process, and (2) the individual researchers had to reveal their biases, interact with others, and produce a critical analysis of their findings through group work.

Moreover, after the identification of the preliminary findings, researchers, development activists, representatives of government agencies and NGOs working in the field of child trafficking, international development partners, and donors were invited to a "sharing workshop". The workshop helped to triangulate study findings, as well as to generate greater ownership of the findings.

Consultative process of the Bangladesh Counter-trafficking Thematic Group

The results of the process are discussed more in-depth below. However, following in-depth discussions, the representatives concluded the following:

- The use of many trafficking definitions tended to limit their scope and not reflect the totality of the problem.
- There are many inconsistencies in the existing human trafficking paradigm that have yet to be resolved in Bangladesh.
- The sector still lacks conceptual clarity even among those working to remedy the problem.
- There is a need to rethink some previous assumptions to restructure and revise/expand our understanding of the problem.

It was recommended that a systematic process to formally "come to terms" with the trafficking paradigm in Bangladesh be adopted in order to address these conclusions. The approach was to be consultative to deepen the knowledge on the basis of continual consultation with people involved in research and interventions regarding trafficking of human beings.

There is a dearth of conceptual frameworks that provide a good overview of the "human trafficking" sector. Such frameworks are needed to help those who are not well versed in the subject to better understand the relationships that exist between various factors and actors within the human trafficking paradigm, and help researchers conceptualize their research more effectively. Unlike reports that describe a problem using text (often in an abstract way), a framework (matrix) can help a person to instantly visualize the interrelated elements of a problem. This makes it possible to bring a group of people "up-to-speed" quickly.

Second-generation thinking on trafficking

Revisiting the Human Trafficking Paradigm: The Bangladesh Experience, Part One: Trafficking of Adults, Bangladesh Counter-trafficking Thematic Group (BCTTG) is the outcome of a consultative research process which began in September 2002. IOM organized a roundtable discussion titled *Anti-Trafficking Initiatives: Bangladesh and Regional Perspectives*. The main objective was to discuss various conceptual and definitional aspects of human trafficking in Bangladesh and South Asia.

To date, the participants in these meetings have included representatives from governments, donors, international governmental organizations, NGOs, universities, and law enforcement agencies. The result was a process document (*Revisiting the Human Trafficking Paradigm: The Bangladesh Experience, Part One: Trafficking of Adults*) and a matrix presenting a thematic paradigm of trafficking. A few of the basic components of this thematic framework are discussed below.

Trafficking and migration nexus: Very few studies explore the nexus between trafficking and migration. However, the matrix developed by BCTTG and a recent paper find that the irregular trade network, especially the irregular migration network, is accessed by rural poor for different migration needs, and the same network is used by the traffickers (Haque, 2004). The studies show that it is very difficult to distinguish trafficked individuals from ordinary migrants before reaching destinations (Bangladesh Counter Trafficking Thematic Group, 2003; INCIDIN, 2002).

Men as victims of trafficking: Apart from sporadic media reporting and a few studies, most researchers throughout and beyond South Asia focus on trafficking in women and children and exclude the issue of trafficking in men.

Deficiencies in existing definitions: The new thematic framework proposes to include the consequence of trafficking as an integral part of the definition of trafficking in persons (Bangladesh Counter-Trafficking Thematic Group, 2003). The new thematic framework notes that the existing definitions usually tend to focus on three basic elements: (1) the movement and trade/sale of a person, (2) the methods used to bring about this movement (e.g. deception, fraud, violence, etc.), and (3) the motives for the action (e.g. forced labour, prostitution, slavery-like practices, etc.). What the definitions do not clearly address are: (1) the actual outcome of the trafficking event; (2) the torture, rape, intimidation, and threats used to ensure that victims comply with their new situation; (3) the slavery-like conditions they must endure over time; and (4) the evolution or temporal nature of the event. In other words, many definitions only address part of the essential elements making up the overall problem or "harm". As research and our understanding and interventions regarding human trafficking expand, the present conceptual frameworks and definitions might also have to change to better articulate the "outcome": commercial sexual exploitation, domestic servitude, and other slavery-like practices (Bangladesh Counter-Trafficking Thematic Group, 2003).

Trafficking as a multilayered process: A study on trafficking in children has revealed that the recruiting agents are not only external criminal agents, but also relatives and community people. In general, for the interviewed children (INCIDIN, 2002), pimps (52%), a relative (17%), and neighbours (8%) appear as the principal recruiting agents. With this in mind, trafficking should not be treated only as a criminal process, but also as a social phenomenon. The chain of traffickers includes members from the victims' families, as well as organized crime gangs and even members of law enforcing and border security forces.

Agency, trafficking, and recovery: The new paradigm determines the question of "agency" (or autonomy and empowerment or choice of producing actions or interventions such as to make a change) as a key element in defining trafficking as well as in qualifying any process of rescue and recovery. From this analysis it appears that loss of agency (with the understanding that there is no one with complete agency, rather there is a continuum of agency) is inherent in trafficking. Moreover, this also leads to the development of a framework to assess whether a programme (may be of an NGO) is regressive or progressive in terms of empowering the survivors. The newly evolved thematic framework also introduces the term "integration" instead of "reintegration". The conceptual understanding regarding this discourse lies in the fact that it may not be in the best interest of the survivors to reintegrate within a context that led to the harm situation; rather, the issue may be of "rebuilding the life". This has a direct impact on designing and implementing monitoring systems.

POLICY INITIATIVES AND THE NEED FOR RESEARCH

The South Asian Association for Regional Cooperation (SAARC) has recently ratified a convention on trafficking in women and children (see Table 6). This *SAARC Convention on Preventing and Combating Trafficking in Women and Children for Prostitution* has recently been sanctioned by the member states. The Convention now needs to be enacted by individual states.

TABLE 6

DRAFT SAARC CONVENTION ON PREVENTING AND COMBATING
TRAFFICKING IN WOMEN AND CHILDREN FOR PROSTITUTION, MAY 1997

Article 1	Definitions
1.	"Child" means a person who has not attained the age of 18 years;
2.	"Prostitution" means the sexual exploitation or abuse of persons for commercial purposes;
3.	"Trafficking" means the moving, selling or buying of women and children (for prostitution) within or outside a country for monetary or other considerations with or without the consent of the person subjected to trafficking;
4.	"Traffickers" means persons, agencies or institutions engaged in any form of trafficking;
5.	"Persons subjected to trafficking" means women and children victimized (or forced into prostitution) by the traffickers by deception, threat, coercion, kidnapping, sale, fraudulent marriage, child marriage or any other unlawful means;
6.	"Protective home" means a home established or recognized by a government of a member state for the reception, care, treatment and rehabilitation of rescued or arrested persons subjected to trafficking.

However, a large proportion of the women and child activist groups and NGOs in Bangladesh and India have strong reservation against restricting the proposed convention only to the area of "prostitution". Discussion with involved institutions revealed the same reservation. NGOs and activist groups all over the region have proposed several amendments to the draft convention.

There is some progress also at national level. In Bangladesh, the Ministry of Women and Children's Affairs (2004) developed a counter-trafficking framework report. It concludes that research offering comprehensive information and analysis is vital for the implementation of counter-trafficking interventions. Studies have already been undertaken in many areas and there is an increasing understanding of the dynamics of human trafficking in Bangladesh as findings are exchanged and integrated into the planning and monitoring of initiatives. The collection of quantitative data remains a challenge, and gender concerns are sometimes absent from analysis, but a commitment to continue learning and building knowledge for all stakeholders is very clear in Bangladesh.

One area highlighted for further scrutiny was the quality of government services. Previous studies found that sometimes safe custody further victimizes those being held. There are some journalistic reports on safe custody but a general lack of any systematic study on the topic. Government shelters for victims of violence do not have the facilities to provide psychosocial support, and authentic information on the status of government shelters is unavailable (INCIDIN, 2002).

ADB's "Combating trafficking" report (2002a) is another attempt at creating a policy framework. The report provides a short analysis of national policies and plans of action for combating trafficking of women and children; offers an outline of national and international regulatory frameworks; indicates legal procedures to prevent trafficking and protect the victims of trafficking; and provides an overview of current practices, procedures, knowledge, and awareness of law enforcement agencies, experiences of the victims, and training materials used by NGOs and different government institutions.

The study identifies that the lack of data and solid body of research have also lead to the creation of certain myths and assumptions about trafficking that need to be questioned, (e.g. that trafficking is usually for the purpose of prostitution, despite evidence that victims of trafficking are often domestic or factory workers). At the same time, the study recommends research to understand why those vulnerable to trafficking migrate in the first place, and how to make migration a positive experience (ADB, 2002a).

These recommendations, especially those from the *The Counter-Trafficking Framework Report: Bangladesh Perspective*, are now being integrated into a process that would lead to a separate National Anti-Trafficking Plan for Action. There is already a National Plan of Action concerning trafficking of children. Moreover, the government is planning to treat the trafficking of women and children separately in the light of the findings of several studies (IOM, 2004). However, the challenge lies not so much in changing policies, but rather in ensuring effective implementation of the existing policies.

DATA ON HUMAN TRAFFICKING: TOWARDS A REGIONAL KNOWLEDGE BASE

There are not many studies conducted from a South Asian perspective. The latest studies look at the problem of trafficking in persons in South Asia by considering India as the major destination country for women and girls from the region (ADB, 2003; IOM, 2001).

The IOM (2001) study notes that there is a need for regional studies to better understand the regional dimension of the trafficking phenomenon. In South Asia, the institutional setup of the research initiatives is neither well connected, nor coordinated. At present, there is no coordination of knowledge and resources. Although there is a contextual and cultural similarity and dependency and a regional feature to the phenomenon of trafficking in persons, there is no collective learning process at the regional level. The experience so far reveals that a regional process to develop a collective knowledge base and sharing among the researchers may enhance the value of the research initiatives.

The ILO project, International Programme on Elimination of Child Labour (IPEC), has formally identified this gap and initiated a process to assess the need for regional coordination among the research agencies and knowledge institutions working on trafficking in persons across South Asia (INCIDIN, 2004).

A regional network of researchers can promote the development of:

- Regional coordination in identifying research problems
- Regional ethical and methodological guideline on research related to trafficking in children
- Regional sharing of databases and knowledge resources on research related to trafficking in children
- Strengthen the capacity of national researchers based on information and experience generated through regional research initiatives.

A regional survey to develop authentic information on trafficked individuals

Several studies used different techniques and methods at different times to collect data on trafficking, Most of the time the secondary data are repeated and unverified and only provide "guesstimates". However, the available studies do contribute to the understanding of the causes, sources, destinations, and consequences of trafficking. But the information available fails to generate a national database. It is difficult to state the nature and extent of the problem accurately. As such, there is an urgent need to carry out a national baseline survey with the aim of developing a South Asian database on trafficking in persons. Given the economic and institutional constraints existing throughout the region, it will be very difficult for individual states to carry out this task alone. Multilateral agencies, such as IOM, could assist and play a crucial role in any such endeavour.

A regional study on the demand side of trafficking in persons

A comprehensive study on the demand side dynamics of trafficking in persons is necessary. There are some media-based studies in which data have been generated through a content analysis, but media reports have not been critically assessed. There are some studies on the demand for trafficked women in the sex industry in South Asia, but the samples of the studies were very small and the analyses were not comparable at a regional level. The Bangladesh Counter-Trafficking Thematic Group also identified the need for such a study. It also identified some of the major actors on the demand side, namely, the third party(ies), the employers of trafficked labour and the consumers who use trafficked labour. ILO, under IPEC, has presently initiated a regional study on the demand side of trafficking in women and children in South Asia. This study is being carried out in Bangladesh, Indonesia, Nepal, Pakistan, and Sri Lanka. The study is expected to identify and analyze different types of demands, demand holders, and factors influencing demands in different sectors in which trafficked women and children are exploited. However, the study will not be able to present a complete overview of regional demand because it is not covering India.

RESEARCH FOR A BETTER TOMORROW

In conclusion, the treacherous path that leads people into the trafficked state requires much more in-depth research and understanding. Presently the South Asian knowledge base on trafficking in persons is loaded with numerous figures on the magnitude of the problem, but almost all are anecdotal and outdated. Although numbers are important for planners, it is high time to start focusing more on the ethnographic aspects of the phenomenon. And before speaking in numbers, there is a need for a comprehensive baseline. There is also a paucity of research initiatives and knowledge on the demand dynamics of trafficked labour. This gap also needs to be addressed both nationally and regionally to enhance the knowledge base and quality of interventions.

The emerging paradigm on trafficking in persons in South Asia is questioning many of the dominant assumptions and definitions. This may also lead to a change in the nature and scope of future research initiatives in the region. The innovative research experience of the region reveals that people's participation (including that of the children) in research enables research initiatives to draw on the community knowledge base. However, the challenge is in bringing these research findings back to the communities.

It is even more challenging to bring the researchers and research resources closer at the regional level. Having access to a shared knowledge base at the regional level can help create a better understanding of a phenomenon such as trafficking, which by nature is not just regional but global. This is a challenge and an opportunity that may help the nations of this region act in synergy to fight trafficking, a crime against humanity that now leaves imprints of tears of pain and shame all over South Asia.

NOTES

1. So far only media reports have mentioned of organ sale. However, no research so far has confirmed the claim.
2. In such cases the selection of factories differs depending on the different definitions of trafficking harms adopted by these research reports.
3. Dowry is defined as any property given or agreed to be given at the time of marriage in consideration for, or in connection with the marriage.
4. ADB, 2003 identifies three sources of data. The paper finds that the fourth category is useful as it contributed in developing the Thematic Framework of the Bangladesh Counter-Trafficking Thematic group.

REFERENCES

Anti-Slavery International
2003   "Trafficking and forced labour of children in the United Arab Emirates (UAE)", United Nations Commission on Human Rights, Sub-Commission on the Promotion and Protection of Human Rights Working Group on Contemporary Forms of Slavery, 28th Session, Geneva.

Asian Development Bank (ADB)
2002a   "Combating trafficking in women and children in South Asia: country paper Bangladesh", ADB, Manila.
2002b   "Combating trafficking in women and children in South Asia: country paper India", ADB, Manila.
2002c   "Combating trafficking in women and children in South Asia: country paper Kingdom of Nepal", ADB, Manila.
2003   "Combating trafficking of women and children is South Asia: regional synthesis paper for Bangladesh, India, and Nepal", ADB, Manila.

Bangladesh Counter Trafficking Thematic Group
2003   *Revisiting the Human Trafficking Paradigm: The Bangladesh Experience*, IOM-CIDA, Dhaka.

Bangladesh National Women Lawyers' Association (BNWLA)
1997   *Survey in the Area of Child and Women Trafficking*, Save the Children and UNICEF, Denmark and Dhaka.

Center for Development and Population Activities (CEDPA)
1997   *Girls' Right: Society's Responsibility, Taking Action Against Sexual Exploitation and Trafficking, Facts on Asia and Country Profiles*, CEDPA, Washington, DC.

Coalition Against Trafficking in Women (CATW)-Asia Pacific
n.d.   *Trafficking in Women and Prostitution in the Asia Pacific*, CATW-Asia Pacific, Quezon City.

Community Action Centre
2001   *Stock-taking of Existing Research and Data on Trafficking of Women and Girls*, Community Action Centre, Kathmandu.

Deutsche Presse Agentur
1996   "Sex tourism spreading from Asia to Latin America, study warns", Deutsche Presse Agentur, 23 March.

Goonesekara, S., and L. Wanasundare
1998   *Commercial Sexual Exploitation of Children in Sri Lanka*, Centre for Women's Research (CENWOR), Colombo.

Haque, Md. S.
2004   *Migration-Trafficking Nexus*, IOM, Dhaka

INCIDIN
2002   *Rapid Assessment on Trafficking in Children for Exploitative Employment in Bangladesh*, February, ILO-IPEC, Dhaka.

IOM
2002   "In search of dreams: study on the situation of the trafficked women and children from Bangladesh and Nepal to India", August, IOM, Dhaka.

2004   *Review of CPCCT, Ministry of Women and Children's Affairs, Government of Bangladesh and NORAD*, IOM, Dhaka.

Ministry of Women and Children's Affairs
2004   *The Counter-Trafficking Framework Report: Bangladesh Perspective*, Ministry of Women and Children's Affairs, Dhaka.

Mukerjee, K.K., and S. Mukerjee
1991   *A Study Report: Female Prostitutes and Their Children in City of Delhi*, Delhi, India.

O'Connell Davidson, J., and B. Anderson
2002   "Trafficking: a demand-led problem?", Save the Children, Sweden.

PEACE
1996   *Protecting Environment and Children Everywhere: Studies on the Commercial Sexual Exploitation of Children in Sri Lanka*, PEACE, Colombo.

Shamim, I.
n.d.   "Mapping of missing, kidnapped and trafficked children and women: Bangladesh perspective", IOM, Dhaka.

UBINIG (Unnayan Bikalpa Niti Nirdharany Gobeshana)
1995   *Trafficking in Women and Children: The Cases of Bangladesh*, UBINIG, Pakistan, Dhaka.

West, J.
1997   "Sri Lankan children for sale on the Internet", *London Telegraph*, New Delhi, 26 October.

WOREC
2002   "Cross-border trafficking of boys", ILO/IPEC, Kathmandu.

Human Trafficking in East Asia: Current Trends, Data Collection, and Knowledge Gaps

June JH Lee*

INTRODUCTION

Migration in Asia is dynamic and complex, especially intraregional movement of people. The volume of migration flows in the region has dramatically increased over the decades in terms of the overall number of migrants hosted by East Asian countries. The increase is alarming because some 30 to 40 per cent of total migration takes place through unregulated channels (Wickramasekera, 2002). It is unknown how much of this migration flow is human trafficking. However, various studies and continuous media reports suggest that human trafficking is widespread throughout the region and on the rise.[1]

Trafficking in persons in East Asia has not been widely studied.[2] This is rather curious because Japan, for example, has a large sex industry employing a significant number of non-Japanese women. As I will discuss later, there are many challenges in conducting research on human trafficking in the region. As a result, literature on the subject, including research-based publications, is rather limited, particularly in comparison with the number of publications on trafficking in South-East and South Asia. Instead, media reports and the United Nations (UN) and other agencies' intervention-oriented studies dominate the literature on East Asian trafficking. Such studies tend to focus on trafficking in women and children for sexual exploitation and highlight serious violations of human rights. Even though these studies are not empirically based and do not present survey results, they still improve the understanding of the trafficking processes, their underlying causes, and impacts on the trafficked persons.

---

* International Organization for Migration, Geneva, Switzerland.

Accordingly, this paper will examine the general trends in human trafficking reported in East Asia from rather disparate sources, identify the main issues and problems raised in the existing information sources, and discuss data collection, research activities, and knowledge gaps.

East Asia includes the People's Republic of China (hereafter referred to as China), Hong Kong Special Administrative Region of China (SAR), Macao SAR, the Democratic People's Republic of Korea (hereafter North Korea), Japan, Mongolia, and the Republic of Korea (hereafter South Korea), according to the classification of world regions in the *UN International Migration Report 2002*. However, Taiwan Province of China (POC), Macao SAR, and Mongolia are not discussed beyond occasional mention, as data on these areas are almost non-existent.

INTERNATIONAL MIGRATION AND WOMEN IN ASIA

For the past two decades, Asia has been characterized by the rapid growth of a market-driven intraregional migration. The end of the cold war, the onset of economic development in China, and the growing global market integration of the region, meant that the more developed parts of Asia, including Hong Kong SAR, Japan, South Korea, and Taiwan POC started to experience severe labour shortages.[3] While none of these governments allow permanent settlement per se,[4] the regional inflows of migrant workers have become firmly established in these countries.

The destination countries of East Asia have fairly restrictive immigration policies, particularly toward the unskilled. Neither Japan nor South Korea allow unskilled foreign workers to hold even short-term jobs.[5] These restrictive policies, coupled with the governments' lack of capacity to manage migration, left the organization of migration in Asia largely to the private sector.

Much of the earlier labour migration flows in Asia included unskilled men. However, starting in the 1990s, the high proportion of women in contract migration became one of the distinctive characteristics of migration in the region (Lim and Oishi, 1996). In the mid-1990s, about 1.5 million Asian women were working abroad both legally and irregularly (Asis, 2002). Overall, female migration in Asia also increased during this period. By 2000, it was estimated that the number of female migrants surpassed that of male migrants in East and South-East Asia (5 million versus 4.9 million). Hence, approximately half of the migrants in East and South-East Asia are women. In South Asia, the corresponding rate is 44 per cent (Zlotnik, 2003), although not all of these women are migrant workers. The flows of female migration show geographical and sectoral concentration. The majority of female migrants are from a rather small number of countries, namely the Philippines, Indonesia, and Sri Lanka. The female migrants are employed predominantly in such unprotected sectors as entertainment and domestic services. It is estimated that about 2 million women from South and South-East Asia work overseas as domestic helpers (Hugo, 1998), and the flow of female entertainers has also grown in recent years, as will be discussed in subsequent sections. These facts have raised much concern.

Against this backdrop, trafficking in women and children is considered to be increasing in the region. The routes, destinations, and modes of trafficking are fairly well known and stories of corruption among public officials and local authorities are common. However, "trafficking" presents a particular challenge to researchers, as the identification of cases is far from obvious, even after the UN Convention Against Transnational Organized Crime provided some conceptual boundaries.

There is a certain pattern to the processes in which either legal male migrants or trafficked women are recruited, transported, and possibly exploited by sets of brokers in both the countries of origin and destination. As Skeldon (2000) observes, there is a "continuum of facilitation" ranging from fairly transparent recruitment at one end to the flow through networks tightly controlled by organized criminal groups at the other.

Both labour migration and trafficking fall between two ends of the continuum, although the latter admittedly involves more illegal practices and exploitation. In addition, unlike "smuggling", which necessarily involves border crossings, "trafficking" also includes internal movement of trafficked persons per the UN Convention. Furthermore, the difficulties of separating trafficking from other forms of migration becomes even more problematic, when we consider the international flows of adopted children and brides who have been abducted from their communities. China is an example of this conundrum as internal bride trafficking has been frequently reported, while systematic research on these diverse forms of trafficking is sorely lacking. "Traditional" bride prices defy any automatic application of concepts such as "profit".

Thus, it is difficult in a practical sense to isolate the movement of trafficked persons, but available information indicates a number of lasting patterns of migrant trafficking within the Asian regions and some variation by subregions (IOM, 2001).

While the UN definition is difficult to absorb, the three core elements of the definition are the activity, the means, and the purpose, where: (1) The *activity* refers to some kind of movement either within or across borders; (2) The *means* relate to the involvement of some form of coercion or deception, and (3) the *purpose* is the ultimate exploitation for profit of a person and that person's loss of self-determination (IOM, 2004a).

As long as these elements are present, I have included various forms of trafficking including forced marriage, in this review. Furthermore, although some elements of smuggling and trafficking are similar, it is useful to make a conceptual distinction for analytical purposes: unlike smugglers, the trafficker has a vested interest in their victims' arrival, hence the payment after the victims have reached the end of the process where she or he is about to be exploited.

In East Asia, countries with well-developed sex industries, including Japan, South Korea, and Hong Kong SAR, are destinations for women from the Philippines, Thailand, several Commonwealth of Independent States (hereafter CIS) countries, Eastern European countries, and South American countries. Within China, a large number of women and children are trafficked for forced marriage or, in the case of infant boys, for adoption. Reportedly, some rural Chinese women and children in southern China are trafficked cross-border to work in the sex industry in Thailand and Malaysia.

There is also increased movement between Asia and other regions; IOM field offices report Moldovan and Romanian women stranded in Cambodia, Peruvian women stranded in South Korea, and Colombian women stranded in Thailand, and even Sri Lankan migrants stranded in Central Asia.

RESEARCH ON TRAFFICKING IN EAST ASIA

Despite the reported growth of trafficking in the world, there are very few indicators that can dependably gauge this activity. Apart from the US Department of State's *Trafficking in Persons* (TIP) report, our literature review suggests that newspaper articles remain the most frequently cited source of information on trafficking in East Asia. There is neither a comprehensive regional report that examines the trafficking situation in the East Asian region as a whole, nor any reputable national reports that can be reviewed and critically evaluated. Needless to say, there is an urgent need to systematically collect reliable indicators of trafficking in the region.

A literature review indicates that most studies on trafficking are qualitative. The few existing surveys (see references) are based on small samples and include participants referred by non-governmental organizations (NGOs). These surveys highlight multiple vulnerabilities trafficking persons face such as deception, abduction, sexual exploitation, forced labour, domestic servitude, forced marriage, confinement, exposure to life-threatening conditions, including sexually transmitted diseases (STDs), HIV/AIDS, or abuse at the hands of the authorities.

Information sources

The following section includes a brief description of materials examined for this paper. This listing illustrates the varied nature of available sources of information on this topic.

Country narratives from: (1) the US Department of State's TIP report; (2) UN reports, including publications by the UN Office on Drugs and Crime; and (3) NGOs, such as Coalition Against Trafficking in Women (CATW), and the Protection Project.

Media reports were also collected: for China, 44 media reports between the years 1995 and 2003 were analysed. Thirteen of the articles were printed in 2003, 20 in 2002, six in 2001, two in 2000, and one each in 1999, 1997, and 1995. Media reports principally came from Agence France Presse (8), the Associated Press (5), and the Deutsche Presse Agentur (7); for Japan, 39 media reports between the years 1997 and 2003 were included in our review. Twenty-five of the articles were printed in 2003, 11 in 2002, and two each in 1999 and in 1997. Media reports principally came from Agence France Presse (4), *Bangkok Post* (5), and *The Japan Times* (4), and the Associated Press (1); and for South Korea, 42 media reports between the years 1994 and 2003 with eight articles from 2003, 24 from 2002, three from 2001, three from 2000 and one each from 1999, 1998, and 1994 were analysed. Media reports principally came from the *Korean Times* (8), the *Korea Herald* (7), Agence France Presse (3), and the Associated Press (4). Finally, several media reports on the rest of the region were also collected.

Reports by intergovernmental organizations such as the International Labour Organization (ILO) and the International Organization for Migration (IOM), and non-governmental organizations (NGOs) such as the Human Rights Watch constitute the majority of the reports on trafficking in East Asia, with the exception of the South Korean case where we found rather significant survey results. Reports specific to particular countries in the region are summarized below.

China

(1) International Labour Organization (2002): as of this writing, this is the only available[6] report on a situation within China based on a survey. However, this

report only discusses two counties of one province in southern China, i.e. Jiang-cheng County and Menghai County in Yunnan province; (2) UNICEF (2001): this report also discusses the forced marriage and adoption in southern China.

Hong Kong SAR

(1) Emerton (2001): this is one of the first reports on trafficking in the area and established the existence of the problem by reviewing reported cases. It also extensively discusses local as well as international laws related to trafficking and provides information on policy approaches taken by the Hong Kong SAR authorities; (2) Emerton and Petersen (2003): this paper discusses human rights violations of Filipino women in the Hong Kong SAR sex industry. It provides comparative information vis-à-vis Filipino women in similar situation in South Korea and Japan.

Japan

The main points of discussion in this paper are drawn from the following reports: Dinan (2002); Human Rights Watch (2000); Molina (2001), which has a detailed description on the organization of the trafficking from Colombia to Japan; Caouette and Saito (1999); and IOM (1997). These publications are fairly comprehensive and present findings from empirical research. The last two reports are based on surveys among the returnees in the Philippines and Thailand, respectively. The information is somewhat dated and the samples are small (i.e. 100 for the Filipinas and 55 for the Thai women).

South Korea

(1) Seol et al. (2003): this research is based on a survey and in-depth interviews, funded by the South Korean Government, and conducted by local university-based researchers; (2) Lee (2002): this is the first English-language report reviewing the subject.

The above reports cover trafficking trends, causes and impacts, and a host of related issues in East Asia. Most of them touch on legal aspects, some more than others (e.g. Human Rights Watch, 2000; Emerton, 2001). To date, there is no report or a systematic evaluation on programme interventions made by governments, NGOs, and/or international organizations.

Research methods employed

The majority of work on trafficking in East Asia is based on interviews with law enforcement agents, local NGOs, and a limited number of trafficked persons.

Most reports identified limited access to trafficked persons as the major obstacle in conducting research. Involving local researchers, NGOs, and gaining support from local communities are identified as critical in facilitating access to even the smallest groups of trafficked persons. The two reports on trafficking to Japan (IOM, 1997; Caouette and Saito, 1999) are based on interviews with returnees, Filipina and Thai, respectively. However, the information elicited from these victims may be outdated given the lapse of time.

Caouette and Saito (1999) used ethnographic research methods to conduct their study. It is worthwhile mentioning that the researchers, Thai and Japanese respectively, paid much attention to establishing trust with the trafficked women so that confidential information could be shared. Also, with the help of focus group discussions[7] and participatory observation, the researchers were able to study both the trafficking and the reintegration processes. However, the sample size was very small and included Thai women from two provinces of northern Thailand. The sample size problem can be partially mitigated by using multiple methodologies and different data sources. A recently completed research project supported by the Ministry of Gender Equality of South Korea seems to be a notable exception among this body of research in that it did indeed use multiple methods including in-depth interview, survey, and participant observation (Seol et al., 2003).

In the Korean study, a team of social scientists including a migration specialist and a women's studies professor carried out research on female migrants in the sex industry in South Korea, which is principally a country of destination. The study has a relatively large sample size (195 trafficked persons) and applies various research methods, including in-depth interviews with 32 trafficked persons and participant observation by trained anthropologists. In addition, the research included a survey of more than 1,000 South Korean men, potential users of sexual services provided by trafficked persons. In addition, the research team carried out a series of interviews with those who returned to the Philippines to examine the reintegration issues.

This study is by far the largest research effort in the region, and is notable for pointing out research challenges, including access to trafficked persons. While Philippine women with entertainment visas live mostly around the US military bases, women from Russia or the CIS countries are scattered throughout the country working in bars frequented by South Korean men. The former group is relatively proficient in English, hence more is known about these women. However, both Lee (2002) and Seol et al. (2003) found that the latter group is larger and faster growing. Furthermore, the study pointed out that numerically smaller groups of trafficked women, without an informal network of their compatriots, were less accessible to the research team.

The study did not include ethnic Koreans from China who enter the country with various visitor visas or possibly without proper documents and work in such places as karaoke joints and massage parlours, allegedly providing sexual services. They are physically impossible to differentiate from other South Koreans and linguistically difficult to identify. Local activists argue that their working conditions are just as exploitative as those of the Philippine and Russian women and should therefore be counted as the victims of trafficking. However, practical difficulties prevented the study team to include this group in their sample.

As laudable as this research effort is, the resulting report has several limitations and ambiguities. For example, the report does not assess how many women are indeed working in exploitative conditions. The report simply indicates that there are cases in which women entered the industry knowingly without being forced and experience few problems.

While the study managed to identify a large number of trafficked persons and carried out in-depth interviews, it failed to examine the critical number of court cases referred to by the Ministry of Justice in response to the 2001 TIP Report's Tier 3 rating (Lee, 2002).[8] The study does, however, examine three court cases and make relevant recommendations.

Additionally, the research did not include discussion of South Korean women reportedly trafficked to Japan and the United States.[9] The Government's position vis-à-vis this group of women remains ambivalent, as the South Korean women are believed to be fully aware of their involvement in the sex industry at destination and their "criminal" acts occur outside the South Korean sovereign territory. It remains to be seen how these research findings will inform the Government's future counter-trafficking activities by, for example, providing an operationalized definition of trafficking.

TRAFFICKING IN EAST ASIA – MAIN ISSUES AND PROBLEMS

The flows of trafficked persons throughout the region are numerous and complex. In reality, there is much more diversity in terms of trafficking typologies and different levels of organized crime involvement, and varying degrees of consent and complicity. Based on a thorough review of data, studies, reports, etc., some generalizations can be made about the scale and routes, forms of exploitation, causes in origin and destination countries, trafficking process, and traffickers.

Scale and routes

Given the clandestine nature of the phenomenon, calculating estimates on the scale of trafficking is next to impossible. However, some direct as well as indirect indicators[10] are available, including police records and the number of visas issued to those working in entertainment industries, and useful in providing rough estimates of the possible scale of the trafficking in the region. Needless to say, however, the former are revealing only to the extent that the number indicates, while the latter does not mean every person with such a visa was trafficked.

As for China, according to a news-clip reported in *Asian Migration News* (2004), statistics from the Public Security Ministry of the Chinese Government show that between 2001 and 2003, the police resolved 20,360 cases of trafficking in women and children, arrested 22,018 traffickers, and freed 42,215 kidnapped women and children.

As for South Korea, the Government reported 100 cases in the years 2000 and 2001 (Lee, 2002). While these cases have not been available for research, a recent study reviewed three such cases and identified problems that prevent trafficked persons from pursuing legal recourse (Seol et al., 2003). Emerton (2001) also examined court cases in addition to Hong Kong SAR's legal environment vis-à-vis trafficking. However, the involved numbers were rather small and did not show any tendency to either increase or decrease.

Both Japan and South Korea have a visa category for entertainers. This has been widely known to be a legal channel that is abused for trafficking women for sexual exploitation. In Japan, the entertainment visa is authorized under the Immigration Control and Refugee Recognition law, while in South Korea it is made available through the provisions of the Departure and Arrival Control Act. In both cases, entertainment visa holders are barred from working as hosts or hostesses at establishments serving alcohol as well as those allowing for a direct contact with customers. However, women entering Japan and South Korea on entertainment visas not only work in the sex industry but also overstay and become irregular migrants.[11] The governments of both countries consider these women criminals; these views have met with much criticism from local as well as international activists (Dinan, 2002).

According to Immigration Bureau Statistics, Japan approved 118,000 applications in 2001 (*Kyodo News Service*, 2002), and 123,322 in 2002 (*Daily Yomiuri*, 2003; for earlier statistics, see Sellek, 1996) under the entertainment visa category. Reportedly, in both years, 60 per cent of the applicants were Filipinas. The equivalent for South Korea is 5,092 in 2001 and 5,285 in 2002 (Seol et al., 2003).

The extent to which female entertainers are involved in the sex industry and suffer from human rights abuse and labour exploitation has not been established. Nevertheless, a recent study conducted by Seol et al. (2003) with 200 cases, indicates that in South Korea the majority of these women are indeed being exploited, including being sexually exploited.

In Japan, the visa issuance figures seem to be accurate and are widely used by the media and counter-trafficking to indicate the scale of trafficking, In fact, the Protection Project (8 October 2003) cited: "40,000 Filipino women enter Japan every year with an 'entertainer' visa, and a large number of them are trafficked" (see also *Japan Times*, 2003a; US Department of State, 2001). In South Korea, activists argue that the figures are much larger, highlighting under-reporting problems.

According to some estimates, as many as 100,000 foreign women are trafficked to Japan every year (Women Overseas Workers Network, cited in IOM, 1997).[12] Reportedly, there are approximately 200,000 illegal female migrants in Japan at any given time. Although 90 per cent come from other Asian countries, there is an increasing number from Latin America, Colombia in particular. Estimates on the scale of trafficking are often vague and they cannot serve as a reliable knowledge base for programme intervention and policy design. Instead mapping of major trafficking routes in a region, identifying "hot spots" and organized crime groups can provide valuable information on the nature of trafficking in a given area. This knowledge can then be used to devise various measures for prevention, victim assistance, and cooperation among field practitioners and government officials.

As Figure 1 shows, based on the review of existing materials, the "hot spots" in the region include the Yunnan province of southern China, north-eastern China with an inflow from North Korea, some coastal provinces of China with a flow from inland remote rural communities, and the Russian Far East to South Korea. A major trafficking route has been established from the countries in South-East Asia, including Thailand and the Philippines, to Japan and South Korea. The flow from South Korea to Japan and the United States has not been studied. A relatively recent flow from Colombia and Taiwan to Japan has started to receive some attention.

Confirming the general understanding, the trafficking routes in the region indicate that origins and destinations tend to come from less-developed to more-developed countries (e.g. from the Philippines and Thailand to Japan and the West), and the continuing importance of sexual exploitation for which victims of trafficking are used.

FIGURE 1

MAP OF TRAFFICKING ROUTES IN EAST ASIA

Source: This map is made based on a review 167 news articles, 17 sources from Internet websites in addition to five national publications including the US DOS report, and so on. The period of reporting in these sources ranges from the mid-1990s to the present. The 167 news articles from sources such as the China Daily, Mainichi Daily News and Xinhua News Agency with one article published in 2004, 61 in 2003, 66 in 2002, 20 in 2001, ten in 2000, four in 1999, one in 1998, two in 1997, one in 1995 and one in 1994. The websites include Stop-traffic and Migration Dialogue, dated after 2000.

Forms of exploitation

Given the high volume of irregular migration in Asia mentioned earlier, men are undoubtedly part of this flow and are vulnerable to exploitation. However, cases reporting male victims are rarely found. Furthermore, men, women, and children are also found in exploitative labour situations, including forcible begging in the streets in southern China. Both men and women find themselves in situations where smuggling turns into debt bondage and becomes trafficking. Initially, migrants may consent to pay smugglers. However, if they are unable to pay all of smuggling fees, the smugglers may "sell" them into indentured labour to recover their costs. This debt bondage can amount to virtual slavery. Organ removal, reported in other parts of Asia (see, for example, IOM, 2004b), has not been found in the examined data sources.

A broad comparison of the various forms of exploitation in selected countries has been illustrated in Figure 2. As can be seen, trafficked persons in China are often forced into the sex industry (14/34 citations – see Figure 2 for more information), trafficked as brides (9) or forced into bonded into labour (6), while in Japan and in South Korea, trafficked persons are almost exclusively exploited in the sex industry (25/29 citations and 25/28 citations, respectively). This corresponds with an observation that Japan and South Korea do not have a comparable demand for foreign domestic workers (Lee, 2003)[13] while they do have an entertainer visa that is known to be (ab)used as a trafficking channel.

FIGURE 2

FORMS OF EXPLOITATION: COMPARISON WITHIN COUNTRIES
(values represent number of citations found)

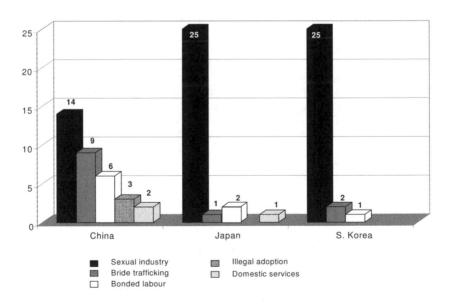

Beyond the overwhelming trend of trafficking for sexual exploitation in the region, a number of reports exist about trafficking for forced marriage in China. This happens mainly internally. However, recently there have been reports of Chinese women being replaced by women kidnapped from Viet Nam and North Korea (ILO, 2002; Human Rights Watch, 2002). Vietnamese women are trafficked to southern Chinese villages, while those fleeing North Korea are deceived or encouraged to marry rural Chinese men in the north-eastern provinces. This indicates, if not the intensity, the geographic spread of the phenomenon within China.

In addition to poverty in rural areas in China, rampant trafficking is often also attributed to a decade-long one-child policy that resulted in gender imbalance, and a universal expectation to marry. Men in communities experiencing severe shortage of women are under strong pressure to find a bride. When they cannot afford to pay the high bride price for local women, they readily resort to purchasing brides kidnapped from other areas. For example, the traditional bride price may be between US$ 1,250 and US$ 2,500, while a kidnapped woman may cost anywhere between US$ 250 and US$ 800 (Marshal, 1999). The purchase of trafficked women thus provides a more cost-effective solution for men in the "marriage squeeze" and yields a high profit for traffickers and middlemen.

According to a report by the United Nations Special Rapporteur on Violence against Women, the kidnapping and sale of women has increased since the mid-1980s and such trafficking accounts for 30 to 90 per cent of marriages in some Chinese villages (Coomaraswamy, 2003). Popular areas of origin for domestically trafficked brides are the poorer areas of Yunnan, Sichuan, and Guizhou where poverty renders women more vulnerable to trafficking (CATW, 1999a). Traffickers generally sell these women in distant areas, such as Shaanxi, Ningxia, Guangxi, Hainan, and Guangdong provinces with large gender imbalances (Pomfret, 2001; Eckholm, 2002).

It is unclear how much of a positive impact the Chinese Government's response to bride trafficking has made on curbing the practice. Nevertheless, the Government has banned sex selection and holds purchasers of brides as well as brokers who kidnap and sell women accountable for trafficking. In fact, the law against trafficking in women in China is as severe as the law prohibiting rape (US Department of State, 2001). Furthermore, public awareness programmes sponsored by the Chinese Ministry of Public Security and UNICEF target rural farmers, warning against domestic bride abuses. However, corruption, weak enforcement measures, and police complicity impede the successful implementation of such laws and programmes, leaving women vulnerable to trafficking for forced marriage in this region.

In "traditional" East Asia and apparently still in some remote rural villages in China, the consent to a marriage proposal has not been that of a bride-to-be. Here, as in the case of seemingly voluntary participation in the sex industry, the question remains whether or not a woman's seeming willingness to marry a man chosen by her parents counts as genuine consent in a culture where women do not choose their own husbands. Even when the concept of "profit" is considered, it still is not straightforward as to whether or not the difference between paying a traditional bride price and buying a wife is wide enough to classify the former as a "cultural practice" and the latter as "trafficking", even if both are against the will of the bride. These questions need more fine-tuned research. In addition, as in the case of the sex industry where the question of individual choice of prostitution or "sex work" as an occupation draws a division among the activists, a similar disagreement may exist among researchers and practitioners.

Causes

Common "push" and "pull" factors reported elsewhere are found underlying the seemingly growing problem in East Asia. Such factors that render persons, especially women and children, vulnerable to trafficking are development processes that marginalize women, in particular from employment and education, gendered cultural practices, gender discrimination, and gender-based violence in families and communities.

General poverty in Chinese inland communities and the traditional preference for male children exacerbated by the Government's one-child policy have been described as the main causes behind the rampant bride trafficking and kidnapping of male babies for adoption in China. If a woman already has a child, she is often forced to have an abortion or be sterilized. Couples failing to comply with the one-child policy regularly face demotion or loss of jobs, extreme fines, or loss of benefits or access to social services. At times, even homes and personal property have been demolished or confiscated for unpaid fines (Methodist Resolution Supporting Human Rights in China, 2004). In addition, gender discrimination at work is unofficial yet common, and in some areas domestic violence is culturally accepted. Those young girls trafficked out of southern China are reported to be from an ethnic minority (ILO 2002).

In the case of South-East Asia and in general, it is true that the so-called push factors in source countries are better studied. In East Asia, however, given the uneven amount of reports existing on Japan and South Korea, the demand side (or pull factors) has received far more attention, both in media and research.

Restrictive immigration policies and laws contribute to the development of underground migration channels, in particular by generating a market for trafficking. Indeed, the migration policies and laws of both Japan and South Korea are considered restrictive in a sense that both countries limit their intake of foreigners as long as the flow is considered "temporary", in spite of the structural labour shortages in parts of their economies. This has been closely linked to the region's high volume of irregular migration, as these two countries are one of the four main destination countries in Asia. Furthermore, globalization is believed to have accelerated the development of such economic sectors in these countries, which demand gender-specific cheap labour, as well as the growth of commercial sex industries in the region. However restrictive the overall immigration policies may be in these two countries, the Japanese and South Korean visa policies (including their entertainer visa) have inadvertently facilitated the inflow of women who end up working illegally in bars and forced to perform sexual services. This observation has generated a fair amount of criticism from both academic researchers and activists.

In South Korea, the presence of US military bases has also drawn considerable amount of attention from both within and outside the country. A close tie between sex trade and militarization[14] in South Korea is one of the recurrent themes in all forms of writings about the phenomenon in and outside of the country (e.g. Enloe, 1993; Moon, 1997; Cheng, 2002). The militarization of Korea and its special tie to the development of the sex industry began during the Japanese colonial rule (1910-1945) of the peninsula, when prostitution was officially recognized, licensed, and even developed on a nationwide scale. This trend continued following the end of Japanese rule to the later establishment of US military bases. In fact, the operation of Rest and Recreation facilities by the US military bases has been cited as creating practices and attitudes that are simultaneously racist and sexist to become pervasive in South Korean society. The operation is purported to be a cause of gender exploitation and violence against both South Korean and foreign trafficked women.

Testimony provided by Donna Hughes (2003a) at the Subcommittee of East Asian and Pacific Affairs of the US Senate Foreign Relations Committee on 9 April 2003 illustrates this view:

> The US military also plays a role in the trafficking of women. In South Korea, there are documented cases of women from the Philippines, the Federation, Bolivia, Peru, Mongolia, China, Bangladesh, Kyrgyzstan, and Uzbekistan being trafficked into bars and clubs around the US bases. Last year, a TV filmed US military police patrolling bars and brothels that held trafficked women. An investigative reporter for *Navy Times* documented that military police have relations with pimps and bar owners where there are trafficked women. (...) Not only does the demand for prostitution result in the trafficking of women for these bars and clubs, the negative local reaction to the abuse

and exploitation by US military personnel provides fodder for anti-American sentiment and interests. (…).

Given that the growing customer base of these trafficked women now includes South Korean men, such notions as foreign sexuality, racism, and power were also explored (Moon, 1997; Cheng, 2003; Hughes 2003b). A good number of social analyses on military prostitution focus on the women who perform sexual services. However, these socio-political dynamics and cultural notions constitute the demand side of the market and indeed are reflected, for instance, in the going prices of the sexual services provided by different nationality/ race groups of trafficked women in South Korea. White women from far-eastern Russia cost most, followed by those from the Philippines, and so on (Seol et al., 2003).

Also noted is the generalized collusion between government officials and criminal organizations, such as *Yakuza* (Human Rights Watch, 2000), which contributes to the reported "little" recognition of the problem by Japanese authorities and keeps trafficking a high-profit, low-risk venture.[15] More discussion will follow.

Trafficking process[16]

As the trafficking process involves multiple stages, the entire process is carried out by a number of people along the route from the countries of origin to destination. In the region, a formalization of the entire process, especially *recruitment*, has been reported.

In the most immediate level in the countries of origin, there are people who can identify potential victims. They tend to belong to the same social network as the victims, either through family lines or other social groupings. In Colombia, those so-called "contacts" are neighbours or acquaintances of the trafficked persons who are also relatives of the recruiters, intermediaries, or managers in Japan (Molina, 2001). In China, they are called *ma zai* (horse boy) (Xiang, 2004).

The more or less formal recruitment is quite usual in the countries of origin such as Philippines and Thailand, where young women are recruited by either or both local and Korean/Japanese recruiters. Hyperbolic job advertisements are common promising jobs abroad as escorts, servers, and dancers, or otherwise "art performers". In addition to advertisements in public media, mail-order catalogues, scholarship opportunities,[17] and various cultural events are also used in trafficking Colombian women to Japan (Molina, 2001).

Less formal means are used to recruit women and children in remote rural villages in southern China for mostly forced marriages (ILO, 2002). However, the ILO report observes that with the growing urban migration of rural young women there coincides a tendency of trafficking with false promises of work. These women end up being forced to provide sexual services in richer neighbouring countries. Furthermore, in the past the internal trafficking for marriage in China from kidnapping to (re)selling trafficked persons was carried out by independent operators. Now, organized crime gangs overseeing the entire process are increasingly dominating the trade. Even some training for sexual exploitation or begging was mentioned in ILO study on the Yunnan Province (ILO, 2002).

The *transportation* stage seems to be one of the least studied stages of the trafficking process, as far as the materials on East Asia is concerned. While the majority of trafficking cases studied to this date in China involve internal trafficking or very porous border-crossings, attention has not been paid to document forgery, etc.[18] A study on the trafficking of Colombian women (Molina, 2001) describes in some detail a transporting process from Colombia to Japan. Colombian foreign affairs ministry reports that many Colombian minors receive forged documents such as passports and national identity cards to enter Japan (Molina, 2001). The passports from Spain, Peru, Brazil, and France are most frequently used and some of the forged passports are made in Hong Kong SAR for less than US$ 2,000. *Control mechanisms* and related human rights violations drew much attention in the studies examined for this paper, as the bulk of the reports are written in order to raise public awareness of the fairly unknown problem with the general public and authorities.

Debt bondage as the major enforcement tactic is commonly reported among those in the sex industries of Japan, South Korea, and Hong Kong SAR. In addition to the fees that trafficked persons incur when being transported to their destination, the debt accumulates fast with arbitrarily imposed fines for being late to work, drinking, having a boyfriend, possessing a mobile phone, etc. (Seol et al., 2003; Dinan, 2002). In Hong Kong SAR, it is required that women pay back the fee within two or three months of their arrival. The fee is usually around HK$ 10,000 to 16,000, while the average monthly income without "escort service" is around HK$ 4,200 to HK$5,100, making it very difficult to pay back the debt in time (Emerton and Petersen, 2003).

Pressure to perform sexual services in bars and clubs around US military bases in South Korea comes from so-called "drink tickets" of which an unreasonable quota to sell such tickets is imposed on those working as bar hostesses (Lee, 2002; Seol, 2003). As most of those working at military camps do so on an entertainer visa, they are by law prohibited to serve customers, and legally allowed only to conduct performances for entertainment. Nevertheless, if the quota is not met, a penalty is imposed. In order to avoid such a situation, the women provide sexual services.

While there are studies on the exploitative working conditions of those forced to provide sexual services, not much has been reported on the situation of those forced into marriage in China. An unusual report by Human Rights Watch (2002) depicts horrendous situations in which North Korean women fleeing their home country find themselves married to a local man (including Chinese national ethnic Koreans) in rural north-east China. Physical and sexual abuse as well as slavery-like forced labour is quite common, as is the constant threat of being reported to Chinese authorities who are certain to deport them back to North Korea, where they would face severe penalties.

Traffickers

From the literature reviewed, the level of criminal organization involvement in sex trafficking in East Asia seems rather high. Caouette and Saito (1999) report that all 55 Thai women studied were sent to Japan through criminal networks and 90 per cent started working in bars upon arrival. Earlier studies among 100 Filipina returnees from Japan (IOM, 1997) also recorded that one-third had worked in bars controlled by a criminal syndicate.

The organized crime group, called *yakuza*, is believed to have initiated the importation of foreign women to Japan in the 1980s, when demand for sex tours had declined in response to the loud protests by feminist groups in the destinations of such tours, namely, South-East Asian countries and South Korea.

In Japan, as Dinan (2002) observes, *yakuza* enjoys acceptance among the population due to their unusually open style of operation (e.g. registered organization with membership list), contribution to community emergencies, and substantial bribes to government officials. This penetration of the crime group into civil society and government has certainly prevented the Government from taking decisive action against trafficking, although there has been some shift in the Japanese legislation, allowing the police to criminalize some *yakuza* activities.[19]

In spite of the deep involvement of such criminal organizations as *yakuza*, in trafficking of women in East and South-East Asia, it is incorrect to assume that trafficking in East Asia is entirely handled by international criminal gangsters. In South Korea, most companies involved in employing foreign entertainers, such as the recruiting agencies, entertainment management companies, and clubs are run like a family company. In many cases, the division of labour among them exists only on paper, while closely related people share the work. These companies use this loose operation to evade at times responsibilities for delayed wages or prostitution charges. Thus far, there is no indication that these companies operate like a mafia-type criminal organization. Nevertheless, frequent mention is made that organized gangsters are involved in trafficking of women from the far north-eastern part of Russia (Seol et al., 2003). However, the UN Trafficking Protocol's own definition of "organized crime" is such that it broadly covers small trafficking networks as well as large, well-established crime syndicates.

Regarding the smuggling and trafficking in and out of China, there is a debate about the nature of the networks, called "snakeheads". While some describe it as a well-organized, highly sophisticated crime syndicate (e.g. Kwong, 1999), some studies dispute this and emphasize that the networks comprise only loosely connected individuals (e.g. Skeldon, 2000; Pieke et al., 2004). However both share the view that snakehead networks are in a way enmeshed in community networks in places of origin and therefore quite difficult for the authorities to root out or even track.

The relationship between snakehead networks and the normal social networks of the trafficked persons still needs to be clarified. Given the complex nature of human smuggling and trafficking in China, both of which often occur after voluntary emigration is initiated, a government crackdown alone may not be a sufficient solution. More research is needed to identify possible mechanisms with the potential to utilize these social networks to empower migrants and prevent them from being victimized (Xiang, 2004). At the same time, however, this overlap of networks means it is unrealistic to expect human smuggling and trafficking to be eradicated altogether any time soon. Instead, the immediate priority for governments and international agencies may be to reduce the human suffering accompanying smuggling and trafficking.

In the majority of reports on trafficking worldwide, there is a widely held assumption that women are trafficked by men. However, several reports in East Asia point out the growing tendency of the operation of female recruiters who also often were former victims themselves (Molina, 2001; ILO, 2002). They are sometimes forced to recruit other women, often their own friends or relatives, to reduce their own debt to the traffickers.

Other groups of women (internationally known as *mama-sans*) also are involved in the daily operation of bars and clubs in South Korea and Japan. These women most often exercise the first line of control over the trafficked persons. As such, most literature on these women in Japan and South Korea depict them invariably as perpetrators of violence, verbal and physical. However, Emerton and Petersen observe in Hong Kong SAR where prostitution itself is legal (2003) that some *mama-sans* are considered to protect the trafficked women's interests. None of the 18 interviewed women in the sex industry reported any form of abuse by their *mama-sans*. The *mama-san* not only brings the customers to the women but also makes sure the male customers pay for the women's service.

It would be interesting to compare this group of women in the three destinations in East Asia and analyse perhaps the factors that affect the apparent difference in the *mama-sans'* behaviour. This alerts us to the important need for more nuanced research and a truly gendered perspective, which locates the dichotomy of the male traffickers/users and female victims in a broader social context.

DATA COLLECTION, RESEARCH ACTIVITIES, AND KNOWLEDGE GAPS

Data gathering and sharing in East Asia

At the international level, a number of international agencies play an important role in data collection on trafficking. There are databases compiled by the International Organization for Migration (IOM), the United Nations Office on Drugs and Crime (UNODC), and the United Nations Children's Fund (UNICEF). These international organizations play a crucial role in raising awareness worldwide. East Asia, however, has been represented neither sufficiently nor accurately in these databases.

Given the sizable irregular migration flows and the increasing complexity of their organization, the governments in the region face significant challenges in managing migration. Regional cooperation has been enhanced over the past several years. During this period human trafficking has become one of the major concerns of both governments and organizations active in the field of migration. In Asia, several regional processes[20] brought together government representatives to share information and improve the dialogue about diverse aspects of irregular migration. As a recent example, in February 2002, the Bali Conference on People Smuggling, Trafficking in Persons and Related Transnational Crime gave regional priority to the issue of, *inter alia*, human trafficking.

These initiatives also include some activities coordinating data collection on trafficking as these regional counter-trafficking strategies emphasize the need to share data and information within the region. In April 2003, the second Regional Ministerial Conference on People Smuggling, Trafficking in Persons and Related Transnational Crime (known as the Bali Process) was held to further reinforce existing legislation and to improve regional cooperation among law enforcement, and to enhance information and intelligence sharing. Section 5.3 under the Plan of Action of Ad Hoc Expert Group I of the Bali Conference identifies the need to establish a process for analysis of migration flows to, from, and within the region through effective international migration data management approaches.

As indicated earlier, the national governments in the region have begun to collect data. China, for example, released figures after some crackdown efforts. Both Japan and South Korea are believed to have fairly reliable data, including information about undocumented migrants. However, the researchers and activists observe that the governments are not willing to share or publicize some of the data. Furthermore, trafficking is a topic on which a consensus is hard to establish, even by the agencies of the same government in terms of its definition and solution.

Nevertheless, collecting reliable data is the essential first step to developing efficient and targeted measures on trafficking in human beings. Data are critically needed that segregate the male, female, and child victims of trafficking in the region. Additionally, improving research and developing analytical tools is also vital, including those on the character and scale of trafficking and the exploitation mechanisms deployed by organized criminal groups.

Research activities in East Asia

Numerous counter-trafficking initiatives, some containing research components, are being undertaken in South-East Asia, especially on the trafficking occurring in the Mekong region (Derks, 2000; Caouette, 2002). By contrast, one cannot find any similar initiative in North-East Asia with the exception of the ILO-IPEC initiative in southern China. In terms of research reports, IPEC-ILO has a programme involving the Yunnan province of southern China (2002) and some international NGOs, along with IOM have produced reports on Japan and South Korea (Human Rights Watch, 2000; IOM, 1997; Caoette and Saito, 1999; Lee, 2002). Nicola Piper points out elsewhere in this volume that the production of a large amount of information and data on trafficking in South-East Asia is due to the enormous activities of donor and UN agencies. A relatively low volume of activities carried out by these agencies in North-East Asia can perhaps be associated with a lack of sufficient information on the phenomenon. Lack of donor interest translates into lack of funding for local researchers, who otherwise might pursue research on trafficking. The fact that the region is known as a destination area[21] might have also contributed to the lack of research, as source countries tend to be better studied than destination countries.[22]

However, the question of why there is not much research on trafficking in this region needs to be examined beyond these practical issues of donor interest and the availability of local expertise, as both Japan and South Korea are quite capable of providing the needed resources. In addition, activists have long criticized the Japanese Government internationally and internally for its lack of action on trafficking. The South Korean Government also has been criticized for not having taken enough actions to improve the situation of women in the sex industry. China also receives its share of criticism regarding its human rights situation in general and women's rights in particular.

China

After some Chinese scholars conducted surveys on internal trafficking of women in the late 1980s and early 1990s, the Chinese Government took various measures in order to crack down on trafficking. However, since then, this topic has not attracted very much attention from scholars.[23] As noted earlier, the Chinese Government collects and releases from time to time figures on court cases involving apprehension and prosecution of traffickers, and women and children released.

Considering the Chinese Government's aversion to outside influence and that the trafficking of women and children occurs mainly within its territory, it is not surprising that few international agencies can make a case to the Government, which will allow them to research and carry out programme activities. The case in point here involves North Korean women reportedly trafficked in the northeastern provinces of China. An even larger group not being assessed[24] includes men and children fleeing from North Korea since the mid-1990s (if not earlier) due to North Korea's failing economy and repeated environmental disasters. The Chinese Government considers this group of North Koreans illegal economic migrants. Accordingly, those who are caught by the local authorities are sent back to North Korea based on the terms of a treaty with the North Korean Government.

Japan

While individual government officials have made comments from time to time, there is no public position or platform relating to trafficking in Japanese Government print or electronic publications. The three *Trafficking in Persons Reports* produced to date have not generated a public response from the Government either. The possibility of a reduction in the trafficking of women to Japan is hence considered severely constricted by the Government's reticence to publicly acknowledge the problem. After the release in 2003 of the *Trafficking in Persons Report*, Human Rights Watch (2003) published their criticism on the report. An entry concerning Japan's Tier 2 rating reads:

Japan: Japan should be placed in Tier 3. Specific legislation prohibiting trafficking does not exist and there is no indication that there will be. In fact, there are special agreements that facilitate trafficking, allowing the admittance of "entertainers" into the country but not unskilled workers. Trafficking cases are not aggressively pursued and penalties are weak. Though the government has funded international programs to increase awareness in other countries, little to nothing has been done to control the growing trafficking issue in Japan.

Kinsey Dinan of Human Rights Watch observed "[t]he Japanese government has been more reluctant to acknowledge that human trafficking exists in Japan, than other countries" (*Financial Times*, 2003). This reluctance has to be understood in a broader context of regional history and politics. Before and during World War II, the Japanese Government invaded a number of countries in the region (including the Philippines and Taiwan POC, two of the main source countries of trafficked persons into Japan) and colonized South Korea. The Government has been accused of systematically forcing women from these countries, particularly from South Korea, into sexual slavery for the benefit of Japanese soldiers at war. This has been criticized as a form of "state-sponsored" trafficking by the South Korean activists claiming that the Japanese Government should acknowledge their war time atrocities involving the South Korean women and make compensation. Considering this context alone, a government-sponsored research project on trafficking may not be realistically expected.

South Korea

By contrast, the South Korean Government has actively responded since the first *Trafficking in Persons Report* in 2001 that included the country among the 23 countries that did not fulfil the minimum requirement set by the US Victims of Trafficking and Violence Protection Act for combating trafficking. The situation related to trafficking research in South Korea and a discussion of some of the factors that might have contributed to the different developments seen in Japan and South Korea are outlined below.[25]

Firstly, in both Japan and South Korea, prostitution is illegal yet widespread. The Ministry of Gender Equality (MOGE) of the South Korean Government conducted a comprehensive survey of the sex industry in 2002 that concluded that as many as 500,000 women, Korean and foreign, engaged in some form of prostitution in the country. The study estimated that the country's sex industry had generated US$ 22 billion in profits that year (US Department of State, 2004). In Japan, it is estimated that the volume of sex industry reaches approximately US$ 83 billion (*Inter Press Service*, 2003; *Financial Times*, 2003), and the figure of "illegal" migrant women in this field amounts to tens of thousands.[26] Both countries have the notorious entertainer visa to facilitate the temporary stay of those deemed qualified to enter the country. As noted, the number of foreign women in the respective sex industries, however, seems to suggest that Japan has a larger share of foreign women working in the sector than South Korea.

The particular attention that has been given to the matter in South Korea started with the publication of the US Department of State's *Trafficking in Persons Report* released on 12 July 2001. This report ranked South Korea in Tier 3, meaning the Government failed to meet minimum standards in attempting to stop the trafficking in human beings, mostly women and children, who are exploited as prostitutes or placed in low-paying jobs with abusive employers.

Upon release of that report, the South Korean Government charged that the US report negatively portrayed South Korea and was not based on an adequate review of the country's situation.[27] The suggestion that South Korea turns a blind eye to such practices shocked Korean government officials, who also readily admitted to the press that they were completely surprised by this report (Lee, 2002: 10). In addition, the Korean Government urged Washington, DC to make immediate changes to the report so as to reflect the "real" conditions in the country, which included, for example, various articles of South Korean criminal law that heavily punish those involved in the sale of human beings for prostitution.[28]

The issue otherwise would have faded from public attention. Yet it continued to linger in part due to constant media attention on human rights violations among migrant workers in South Korea, including those in the sex industry. In addition, the alleged link of the onset of international trafficking involving those from the Philippines with the existence of the notorious Rest and Recreation facilities of the US military base in South Korea kept some US media interest in the South Korean trafficking case.[29]

The then newly established Ministry of Gender Equality (MOGE)[30] in the South Korean Government took up the issue and in 2003 commissioned a survey to study the foreign women engaged in the South Korean sex industry. In September 2003, the Ministry also organized an international conference[31] with the Justice Ministry. A wide range of South Korean authorities, representatives of national governments in the Asia Pacific region, international organizations, and other experts from national and international NGOs contributed to this meeting that focused particularly on identifying the needed action and relevant target groups for further awareness raising on trafficking in the region.

Further impetus was given to the issue after the appointment of a new minister, Madame Eun-hui Ghee, who had working experience as an activist to abolish prostitution. With the MOGE initiative, the South Korean national assembly passed in March 2004 a draft law, Prostitution Victims Prevention Act,[32] which heavily criminalizes the acts of intermediaries in the sex industry. Whether or not this Act will qualify the South Korean Government as a government with a decent anti-trafficking law will have to wait until legal experts can fully examine its contents. Nevertheless, it does include a clause in which a temporary delay of deportation can be granted on a case-by-case base if a designated deportee is cooperating with law enforcement bodies in an investigation.

In sum, such factors as a willing government, an active civil society, and perhaps a fortunate turn of events within South Korean politics plus a little outside pressure seemed to have contributed to recent favourable developments. It is particularly positive that the MOGE has started its efforts by commissioning the unusually large survey study among non-Koreans in the sex industry. However, much work is needed to transform the research results into a knowledge base that can be operationalized for local policy purposes, as well as for the various government agencies and NGOs who would participate, along with others, in assisting trafficked persons. Furthermore, the earlier mentioned lack of cooperation among the South Korean Government agencies, in particular the national police force, needs to be improved.

Remaining gaps in knowledge

To date, research studies on trafficking in women in East Asia have been descriptive, qualitative analyses based on interviews with trafficked persons, government officials, and representatives of civil society. These descriptive studies have been crucial in understanding the operation of traffickers and the impact on victims, but they provide no systematic way to estimate the precise magnitude of the problem.

The research needs are many in East Asia, specifically:

- A more comprehensive understanding of trafficking in China has to be established through research, particularly with the growing regional economic disparities within the country. More up-to-date research on Japan is also urgently needed to develop counter-trafficking activities.
- More research and exchange of information on trafficking in children is another area that is lacking in the region, especially given the tendency of younger victims being reported.
- More in-depth analyses of the root causes, supply and demand, trafficking networks, and the economic consequences of the various kinds of trafficking in human beings are needed. As suggested earlier, a gendered analysis is needed involving both men and women in the process.

- Research dealing with the Internet needs to be initiated,[33] as the Internet is a space through which a lot of trafficking-related activities are presumed to happen according to some media in South Korea.

Despite the clandestine nature of the phenomenon, it is absolutely crucial to develop reliable measures of trafficking activity; without such measures, the governments and the international community cannot evaluate the performance of their counter-trafficking activities. The success in identifying indicators and measures of trafficking depends on the accurate conceptualization of the framework and definitions of trafficking. One of the factors hindering research and policy on trafficking has been the lack of definitions and clarity in distinguishing among different phenomena involving movement of people across borders. The United Nations Convention Against Transnational Organized Crime and its supplementing Protocols[34] does provide the bases for a conceptual framework for trafficking that is differentiated with smuggling, but not without some critical caveats.[35]

As far as Japan and South Korea are concerned, it is not entirely unrealistic to develop a trafficking process model for sexual exploitation, given qualitative information on the various stages in the process through which women are taken from source countries to the sex industries of these two countries. The information does show remarkable similarity in the process of recruitment, transportation, deployment, and control. This is because the overwhelming majority of the trafficking cases to the two countries is, as shown earlier, for sexual exploitation with quite a high level of involvement by criminal organization. This model can (at least during the start-up and set-up phase) exclude trafficking for labour exploitation, domestic service, or organ removal. In terms of migration data in general, both South Korea and Japan have advantages, as the former has heavily defended land borders and the latter is an island, which make the monitoring of arrivals and departure relatively easier.[36]

Additionally, as unfortunate as it may be, these countries both do have data on their issuance of entertainer visas, and their estimates of overstayers are fairly reliable and can be used at least in a longitudinal analysis. Furthermore, South Korea conducted a de facto regularization exercise in 2002 and is going through a process in which undocumented migrants can register and benefit from an upcoming employment permit system. This series of factors puts this Government in a rather unique position of knowing precisely the composition of the foreigners residing in its territory in an irregular situation.

Still, further government cooperation is needed in accessing data on court cases in order to be able to accurately know the profile of trafficked persons as well as that of the traffickers. Additionally, interviews with the incarcerated traffickers would be of enormous importance to verify the qualitative information gathered mostly from trafficked persons.

NOTES

1. This is only a general perception, as there is no way a precise figure can be generated about the extent of trafficking. The perception is generated partly due to growing public interest and frequent coverage in various media.
2. This paper will not discuss the already much-studied irregular migration out of the region that originates from the People's Republic of China. Furthermore, it should be noted that even after the United Nations provided definitions distinguishing "smuggling" and "trafficking", the usage of both terms, often in one article, continues in some media reports on China.
3. In China, external migration remains insignificant despite much attention to its outflows to North American and European countries, while the size of internal migration to emerging urban centres has exponentially grown since the 1990s.
4. These governments, however, do facilitate the settlement of highly skilled professionals.
5. In August 2004, the South Korean Government started an employment permit system, which allows temporary employment of foreigners up to one year (renewable up to two times).
6. Several Beijing-based researchers contacted during the preparation of this paper are not aware of any English literature on trafficking. The Chinese Women's Federation did do some research related to government practices in the Yunnan province (in Chinese), however, this too was unavailable at the time of this writing.
7. One focus group meeting was inadvertently held in the house of a woman who was later identified as a former pimp and broker. This was found to affect the conversations and the relationship among the women and the researchers. For this and other reasons, data from a focus group discussion needs to be handled with much care.
8. While preparing my paper (Lee, 2002), I contacted the Ministry of Justice who was at the time preparing the written response to the US report. The Ministry official mentioned that collecting related court cases would involve enormous work internally within the Ministry as information on such cases was not centralized and is spread throughout the country's local courts.
9. Both 2002 and 2003 TIP Report mentioned that some South Korean women are trafficked to Japan and North America. Some of the recent media coverage on this includes Crecente (2003) and Fox News (2004). It is well known and supported by the Ministry of Justice, GOJ with their statistics that a good number of South Korean women (most of them overstayers) are found in the Japanese sex industry, although the South Korean Government (and possibly the Japanese

Government) do not seem to think these Koreans are trafficked (personal communication with the government officials).

10. In general, statistics are most easily available for offender and victim-related data. These data can be obtained from police records, prosecution, and court statistics. Victim-related data might be available from NGOs and international organizations. There are direct indicators, such as criminal justice statistics, which show the offences committed. But there are also indirect indicators, such as the number of visas issued for people working in the entertainment business, which is often the destination of trafficked persons. Data collection efforts should include both direct and indirect indicators.

11. For example, it is reported that "among the total 30,000 Thai women living in Japan, only around 8,000 had legal visas, while most of them were tricked by Japanese Yakuza gang into working as prostitutes", cited in Protection Project, 22 August 2003, and "Large number of Thai women forced into Japanese sex trade", *Chinese Media People's Daily*, 19 August 2003.

12. This number is also used in a more recent reference, Babidor (2003). Babidor confirmed that this estimate is based on personal communication with her informants in Japan who are involved in migrant worker and trafficking issues.

13. With rising affluence and increased participation of women in the labour force, a market for foreign domestic workers has been established in many countries. Filipinas are widely popular as domestic help in the Middle East as well as in Hong Kong SAR in East Asia.

14. Militarization is "an act of assembling and putting into readiness for war or other emergency", according to www.cogsci.princeton.edu/cgi-bin/webwn. Militarization may suggest a society dominated by military values, ideology, and patterns of behaviour. This definition accounts not only for the role of the army itself but also the authoritarianism, oppression, and violence that become a routine part of state affairs. For a detailed discussion on militarization, see Enloe, 2000.

15. The Government of Japan has started paying attention to trafficking and ratified *Japan's Action Plan of Measures to Combat Trafficking in Persons* in December 2004.

16. A trafficking process can range from the recruitment of migrants and their possible training and preparation, the transportation of the migrants to their country of destination, to the final insertion of the migrants into the exploitative work.

17. These opportunities are advertised in a catalogue form. The destination for such scholarships is the United States travelling via Japan.

18. This is certainly not the case for international migration of the Chinese, especially smuggling (e.g. Chin, 1999).

19. For example, the Law Concerning Prevention of Unjust Acts by Violent Group Members that went into effect in 1992, cited in Dinan, 2002.

20. Many regional consultative processes have emerged over the past decade or so to address migration related issues. These processes have focused on irregular migration, and often singled out specific topics such as trafficking or smuggling. An overriding concern is to ensure jointly that such aberrant forms of migration do not pose security problems and contribute to regional destabilization.

Regional processes bear witness to the fact that, while border management remains a sovereign issue, governments acting alone can no longer effectively deal with migration. The processes vary greatly, but they generally share a common objective and a commitment of the participating countries, despite their non-binding character.

21. For example, Kangapunta (2003) notes "East Asia is slightly higher as a receiving area than it is as an origin or transit region. Countries cited as destination countries in East Asia were China, Taiwan POC, Hong Kong SAR, Macao SAR, Republic of Korea, and Mongolia." In this paper based on media coverage, Japan, the best-known destination in East Asia is missing, demonstrating the fact that proper research must complement media reports.

22. In Europe, Sweden and the Netherlands have national rapporteurs who publish every year reports on known cases of trafficking. The German police keep some related information.

23. Biao Xiang made this observation after consulting several researchers in Beijing early 2004.

24. UNHCR Beijing has asked reportedly for the Chinese Government's cooperation on their situation assessment efforts.

25. For the sake of a fair comparison, one should note that the Japanese population was 127,096,000 in 2000, while that of South Korea was 46,740,000 in the same year.

26. According to *Inter Press Service*, 24 January 2003, the Justice Ministry of Japan reports that as of January 2002, there are around 224,067 overstayers in Japan, of which 105,945 are women, More than 46 per cent of these women work as bar hostesses and prostitutes (i.e., 103,371), the rest as waitresses and factory workers. By nationality, South Koreans comprise 25 per cent of these overstayers followed by the Philippines and Thailand.

27. A summary of the South Korean Government's rebuttal to the points made or implied in the US *Trafficking in Persons Report 2001* is included in the appendix of Lee, 2002.

28. The second *US Trafficking in Persons Report* (2002) ranked South Korea as a Tier 1 country. This has not stopped the criticism from local NGOs. I have received repeatedly questions on the base of this change from mainly the US and South Korean media.

29. I was interviewed by the local correspondents of *Newsweek* and *Time* magazines in this very linkage and possible collusion between the US military and South Koreans including bar owners around the military camps. Local activists were interviewed as well. Both news magazines, however, either cancelled or changed the core argument of their intended articles on the subject.

30. The Ministry of Gender Equality, Government of Republic of Korea was established on 29 January 2001.

31. The Expert Group Meeting on Prevention of International Trafficking and Promotion of Public Awareness Campaign was held in Seoul, South Korea, from 22-23 September 2003. Meeting materials can be accessed at www.mogego.kr/eng/trafficking/index.jsp.

32. The translation is mine as the official English translation of the Korean law is not yet available.
33. For example, Raymond and Hughes (2001) drew qualitative data from men's writing on the Internet about their procurement of women and their description of the sex industry.
34. *Protocol against the Smuggling of Migrants by Land, Sea and Air*, and *Protocol to Prevent, Suppress and Punish Trafficking in Persons, Especially Women and Children*, both supplementing the *United Nations Convention Against Transnational Organized Crime*. Japan and South Korea are the only two signatories for both protocols in East Asia. However, it should be noted that "being a signatory" of an international convention does not mean that the state party is immediately obliged to follow the contents of such a convention. The international convention does not take effect until the national legal regime has been adjusted accordingly.
35. For example, it is widely acknowledged that a term such as "organized crime" is too widely defined by the Convention, as it defines a criminal group as "three or more people working together to commit one or more serious crimes for material benefit".
36. In addition, the vast majority of migrants in both Japan and South Korea are workers, legal or illegal, with a small number of non-working dependants. These dependants are the spouses and/or children of legal migrants who belong to various professional ranks of the economy. However, it is noted that there exists a small but growing population of children by undocumented migrant parents.

REFERENCES

Agence France Presse
    2001   "Six executed in one of China's largest trafficking in women cases", Agence France Presse.
    2002   "American, South American on trial in China for human trafficking", Agence France Presse.
    2002   "China executes traffickers in women", *Agence France Presse*.
    2002   "Five jailed for trafficking Vietnamese women to China", Agence France Presse.
    2002   "New report highlights plight of trafficked women in S. Korea", Agence France Presse.
    2002   "Vietnam police bust China-US people smuggling ring", Agence France Presse.
    2003   "China sentences five for trafficking in women and children", Agence France Presse.
    2003   "Hundreds arrested in Chinese human-smuggling crackdown", Agence France Presse.
    2003   "Japan criticized for being soft on human traffickers", Agence France Presse.

2003   "Japan gives 1.21 million dollars to stop trafficking from Vietnam, Cambodia", *Agence France Presse*.
2003   "Philippines uncovers human smuggling syndicate", *Agence France Presse*.
2003   "Police arrest 18 for trafficking women", *Agence France Presse*.
2003   "Prisoner abuse, human trafficking cited in US human rights report on Japan", *Agence France Presse*.
2003   "South Korea bans Filipino dancers over prostitution fears", *Agence France Presse*.
2003   "Trafficked Thai woman tells UN meet of decade-long Japanese ordeal", *Agence France Presse*.
Asian Migration News
2004   "Anti-trafficking campaign", *Asian Migration News*, 1-15 March.
Asis, M.M.B.
2002   "Women migrants in Asia: the hands that rock the cradle", presented at Globalization and International Migration: Asian and European Experiences, 12-13 March, CERI-Science – Po, Paris.
Associated Press
2000   "Philippines raises concern over treatment of Filipino women in Malaysia, South Korea", Associated Press.
2001   "Indictments announced in South Korean, Chinese smuggling ring", Associated Press.
2001   "Sex trial to get underway", Associated Press.
2001   "Six executed in China for trafficking women, children", Associated Press.
2002   "China says it's working hard to end trafficking in women and children", Associated Press.
2002   "FBI busts Asian prostitution ring", Associated Press.
2002   "From soaplands to streetwalkers: Japan's sex industry sells dreams, desperation", Associated Press.
2002   "Women trafficked to South Korea to provide sexual services to US servicemen", Associated Press.
2003   "10 Chinese nationals on human trafficking charges", Associated Press.
2003   "China, Taiwan cooperate in prostitution case", Associated Press.
Babidor, S.L.
2003   "Sexual abuse and human trafficking in Japan", UCLA International Institute, 17 November.
Bangkok Post
1997   "More foreign workers join sex industry as fewer Thai girls enter flesh trade", *Bangkok Post*.
2002   "Embassy in Japan moves to stem influx labourers, prostitutes 'hurt national image'", *Bangkok Post*.
2003   "Sex slaves could get cheap tickets home", *Bangkok Post*.
2003   "Most women from Chiang Rai, Korea", *Bangkok Post*.
2003   "Cracks in the melting pot", *Bangkok Post*.
Caouette, T.
2002   *Trafficking in Women and Children in the Mekong Sub-Region (UNIAP), Mid-term Evaluation Report*, United Nation's Inter-Agency Project, Bangkok.

Caouette, T., and Y. Saito
  1999   *To Japan and Back: Thai Women Recount their Experiences*, International Organization for Migration, Geneva.
Cheng, S.
  2002   *Transnational Desires: "Trafficked" Filipinas in US Military Camp Towns in South Korea*, Ph.D. Dissertation, Department of Anthropology, Oxford University.
  2003   "'R and R' on a 'hardship tour': GIs and Filipina entertainers in South Korea", *American Sexuality Magazine*, 1(5).
Chin, K-L
  1999   *Smuggled Chinese: Clandestine Immigration to the United States*, Temple University Press, Philadelphia.
China Daily
  2000   "British police arrive in China to probe deaths of illegal immigrants", *China Daily*.
  2001   "Prosecutor demands up to 20 years imprisonment in Dover immigrants trial", *China Daily*.
  2001   "ROK pledges to punish snakeheads", *China Daily*.
  2001   "South Korea apologizes for deaths of dumped Chinese", *China Daily*.
  2002   "Joint police net nabs human smuggling kingpin", *China Daily*.
  2002   "Poverty breeds woman trafficking," *China Daily*.
  2002   "Program to cut human trafficking", *China Daily*.
  2002   "South Koreans jailed in fatal stowaway incident", *China Daily*.
  2003   "Baby smuggling cases shock public", *China Daily*.
  2003   "Border police foil human smuggling bid", *China Daily*.
  2003   "Calls to curb cross-border human trafficking", *China Daily HK Edition*.
  2003   "Human trafficking gang smashed", *China Daily*.
  2003   "Life jail for people smuggling kingpin", *China Daily*.
  2003   "Project to crack down on human trafficking", *China Daily*.
Coalition Against Trafficking in Women (CATW)
  1999a   "The factbook on global sexual exploitation", CATW.
  1999b   "Trafficking in women and prostitution in the Asia Pacific", CATW.
Coomaraswamy, R.
  2003   "Report of the Special Rapporteur on violence against women: trafficking in women and forced prostitution", UNHCR, Geneva.
Crecente, B.D.
  2003   "Sex-slave underworld Korean women seek new life in US, end up in Colorado brothels", *The Rocky Mountain News* (Colorado), 22 November, www.rockymountainnews.com/drmn/local/article/0,1299,DRMN_15_2449170,00.html.
Daily Yomiuri
  2003   *Daily Yomiuri*, 5 October.
Derks, A.
  2000   *Combating Trafficking in South-East Asia: A Review of Policy and Programme Responses*, Migration Research Series, IOM, Geneva.
Deutsche Presse-Agentur
  2002   "China to try gang accused of smuggling 730 people to Japan", Deutsche Presse-Agentur.

2002   "China, Vietnam plan to combat cross-border sex trafficking", Deutsche Presse-Agentur.

2002   "Police break up huge human trafficking ring", Deutsche Presse-Agentur.

2002   "Police bust Vietnam-China prostitution ring", Deutsche Presse-Agentur.

2002   "Poverty, policy fuel China's trade in women and children", Deutsche Presse-Agentur.

2002   "Vietnam jails five for trafficking women to China", Deutsche Presse-Agentur.

2003   "Web-based child prostitution doubles in Japan in 2002", Deutsche Presse-Agentur.

Dinan, K.A.
2002   "Trafficking in women from Thailand to Japan: the role of organized crime and governmental response", *Harvard Asia Quarterly*, 6(3).

Eckholm, E.
2002   "Desire for sons drives use of prenatal scans in China", *New York Times*, 21 June.

Emerton, R.
2001   "Trafficking of women into Hong Kong for the purpose of prostitution: preliminary research findings", Occasional Paper 3, Centre for Comparative and Public Law, Hong Kong.

Emerton, R., and C. Petersen
2003   "Migrant nightclub/escort workers in Hong Kong: an analysis of possible human rights violations", Occasional Paper 8, Centre for Comparative and Public Law, Hong Kong.

Enloe, C.
1993   *The Morning After: Sexual Politics at the End of the Cold War*, University of California Press, Berkeley.

2000   *Maneuvers: The International Politics of Militarizing Women's Lives*, University of California Press, Berkeley.

Financial Times
2003   "Tokyo under fire for turning blind eye to trafficking in women", *Financial Times*, 6 February.

Fox News
2004   "Smuggled South Koreans turn to sex slavery", Fox News, 20 March.

Hughes, D.M.
2003a   "Trafficking of women and children in East Asia and beyond: a review of US policy", testimony before the Subcommittee of East Asian and Pacific Affairs Senate Foreign Relations Committee, 9 April.

2003b   "The driving force of sex trafficking: the demand", Vital Speeches of the Day, 69(6): 182-184.

Hugo, G.
1998   "International migration of women in South-east Asia: major patterns and policy issues", in C.M. Firdausy (Ed.), *International Migration in South-east Asia*, The South-east Asian Studies Regional Exchange Program, The Toyota Foundation and the Indonesian Institute of Sciences, Jakarta.

Human Rights Watch
2000   "Owed justice: Thai women trafficked into debt bondage in Japan", *Human Rights Watch*, New York.
2002   "The invisible exodus: North Koreans in the People's Republic of China", *Human Rights Watch*, 14(8)C.
2003   "US State Department trafficking report undercut by lack of analysis", Human Rights Watch, New York, 11 June.
Inter Press Service
2003   "Japan: another risk for sex workers: illegal status", Inter Press Service, 24 January.
International Labour Organization-International Programme on the Elimination of Child Labour (ILO-IPEC)
2002   *Yunnan Province, China: Situation of Trafficking in Children and Women*, ILO, Bangkok.
International Organization for Migration (IOM)
1997   "Trafficking in women to Japan for sexual exploitation: a survey on the case of Filipino women", IOM, Geneva.
2001   *Trafficking in Migrants*, quarterly bulletin No. 23, April, IOM, Geneva.
2004a   *Direct Assistance for Victims of Trafficking: IOM Handbook*, IOM, Geneva.
2004b   "Trafficking in persons: an analysis of Afghanistan", IOM, Geneva.
Kangapunta, K.
2003   *Desk Review for the Programme of Action Against Trafficking in Minors and Young Women from Nigeria into Italy for the Purpose of Sexual Exploitation*, United Nations Interregional Crime and Justice Research Institute (UNICRI), UNICRI/UNODC Project on Trafficking.
Korea Herald
2000   "10 arrested in connection with Russian prostitutes", *Korea Herald*.
2002   "Foreign female victims of abuse eligible for free aid", *Korea Herald*.
2002   "Government to tighten rules on entertainment visa applicants", *Korea Herald*.
2002   "Korean survey of sex workers on legalization", *Korea Herald*.
2002   "Korea's saddest profession", *Korea Herald*.
2002   "Police bust human smuggling ring", *Korea Herald*.
2002   "Seoul enhances protection of women's rights", *Korea Herald*.
Korean Times
2002   "Activist to testify at US hearing on human trafficking: South Korean activist will testify at US congressional", *Korean Times*.
2002   "Diary of Filipino victim of forced prostitution", *Korean Times*.
2002   "Government to rehabilitate women sex workers", *Korean Times*.
2002   "Lawsuit represents test case for protection of human rights", *Korean Times*.
2002   "Most female E-6 visa holders work in nightspots", *Korean Times*.
2002   "Priest calls on Philippine Government to act against human trafficking", *Korean Times*.
2002   "Prostitutes use visitors visas to enter Korea", *Korean Times*.
2003   "Local film series targets US military", *Korean Times*.

Kwong, P.
  1999   *Forbidden Workers: Illegal Chinese Immigrants and American Labour*,
          New Press, New York.
Kyodo News Service
  2002   "Trafficking of Female Foreign Workers Increasing", Kyodo News Serv-
          ice, 19 July.
Lee, H-K
  2003   "Gender, migration and civil activism in South Korea", *Asian and Pacific
          Migration Journal*, 12(1-2): 127-153.
Lee, J., JH
  2002   *A Review of Data on Trafficking in Korea*, IOM, Geneva.
Lim, L.L., and N. Oishi
  1996   "International labour migration of Asian women: distinctive characteris-
          tics and policy concerns", in G. Battistella and A. Paganoni (Eds), *Asian
          Women in Migration*, Scalabrini Migration Center, Quezon City.
Mainichi Daily News
  2001   "Boat crew reeled in over human-smuggling", *Mainichi Daily News*.
  2001   "Coast guard sinks mass human-smuggling attempt", *Mainichi Daily
          News*.
  2001   "Human-smuggling ad tempts Chinese couple", *Mainichi Daily News*.
  2001   "Indonesian human-smuggling scheme blown open", *Mainichi Daily
          News*.
  2002   "Bust on forced prostitution ring nets big catch", *Mainichi Daily News*.
  2002   "Chinese gang boss raked in 40 mil. yen cut from crimes", *Mainichi Daily
          News*.
  2002   "Chinese target weak within own society in Japan", *Mainichi Daily News*.
  2002   "Coast guard, cops, and customs raid human smuggling ship", *Mainichi
          Daily News*.
  2002   "Police crack people-smuggling ring, net 52 Chinese", *Mainichi Daily
          News*.
  2002   "Smuggled Chinese destined for Tokyo hideout", *Mainichi Daily News*.
  2003   "Colombian stripper's deportation highlights slave trade in Japan",
          Mainichi Daily News.
  2003   "Filipinas sent to Japan forced into prostitution: survey", *Mainichi Daily
          News*.
  2003   "Gangsters suspected in brutal murder of young family", *Mainichi Daily
          News*.
  2003   "Japan faces international probe over sex slaves", *Mainichi Daily News*.
  2004   "International marriage scams on the rise in Japan", *Mainichi Daily News*.
Marshal, S.
  1999   "Vietnamese women are kidnapped and later sold in China as brides",
          Wall Street Journal, 2 August.
Methodist Resolution Supporting Human Rights in China
  2004   Methodist Resolution Supporting Human Rights in China, 2 March.
Molina, F.F.
  2001   "Japan, the mecca for trafficking in Colombian women", http://www.
          december18.net/web/general/page.php?pageID=45&menuID=5 8&lang=
          EN&seclang=0.

Moon K.
1997   *Sex Among Allies: Military Prostitution in U.S.-Korea Relations*, Columbia University Press, New York.
Pieke, F.N., et al.
2004   *Transnational Chinese: Fujianese Migrants in Europe*, Stanford University Press, California.
Pomfret, J.
2001   "In China's countryside, 'it's a boy!' too often", *Washington Post*, 29 May.
Protection Project
2002   "A human rights report on trafficking of persons, especially women and children: Japan", *Protection Project*.
Sellek, Y.
1996   "Female foreign migrant workers in Japan: working for the yen", *Japan Forum*, 8(2): 159-175.
Seol, D.H.
2003   "International sex trafficking in women in Korea: its causes, consequences, and countermeasures", Expert Group Meeting on Prevention of International Trafficking and Promotion of Promotion of Public Awareness Campaign.
Seol, D.H., et al.
2003   *The Current Situation of Migrant Women Employed in the Sex and Entertainment Sector of Republic of Korea* (English translation of a report written in Korean, *Oeguin Yeoseong Seongmaemae Silt'aejosa*), Ministry of Gender Equality, Republic of Korea.
Skeldon, R.
2000   *Myths and Realities of Chinese Irregular Migration*, Migration Research Series, International Organization for Migration, Geneva.
Stop-traffic
2001   "Philippines: child trafficking rises in Asia – ILO", Stop-traffic electronic list, http://www.stop-traffic.org.
2002   "Government targets abuse of entertainer visas", Stop-traffic electronic list, http://www.stop-traffic.org.
2003   "Sex trade exploitation: destination Japan", Stop-traffic electronic list, http://www.stop-traffic.org.
The Japan Times
2002   "Foreign brides fill the gap in rural Japan", *The Japan Times*.
2003a   "Japan not attacking root causes of abused, exploited foreigners: experts", *The Japan Times*.
2003b   "The foreign angle", *The Japan Times*.
2003c   "Passports targeted by sex traffickers", *The Japan Times*.
United Nations Children's Fund (UNICEF)
2001   *Children on the Edge*, UNICEF.
2003   *End Child Exploitation: Stop the Traffic*, UNICEF.
United Nations Office on Drugs and Crime (UNODC)
2002   "Countering child trafficking: a united response to a global problem", *United Nation Office on Drugs and Crime*.

US Department of State
  2001 "Global trafficking in persons report 2001: Peoples Republic of China", US Department of State, Washington, DC, July.
  2003 *Trafficking in Persons Report*, US Department of State, Washington, DC.
  2004 *Country Reports on Human Rights Practices 2003*, US Department of State, Washington, DC, 25 February.
Wickramasekera, P.
  2002 "Asian labour migration: issues and challenges in an era of globalization", International Migration Papers 57, International Labour Office, Geneva.
Xiang, B.
  2004 "Network failure", paper presented at the 5th Conference of the International Socicty for the Study of Chinese Overseas, 10-14 May, Elsinore (Helsingør), Denmark.
Xinhua News Agency
  2000 "HK urges joint efforts in striking human trafficking", Xinhua News Agency.
  2001 "East China province clamps down on human smuggling", Xinhua News Agency.
  2003 "ASEAN, China to intensify cooperation against transnational crime", Xinhua News Agency.
  2003 "Chinese police nab gang that sold 24 babies to wealthy clients", Xinhua News Agency.
  2003 "Human trafficking case adjudicated in east China city", Xinhua News Agency.
  2003 "ILO, China join to combat trafficking in children and women", Xinhua News Agency.
  2003 "Japan, ASEAN sign partnership declaration", Xinhua News Agency.
Zlotnik, H.
  2003 "The global dimensions of female migration", *Migration Information Source*, www.migrationinformation.org/Feature/display.cfm?id=109.

A Problem by a Different Name?
A Review of Research on Trafficking in South-East Asia and Oceania

Nicola Piper*

INTRODUCTION[1]

Trafficking in human beings is a global phenomenon which has been subject to increasing international attention in recent years. Anti-trafficking initiatives have mushroomed, globally and regionally, and trafficking projects have become an important item on international development agencies' agendas (Marshall, 2001).[2] Global and regional responses have been phenomenal, so much so that "(f)rom a poorly funded, NGO women's issue in the early 1980s, human trafficking has entered the global agenda of high politics, eliciting in recent years significant legislative and other action from the United States Congress, the EU and the UN" (Wong, forthcoming). These global developments constitute an important background to the issue of researching and generating data about trafficking in general, and specifically in the Asia Pacific region.

Asia constitutes a region often described as a hub of trafficking in persons, particularly for the purposes of sexual exploitation. The largest number of children and women trafficked are said to be *within* or *from* Asia.[3] In this sense, trafficking is not only a national and international issue, but also essentially a regional issue. As a result, a number of anti-trafficking initiatives have been instigated in the Asia Pacific, resulting in all governments in this region taking some kind of interest in, and steps toward, tackling this problem (Marshall, 2001).[4] At the same time, the lack of systematic research (as opposed to paying mere lip service to this issue) has been widely commented upon. As a result, reliable data on the trafficking of humans that would allow comparative analyses and the design of precise countermeasures is scarce. In this sense, the

* Asia Research Institute, National University of Singapore, Singapore.

findings from this research confirm findings from other regional contexts (such as, for example, Kelly, 2002). At the same time, there are some notable differences which distinguish Asia from other parts of the world.

The specific part of the Asia Pacific region dealt with in this paper, South-East Asia and Oceania, has been of great interest to scholars analysing domestic and international migratory flows for quite some time, by paying more or less attention to the specific issue of trafficking. Oceania has been subject to very little research in the context of trafficking. Existing studies mostly revolve around refugee movements, and in Australia and New Zealand, in particular, around issues of integration and multiculturalism in the context of settlement migration. South-East Asia, by contrast, has been highlighted in the existing literature as having great significance with regard to extensive intra-regional trafficking taking place around Thailand – one of the major source, transit, and destination countries for trafficking in women and children for the purpose of sexual exploitation. Another country that has emerged as a sending, receiving, and transit area for both domestic and international trafficking is Indonesia, but unlike the Greater Mekong subregion,[5] it has not been subject to much research in this particular regard. The Philippines is also a source country of great significance. In Thailand and the Philippines, connections have been made in the (mostly feminist) literature between trafficking for sexual exploitation and prosperous sex tourism as part of both countries' economic developmental policies. Cambodia has more recently become subject to attention for a more specific sex tourism, namely that of *child* sex tourism. A vast range of projects and programmes – largely sponsored by United Nations (UN) agencies and international donors – have been instigated on various aspects of trafficking in the Mekong subregion and the Philippines. Indonesia, on the other hand, has not yet been given as much attention by donors in this regard. Overall, there is quite an extensive literature on all sorts of aspects of trafficking on South-East Asia available – at least as far as the source countries are concerned.

By contrast, countries which are usually classified as "destination countries" in the region under investigation here – i.e. Malaysia, Singapore, Australia, and New Zealand – are more known in the context of receiving foreign migrant workers and have to a far lesser extent been subject to analysis in the specific context of trafficking – which does not automatically mean that trafficking does not occur. Even less is known about the Pacific Islands in this regard. Most of the literature on Fiji, Samoa, Tonga, and other Polynesian islands deals with labour *out*-migration (Bedford et al., 2002). These islands have, however, been described as "potentially vulnerable" to trafficking.[6] East Timor is another potential source country which deserves attention in the near future.[7] As so little is known and written about trafficking to, between, and from these islands, the remainder of this paper will not discuss this subregion any further. To do so, a separate research exercise is needed.

This article has the main objective to review existing research and literature on trafficking in South-East Asia and Oceania in the larger context of regional migration patterns. It attempts to identify key themes and critically assess the knowledge base and gaps that emerge from this review. The major issue areas which are being addressed are: (1) quantification and definitional issues, and (2) resulting responses to trafficking by policy makers and law enforcers. Data and studies from this region confirm findings from other regions in many respects: (1) trafficking in humans emerges as a complex phenomenon that requires multi-dimensional responses; (2) despite its high and growing profile, statistical data and precise figures do not exist; and (3) although our understanding of the processes, dynamics, and underlying causes of human trafficking has substantially improved, it remains largely fragmented. Reflecting the feminization of migratory movements in general and the growing demand and supply in the sex industries, it appears as if women comprise the bulk of those trafficked. There are, however, also some region-specific issues and trends which yield different findings from studies in other regional contexts.

BACKGROUND

Approach and methodology

Although clearly also an internal problem, trafficking of South-East Asians within the same region, as well as to Oceania, cannot be divorced from broader international migration patterns and policies as well as specific characteristics that have been widely acknowledged globally: the "feminization" as well as "illegalization" of labour migration. In addition, South-East Asia is also characterized by high incidences of child migration, domestically and across borders. Despite the rapid rise in women's participation in these migration flows, the discussion of trafficking cannot exclude male victims. In light of the Asian region being notorious for its large numbers of irregular migrants with few legal channels available, there is evidence of men migrating under precarious conditions that can be classified as trafficking. In addition, women and children are not only trafficked for sexual exploitation, but also for other types of work. Among the various studies on child trafficking, reference has in fact been made to boys as well as the trafficking of girls for non-sex work (Archavanitkul, 1998).

To take a perspective on trafficking located within broader migration pattern and policies has often been criticized for disregarding human rights issues. However, this does not have to be so. There is in fact an increasing literature analysing the various exploitative and abusive aspects of migration, pointing to the violation of international standards set by various United Nations (UN) and International Labour Organization (ILO) conventions (e.g. ILO, 2004; Pécoud and de Gucheneire, 2004; Satterthwaite, forthcoming; Piper, forthcoming). In this literature, the emphasis is not only on the movement aspects but also on the exploitative aspects of the processes and outcomes of such movement. Furthermore, studies focusing on trafficking for sexual exploitation have pointed to the serious violations of women's human rights. Thus, Gallagher's argument is fully agreed with here that "human rights are not a separate consideration or an additional perspective. They are the common thread" (2001: 1004).

With trafficking being strongly linked to the issue of sexual exploitation, this involves a debate which revolves around two fundamentally opposed views regarding the legitimacy of the sex industry, and thus, also around the choice of terminology. In this way, whether to speak of "prostitution" as opposed to "commercial sex work", often reflects the ideological position of the speaker/author. It is, in particular, the issue of "consent" which is highly contested, with some proponents arguing that a woman never consents to working in prostitution and that she is driven by socio-economic circumstances seriously limiting her choices. This is a somewhat broader (and older) debate, full engagement with which is beyond the scope of this paper. Instead, this review follows Surtees (2003: 63) in choosing to speak of commercial sex workers (rather than prostitutes) to avoid projecting any negative associations on individuals involved in this type of income-generating activity, and also to make the comparison, in terms of trafficking, with other forms of forced labour.

The literature and data search undertaken for this paper involved desk research as well as fieldwork. The desk research revolved around detailed Internet searches on: (a) anti-trafficking programmes and projects by various UN and donor agencies; (b) literature searches through e.g. the *Violence Against Women Online Resources*; (c) contacting NGOs, academics, and government officials via e-mail; and (d) use of survey questionnaire data compiled as part of the BALI Process.[8] Identification of existing studies was limited to publications in the English language and can, thus, not claim to be exhaustive. Fieldwork was conducted between December 2003 and April 2004 in Australia, New Zealand, and Fiji involving informal, semi-structured interviews with government officials, national commissions for human rights, academics, and senior staff members of relevant NGOs. In addition to e-mailing informants, some of the information-seeking efforts in Australia involved telephone conversations.

Data from an earlier field trip to Cambodia and Viet Nam, undertaken in March and April 2002 on a different project investigating NGOs' involvement with trafficking issues, are also included in this paper.

Regional migration flows and policies

Over the last few decades, the economies and labour market conditions in the region under discussion have undergone considerable changes. Intensified migration pressures have resulted in the supply side of migrant labour out-balancing the demand, resulting in reduced financial benefits for migrants because wages have been pushed down and recruitment fees up. On the labour-sending side, new source countries have emerged (such as Viet Nam and Cambodia), resulting in increased competition at the destinations. Certain abuses have become more common, such as the non-payment of wages. This might, to some extent, reflect the current state of the economy in many receiving countries where unskilled migrants are usually employed either in small- and medium-sized companies, which typically take the brunt of increased global competition, or as domestic helpers in middle-class households, which are also suffering from decreased economic growth, such as in Hong Kong Special Administrative Region of China.[9] At the same time, transition from socialist to free market systems and economic growth in some countries have brought about socio-economic disparities resulting in the re-emergence of prostitution – with some enjoying higher incomes to take advantage of the feminization of poverty driving women into prostitution (Piper and Yeoh, forthcoming).

Overall, the costs of migration have become disproportionately borne by the migrants themselves. The situation of increased competition and increasingly higher costs incurred results in greater debts and fewer benefits for the women and men involved. There is evidence, for example, that Thai women working in Germany's sex industries could make good money in the 1970s and 1980s, but over time working conditions changed and deductions from their salaries increased (Skrobanek et al., 1997). Similar evidence exists in the context of male migrant workers, such as Indonesians in Malaysia (Jones, 2000) and Bangladeshis in Singapore.[10] This is related to economic boom and busts in destination countries, and increased involvement of recruiters/brokers over time.

Trafficking has to be seen as part and parcel of the reality of these broader migration patterns, particularly undocumented flows. The overall numbers of undocumented migrants leaving Asia are small compared with the numbers moving within Asia (Skeldon, 2000). The stock of undocumented migrants is at least equal if not higher than that of legal labour migrants (Wong, forthcoming). Thus, most labour migration within Asia is arranged through the medium of brokers or recruiters, at the origin as well as destination country, under a wide range of scenarios (Skeldon, 2000) reflecting the unavailability of legal channels, let alone settlement policies. The flows of trafficked people throughout this region seem to occur on a comparatively large scale and are of a very complex nature in the sense that there are several human trafficking typologies at work, with different locations, different levels of criminal activity (more or less organized), different degrees of consent and complicity, and with different sources and destinations.

In addition, globalization processes have increased the awareness of opportunities outside the country of origin. However, despite severe labour shortages in certain sectors in the destination countries, the unavailability of legal migration channels has resulted in an increased shift from legal to illegal practices (Skeldon, 2000).

In most of the existing literature, trafficking is related to the increased demand and supply of mainly women in the sex industries in South-East Asia and Oceania. In addition to prostitution, the "trade in brides" as well as domestic work have also been included in the discussion of trafficking, albeit to a far lesser extent in the context of Oceania. Specific to the Asian regions seems to be another category of trafficking about which more is being written, and that is the trafficking of children for begging, as domestic workers, for adoption, as brides, and in other forms of labour (Marshall, 2001; Archavanitkul, 1998).[11]

To sum up, Asia-specific features revolve around the large scale of undocumented or irregular labour migration, which results in a blurred distinction between trafficking and smuggling; the widespread movement of women as wives and domestic workers, in addition to sex and entertainment work; the trafficking of children for labour, sexual exploitation, and adoption; and the strong link between prostitution, sex tourism, and militarization.

Oceania's specific features are the relative insignificance of trafficking in numerical terms which is largely due to its geographic remoteness and inaccessibility, but also to its different migration policies (such as family unification and refugee migration which are two channels absent in South-East Asia) and "demand" structure. But even within Oceania, there are variations. Australia appears to experience larger incidences of trafficking than New Zealand.

RESEARCHING THE PHENOMENON OF HUMAN TRAFFICKING

When reviewing existing studies and addressing the issue of "doing" research and generating knowledge that is based on defining a problem such as "trafficking", it is important to look at the academic and research environments in the countries at issue as well as the sources of funding in order to raise the following questions: are there differences between destination and source countries?

Is the research mainly conducted by government departments, NGOs, or academic institutions? Is the research conducted in source countries host country and/or donor driven? All of these issues are assumed to have an impact upon definitions, data, and analysis.

A review of the existing literature shows that certain countries are better researched than others. In the Asia Pacific region, this mainly refers to source countries, but even there it is the Mekong subregion which is particularly well researched. This has to do with the fact that any research on trafficking tends to focus on commercial sexual exploitation with Thailand, which is regarded as *the* hub for the sex trade. Cambodia has been an important focus of many UN activities since the UN Transitional Authority in Cambodia period, and trafficking of children has been identified as a specific problem. Indonesia is better known for "exporting" labour migrants (such as domestic and construction workers), with little attention given to trafficking for sexual or any other exploitation. The focus of NGO advocacy and service provisioning in these countries seems to follow the same pattern: there is quite a large number of NGOs in the Mekong subregion engaged in trafficking, but in Indonesia, most NGOs are concerned with migrant labour issues.

Studies on trafficking in the context of Oceania are the scarcest – a fact also confirmed by the bibliography of trafficking compiled by the *Violence Against Women Online Resources* which does not list a single study on Australia, New Zealand, or the Pacific Islands.[12]

Academic research

Existing studies on trafficking issues can be divided into two broad categories distinguishing those coming from a sexual violence perspective (and thus with a focus on commercial sexual exploitation) and those taking migration as their starting point (the latter can be further subdivided into gender and non-gender analyses). Both perspectives agree on the exploitative and abusive practices, often making reference to human rights violations, but the former perspective typically results in an alarmist tragic victim discourse, whereas the latter tends to look at practical measures which can be used to combat exploitation – one of which is the promotion of the rights of sex workers. The disagreement on the definition of the problem has implications for assessing the extent of trafficking in numerical terms. As a result, recommendations and suggestions for solutions to tackle trafficking also tend to differ.

Scholars coming from a sexual violence perspective exclusively focus on women and children, whereas those writing from a migration perspective also acknowledge the possibility of trafficking taking place in non-sexual contexts and, thus, including male victims. However, despite this recognition by the latter, very little concrete research has been carried out that would have a clear focus on these other (non-sexual) types of trafficking or that would offer a comparative analysis of trafficking in a "non-sex trade" context with trafficking for the purpose of sexual exploitation. Invariably, it is commercial sexual exploitation that ends up being the main subject of theoretical and empirical works. This begs the question, why? Part of the answer seems to be that trafficking research has been dominated by feminist approaches – which explains the focus on sexual exploitation of women and children – and the enormous gains and influence achieved by the political activism of the feminist movement that managed to place "violence against women" firmly onto the agenda of international and national policy makers (Meyer and Pruegl, 1999); and, partly resulting from this, the emergence of a gendered understanding within public and policy makers' discourse associating men with being smuggled and only women and children with being trafficked (Hemming, 2004).

Since the 1990s, feminist researchers have intensely discussed feminized migration in Asia in relation to the increasing incidences of trafficking in women and "mail-order brides" on the one hand, and growing sex tourism on the other (Barry, 1995; Enloe, 1989; Hall, 1992; Matsui, 2000; Truong, 1990; Wijers and Lap-Chew, 1997; Constable, 2003; Hill Maher, 2003). In these debates, researchers have established a link between internal migration and sex tourism as a gendered phenomenon. This is because increasing numbers of migrant women engage in sexual labour in major tourist sites in search of better economic opportunities unavailable in their home communities. Throughout the post-World War II era, the presence of American military bases and frequent eruption of regional wars in East and South-East Asia gave rise to a prosperous sex industry (Enloe, 1989; Pettman, 1997). With the advent of the age of global tourism since the 1970s, the sex industry has expanded rapidly as an integral part of the tourist industry. Under heavy pressure to repay their foreign debts, governments of Thailand, the Philippines, and Indonesia have promoted tourism as a national policy (Phongpaichit et al., 1998; Bell, 1998). Consequently, with abundant labour supplied by local and migrant women, sex tourism boomed in these countries' metropolises and resorts, drawing massive numbers of male tourists from Japan, Australia, Europe, and North America (Enloe, 1989; Bulbeck, 1998; Matsui, 1999). There has, thus, emerged a vast literature on various aspects of the rapidly expanding entertainment and "sex sector" (to use Lim's phrase, 1998).[13] The more recent economic reforms in former socialist countries such as Viet Nam and China have also resulted in the revival of local sex industries, triggering internal and international migratory flows (Piper and Yeoh, forthcoming). In addition, child sex tourism has also been identified as a burgeoning problem, particularly in countries like Cambodia (Archavanitkul, 1998). The causes, patterns, and outcomes of child trafficking appear to have many parallels with trafficking of adult women – in the sense that "real" abductions are rare, but deception, various levels of violence, debt bondage, and slavery-like conditions pose serious problems. Internal migration of women who often end up in prostitution because of the lack of other opportunities has also been attributed to environmental and developmental problems, as in Thailand (Mensendiek, 1996).

In this sense, accelerated globalization processes have contributed to movements across borders by women ending up in the sex and entertainment industries in the economic powerhouses of this region as well as beyond. Partly in response to transnational feminist campaigning and widespread public criticism against sex tourism, the numbers of East Asian men travelling abroad to purchase sexual services decreased, but at the same time the introduction of the so-called "entertainer" or "artist" visa by Japan and Korea resulted in the "import" of foreign women (Piper, 1999). On the whole, global trafficking in women appears to have surged sharply in East and South-East Asia. Since the late 1970s, networks of recruiters/traffickers throughout the region have begun to transport women (and children) from Thailand and the Philippines to Japan and Korea, and from Burma, Laos, and Cambodia to Thailand and Malaysia (Singhanetra-Renard, 1996; Matsui, 1999; Asia Watch, 1993; Caouette and Saito, 1999).

Parallel to the emergence of this literature, numerous studies on international labour migration have been produced, with increasing attention being paid to irregular flows and the documentation of abusive practices involved, but these two strands of literature – trafficking and irregular migration – have hardly engaged with each other which might to some extent explain the little recognition of male victims of trafficking. What does happen at times is that reports or research papers start off by acknowledging the fact that victims of trafficking can be male and female, in a sex and non-sex work context, but subsequently they all focus on trafficking in the context of sexual exploitation and thus, on women and children. This has been explained by the difficulty of "separating trafficking from other forms of labour migration" and men being "arguably less open to exploitation than women" (Skeldon, 2000: 17). In fact, when men are brought into the discussion, the distinction between trafficking and smuggling becomes even more blurred than when the focus is on women only, especially for sexual exploitation. As it stands, the evidence of male victims is mainly anecdotal. For Australia, a recent report by an NGO has identified a comparatively small number of male victims (Project Respect, 2004). The same is true for trafficking of women in a non-sex context. According to the National Commission for Human Rights in New Zealand, in 1999 there were seven Thai women freed from slave labour conditions in an Auckland factory.[14] An Indonesian NGO has also reported women trafficked to perform non-sex work.[15] The final report by GPAT (2003b) mentions the case of two male Filipino victims held against their will and forced into slave-like conditions on a Malaysian plantation. Personal interviews conducted with Bangladeshi male workers in Malaysia[16] have shown that there are cases of men that fulfil the criteria of the UN's definition of trafficking (deception, coercion, debt bondage, slavery-like conditions). In spite of this, men have been treated as "the invisible dimension of trafficking" by researchers (Skeldon, 2000: 17), and it is only women and children who are clearly acknowledged as victims of trafficking. This, however, often results in an indiscriminate categorizing of any individual in the sex and entertainment industries as a "trafficked victim" without a more sophisticated distinction of the very complex and hierarchical nature of the industries and processes involved.

More recently, trafficking has also been researched from a health perspective (Piper and Yeoh, forthcoming) which is not surprising considering the rising numbers of HIV/AIDS infected individuals in South-East Asia and the many projects funded by the World Health Organization (WHO) and UNAIDs, especially in the Mekong subregion. A clear link has been made by WHO between migration and health concerns (WHO, 2003). Going beyond HIV/AIDS, a recent comparative study on five countries has provided a comprehensive insight into the array of health problems women trafficked into sexual exploitation experience (Raymond et al., 2002).

Trafficking is also subject to academic analysis in the context of the 2000 UN Convention on Transnational Organized Crime and related protocols – from a critical human rights perspective (Gallagher, 2002) or a more legalistic/criminological perspective (Schloenhardt, 2001). However, the extent to which organized crime is involved is questionable. At least within the Mekong sub-region, trafficking appears to resemble more of a cottage industry (carried out at home) rather than organized crime, with local recruiters being seen as providing a service to the community (Marshall, 2001). In the Malaysian context, it has also been found that the involvement of organized crime networks is minimal (Wong, forthcoming). It seems as if shorter distances to a neighbouring country do not require a sophisticated crime network, unlike the crossing of larger distances.

There are no studies on the trafficking of organs in South-East Asia and Oceania. This is, however, a category of trafficking included in the UN Convention on Transnational Organized Crime. There is only anecdotal evidence of repatriated corpses which were found to have some internal organs missing.[17]

In many receiving countries, local academic communities often ignore the issue of trafficking. This is most certainly true for Malaysia (Wong, forthcoming) and Singapore where there are no leading academic institutions which conduct research on trafficking. Key informants in Australia have mentioned this with regard to academic institutions there also. Likewise in New Zealand, no researchers working on trafficking could have been identified. Reasons for this lack of research include: denial that such exploitative, or slavery-like, conditions exist; no funding opportunities because of little political interest; and lack of understanding of trafficking as a whole. This, however, means that there is a serious lack of experts.

Policy makers and non-governmental studies

The "international career" of concerns for trafficking has been remarkable with the mushrooming of NGOs devoted to this issue as well as the extensive involvement of the UN as well as international development agencies (Wong, forthcoming). The fact that the United States, the European Union, and the United Nations – in their capacity as the three most important sources for donor funding and development aid – are the driving force behind projects and programmes on trafficking in the Asia Pacific cannot be denied.[18] These forces – NGOs and donors – most certainly also explain the increased reaction, if not interest, on the part of source countries' governments to take some kind of action against trafficking.

A vast amount of programmes and projects in this region have produced a lot of data. In 2001, within the UN Economic and Social Commission for Asia and the Pacific (UNESCAP) region, there were six projects run by UNESCAP itself, two projects by the International Programme on the Elimination of Child Labour (IPEC)/ILO, eight by the International Organization for Migration (IOM), four by the UN Educational, Scientific and Cultural Organization (UNESCO), four by the UN High Commissioner for Refugees (UNHCR), 32 by the UN Children's Fund (UNICEF), and two by the UN Development Fund for Women (UNIFEM).[19] Many of these programmes focus on the Mekong subregion. Research institutes like the UN Interregional Crime and Justice Research Institute (UNICRI) have also been involved in projects in this region. The most comprehensive programme on trafficking in the Mekong region, involving most UN agencies, is the UN Interagency Project (UNIAP) headquartered in Bangkok with regional offices in Viet Nam, Cambodia, and Laos.

Most research conducted on trafficking of children appears to be instigated by UNICEF and IPEC-ILO as well as by NGOs such as ECPAT, Save the Children, and the International Catholic Migration Commission. Most of this research concerns the Mekong subregion, but more recently also Indonesia (Rosenberg, 2003). Data on internal child trafficking for domestic work in Jakarta have found that these children rarely experienced any extreme forms of exploitation. A project investigating child trafficking in Bali could not find any evidence of trafficking, despite the occurrence of internal migration by children. A study undertaken for IPEC/ILO found that the actual procedures through which children are recruited seem to follow the same pattern as for adults, and that the most vulnerable are minorities, the lower castes, and children of undocumented migrants (Archavanitkul, 1998). The types of exploitation seem also similar to adult trafficking: (1) low remuneration and excessive hours of work, (2) hazardous work conditions, and (3) physical and mental abuses. Trafficking children into begging has been identified as a new form of bonded labour, and trafficking of girls into prostitution is also seen as a comparatively new phenomenon that had not existed before 1970 in some countries in the subregion. There is evidence of a small number of boys trafficked into the sex business (Archavanitkul, 1998). Unfortunately, no study exists which links trafficking of children to trafficking of adults, although data from interviews with adults often indicate an early involvement in internal trafficking for sex work at the age of a child which subsequently led to further trafficking – often across international borders – as an adult.

Ethnographic community-based research has been carried out by Trafficking from Community to Exploitation (TRACE), a research network comprised of six researchers in Laos and Thailand respectively. UNESCO has conducted field-based research in connection with a project on the citizenship of Thai hill tribe villages based on the argument that the lack of citizenship rights is one of the root causes exposing minorities in particular to the risk of trafficking. In fact, UNESCO has been working on a website which is to function as a clearing-house of trafficking data and information for Asia.[20]

As laudable as these initiatives might be, the lack of an overall coordinating body – similar to UNAIDS – might mean that much duplication and little exchange between individual agencies is occurring. Many of these programmes are host/donor country driven with many donors (such as DfID, AusAID, SIDA, CIDA, GTZ, DANIDA, USAID, etc.) channelling funds through UN agencies or NGOs for trafficking projects, directly or indirectly. But not all of these projects or programmes include a research component, and even if they do, it is not always independent research.[21] Likewise, it is not always clear why a certain country has been chosen over another.[22] The UNIAP has been designed to address many of these problem areas. Its activities so far, however, have been described as a "stock taking" exercise rather than one which produces original research to fill the gaps that still exist.[23] An independent evaluation report lists in detail the positive outcomes achieved so far and areas subject to improvement (Caouette, 2002). In general, with little own research components, many projects depend on secondary data and are thus hampered by the unavailability of reliable data with governments often reluctant to disclose their data (if gathered at all).

Regarding the link between donor/UN and local researchers, two other issues have arisen: one concerns the fact that independent research institutes some-times do not exist, such as in Cambodia, or where they do exist, they have serious difficulties surviving economically and thus heavily depend upon donor funding; the other issue concerns the seemingly little interest by donor/UN agen-cies in involving local researchers. The donor sector thus appears to create "jobs for the boys" without engaging in local capacity building.[24] Hence, more independent evaluation and assessment of these projects and the way they are designed and carried out needs to be done.

The enormous activity of donor/UN agencies largely explains the production of information and data as far as the source countries are concerned. By contrast, the situation at the destination countries in this region is very much under-researched. At the receiving end, governments' programmes or anti-trafficking initiatives do not usually include a research component or funding for thorough research. A good example is that of the AUS\$ 20 million initiative recently implemented by the Australian Government: most of this funding goes to the Australian Federal Police for training and the locating of an officer in Bangkok as well as for an awareness campaign and for victim support services. Not a single Australian dollar goes to independent research or to NGOs active in this field.

There are also a huge number of local NGOs in South-East Asia devoted to trafficking issues, offering welfare services, awareness raising campaigns and engaging in advocacy. Many conduct their own research, but based on budget-ary and staffing constraints, the end products are limited. Larger NGOs, such as the Global Alliance Against Trafficking in Women (GAATW) branch in Bangkok and the Coalition Against Trafficking in Women (CATW) in Manila, have been able to produce more comprehensive research due to their networks with local and international researchers. It is interesting to note that most of these NGOs are either feminist/women organizations or NGOs concerned with children; there is not a single NGO advocating for male victims of trafficking – which also explains the general focus on the trafficking of women and children for sexual exploitation.

Very little research has been undertaken by trade unions. Only two reports could be identified: one written for the International Confederation of Free Trade Unions

(ICFTU) on the contributions of the union movement to the problem of commercial sexual exploitation of children (Grumiau, nd); the other for the ILO on
the role of employers and workers' organizations in taking action against trafficking of children (Smith, 2001). Both reports draw on examples from the
Asian region (Mekong subregion, Philippines, Nepal).

To sum up and conclude this section, it cannot be said that there is a general
lack of research in the region investigated here. Source countries of trafficking
tend to be better researched than countries of destination. This is most certainly
related to UN and donor agencies' interests and funding opportunities. However, the research which has been conducted – as important as it is – remains
fragmented and typically offers only a snapshot[25] in four main regards: (1) geographically (ethnographic work in one specific village or community; or one
specific country without cross-locale or cross-national comparison); (2) typo-
logically – i.e. one type of trafficking only (children or women and often in the
context of sexual exploitation only); (3) periodical timing – one specific and
short time period during which research is carried out (no longitudinal or life
course analysis type of studies)[26] makes the identification of victims problematic as establishing networks and a relationship of trust is crucial to NGOs,
government officials, and the victims themselves; this requires a lot of time;[27]
(4) disciplinary terms – no interdisciplinary studies, using multi-methods, exist.[28]
One recent study on women trafficked for sexual purposes in five countries
(Raymond et al., 2002) is an exception to this, offering a multi-methods as well
as an interdisciplinary approach by having a research team comprised of
researchers with different disciplinary backgrounds. Trafficking is a dynamic
phenomenon, but most research tends to be of a static rather than longitudinal
nature (Marshall, 2001). Methods used are mostly qualitative involving the use
of secondary data and interviews with government officials, NGO representatives, and a relatively small sample of individual victims, the latter reflecting the
general difficulty of "accessing" victims of trafficking. Also, research on trafficking is rarely contextualized with other social problems whose research
encounters similar problems with regard to the production of exact data, such
as drug abuse, domestic violence, rape, child prostitution,[29] etc. Important lessons could be drawn from such studies.

Because of the snapshot nature of most research, contradictory findings emerge,
particularly with regard to the extent of serious violence involved in trafficking.
The report by Raymond et al. (2002) lists an extensive range of various types of
violence experienced by trafficked women, whereas GPAT reports less severe
forms of violence being the norm. This might be related to different contexts,
i.e. to differing experiences in the source as well as destination countries and
also to differing experiences by different types of trafficked victims.

Overall, it can be said that our qualitative understanding of dynamics, patterns, and impacts involved in trafficking – despite its sketchiness – has improved, but the problem of producing reliable statistical data (that would allow comparative analysis) still remains. Apart from "practical" reasons, the production of quantitative data is in many ways related to the definition of the problem and, thus, to the very nature of the problem.

A note on gender research

With men usually being treated as "smuggled" labour migrants and the trafficking category being reserved for women (and children), this clearly points to assumptions about the sexes and, thus, the need for a gendered analysis. "Gender" as such does not necessarily mean "women" only, but refers to women in relation to men. There is, however, a tendency in gender research to be centred on women and rarely on the two genders defined in relation to one another (Carling, 2001). Because the starting point in social scientific research has traditionally been men's subject position, much of "gender" research has come to mean a focus on women with the quest to make women visible. This has been, and still is, a very important undertaking, but the move from "women per se" to "women in relation to men" has so far rarely been made which is reflected in the numerous empirical case studies hardly ever including male respondents. Even the concept of "victimhood" hardly ever includes men as potential victims of socio-economic pressures and structures leading to their being trafficked. In the context of trafficking research, it would, for instance, be valuable to gain insights into (female and male) local recruiters or brokers' roles and the type of constraints they might encounter.[30] Similarly important would be a project on male customers of prostitutes to fully understand the demand for, and use of, paid sexual services. In this sense, gender has not sufficiently been approached as a "relational" concept.

A second problem area – as pointed out by Carling (2001) – is the generally held assumption that women-in-general are oppressed everywhere by men-in-general. However, gender relations are always mediated by other socially constructed categories such as class, age, "race", and ethnicity. There are many different classes and nationalities of women, and they do not constitute a monolithic category (Piper and Roces, 2003). Hence, what is required is the examination of migrant/trafficked women vis-à-vis other women, such as their female employers (an issue raised by Anderson, 2001; Chin, 1997; and Macklin, 1994 in the context of domestic workers), female recruiters, female NGO representatives (raised by Cheng, 2002), and female politicians/government officials. We do not know the role, motivations, and constraints of female *mama-sans* (brothel or hostess club owners) and other female employers who are perpetrators of violent acts (such as female employers of domestic workers).

In other words, the "gender and trafficking" problem needs to be integrated into a larger socio-economic and cultural context of men-women relations and women-to-women relations. This perspective is also confirmed by a recently held session organized by the UN Commission on the Status of Women titled "The role of men and boys in achieving gender equality" held in March 2004. The emphasis is on considering "men and boys not just as beneficiaries of women's work or holders of privilege or perpetrators of violence against women, but also explicitly as agents of change, participants in reform, and potential allies in the search for gender justice" (Connell, 2004: 2). This position is highly controversial within sections of the women's movement fearing that "working with men and boys is diluting, diverting and even trivializing" women's struggle (Wainaina, 2004: 3), but projects which include men and boys in their strategies to achieve gender equality have shown compelling reasons for involving male counterparts to move the empowerment of women forward (Wainaina, 2004: 3).

To sum up, there is in fact a wealth of documented experience, research, and analysis on sex work and sex trafficking of women and children, especially into and out of Thailand as well as the Mekong subregion. Studies cover a spectrum of trafficking issues: trends; causes; abusive practices; and policy and programme interventions by multilateral institutions, states, and NGOs. This might give the impression of an exhaustive treatment, but certain gaps remain. D'Cunha (in Raymond et al., 2002: 124), for instance, has pointed out that it is particularly "the nature of violence intrinsic to the institution of prostitution and sex trafficking" that begs further attention. In other words, it is the deconstruction of the sex and sexuality of prostitution for women and clients that remains inadequately addressed. Her own study contributes to the development of a deeper understanding of the terms "consent" or "choice" as well as the documentation of cumulative and related violations. Other gaps involve the socio-economic contexts of gender relations, showing the extent of constrained choices or "survival strategies" (to use D'Cunha's term) of men and women involved in trafficking. Thus, we need more investigation into the pre-trafficking situation (evidence of child abuse, broken families, socio-economic pressures on men and women, etc.). In addition, it is also necessary to further research what happens after trafficked victims return to their country of origin.[31]

STATISTICAL DATA AND DEFINITIONS

Quantifying trafficking

It is a universally agreed upon fact that accurate figures are impossible to come by. One of the earlier studies on trafficking stated that finding reliable statistics on the extent of trafficking is virtually impossible and attributed that to two main reasons: (1) lack of systematic research, and (2) lack of a precise, consistent, and unambiguous definition of the phenomenon (Wijers and Lap-Chew, 1997: 15). As a result, there are practical as well as definitional (or ideological) reasons involved in the problem of quantifying trafficking. On a practical level, when drawing parallels to undocumented migration and issues revolving around various forms of sexual violence in general (such as rape, domestic violence, incest), particularly in countries where talking about sexuality constitutes a strong taboo and legislation to address all forms of sexual violence are not in place, it is not surprising that accurate numbers are elusive. It is also a well-established fact that the under-reporting of any crime or illicit practices is a common problem everywhere in the world.[32] It has also been shown that victims of trafficking do not report their experiences because they do not trust authorities – neither in their country of origin, nor at the destination (GPAT, 2003a). In addition, budgetary constraints in the source countries, sometimes confounded by the lack of experts, obstruct setting up the infrastructure needed to collect statistical data.

In a more specific context, recent studies carried out by GPAT of trafficked victims from the Philippines to destinations such as Malaysia, Italy, and Australia, have noted that reliable data on migrant smuggling and human trafficking are scarce. A recent Australian study also concludes that there is limited evidence available regarding the incidence and nature of human trafficking (David, 2000).

In the absence of reliable data, all that can be produced are estimates or "guesstimates". And even there, a huge gap between government and NGO estimates is common, mainly because of definitional inconsistencies. Governments usually claim to base their estimates on the definition of trafficking as promoted by the UN which is based on the notion of initial intention, but most NGOs measure trafficking based on the outcome only. Even among NGOs, however, there is disagreement, typically reflecting their differing positions vis-à-vis prostitution or sex work. To illustrate this, the Australian case offers a good example: the Project Respect NGO estimates that up to 1,000 trafficked foreign women are in the Australian sex industry under contract at any one time, whereas another NGO, Scarlet Alliance, presents a much lower estimate of less than 400 foreign women in any one year. The figure of approximately 300 foreign women in the sex industry seems generally accepted, of whom a much smaller number is said to be in servitude, and thus fitting the UN definition of trafficking (Parliamentary Joint Committee on the Australian Crime Commission, 2004).

The low numbers quoted by governments also has to do with their reliance on the actual numbers of complaints (i.e. victims coming forward) which significantly understates the problem (Carrington and Hearn, 2003) as lamented by NGOs. In addition, there are also intra-governmental discrepancies regarding figures as a result of the lack of coordination among the various ministries, as in Malaysia where the police are said to have one set of figures, while the Immigration Department has its own data which do not match.

Concerning governments' narrow definition of trafficking victims, scholars coming from a migration or general human rights' perspective have argued that the approach to, and interest in, trafficking on the part of destination countries' governments has to be seen in the context of the "politics of migration control" (Gallagher, 2001; Wong, forthcoming). This also explains, at least partially, the reluctance on the part of destination governments to broaden their definition of trafficking, and thus, the overall figures, as they do not want to be seen as lacking control of their borders. The situation in source countries is slightly different: governments do not want to admit to the large numbers of trafficked, and thus illegal, persons, mostly for diplomatic and/or political reasons. A high occurrence of trafficking for the purpose of sexual exploitation is also seen as highly stigmatizing and embarrassing for source countries. Moreover, as argued by Jones (2000), sending countries are mainly interested in making money out of migrants (through charging recruitment and other fees) and hence do not want to officially recognize this as trafficking and, thus, as a criminal and moral matter that should be combated. At the same time, source countries have come under pressure (mostly exerted by the destination countries, and often through donor funding) to implement anti-trafficking initiatives. In Asia, this can be seen in the BALI process for instance.

This still leaves the widely observed problem of the absence of an agreed upon definition of trafficking. Despite the passage of the UN Convention Against Transnational Organized Crime and its three additional protocols, which establish a now widely accepted definition of trafficking, many fundamental questions remain unanswered at both the theoretical and practical levels (Gallagher, 2001).

It is interesting to note that despite the problems with establishing clear figures, the trafficking phenomenon has been described as being on the rise globally. In the context of Thailand, however, it has been noted that the number of trafficked victims is actually *decreasing*. On a positive note, this has been related to demographic changes and the drop in the overall birth rate, lowering the availability of children and young women for trafficking. These changes are somewhat connected to Thailand's overall socio-economic development in recent years, resulting (among others) in the improvement of education for women (Skeldon, 2000). On a negative note, this decrease has seen a corresponding increase in the number of foreign girls trafficked for sexual exploitation, the majority from Burma, followed by Yunnan. The number of foreign children as beggars has also risen, mostly Cambodians (Archavanitkul, 1998).

Definitional issues   who is trafficked and what for?

The above section still leaves the issue unanswered as to why men are absent from official figures or "guesstimates" of trafficking. More and more studies seem to find that numerically speaking, trafficking for labour outside of the sex trade also constitutes a significant problem. David Feingold from UNESCO even goes so far as saying that approximately 90 per cent of trafficking in Indonesia is labour trafficking (Silverman, 2004).[33] Existing research on trafficking in children also finds that more children are trafficked for labour than sexual exploitation. "Trafficking for labour" clearly includes men and women, boys and girls. This means that there is evidence to support the argument for an all-inclusive, broad definition of trafficking going beyond sexual exploitation alone.

To include men and women into trafficking for non-sex work, however, would in law enforcement terms (regarding anti-trafficking laws) mean that larger numbers than currently acknowledged, or assumed, would be involved, potentially creating a bigger administrative and budgetary burden than at present. It is highly unlikely that destination countries would agree to this. Hence, a narrow approach focusing on "worst forms" seems more realistic in legalistic terms. There is no doubt that trafficking in the context of sexual exploitation constitutes the worst form of trafficking. In this regard, one can draw a parallel to the debate on child labour, as suggested by Skeldon (2000): there are many forms of child labour, more or less exploitative, happening in specific socio-economic contexts in which a total ban on child labour would actually have detrimental effects unless alternative opportunities for income generation are created. Hence, it is the worst forms of child labour that need tackling. Similarly, it is the worst forms of trafficking that require urgent attention and that can realistically be met by legislative means. If we take trafficking for sexual exploitation as the worst form, and given that gender inequality is one of the overarching root causes (Brown, 2001; Dargan, 2003), the interacting socio-economic and political structures, processes, and relationships involved in trafficked women's experiences need to be addressed.[34]

Law enforcers approach to identifying victims

A narrow approach to the enforcement of anti-trafficking legislation (in the sense of "worst forms"), however, does not automatically mean a narrow approach to policy making on trafficking in general. To address the root causes of trafficking and to prevent re-trafficking, a comprehensive, multi-layered approach is required tailor-made to the specific circumstances in the source and destination countries. As it stands, however, this is not happening.

Considering that receiving governments' number one priority is illegal immigration, it does not come as a surprise that victims of trafficking tend to be prosecuted under Immigration Acts, as in Malaysia, Singapore, and Australia until recently. This is reflected in the fact that the lead agencies responsible for smuggling and trafficking are typically immigration departments or home affairs departments, and never Ministries of Labour which would focus on the monitoring of labour standards at work sites rather the visa status of the foreign worker. The common practice of giving priority to the victims' immigration status, thus, results in neglect for the work-related abuses they have endured.

In the context of the UN Convention Against Transnational Organized Crime (more widely signed or ratified than the migrant worker specific ILO or UN conventions), Gallagher argues that the regime established by this instrument (whereby trafficked persons are accorded greater protection and therefore impose greater financial and administrative burden than smuggled migrants) creates a clear incentive for national authorities to identify irregular migrants as smuggled rather than trafficked. In addition, neither the protocol on smuggling nor the one dealing with trafficking provides clear guidance on the issue of identification. Gallagher refers to this as a "significant, and no doubt, deliberate weakness" (2001: 1000). According to the Advisory Council of Jurists of the Asia Pacific Forum (2002), international law generally does not articulate the nature and extent of the obligation of states to identify trafficked persons. Article 18 of the 1949 Trafficking Convention requires states to have a declaration taken from aliens who are prostitutes in order to establish their identity and civil status. Although not explicitly articulated, the requirement to identify trafficked persons is implicit in the provisions of the Trafficking Protocol (art. 6, 9, 13). But according to Gallagher (2001), the definition of smuggling in the Smuggling Protocol is so broad that it can be applied to all irregular migrants whose transport has been facilitated. This leaves only a small number of trafficked persons who enter the destination country legally who would not be considered smuggled migrants. It is individual states who retain the capacity to decide who is smuggled and who is trafficked, and there is no independent institution in charge of this.

Even if the UN definition of trafficking was to be imposed as the golden rule, it could be argued that the overall size of the problem would be even lower than stated by (destination) governments' estimates. The primary reason for this is that the definition could be interpreted as being initiation-based – that is, what the intention of the recruiter or broker was at the time when the recruitment or transport was transacted. Many cases of alleged trafficking, however, are cases of contract substitution, and accordingly are subject to civil, not criminal remedies, and thus they fall out of the trafficking basket. It is extremely difficult to prove this initial intention. According to this interpretation, the number of trafficked victims would be even smaller than commonly acknowledged or assumed.[35]

In Australia where the government has passed a AUS$ 20 million anti-trafficking package, increased training and awareness among law enforcers has in fact taken place. It is nonetheless difficult to prove the various criminal offences as stipulated by the UN Convention Against Transnational Organized Crime. To identify a woman as a victim of trafficking, the individual has to come forward and claim to be such. Compliance raids on brothels tend to be rather unsuccessful in identifying victims as they (1) can only be carried out if serious suspicion of the involvement of illegal migrants exists;[36] and (2) the women have to be seen as "working" (i.e. offering their services and are hence seen as breaching the conditions of their visa), which is difficult as most brothel owners are warned prior to such raids being carried out and usually manage to hide the women. Even when a woman is "found" or comes forward, prosecution is difficult because most women knew what sort of work they would be doing, that they would be in the country for a short while, and incurring some sort of debt. To capture the issue of debt bondage and slavery-like conditions (no freedom of movement, unexpected increase of the debts, no control over the number and choice of customers), the law must be tightened.

Other countries in the region under discussion have also passed anti-trafficking legislation, most notably the Philippines and more recently Thailand, but it remains to be seen how well such laws are implemented.[37] All of this points to serious limitations of a pure law enforcement approach – which has been highlighted by researchers, such as Schloenhardt, who writes that "criminal law and its enforcement cannot substitute the structural and political changes that are necessary to address the more fundamental causes of human trafficking" (2000). In addition, all existing anti-trafficking legislative efforts narrow the scope of trafficking victims to women and children for the purpose of sexual exploitation. No government is seriously interested in tracking down trafficked victims in construction, agriculture, factories, or any other sector.[38]

As touched upon above, the migration framework to trafficking points to factors that compels individuals to leave their community or country of origin. The human rights framework is concerned with the lack of appropriate and adequate legal structure that criminalizes the traffickers rather than the trafficked, protects the human rights of the trafficked, and provides support to the victims (Ucrarer, 1999). As the situation in South-East Asia (as elsewhere) has shown, these two perspectives – migration and human rights – need to be linked. Thus, any policy approach that uses only one will be ineffective.

Another issue that has implications for the identification of victims is an issue that has appeared in Malaysia: the link of missing persons and trafficking. In Malaysia, figures obtained from the police on missing persons in 2003 show that the majority were female between the ages of ten and 17, with 1,405 cases reported. Of that, 983 were found. Although there is no conclusive evidence, among the three possible scenarios trafficking constitutes one. A UNICEF spokesperson is quoted as commenting on the issue of "untraceable children" that "in some places, the child may never have been registered at birth so there is no official record of their existence. Children without an official name and age are very vulnerable to exploitative labour, including prostitution. Since they have no birth record, they cannot be registered as "missing."[39] The issue of registration and citizenship provided at birth should thus be a clear right. This is also an important case.

All of this shows that a pure "law enforcement" perspective is far too narrow to address the multi-layered issues implicated in trafficking. A comprehensive rights-based approach might prove far more useful.

Problems encountered in researching trafficking

Limitations and/or problems experienced when researching trafficking are clearly linked to the nature of trafficking involving many practices deemed illegal and illicit. This relates first and foremost to the difficulties that are encountered when attempting to locate trafficking victims – a problem remarked upon in many studies, including those that involve local researchers (GPAT, 2003a, 2003b; Caouette and Saito, 1999; Darwin et al., 2003; Raymond et al., 2002). Another serious issue is the uncooperative stance taken by many governments which do not disclose any information on trafficking (for Indonesia e.g., see Raymond et al., 2002; it is in fact noted that the Indonesian Government might not even collect such data).

GPAT (2003b) listed in its final report the major problems identified during its course of study as follows:

- lack of agreement or confusion on the definition of "trafficking",
- lack of recognition or denial of the problem coupled with criminalization of the victim.

Those two go hand-in-hand. Due to the fact that there are no anti-trafficking laws in many countries under study,[40] or even where they exist implementation remains a problem, it is not surprising that individuals working within governmental bureaucracies either have difficulty recognizing this problem or are reluctant to take concrete action. In addition, unsympathetic attitudes on the part of government officials towards trafficking victims, to different degrees according to country context or parts of a country, contribute to the non-recognition of the nature of this problem.

In addition, the following issues aggravate the situation:

-   lack of government experts or focal points in destination countries,
-   difficulty in accessing case files and victims,
-   limited validity and quality of data.

This relates, for instance, to the interviews with individual victims: if they were conducted with women "still under the control of the sex clubs", it is impossible for researchers to use structured questionnaires. When interviews are conducted with "returnees" or repatriated victims, the data might be skewed the more time has passed since returning. In addition, the samples are often relatively small, without any large-scale quantitative type of surveys done. Lacking expertise in both the research field and within government agencies also contributes to the list of problems.

The lack of accurate statistics available on the magnitude of human trafficking is closely related to the general problems identified when researching trafficking:

-   countries often lack mechanisms for registration and data collection;
-   the use of different definitions and laws, or the lack thereof, with respect to trafficking;
-   much of the trafficking in human beings takes place within communities and countries; border control checks are thus useless against this form of trafficking (all three points were listed in GPAT's final report, 2003b).

But the above is only part of the larger story regarding problems with researching trafficking.

WHERE TO GO FROM HERE? CONCLUDING REMARKS

Despite the improvement of our qualitative understanding of the causes, patterns, and processes involved in trafficking, a number of gaps in our knowledge remain. Quantifying the extent of trafficking is an impossible task, largely based upon the use of inconsistent definitions and the very nature of trafficking itself.

What the review of existing literature and interviews with policy makers and law enforcers have shown is that the chasms between an all-inclusive conceptualization of trafficking and the narrow definition of legalistic approaches cannot easily be wedded. To overcome this situation and move forward, it is the very root causes of trafficking that need to be placed at the centre of analysis and policy making. To do so, it is not only empirical gaps that are left to be filled, but conceptual and methodological innovations are also needed.

To move beyond the "snapshot type" of existing research as well as beyond an ideologically dividing and criminalizing discourse on trafficking, new conceptual tools and methodologies are needed to capture the complexities of the "trafficking" phenomenon which would lead to a set of principles offering a new way of thinking about trafficking and moving toward a new normative agenda. As indicated above, the two approaches to trafficking (1) trafficking for sexual exploitation and (2) irregular migration have dominated the conceptual debate to date and have reached an impasse. This debate can only be moved forward in a meaningful manner (and yield important policy recommendations) if it concentrated on addressing the root causes of trafficking by establishing a link between internal and international trafficking – something which has largely been neglected. This neglect underpins the above argument that much trafficking research is donor-driven and thus first and foremost concerned with illegal migration. To address the root causes means to address issues with development in general and social development in specific. This would require engagement with the development literature and gendered perspectives thereof. To take this matter to a higher level of abstraction, the fairly recent concept of "human security" is suggested here as a normative framework that could shape future research on trafficking, conceptually and empirically.

The concept of "human security" was first introduced by UNDP in its 1994 Human Development Report and has since been elaborated on by the Commission on Human Security (CHS, 2003) as well as by the ILO (2004), albeit with a focus on economic security. The objective of the CHS was to generate a dialogue between the human development and human security communities to develop a practical policy agenda to examine how building human security is an essential contribution to the development process. As a consequence, in recent years, the debate has shifted as both security and development actors have been strongly encouraged, and some have actually begun, to incorporate a human dimension into their policies to expand the debate from a near-exclusive focus on economic growth and development to incorporate issues such as social and human aspects of development and politico-economic governance.

In the specific context of human trafficking, the concept of human security should best focus on the aspect of *in*security. This would allow for an integrated approach to the three major types of migration that lead to many abusive and exploitative practices: (1) undocumented labour, (2) refugee migration, and (3) human trafficking. A future research agenda should be built around the broad objective of investigating human insecurity as the root cause leading to migration (and thus focus on countries of origin). One such dimension to this is discrimination on the basis of gender. Gender-specific economic, social, and cultural insecurities explain to a great extent different motivations to, and modes of, migration. For instance, there is some evidence that in the case of women, it is often not purely economic hardship as such that leads to migration and trafficking, but also such aspects as violent marriages or family relations and stigmatized status as a widow or single mother. This also shows that inadequate social policy and social welfare provisioning is an important source of insecurity. A team of development, social policy, and (internal and international) migration experts need to get together to draft a research project that maps and analyses various forms of migration from a regional perspective to investigate the gendered patterns and to establish indicators of insecurity causing migratory movements of vulnerable people. This could yield data on the worst forms of trafficking that would inform policy making, but would also help to address other precarious scenarios of migration.

NOTES

1. I would like to sincerely thank all those informants who kindly agreed to be interviewed and/or to assist via e-mail in the collection of materials and data for this report. This was partly only possible with the help of other colleagues in identifying key persons and organizations. My gratitude, therefore, goes to Professor Richard Bedford (University of Waikato, New Zealand), Dr. Riwanto Tirtosudarmo (LIPI, Jakarta), Dr. Dang Anh (Department of Sociology, Hanoi), Mr. Chan Sophal (CDRI, Phnom Penh), Ms. Kathy Richards (ACFID, Canberra), and Dr. Sallie Yeah (RMIT, Melbourne). A special "thank you" also goes to all those dedicated NGO representatives who kindly took the time to reply to my e-mails and to put me in touch with other NGOs or individuals. I also would like to extend my gratitude to Ms. Judy Hemming for her research assistance. Last but not least, I have benefited from the useful comments of two anonymous referees.

2. To what extent these are informed by thorough research is of course a different matter.

3. This statement was made by the regional director for the East Asia and Pacific region of UNICEF See www.emedia.com.my/Current_News/MM/Sunday/Frontpage/20040418082107 (18 April 2004).

4. Such as the Asia Pacific Consultation, the Manila Process, the BALI process, workshops run by the Mekong Regional Law Centre, potentially a new ASEAN

Trafficking project sponsored by AusAID, various one-off initiatives addressing irregular migration, ARIAT, Asia pacific Seminar of Experts on Migrants and
Trafficking; moves continue to put trafficking onto the agenda of regional
forums such as APEC and ASEM.

5. Comprised of six countries: Cambodia, China, Laos, Myanmar, Thailand, and
Viet Nam.

6. Personal conversation with IOM office in Canberra, April 2004.

7. This was pointed out by an Australian Federal Police agent (personal
conversation, April 2004).

8. This is an Australian-Indonesian initiative launched in 2002 and refers to the
Regional Ministerial Conference on People Smuggling, Trafficking in Persons
and Related Transnational Crime in Bali which have taken place twice. The
countries covered by the survey questionnaire are: Singapore, Malaysia,
Philippines, Thailand, Indonesia, Laos, Fiji Islands, and Myanmar. Viet Nam
and Cambodia seem to have not replied to the questionnaire as their responses
were unavailable.

9. In Hong Kong Special Administrative Region of China, for example, there were
several attempts by the government to lower the minimum wage guaranteed to
domestic workers by law.

10. I owe this information to Mr. Mizanur Rahman whose PhD thesis on Bangladeshi
workers in Singapore will soon be finalized (National University of Singapore).

11. Trafficking of children for the purpose of camel jockeys seems to be limited to
South Asian children taken to the Middle East and thus not a phenomenon that
occurs in South-East Asia.

12. This bibliography, however, was compiled in 2001 while, or just before, crucial
publications on Australia have been produced. See e.g. Meaker, in Thorbeck
(2002), Carrington and Hearn, 2003; David, 2000; Tailby, no date.

13. See also "Bibliography of Trafficking" compiled by Yukiko Nakajima, *Violence
Against Women Online Resources*, http://www.vaw.umn.edu, 2002.

14. E-mail communication with a staff member, March 2004.

15. This information comes from Migrant Care in Jakarta, received through e-mail
communication in April 2004.

16. I conducted these interviews in April 2003 in connection with a project on
migrant workers' rights.

17. This has been verbally transmitted to me by NGOs in Indonesia and the
Philippines.

18. In this context, a note on the US State Department's TIP report seems
appropriate. Since the passage of the Victims of Trafficking and Violence
Prevention Act 2000, the State Department is required to produce an annual
report on all UN countries on the state of anti-trafficking initiatives by
classifying countries according to a three tier system. Critical voices have
commented upon this report being coloured by the political interests of the
United States and not at all approached by any considerations or sensitivity
for gender. But because classification in the bottom tier results in economic
sanctions, countries are compelled to comply with US demands. However, that
does not necessarily result in policies with positive outcomes for the victims,

or potential victims. For a detailed critique, see www.hrw.org/press/2003/06/us062703ltr.htm.

19. For more detail, see http://www.unescap.org/wid/04widresources/03traffick/trafficking-directory-updated.pdf.
20. See www.unescobkk.org/culture/trafficking.
21. Personal conversation with Vietnamese researcher, Hanoi, April 2002.
22. Critical voices in a recent trafficking project involving the Philippines have indicated their surprise over the choice of the Philippines where there is very little evidence of trafficking (as defined by the UN) as opposed to other countries in this region where trafficking might be a more serious problem (personal communication with researchers, March 2004).
23. Claim made by a Vietnamese researcher involved in the Vietnamese component of this project (March 2002).
24. Claim made by a Vietnamese researcher involved in the Vietnamese component of this project (March 2002).
25. This has also been referred to as "quick and dirty" studies by social researchers (Kelly, 2002).
26. One exception is Kinsey Dinan's report on Thai women in Japan, written for Human Rights Watch. This report covers the period from 1994 to 1999 and points to changes and new developments.
27. Some studies have been able to build upon trust relationships due to the researchers' long-term involvement in NGO work, etc. (Archavanitkul, 1998).
28. The need for a multidisciplinary approach has also been pointed out by Van Impe (2000).
29. As for example the study by Grant et al. (2001).
30. Research on recruitment agencies in Sri Lanka, e.g. has shown that such agencies often go broke because they do not receive payments of debts by migrants (personal conversation with the researcher, November 2003).
31. I owe this last point to Dr. Sallie Yeah (RMIT, Melbourne) who has been involved in drafting a research project with IOM in Manila on this very issue.
32. This under-reporting is said to amount to at least 30 per cent (Grant et al., 2001).
33. This can be found at http://japan.usembassy.gov/e/p/tp-20030912b3.html, 14 April 2004.
34. For a more detailed discussion of these gendered structures, processes, and relationships, see e.g. D'Cunha (in Raymond et al., 2002) and a case study on West Java done for ICMC Indonesia, no date.
35. This information is based on an e-mail exchange (April 2004) with a data and methodology expert (who prefers to remain anonymous) who was involved in assessing trafficking projects in South-East Asia and Australia.
36. As sex work as such is legalized in most Australian states, the criminal offence is illegal immigration only.
37. For a more detailed discussion, see Dixon and Piper, 2004.
38. A recent initiative in the Mekong Subregion called COMMIT (Coordinated Mekong Ministerial Initiative Against Trafficking), assisted by UNIAP, takes a comprehensive view on human trafficking "including trafficking for all end

purposes and involving women, children and men". It remains to be seen, however, how this will be realized and implemented.

39. Same as above: www.emedia.com.my/Current_News/MM/Sunday/Frontpage/ 20040418082107 (18 April 2004).
40. As evident from a recent survey of legislation in place done as part of the BALI process.

REFERENCES

Archavanitkul, K.
  1998   *Combating the Trafficking in Children and their Exploitation in Prostitution and Other Intolerable Forms of Child Labor in Mekong Basin Countries*, a research report submitted to ILO/IPEC, Bangkok.
Bedford, R., et al.
  2002   "International migration in New Zealand: context, components and policy issues", *Journal of Population Research and NZ Population Review*: 39-65.
Brown, L.
  2001   *Sex Slaves: The Trafficking of Women in Asia*, Virgo Press, London.
Caouette, T.
  2002   *Trafficking in Women and Children in the Mekong SubRegion (UNIAP)*, Mid-term Evaluation Report, UNIAP, Bangkok.
Caouette, T., and Y. Saito
  1999   *To Japan and Back*, IOM, Geneva.
Carrington, K., and J. Hearn
  2003   "Trafficking and the sex industry: from impunity to protection", Current Issues Brief No. 28, www.aph.gov.au/hansard and www.parlinfoweb. aph.gov.au.
Commission on Human Security (CHS)
  2003   *Human Security Now*, CHS, New York.
Connell, R.W.
  2004   *The Role of Men and Boys in Achieving Gender Equality*, 48th Session of Commission on the Status of Women, United Nations, New York, 1-12 March.
Dargan, P.
  2003   "Trafficking and human rights: the role of national human rights institutions in the Asia Pacific region", The Asia Pacific Forum of National Human Rights Institutions, Stop the Traffic 2 Conference, Melbourne, 23-24 October.
Darwin, M., et al.
  2003   *Living on the Edges: Cross-Border Mobility and Sexual Exploitation in the Greater South-East Asia Subregion*, Centre for Population and Policy Studies, Gadjah Mada University, Yogyakarta.

David, F.
2000   "Human smuggling and trafficking: an overview of the response at the federal level", Australian Institute of Criminology Research and Public Policy Series, No. 24.

Dixon, J., and N. Piper
2004   "Trafficking in humans and victim support initiatives: insights from South-East Asia and Oceania", background paper prepared for IOM, Geneva.

Gallagher, A.
2001   "Human rights and the new UN protocols on trafficking and migrant smuggling: a preliminary analysis", *Human Rights Quarterly*, 23: 975-1004.
2002   "Consideration of the issue of trafficking", Background Paper, The Asia Pacific Forum of National Human Rights Institutions, Sydney, 11-12 November.

Global Programme against Trafficking in Human Beings (GPAT)
2003a   *Coalitions Against Trafficking in Human Beings in the Philippines*, United Nations Office on Drugs and Crime, Vienna.
2003b   *Coalitions Against Trafficking in Human Beings in the Philippines: Research and Action Final Report*, United Nations Office on Drugs and Crime, Vienna.

Grant, A.
2001   "The commercial sexual exploitation of children", *Journal of the Institute of Criminology*, 12(3): 269-287.

Grumiau, S.
n.d.   *Commercial Sexual Exploitation of Children: The Situation in Thailand, Cambodia and the Philippines: What Can the Trade Union Movement do to Help?*, International Confederation of Free Trade Unions (ICFTU).

International Labour Organization (ILO)
2004   "Economic security for a better world", ILO Socio-economic Security Programme, ILO, Geneva.

Joint Committee on the Australian Crime Commission
2004   "Trafficking in women for sexual servitude", Proof Committee Hansard-Commonwealth of Australia, Canberra, 26 February.

Jones, S.
2000   *Making Money off Migrants: The Indonesian Exodus to Malaysia*, Asia 2000 Ltd, Hong Kong.

Kelly, E.
2002   *Journeys of Jeopardy: A Review of Research on Trafficking in Women and Children in Europe*, IOM, Geneva.

Marshall, P.
2001   "Globalization, migration and trafficking: some thoughts from the South-East Asian region", Occasional Paper No. 1, Globalization Workshop in Kuala Lumpur, UN Inter-Agency Project on Trafficking in Women and Children in the Mekong Subregion, 8-10 May.

Parliamentary Joint Committee on the Australian Crime Commission
    2004   "Inquiry into the trafficking of women for sexual servitude", Common-
            wealth of Australia, Canberra, http://www.aph.gov.au/Senate/committee/
            acc_ctte/sexual_servitude/index.htm.
Pécoud, A., and P. de Guchteneire
    2004   "Migration, human rights and the United Nations: an investigation of the
            obstacles to the UN Convention on Migrant Workers' Rights", *Global
            Migration Perspectives No. 3*, Global Commission for International
            Migration, Geneva.
Piper, N.
            "Rights of foreign workers and the politics of migration in South-East
            and East Asia", *International Migration*, forthcoming.
Piper, N., and B. Yeoh (Eds)
            "Meeting the challenges of HIV/AIDS in South-East and East Asia", *Asia
            Pacific Viewpoint*, special issue, forthcoming.
Raymond, J.G., et al.
    2002   *A Comparative Study of Women Trafficked in the Migration Process –
            Patterns, Profiles and Health Consequences of Sexual Exploitation in
            Five Countries (Indonesia, the Philippines, Thailand, Venezuela and
            the United States)*, CATW.
Rosenberg, R. (Ed.)
    2003   *Trafficking of Women and Children in Indonesia*, ICMC, ACILS, and
            USAID, Jakarta.
Satterthwaite, M.
    2005   "Crossing borders, claiming rights: using human rights law to empower
            women migrant workers", *Yale Human Rights and Development Law
            Journal*, 8, forthcoming.
Schloenhardt, A.
    2001   "Trafficking in migrants, illegal migration and organized crime in Australia
            and the Asia Pacific region", *International Journal of Sociology of Law*,
            29: 331-378.
Skeldon, R.
    2000   "Trafficking: a perspective from Asia", *International Migration*, 38(3):
            7-30.
Smith, S.
    2001   "The role of employers and workers' organizations in action against the
            worst forms of child labour, including the trafficking of children into labour
            and sexual exploitation", Background Paper for ILO-Japan Meeting on
            Trafficking of Children for Labour and Sexual Exploitation, Manila,
            Philippines, 10-12 October.
Surtees, R.
    2003   "Commercial sex workers", in R. Rosenberg (Ed.), *Trafficking of Women
            and Children in Indonesia*, ICMC, ACILS, and USAID, Jakarta.
Tailby, R.
    n.d.   *A Cross-Analysis Report into Smuggling and Trafficking Between the
            Philippines and Australia*, Coalition against Trafficking in Human Beings

in the Philippines-Phase 1, United Nations Global Programme against Trafficking in Human Beings.

Van Impe, K.

2000   "People for sale: the need for a multidisciplinary approach towards human trafficking", *International Migration*, Special Issue 2000/1.

Wainaina, N.

2004   "The role of men and boys in the prevention of HIV/AIDS and in combating gender-based violence", 48th session Commission on the Status of Women, United Nations, New York, 1-12 March.

Wijers, M., and L. Lap-Chew

1997   *Trafficking in Women Forced Labour and Slavery-like Practices in Marriage Domestic Labour and Prostitution*, Foundations Against Trafficking in Women (STV), Utrecht.

Wong, D.

"The rumour of trafficking: border controls, illegal immigration and the sovereignty of the nation-state", in W. van Schenden and I. Abraham (Eds), *The Criminal Life of Things*, University of Illinois Press, Chicago, forthcoming.

"You Can Find Anything You Want": A Critical Reflection on Research on Trafficking in Persons within and into Europe

Liz Kelly*

INTRODUCTION

The title of this paper – a direct quote from an economically successful Turkish male prostitute user (Erder and Kaska, 2003: 65) – encapsulates attitudes underpinning the treatment of human beings as commodities. Yet, at the same time, we cannot "find anything we want" in the research on trafficking, which continues to be deficient in a number of respects. This paper takes a critical look at the current state of research with respect to Europe; given that trafficking occurs into and out of Europe to other regions of the globe, and that new concepts and theoretical perspectives transcend locality, "Europe" has been interpreted broadly. It both stands alone and acts as a companion piece to *Journeys of Jeopardy* (Kelly, 2002), extending that overview not only in terms of recent publications and more complex frameworks, but also through an attempt to move beyond the focus on trafficking for sexual exploitation to include that for domestic service and labour exploitation.[1] The majority of published material still focuses on sexual exploitation and few investigations include more than one form (for exceptions, see Anderson and O'Connell Davidson, 2003; Kelly, 2005). Emphasis here has also been placed on conceptual framings and frameworks that could enhance future work.

The scale of publications on trafficking in persons has grown hugely in the last decade, reflecting and constructing a context in which funding for counter-trafficking efforts has also increased substantially. As the issue gained policy recognition and financial resources were mobilized, many more players entered

* Child and Woman Abuse Studies Unit, University of North London, United Kingdom.

the increasingly competitive field of non-governmental organizations (NGOs) and international non-governmental organizations (INGOs) activity. While the engagement in research and documentation of international bodies, including at least five United Nations (UN) agencies, is welcome, it does not necessarily ensure a deepening of the knowledge base. Publications may primarily reflect a claims-making process, vying for influence over how the issue is understood and where it is located intellectually, symbolically, and materially. This paper argues for a widened framing and a more interdisciplinary approach to the issue of trafficking in order not only to enhance intellectual understanding but also to provide firmer ground on which to build and assess counter-trafficking strategies.

No claim is made to have undertaken a comprehensive review of all recently published European research. Although a large number of Internet and academic database searches were undertaken, only material published in English has been included. With that said, a substantial amount of material was critically analysed, with much of it falling into the patterns noted in *Journeys of Jeopardy* (Kelly, 2002): single country studies (see, e.g. Erder and Kaska, 2003; Hughes and Denisova, 2001; Human Rights Watch, 2002) or regional overviews (see, e.g. Apap, 2003; Chammartin, 2003; Hunzinger and Coffey, 2003; Zimmerman et al., 2003) documenting and reflecting upon existing efforts and interventions. The sections that follow address: continued methodological deficiencies, including the perennial question of defining trafficking; the current knowledge base with respect to trafficking for sexual exploitation, domestic service, labour exploitation, and trafficking of children; the construction of hierarchies of worth; and new approaches to the study of traffickers and exploiters; it concludes with an argument for a recasting of the future research agenda.

WEAKNESSES AND LIMITATIONS IN DATA AND METHOD

A considerable proportion of trafficking research is funded/commissioned/conducted by international organizations as one element of counter-trafficking programmes. Establishing an evidence base for interventions is to be commended, but most such commissions have short time lines and require policy relevant findings and conclusions. Pure research studies and detailed research evaluations continue to be extremely rare, and a limited number of established social scientists are involved in exploring the contours of human trafficking. These patterns contribute to several methodological weaknesses in the field.

The majority of published studies continue to say little, if anything, about the methods used to collect and analyse the data they present, restricting this part to a page or a short appendix (see Kelly, 2002). In some cases it is evident that the authors have limited research training, illustrated by a number of omissions including a lack of critical assessment of official statistics, a failure to draw on qualitative material in anything other than an illustrative way, and no discussion of the limitations of method and data. There is also confusion with respect to methodology, methods, tools, and analysis, resulting in minimal documentation of how research was undertaken. For example, there is never any discussion of how interviews are conducted with women who speak a range of languages, or how translation affects the depth and quality of data. Few multi-country/regional studies present data in a comparative way that identifies similarities and differences, opting for the basic route of taking each nation as a separate case.

Other methodological challenges are inherent to the topic, as the illegality of trafficking in persons ensures that accurate measures of extent will elude researchers, however much policy makers and politicians may seek them (Kangaspunta, 2003). What can be presented, however, are "best estimates", the accuracy of which depends on the sources relied on and assumptions made. Unfortunately, few estimates of scale include the background information and thinking underpinning the calculation, denying readers the opportunity to assess the claim.

The lack of methodological transparency provides little foundation for assessing the depth and quality of research and denies the entire field opportunities for learning and knowledge transfer. A 2003 UN Children's Fund (UNICEF)/UN Inter-Agency Project on Human Trafficking in the Greater Mekong Subregion (UNIAP) project in Thailand, for example, used participatory research methods to develop research capacity in villages that simultaneously act as a way to trace women and girls who have been trafficked. The interim report contains hints that implementation has been problematic, but the absence of detail means that neither methodological nor practical lessons can be learned.

The recurring problem of definition

The question of definition continues to vex researchers and practitioners in this field. While the definition in the UN protocol has provided a baseline,[2] specifying that cases of trafficking involve the three elements of recruitment, movement/receipt, and intention to exploit, this has not resolved the debates (Anderson and O'Connell Davidson, 2003) which coalesce around unresolved positions on the issues of migration, prostitution, and agency. This preoccupation has deflected attention from a range of other questions about which it might be possible to generate new and revealing knowledge, such as why so little attention has been paid to trafficking which does not involve children and/or sexual exploitation, and how a wider framing might change what we think we know about the prevalence and patterns involved. At the micro level there has been hardly any empirical investigation of how members of civil society and those whose labour and trust has been exploited define trafficking, yet this has direct effects on whether people seek advice or help, and will determine how they respond to questions intended to discern if they have been trafficked or "merely" smuggled. How service providers and state agents define trafficking, and especially the extent to which they introduce additional requirements which do not appear in the protocol in order to construct a category of "deserving" victims or ration scarce resources, is seldom studied in any depth, although published material does document these practices (Kelly, 2002).

While the UN protocols on trafficking and smuggling attempt to make clear, and to an extent absolute, the distinctions between the two practices, a number of studies are highlighting that this is a fiction (see Kelly, 2002). From the perspective of victims trafficking is a process within which, in most instances, they believe they are making an agreement to be smuggled; the exploitation aspect may only be evident at an end point, where someone demands payment they think they are owed or discovers that promised remittances have not been sent to their family (Kelly, 2005). What we know about both smuggling[3] and trafficking suggests that it would be more accurate to view them as a continuum, shading into and out of one another across a number of dimensions (ILO, 2003b; IOM, 2004; Anderson and O'Connell Davidson, 2003). There are both overlaps and transitions from smuggling to trafficking, made more likely where the journey is lengthier since this increases the opportunities for exploitation and the size of debt on arrival. Many who are smuggled rely on third parties for employment in the destination country, which increases the potential layers of control that can be used to create conditions of bondage (Shelley, 2001). A diagrammatic representation of some of the overlaps is presented in a recent study of Afghanistan (IOM, 2004), and could certainly be extended.

This study also introduces the concept of "trafficking-like practices". A number of these – child/early/forced marriage, kidnapping, bride price, and exchanging women as a way of settling tribal disputes – are already specified as "harmful traditional practices" within UN definitions of gender-based violence. Where local custom, sometimes supported by law, treats women so explicitly as property, their commodification through trafficking is facilitated. Other less gender-specific aspects involve kidnapping and holding young migrants ransom while exploiting their labour and/or sexuality (IOM, 2004), practices that have also been documented in Central Asia (Kelly, 2005).

THE CURRENT KNOWLEDGE BASE

The difficulties of establishing accurate baseline estimates for any form of trafficking, at global, regional, or national levels, have been well documented, as has the need for more careful explication of how figures are determined (Kangaspunta, 2003; Kelly, 2002; Laczko, 2002). Assessing what data we do have is made more complex by the fact that governments, the media, and even researchers continue to conflate migration, asylum, refugees, trafficking, and smuggling. Indeed it may prove impossible to resolve this conceptual confusion, since in some instances it serves political and ideological ends (Laczko, 2002), and in others represents a sincere attempt to reflect the complexities of lived experiences.

In 2003 the UN Educational, Scientific and Cultural Organization (UNESCO) undertook the useful exercise of compiling and comparing the worldwide estimates for trafficking, and while the actual presentation of the data (found at: www.unescobkk.org/culture/trafficking, Factsheet 1) leaves much to be desired, it nonetheless reveals a range of figures that differ by factors of between two to five. The highest estimate of 4 million trafficked persons per year globally has been used by International Organization for Migration (IOM), United States Agency for International Development (USAID), and the UN. However, graphically documenting this variation is simply a first step. It is difficult to move on to postulating why estimates differ so markedly since contextual information, such as whether the figures cover all forms of trafficking in persons or only sexual exploitation, is lacking. The global estimates in successive US Department of State Trafficking in Persons reports (US Department of State, 2002, 2003, 2004) have declined year on year, as shown below:[4]

2002	700,000-4 million
2003	800,000-900,000
2004	600,000-800,000

These adjustments can be related to both the widespread critique of the absence of documentation accompanying such figures and the development of more "evidence-based" approaches to estimation. The lack of detail about the shifts[5] and why estimates continue to fall is regrettable because it precludes academic exploration and permits continued speculation about "advocacy numbers".[6] Adding to the lack of clarity is the fact that while the overall framing of the report is trafficking in persons, most of the content and data are confined to sexual exploitation. Including other forms of trafficking would increase estimates considerably, and if documented by region and form of trafficking, probably heighten awareness of intra-regional flows.

Even establishing seemingly simple facts, such as how many victims have been assisted in a region, produces complex methodological challenges, including how to avoid double counting individuals. An attempt to establish a sound methodology addressing this question in south-east Europe (Hunzinger and Coffey,

2003) for the previous year encountered a number of complex problems with respect to record keeping. Some have argued that the small numbers of identified victims, in this instance 5,203, demonstrate that estimates of scale, such as those cited above, are wildly inaccurate (Chapkis, 2003). The report, however, makes clear that apart from under-detection and under-reporting, in resource poor contexts a filtering process determines who receives assistance.

Flows and/or hot spots

Global trafficking flows echo patterns of the globalization of labour migration, albeit in contexts where increasingly strong immigration controls create irregular migration and through this the markets for facilitation and smuggling. At the same time, however, movements are not simply between the global north and south, with greater but less documented flows taking place within regions (Kelly, 2002; Kelly, 2005).

The strongest flows now are taking place *within* Europe – a shift from the picture in previous decades, where trafficked women came primarily from Asia and South America. This illustrates the dynamism of trafficking, with rapid shifts in countries of origin and routes reflecting the ability of traffickers to respond quickly to changing political and economic conditions and counter-trafficking responses (Shelley, 2002b). At the same time, there are still large flows into Europe from other continents, including Africa (Pearson, 2003). One recent aspect of the changing context has been the accession of ten states into the European Union, a number of which had been identified as source, but primarily transit, countries in the 1990s (Kelly, 2002). The adjustments in border regimes required for accession have led to a decline in trafficking from or through Hungary and Slovenia, accompanied by increased recruitment in, and transit through, Romania and Serbia (Hunzinger and Coffey, 2003).

The documentation of routes and flows is a migration framing, drawn from classical demography. Asking similar questions but using the criminological framing of crime mapping and "hot spots" might produce additional insights. Explaining what it is about a particular location at a particular moment in time that makes it favourable has been a route criminologists have used to discover both intervention points once the pattern has developed, and opportunities for prevention and early intervention. Examining the emergence of Turkey as a "hot spot" would involve discussion of its strategic location, large landmass, increasing economic activity, and open visa regime to facilitate tourism. A less obvious aspect affecting Turkey currently involves "ocular" or "shuttle" migrants – small-scale female traders/entrepreneurs from many countries in Eastern Europe and Central Asia who regularly travel to Greece, Turkey, and the Gulf states to purchase goods for re-sale at home. There are complex, and as yet poorly understood and documented, connections between these patterns and trafficking in persons (Kelly, 2005).

Increasing reference to significant flows to the Gulf states of migrant labour and trafficking for domestic service, the sex industry, and other forms of bonded labour is evident. There are an estimated 20,000 to 25,000 Ethiopian domestic workers in Lebanon alone (Pearson, 2003), many of whom are illegal because there are only three state-registered employment agencies in Ethiopia. Increased case-based documentation of trafficking is evident, but limited research/ documentation has been undertaken, with what little has been published focusing on the legal context (see, for example, Mattar, 2001) or the use of children as camel jockeys (Mattar, 2003a). Two recent exceptions include a discussion of the range of trafficking (Mattar, 2003a) and a short journalistic piece by Donna Hughes (2004) on the extent of organized prostitution in Iran. Fifty prosecutions – many large scale – took place between 2000 and 2003, revealing extensive internal trafficking and trafficking of Iranian girls and women into the EU (France, UK), the other Gulf states, Pakistan, and Afghanistan.

Accounting for why the Gulf constitutes a "hot spot" with respect to all forms of trafficking deserves more attention, including the complexities and tensions with respect to Islam and the purchase of sexual services. Prostitution was legal in many Arab countries during the first part of the twentieth century (Mattar, 2001), while more recently most systems of Islamic law have defined it as a form of adultery, for which both parties are criminally liable. The possibility that women could also be prosecuted acts as a powerful disincentive for any Muslim woman to report/give evidence against traffickers. Shi'a Muslims, however, have in some instances invoked the notion of temporary marriage as a legitimizing Islamic framework for prostitution, especially the model where one man takes ownership of women for a period of weeks or months. Ethiopian trafficked women, for example, are divided upon arrival to the United Arab Emirates (UAE), with the most "attractive" reserved for individual contracts.[7]

In temporary marriages, the marriage itself may be entered into orally, without witnesses or registration. Moreover women in temporary marriage have no right to divorce; nor are they entitled to inheritance. Meanwhile men may terminate the agreement at any time. It has been argued that temporary marriages make women vulnerable to sexual exploitation and are very often used as a legitimate means to force women into prostitution (Mattar, 2003: 726).

Officials from the Iranian Ministry of the Interior have proposed legalizing brothels which were to be called "morality houses", using the temporary marriage custom, as a way to deal with burgeoning prostitution in Iran (Hughes, 2004: 2).

Trafficking for sexual exploitation also occurs in Lebanon, which has a less restrictive social policy, including a state-controlled brothel regime.[8]

The large movements into Israel also deserve attention, given that during conflict the movement tends to be outward. Of the 400 women detected in 2000 (Levekron, 2001) the vast majority came from Ukraine, Russia, and Moldova, and although 70 per cent knew they would be working in prostitution, they had not previously been active in the sex industry. One of the situational factors at work in Israel is the presence of a significant Russian diaspora, of which a minority of the members are organized crime bosses. Routes into Israel have become more complex as efforts to limit trafficking have increased: one involves arriving in Egypt as a tourist from Moscow and then being taken across the desert for days by Bedouins. Recent accounts of women travelling this route document rape and being held in the desert for several months (Kelly, 2005).

New trends in trafficking for sexual exploitation

Journeys of Jeopardy (Kelly, 2002) outlined the major flows of trafficking for sexual exploitation within and out of Europe at the turn of the twentieth century, noting the increased relevance of intra-regional flows, and posing the question of whether trafficking routes and "hot spots" extend sex markets, which in turn increase the demand for trafficked women. A number of recent reports support this analysis, especially with respect to the Balkans (SEERIGHTS, 2003; O'Brien et al., 2004). An Amnesty International press statement in May 2004 asserted that the sex industry in Kosovo had not only grown ten times since the early 1990s, but also that the majority of women within it were trafficked. The emergence of extensive sex markets in the poorest countries in Europe has taken place in the nexus between the poverty of transition, conflict, gender inequality, and human trafficking routes.

Sex industries in the West continue to expand, while being less able to recruit nationals to work within them, thus creating a strong market for both migrants and trafficked women. Sex markets are increasingly diverse and wide ranging, with a small top end where the financial rewards can be substantial, and a large middle and bottom end, where conditions vary, and in some instances can only be described as sexual slavery (Bindel and Kelly, 2003). Turkish research confirms and illustrates these processes:

> ...this was a very diversified field where highly organized international syndicates, relatively small networks working through intermediaries and local pimps, as well as independent sex workers all interacted, characterized by illegality and various degrees of deception, mistreatment and exploitation (Erder and Kaska, 2003: 61).

This study is unusual in the breadth of data drawn on, including interviews with two customers who admit to knowing that women are exploited, controlled, and lack freedom. One customer even revealed that he was considering purchasing a trafficked woman for his personal use, reflecting patterns noted in the Gulf (see earlier) and in Bosnia (Kelly, 2002). The extent of this practice in Europe is unclear, as is the recent documentation of pimps/traffickers "renting" women to men, who then pimp the women themselves.[9]

The first documentation of those assisted in the UK shelter (Poppy Project, 2004) is to be commended for its transparency and detail. Data collection is explained as a process, with initial entries subsequently updated as more detail emerges and as women trust the project enough to reveal aspects of the truth which they fear may discredit them. The data also confirm that narrow definitions act as a filter into support, with strict rules by the Home Office (alongside personal choice) meaning that less than half of those referred in the first year (n=114) receive assistance (n=46) and less than one-quarter receive shelter (n=26). Three-quarters come from Europe, both accession and CIS states. The systematic collection of data on gender violence before and during trafficking is also welcome and shows that before they were trafficked, more than one-third (38%) report being subjected to multiple forms; almost half (46%) were sexually abused/raped; one-third (31%) were sexually abused as children; two-thirds (62%) experienced physical assault; and almost half (46%) experienced domestic violence, primarily as children living with it. A range of traumatic symptoms have also been documented, with almost all (92%) reporting mental distress, including:

> ...near universal problems with sleeping/nightmares, anxiety and fear and common problems with loss of appetite and controlling aggression. Many women also talked about experiencing panic attacks, memory problems, self blame... flashbacks... thoughts of suicide, self-harm and crying constantly. One woman articulately sums this up as feeling like she is "screaming inside all the time" (Poppy Project, 2004: 7).

These data echo the experiences of shelters in countries of origin working with women who have been returned. The SEE overview of assistance concluded that 95 per cent of their service users needed treatment for sexually transmitted infections (STIs) and many needed intensive psychological support, but the most extensive counselling currently on offer was limited to three to four weeks (Hunzinger and Coffey, 2003: 22). The inadequacy of such provision is confirmed by an overview (Rousseaux, 2003) of the psychological impacts, with links to the most recent work on trauma and clinical practice regarding torture, child sexual abuse, and domestic violence. The disconnection from others, a feature of trauma, is accentuated in contexts where victimization carries shame for victims, and has serious implications for reintegration in contexts where not only is there minimal support, but it is also taboo to discuss mental distress and/or and the realities of sexual exploitation (Bales, 2003).[10] The Afghanistan study (IOM, 2004) presents an important challenge for counter-trafficking work, which must refocus shame so that it both attaches to perpetrators and ceases to be a deterrent to seeking support.[11] That it arises so strongly in this report is partly the outcome of the level of shame in an honour culture functioning as a huge deterrent to women reporting trafficking and any form of sexual violence, although shame attaches to victims of all forms of sexual violence across various cultures and contexts.

A note on domestic service

This section does not seek to review the burgeoning connections between migration and domestic service (see Anderson, 2000 for an overview) but points to what indicators currently exist regarding the links between trafficking and systems of inequality. Reflecting patterns highlighted earlier, there are movements between continents alongside intra-regional flows. Crossovers with child trafficking are also strong, connected to long-standing indigenous patterns of child servants and internal trafficking. The majority of those involved are female, reflecting the virtual global allocation of household and personal care work to women. The largest and most sustained international flows appear to be into Arab countries (Mattar, 2003) and within Asia (from Indonesia to Malaysia, for example). Movements into Europe are also strong, but there is limited documentation about the relative numbers with legal permits, and those who are irregular and/or trafficked. The increased use of migrant labour for private care of the disabled and elderly in developed countries is also extending the market (Ehrenriech and Hochschild, 2003).

The privatized nature of domestic work provides fertile ground for exploitation, and trafficking is one variant in a wider system of ill-treatment by recruitment agencies and individual employers. Recruitment agencies are known for charging excessive fees (Anderson and O'Connell Davidson, 2003a: 14) and failing to fulfil contracts which state they will find another employer if serious problems are encountered. Many domestic workers work in a form of debt bondage, that is, they work for nothing to pay off transportation and arrangement fees. This parallels the practices of brothel owners (Kelly, 2002) who evade their financial responsibilities by finding reasons to fire workers when they are due to be paid their wages and the return fare home (Anderson and O'Connell Davidson, 2003a: 15; Chammartin, 2003). Another parallel is the scale of exploitation inflicted on all domestic workers, legal and illegal, ranging from excessive work hours to control of movement (often including removal of papers) and sexual abuse by male members of the household (Anderson and O'Connell Davidson, 2003b).

A major problem with domestic work is that it is rarely recognized as a form of labour. In most of the Gulf states, for example, such a law would be regarded as an intrusion into the privacy of the family, and domestic workers are defined as members of the household (Matter, 2003b). Discussions about bringing domestic workers within labour law frequently flounder in developing countries, as recently happened in Ethiopia, with difficulties centring on how to define it, and draw boundaries between this and systems of family fosterage. Such arguments, however, do not hold for Western destination countries where inclusion is also resisted (Anderson and O'Connell Davidson, 2003b). There is a clear need for more detailed exploration of trafficking for domestic work in Europe, and for deeper connections to be made across the trafficking and labour exploitation literatures.

A note on labour exploitation

Trafficking for labour exploitation is used to refer to workers who are in less privatized sectors of economies, including agriculture, construction, and manufacturing (including low-tech/craft production). In much of the literature, reference is made to the preponderance of men in this form of trafficking, although recent data (Kelly, 2005) and the feminization of migration more broadly, point to the presence of large numbers of women, especially in the intra-regional movements.

Underpinning trafficking for labour exploitation in Europe is the demand for cheap and malleable labour for businesses which are no longer competitive and can be relocated (agriculture, garments) and those that cannot (construction, catering) (ILO, 2003b). Significant sectors of western European industry are now dependent on migrant labour, both legal and illegal, especially agriculture in the UK, France, Spain, Switzerland, and the Netherlands. There are also large numbers involved in the garment and shoe industries in Italy and France, where both national pride and premium prices accompany labels that state "made in Italy" or "produced in France".

In other parts of the world historic and contemporary practices of slavery, bonded labour, child labour, and labour camps have much in common with, and could be understood as precursors of, trafficking. One example here is the construction industry, which is now dominated by a small number of major companies that subcontract to a globalized workforce. Depending on where the contracts are located the workforce will experience various forms of restriction and exploitation. Currently, many projects in Russia use bonded/trafficked male workers, with those from Central Asia the most likely to be trafficked and earning the lowest wages. They are also often required to live in walled-off sites, within a version of the gangmaster system (Kelly, 2005; ILO, 2003a).

The "gangmaster" system has been subjected to increased scrutiny in the United Kingdom, partly in response to revelations after the death of a group of Chinese cockle pickers in 2004, although research had already documented its revival and expansion (ILO, 2003b). Based on a nineteenth-century tradition (ILO, 2003b: 13), there are documented connections with organized crime. Workers, who are a combination of legal and illegal migrants, have to pay 150 euros for a gangmaster's telephone number and a fee of about 400 euros to arrange work and accommodation. Work is seldom guaranteed, and wage rates are significantly less than the national minimum wage. Low wages, and the extortionate charges for transport and accommodation, make it difficult to get out of debt. In a case study based on agricultural work in the Midlands (ILO, 2003b) not all of the undocumented workers had been trafficked, but all were subjected to labour exploitation by virtue of their vulnerable position, and were undoubtedly trapped in a form of bonded labour (ILO, 2003b: 25).

The extent to which the definition of trafficking applies to labour exploitation of migrant workers has not received the same level of attention as the application to sexual exploitation. Some of the dilemmas and anomalies concern whether an unbroken chain needs to exist between recruitment and eventual exploitation, as there appears to be more fragmentation in this area, with some agencies facilitating smuggling and promising jobs in the destination, but abandoning people there with no resources or papers (Kelly, 2005). This "position of vulnerability" is exploited by unscrupulous employers who appear aware of these deceptive practices to the extent that they frequent the locations where migrants are dropped. One difference with respect to sexual exploitation appears to be that fees are more likely to be paid/required before departure and are often borrowed from family members. It is the responsibility for this debt which acts as a barrier to seeking help or reporting exploitation.

A note on child trafficking

The knowledge base on children is even less strong than that on adults, with the most significant movements taking place outside Europe. While children's charities in many European countries continue to publish studies of child trafficking and document cases of minors being trafficked into the sex industry, there is little evidence that the scale has increased markedly in recent years. While traffickers and exploiters can earn premium prices on girls, having sex with minors has become less acceptable in much of Europe. As Julia O'Connell Davidson (1998) argues, while there is a small market for sex with children, many customers in the larger adult sex market are not that discriminating about age. This logic suggests that young women, aged 13 to 15, are the most likely recruits for the western European sex industries. One recent study (O'Brien et al., 2004) highlights the difficulties of tracing these patterns, as the seven countries examined – Albania, Belarus, the Czech Republic, Moldova, Romania, Russia, and the Ukraine – currently lack the capacity to ensure accurate official record keeping and thus cannot identify children as a separate category.

Too little attention has been paid to the trafficking of children into domestic service and other forms of bonded labour within Europe, although substantial documentation of it in other regions can be found through the International Labour Organization (ILO) and UNICEF, including analysis of how complex and intersecting local traditions and practices with respect to slavery, child labour, and fosterage can provide contexts in which trafficking can emerge and become embedded. Perhaps most important, however, is the limited attention that has been paid to how living in a context with high levels of irregular migration affects children, who may become involved in trafficking as a family group, through being sold or being present in the contexts where daily recruitment takes place (Kelly, 2005). Beyond these direct engagements is a much wider impact of trafficking and migration on the far greater numbers of children whose parents have sought employment elsewhere. They are vulnerable here to neglect and mistreatment by the adults in whose care they are left, especially when parents do not or cannot remit money for their upkeep.

The feminization of migration at the close of the twentieth century has led feminist commentators to ask whether the relative freedom of women in the West is being bought at the cost of exploitation of those from the South (Ehrenreich and Hochschild, 2003). Within the globalization of household labour, particular nationalities, rather than women per se, are being constructed as "naturally" suited to this work (Ehrenreich and Hochschild, 2003), sometimes travelling half way around the globe to care for other women's children, while leaving their own in the care of impoverished relatives. This disjunction of childhoods has prompted questions about whether a "care deficit" is emerging in the global South, and what the consequences of this will be for the current generation of children.

HIERARCHIES OF WORTH

Comparing findings across studies highlights differential pricing regimes both for the range of services and journeys, but also what is charged in the same country for individuals from different countries of origin. Further attention to the economics of human trafficking is surely needed, where short journeys into neighbouring countries (for example by boat from Morocco to Spain or Mexico to the United States) may cost 500 euros, whereas lengthy and more complex processes of moving people, for example, from China to western Europe or the United States can cost up to 30,000 euros (Banerjee, 2003). The lengthier and more expensive the journey, the greater the indebtedness and dependency of the migrants, which in turn creates higher levels of vulnerability to exploitation. At the same time, it may be that some networks are more interested in smuggling than trafficking, or vice versa. Explicating the macro- and microeconomic factors involved, from the perspective of traffickers and trafficked persons, should be a research priority. It may be, for example, that the premium prices for travel into western Europe create more extensive conditions of exploitation.

The pattern of sale and resale of women trafficked into the sex industry seems increasingly common in Europe. In the recent Turkish study a trafficker openly admitted that women are sold in "sales-like auctions" (Erder and Kaska, 2003: 63); literally dealing with women as commodities has also been documented in Bosnia and Kosovo (see also Corrin, 2000, Human Rights Watch, 2002). A more common pattern is revealed in the accounts of trafficked women, some of whom talk of being sold more than 20 times (Kelly, 2005). It is unclear whether this is a way sex businesses circulate women and/or a mechanism to ensure maximum exploitation, as it ensures debts are never paid off. The differential pricing of trafficked persons – across various forms of human trafficking – reflects processes of both commodification and racism. For example, higher prices are charged (and wages paid) to Filipina maids in the Gulf states than those from Sri Lanka, sex business owners pay more for Slavic women than those from the Caucasus (Shelley, 2002b), and hierarchies exist in relation to the bonded labour systems in construction in Russia (Kelly, 2005). The "worth" of persons is thus reduced to a financial calculation, with meanings and consequences at the level of identity and the symbolic rarely noted.

The emphasis on assessing assistance and documenting the experiential aspects of trafficking, perhaps accompanied by a view of victims as lacking agency and therefore unable to escape, has meant that very limited work has addressed ways people extricate themselves from exploitation. Owing money that one has borrowed from one's relatives appears to entrap in a particularly remorseless way, and applies across all forms of trafficking (Kelly, 2005), as returning with nothing, not even enough to repay the debt, is unacceptable to many, involving too great a loss of face and/or irresolvable guilt at having not only failed to improve family fortunes but made them worse. In such contexts being re-trafficked may be preferred to returning empty handed to one's family/community.[12]

Some routes out of exploitation are also problematic. Most studies that address law enforcement responses reveal that significant proportions of the women detected in prostitution are treated as illegal migrants, and are frequently held in prisons and detention centres for weeks and months. This becomes especially daunting for women from countries without diplomatic missions in destination countries and who have yet to negotiate reciprocal arrangements with other countries. Similarly, some countries of origin often cannot afford, or choose not, to fly their citizens home, preferring to issue bus and train tickets – much more possible across Europe than some other routes – which in turn make people much more vulnerable to re-trafficking (Hughes and Denisova, 2001: 15). One journalist, Martin (2003), presents strong evidence that corrupt officials alert traffickers when women are being returned. Such treatment indicates perceptions of these women as "worth less" than others; the combination of irregular migration and prostitution somehow not only excusing treatment that is the opposite of that expected under the UN protocol, but also justifying states taking less than swift and determined efforts to identify and ensure the return of their citizens. It is a link between women's NGOs in Israel and Uzbekistan that identifies trafficked Uzbek women in Israeli prisons, some of whom have been there for months, and even years.

"IS IT A CRIME TO SELL WOMEN?
THEY SELL FOOTBALLERS DON'T THEY?":[13]
A FOCUS ON TRAFFICKERS AND EXPLOITERS

It is less than simple to study traffickers who have every reason for wishing to remain hidden from scrutiny (Tailby, 2001). Adding to the difficulties is the fact that trafficking is a dynamic, moving target, connected to local circumstances, while adapting rapidly to global shifts in opportunities and enforcement (UNDOC, 2003). What we do know is that there are large, complex, and transnational groups alongside more nebulous networks that form alliances for particular projects, and smaller emergent groupings that tend to operate in specific locations (Bagley, 2001). In this section more recent insights and questions are explored alongside two typologies that deserve empirical testing and extension.

One connection worthy of more detailed research is the extent to which the scale of human trafficking is associated with established organized crime networks and corruption, including what the precise mechanisms involved are and whether these extend across all forms of trafficking in persons. Correlations with respect to high flows for trafficking for sexual exploitation and regional reputations for corruption and organized criminal networks have been noted across the globe (e.g. Ukraine (Hughes and Denisova, 2001), Nigeria (Pearson, 2003), and Thailand (Phongpaichit et al., 1998)). The Thai study is to be commended for the attempt to investigate the connections more explicitly, including heavy financial investments in political parties and individual politicians to ensure counter-trafficking efforts are ineffective.[14] The extensiveness of organized crime, and its penetration of the political sphere, have prompted complex questions about the state and civil society, especially in transition states (Kleveman, 2003).

Emerging data suggest a strong presence in Western democracies with, for example, police in the Netherlands reporting that between 1997 and 2000 there were 1,350 people traffickers operating, earning 118 million euros, while 65 per cent of the women they exploited earned nothing (cited in Hughes and Denisova, 2001: 16).

Whether human beings are treated like any other commodity is a moot point; it may apply to those who specialize in recruitment and transportation, but within a more integrated system where traffickers also profit from the exploitation element, a less cavalier attitude to the welfare of individuals is probably pre-ferred. With respect to sexual exploitation in Europe it is currently thought that women are usually sold by middlemen when they come from south-eastern Europe (SEE) (Hunzinger and Coffey, 2003), although Albanian traffickers have increasingly taken over sex businesses along their trafficking routes. How these patterns are reflected with respect to domestic service and labour exploitation is unclear, although integrated models appear common in trafficking from China. While lacking sound economic data on the scale of earnings/profit involved in either smuggling or trafficking, Shelley (2001) reports on translation of accounts of Chinese traffickers, who were primarily transporting men for labour exploit-ation. They made 90 per cent profit on each person, with the largest expenses being bribes to officials en route and very high payments to a US lawyer.

All of these aspects of organization and practice feature in the two typologies that follow: one from the UN Drugs and Crime (UNDOC) (2002) section cov-ers organized crime in general whereas Louise Shelley and her colleagues (2003a) focus on trafficking in persons. Each model has five variants, and summaries are presented in Table 1. UNDOC argue that assessments by police and others have underestimated the harm caused by smaller groups, and consequently paid insufficient attention to them (2002: 33). Russian (perhaps even CIS) groups are considered unique since they involve former senior security staff, who al-ready have extensive experience in evading legal controls alongside expertise in practices such as money laundering (Shelley, 2002b). Both note differences between integrated groups that control the entire trafficking process and those who sell/facilitate only one part of the process. Louise Shelley (2002b) emphasizes that the least investment the traffickers have in the person, the more brutal they are prepared to be, although the Balkan groups appear to be an exception, combining integration and excessive cruelty. There is a clear need to develop and expand upon these outlines through integrating other forms of human trafficking more strongly and interrogating features thought to represent differences and similarities between them. A stronger typology, which also has purchase on regional differences and organizational forms, would aid the develop-ment of more nuanced law enforcement and prevention strategies.

TABLE 1

TWO TYPOLOGIES OF ORGANIZED CRIME/
HUMAN TRAFFICKING NETWORKS

UN Drugs and Crime Typology Organized Crime	Louise Shelley Typology Human trafficking
Standard Hierarchy (most common – China and Eastern Europe) - Single leader - Clear hierarchy - Internal discipline - Named group - Social/ethnic identity - Violence integral - Influence/control over particular territory	Natural Resource Model (post-Soviet organized crime) - Primarily trafficking in women - Use like natural resource - Sell to near trading partners - High violence and human rights abuses - Often "break" women before leave country of origin

Regional hierarchy (Japan and Italy)
 	
- Single leader
- Line of command
- Some regional autonomy
- Geographical reach
- Multiple activities
- Often social/ethnic identity
- Violence integral
	Trade and Development (China)
	
	- Mainly smuggling of men for labour
	  exploitation, 10 per cent women
	- Control all stages to maximize profit
	- Some profit invested in legitimate
	  entrepreneurship in Thailand and China
	- Less abuse and violence as have
	  investment in continued profit

Clustered hierarchy (least common)
 	
- Number of groups
- Stronger as network
- System of governance
- Some autonomy
- Link to a social/historical context
	Supermarket – low cost, high volume
	(Mexico)
	
	- Facilitate illegal entry across border
	- Small fees, large numbers
	- Extent of failures, need for multiple
	  attempts keeps fees low
	- Investment patterns similar to those of
	  migrants – into land and property

Core group (3 in western Europe)
 	
- Core group surrounded by loose
  network
- Limited numbers
- Tight, flat structure
	Violent Entrepreneurs (Balkans)
	
	- Almost all trafficking in women
	- Middlemen for Russian organized crime
	- Increasingly integrated as take over
	  sex businesses in destination countries
	- Involvement of top level law enforcement
	  in own countries
	- Use profits to finance other illegal
	  activities, and invest in property and
	  business elsewhere
	- Considerable violence

Criminal network
 	
- Linking activities of individuals
- Position by virtue of networks and skills
- Personal loyalties
- Alliances around projects
- Low public profile
	Traditional slavery with modern technology
	(Nigeria and West Africa)
	
	- Multi-faceted crime groups
	- Use female recruiters and trade in girls
	  and young women into street prostitution
	- Small amounts returned to local operators
	  and families to maintain flow

An emergent theme is the potential link between organized crime,[15] globalization, trafficking, and global security. This is a major issue for Europe, both in terms of the countries where crime groups are based, where the illicit economy acts as a break on both the movement out of economic transition and democratization processes, and on the Western countries where organized crime has taken advantage of diasporas to put down roots. The Netherlands, for example, has identified 100 different ethnically organized crime groups operating within its borders (Shelley, 2003b). The links to global insecurity in terms of terrorism are more distal, with an overview essay pointing out that while traffickers and terrorists might use the same methods, they have entirely different, and incommensurate, ends (Shelley and Picarelli, 2002). The researchers do, however, conclude that "transnational criminals are the major beneficiaries of globalization" (2002: 306), and that there is considerable power and destabilizing potential, not just in terms of the growing illicit global economy, but also the stakes that some groups now have in national economies through the privatization of state assets in the 1990s. At the same time, the major activities of organized crime continue to be smuggling/trafficking of goods and people. The scale of money made from these activities is hard to gauge, but one estimate of money laundering is between US$500 billion to a trillion annually (Shelley et al., 2003: 152). There are also seeds of exploration of what happens to the proceeds, both the earnings of those who are smuggled and trafficked, and the profits accrued by traffickers. With respect to the former research on remittances, while demonstrating its importance for many economies, it has yet to demonstrate that trafficked persons are able to remit at the same levels as irregular migrants (Sen and Kelly, 2004). In terms of traffickers, their income has been a source of development capital in Asia, which has not been the case in the former Soviet Union, reflecting the short-term, raider mentality that followed privatization of state-run business. In this case, trafficking has also drained human capital, as a high proportion of those trafficked are educated women (Shelley, 2002b: 215).

More sophisticated understandings

The last three years have witnessed the emergence of more sophisticated approaches to trafficking, with studies placing it within both localized anthropological and historical perspectives, and drawing more on contemporary political economy. Regional patterns have been connected to cultural attitudes on labour, gender, and childhood along with more specific trade and geographic links between origin, transit, and destination countries. Criminal networks have historic roots – of kin, ethnicity, or tribe – coupled with alertness to contemporary conditions and practices. As Shelley (2003a) points out, the scale of human trafficking requires highly paid facilitators in destination countries, employers prepared to use exploited labour and the collusion, if not corruption, of the private sector. The conditions needed to facilitate trafficking, therefore, require the combination of a favourable political economy, cultural supports, and the criminal element.

A variety of concepts from political science have provided useful windows on the processes involved in trafficking, including illegal/unregulated markets (Anderson and O'Connell Davidson, 2003b; Aronowitz, 2001), and the impacts of trafficking and organized crime on political systems, sovereignty, and political economy (Long, 2002). In terms of political economy, Shelley (2002b) analyses a "transnational political criminal nexus", which she conceptualizes on multiple levels, that facilitates trafficking. At the most extreme end of the continuum are states which can be said to have been criminalized,[16] and where civil society has been weakened/corrupted (Stoecker, 2003) to the extent that large numbers of people are implicated in the trafficking process. At the other end are societies, such as the Netherlands, where the sex industry has become a significant element in the national economy, and is difficult to challenge/regulate for that reason.[17] Most states are positioned at points in between, with the extent of corruption not just undermining the effectiveness of law enforcement,[18] but also corroding trust in governance, engendering fatalism in disaffected and disempowered citizens (SEERIGHTS, 2003). One commentator notes that in the CIS states "democratic transition has been derailed by institutionalized corruption and organized crime penetration of the state" (Shelley, 2002a: 73) and that this has facilitated trafficking.[19]

Documentation of conducive contexts often links the strategic location of a country/area/region and aspects of poor/inadequate legal regulation. For example, the absence of regulation of prostitution in the Czech Republic enabled huge growth of a sex market along the extensive border with Germany, in what is now termed a "brothel belt" (O'Brien et al., 2004). Estonia was similarly positioned with respect to Scandinavia. War and conflict have also been implicated, as they increase vulnerability and decrease protection, especially where civilian populations, predominantly women and children, begin to move (Moore, 2001). Internal displacement that includes border crossings offers opportunities for traffickers. Disorganized post-conflict situations seem to be especially conducive, most extensively documented in Europe in the break up of former Yugoslavia (Human Rights Watch, 2002; Amnesty International, 2004). The late twentieth-century twist, regretfully acknowledged by the UN (2005), has been the involvement of "peacekeepers" – both the military and the civilians employed for security and reconstruction – as customers and in a few documented cases, as traffickers. While there is documentation of staff being removed from their posts, very few prosecutions have taken place, and it is unclear how attempts to regulate the behaviour of soldiers and staff of international agencies through codes of conduct are being implemented and monitored (Human Rights Watch, 2002).

At the cultural level, practices based on inequalities of gender, generation, and ethnicity – such as bride price, dowry, ritual prostitution,[20] child marriage, and fosterage – also provide fertile ground for trafficking (Banerjee, 2003; IOM, 2004). Where a social group is marked in this way through traditions and status hierarchies, there are no easy transitions to alternative livelihoods, making the girls from this group especially vulnerable to recruitment. Two studies explore prostitution regimes and the links to trafficking (Bindel and Kelly, 2003; Regeringskansliet, 2003). Both argue that legalization of brothel prostitution has not, and cannot, provide a solution to trafficking: trafficking is as, if not more, frequent in countries with elements of legalized prostitution and trafficked women end up in the less safe contexts of the street or illegal brothels.

One area where more sophisticated understandings are still needed is in the representation of, and research with, those who have been trafficked. The deployment of the concept of "victim" is too often within a context that implicitly suggests powerlessness. In fact, most trafficking victims continue to exercise agency, but in contexts where their options and possibilities are severely constrained. There is little documentation to date of how people escape – sometimes in mundane ways, others are more dramatic – and the routes by which they manage to return to their families/communities. While diasporas have been discussed with reference to traffickers, there is some documentation (Kelly, 2005) of migrants from the same countries/ethnic groups acting as support networks and even providing small amounts of money to enable return, or acting as facilitators into slightly less exploitative conditions.

OUT OF SIGHT, OUT OF MIND

Journeys of Jeopardy noted the lack of research evaluation of counter-trafficking initiatives, and the tendency of publications to do little more than describe current provision. Recent publications continue this trend, albeit organizing material under the US Department of State *Trafficking in Persons Report* framework of prevention, prosecution, and protection (Goodey, 2003; Smatt, 2003). Other overviews document protection in ten European countries (Apap, 2003), or support and return programmes (Stiftelsen Kvinnoforum, 2003; van der Kleij, 2002). None of these reports involves the development of a methodology which would allow evaluation and comparison of interventions.

Law enforcement responses across Europe continue to be understaffed and under-resourced (Laczko, 2002) even in rich Western countries. A critical analysis of Plans of Action in SEE argues they are steps forward, but lack a clear strategy, sustainable structures, or specified tasks and timelines (Hunzinger and Coffey, 2003: 19), with those who carry the counter-trafficking brief in ministries and agencies having this in addition to many other responsibilities. Policy tensions between Ministries continue to undermine counter-trafficking efforts. For example, in Turkey (Erder and Kaska, 2003) law enforcement have to defer to the Ministry of Tourism, which has responsibility for the hotels and bars where much prostitution takes place; a senior official in the Ministry commented that he was just fulfilling the enormous demand for entertainment visas.

Service development in SEE was linked to whether countries were primarily origin, transit, or destination. Countries of origin mainly had return programmes, whereas those with transit and destination outcomes focused on repatriation. The primary services were shelter-based, with 26 in the region, and a total of 300 bed spaces. Most are short-term, with average stays of between two weeks and two months (Hunzinger and Coffey, 2003). Most are funded by international donors, with local NGO implementers and minimal engagement by national governments; provision is primarily for those who are willing to return to their countries of origin and little, if anything, caters specifically for minors. There is minimal follow up of women who are returned and only three reintegration centres in the entire region – Albania, Romania, and Moldova – with one allowing stays of up to two years, and the others limited to three months. Little educational input is provided, although there has been some increase in vocational and employment components recently (Hunzinger and Coffey, 2003: 23). Legal advocacy is rare, and the majority of trafficked women who give court testimony in SEE have never had legal advice. Most states in the region signed a commitment in 2002 in Tirana to regularize the status of victims and provide temporary residence permits (Hunzinger and Coffey, 2003: 24), but like their EU neighbours with respect to a similar directive, the majority have yet to fulfil this commitment. Given the lack of employment and access to housing for women in the region, let alone the impact of sexual exploitation, one can conclude that despite a large amount of positive rhetoric from the EU and politicians there remains a systemic failure to provide adequate support to trafficked women who are returned from western to central and Eastern Europe.

This limited investment in support and law enforcement is all the more regrettable, as evidence continues to show that high quality and extensive NGO support can enable women to press charges: The Hearth in Vlore, Albania, has supported women to press charges against 497 individuals (Martin, 2003), although only seven cases have been brought by the police to court. There are also indications that hotlines may be a cost-effective intervention (Kelly, 2002).

OLD DEBATES, NEW DIRECTIONS

While discussions of trafficking have moved into new and more sophisticated domains, currently it is not clear whether this will result in a more informed interdisciplinary exploration or merely more complex competition for discursive control of the issue.

Unresolved debates about prostitution, especially as rehearsed within feminist/ gender studies, continue to be played out through the lens of trafficking. For example Jo Dozema (2002) criticizes the UN protocol on the grounds that it precludes the choice to migrate for sex work, Laura Agustin (2003) appears to want to abandon the concept of victimization altogether, and Wendy Chapkis (2003) argues that the Trafficking Victims Protection Act in the United States created a moral panic. Within these exchanges the voices of trafficked women themselves are muted to say the least, and many have no opportunity to participate because speaking out can literally endanger their future safety, as their inclusion in their own communities requires that they pay a further price of not discussing what they have endured (Bales, 2003; Kelly, 2002). Women trafficked from Islamic countries face being charged with adultery, including those who, without realizing the implications, convert in order to legitimize temporary marriages. In other contexts, such as Afghanistan, the current security situation and gender order continue to limit women's autonomy and undermine opportunities for denouncing sexual exploitation (IOM, 2004). It is, however, imperative that those who are subjected to trafficking are part of the debate, meaning that research offering confidentiality, conducted by independent researchers, continues to be a priority.

Most exploitation takes place in destination countries, many of which are proud of their human rights records – this surely makes it even more vital that the issue of demand is addressed (see also ILO, 2003b), and that this extends to demand for exploitable labour, rather than only those who are trafficked (Anderson and O'Connell Davidson, 2003). We also need to make more links, not only across forms of human trafficking but also with other areas, such as child marriage (Mikhail, 2002) and sustainable development agendas (Laczko, 2003; Poudel and Smyth, 2002). Just as the Bangladesh Thematic Group (2004) argues for a new generation of concepts, we need a new generation of research, asking slightly different questions and a more inclusive sense of the research field.

Rather than repeat studies focused on countries or region, we need to move on to explore identified questions and issues which may cut across the preferred distinctions between trafficking and smuggling. For example, we need to investigate the illegal/sham employment and travel agencies that facilitate smuggling and act as agents/brokers for traffickers. A multi-country study of how these groups operate, especially the extent to which they are implicated across all forms of smuggling and trafficking of human beings, or whether there are specializations, would enhance our understanding; as would a critical assessment of the reluctance of many governments to regulate their operation. Conducting a prospective study of assistance and return for a large enough sample over time, so that differences in experiences, inputs, and outcomes could be systematically tracked, would not only enhance understanding of whether any of the current provision actually "works", but also offer information on the ways informal networks respond and the longer-term support needs that people have, neither of which have been systematically documented. Similarly, undertaking ethnographic research in specialist law enforcement units in origin, transit, and destination countries would undoubtedly illuminate why so few successful prosecutions are mounted.

The examples above are part of a call for research agenda that is driven by the wish to answer a troubling question and/or draw on methodological and theoretical frameworks from a range of academic disciplines. Donors and funders may need convincing with respect to the knowledge gains from such investments, and that studies addressing all forms of trafficking in persons might provide critically important insights. For instance, understanding the scale of irregular migration (and trafficking) into domestic work and other unskilled sectors offers a different position from which to assess deceptive recruitment into the sex industry: this is the context in which women are making decisions about offers, and judging their veracity, where smuggling is extensive and cheap female labour widely sought. Extending our thinking also requires recognizing that many will continue to accept offers of work, despite prevention campaigns, because the scale of need and of recruitment is so extensive.

Social researchers also have to continue to ask the hard questions. An emerging consensus between major UN agencies and some academics appears to be that managed migration will provide the best solution to trafficking. There are strong arguments for more transparent and open migration regimes, but the assertion that this constitutes a counter-trafficking strategy needs to be subjected to serious scrutiny. While managed migration could have an impact on smuggling, if the legitimate routes expanded substantially, it is rather optimistic to presume that the organized crime groups would simply disappear. The integrated trafficking model, where traffickers make profit from both the movement and later exploitation of the trafficked person would seem the least likely to be affected. Such a perspective also fails to ask critical questions about demand itself. Bridgit Anderson and Julia O'Connell Davidson (2003a) argue that demand is culturally and socially constructed – it has to be created and grown for a market to exist and expand. Human beings ...*have to learn to imagine that it would be pleasurable to pay a stranger for sex, that it would be convenient and pleasant to have another person to clean up after them* (2003a: 25).

Accepting the patterns of globalized labour also involves accepting processes of racism and "otherization" that are built into current patterns of migrant labour:

> Women and girls who belong to groups that are in general socially devalued, and socially and politically and economically marginalized are also devalued by both employers and clients, and thus socially constructed as the "natural" or "ideal" occupants of the lowest positions in domestic and sex work (2003a: 27).

The question we all have to ask is whether managed migration will serve to normalize patterns based on systematic inequalities, while offering little change for those who continue to be smuggled and/or trafficked. The current knowledge base suggests that the levels of exploitation can be gross, the assistance sparse, and the consequences negative for the health and welfare of the individual and their family.

NOTES

1. These distinctions in part reflect those found in other literature, and also specify different contexts in which individuals are exploited.
2. (a) "Trafficking in persons" shall mean the recruitment, transportation, transfer, harbouring or receipt of persons, by means of the threat or use of force or other forms of coercion, of abduction, of fraud, of deception, of the abuse of power or of a position of vulnerability or of the giving or receiving of payments or benefits to achieve the consent of a person having control over another person, for the purpose of exploitation. Exploitation shall include, at a minimum, the exploitation of the prostitution of others or other forms of sexual exploitation, forced labour or services, slavery or practices similar to slavery, servitude or the removal of organs;
   (b) The consent of a victim of trafficking in persons to the intended exploitation set forth in subparagraph (a) of this article shall be irrelevant where any of the means set forth in subparagraph (a) have been used;
   (c) The recruitment, transportation, transfer, harbouring or receipt of a child for the purpose of exploitation shall be considered "trafficking in persons" even if this does not involve any of the means set forth in subparagraph (a) of this article.
3. There is far less research and commentary on smuggling.
4. The fall in baseline estimates and more muted rhetoric is reflected in claims about the extent of profit derived from human trafficking; most recent publications place it second to drugs and arms, rather than equalling or exceeding them (Shelley, 2001).
5. The 2003 report states "The new figures were generated from a database that examined reports of specific trafficking incidents, counts of repatriated victims, estimates for victims worldwide, and victim demographics derived from analysis

of information from press, governments, non-governmental and international organizations, and academic reports from 2000 to the present" (2003: 8)

6. The author has reviewed two academic journal papers in 2004 that made this argument, although neither has appeared in print to date.

7. From an interview with an IOM staff member in February 2004, in preparation for a training course in Addis Ababa.

8. They are allowed in specified areas, anyone working in them has to be at least 21 years old and undergo regular medical examinations.

9. This is the pattern represented in the film Lilja 4-ever (2002).

10. This is further illustrated by research from Thailand, where despite three decades of families living off income from sisters, daughters, and mothers who worked in the sex industry, it is still considered shameful to have been in prostitution, and many women find it impossible to reintegrate and/or marry. Rather than face such isolation "at home", they stay in Japan, "choosing" to be part of an ethnic group that is marginalized, segregated, and discriminated against (Chuntjitkaruna, 2000); they take a Japanese name, but stay in their tiny apartment most of the time, for fear they may be detected and deported.

11. There are important knowledge transfers and lessons here from work on other forms of violence against women, where some elements of victim blame have been successfully undermined, while others persist.

12. There is little documentation of this in the literature, but the author has heard accounts of such calculations by recently returned women and men from front line workers in Africa and Central Asia.

13. An Albanian trafficker cited in Martin (2003).

14. The extent to which there is systematic corruption in the international and NGOs sectors has not been studied (Shelley et al., 2003), although an exploratory examination has been commissioned by IOM.

15. A useful definition is that used by the FBI: "continuing and self-perpetuating criminal conspiracy, having an organized structure, fed by fear and corruption and motivated by greed" (cited in Shelley et al., 2003: 145).

16. Sometimes referred to as "kleptocracies".

17. Hughes and Denisova (2003: 16) cite figures from the Dutch police which suggest it accounts for 5 per cent of the national economy.

18. An example here is provided in a paper by Kathleen Maltzhan (2002), through the story of Ella, who escaped a brothel in the Philippines. She was determined that the many other women there should also be freed, and after huge efforts convinced an NGO to act and demand the police act. Unfortunately the traffickers were warned on two separate occasions, so that when the raids took place everyone had been removed.

19. A similar argument is made about Thailand in Phongpaichit et al., 2003. Publication of the book was delayed following intimidation of the authors.

20. Including *devadasi*, *basavi* and *jogin* in India, *trokosi* in Africa, and *Kamayani* in Nepal where certain tribes provide concubines for the royal family.

REFERENCES

Agustin, L.
2003   "Forget victimization: granting agency to migrants", *Development*, 46(3): 30-36.
Anderson, B.
2000   *Doing the Dirty Work? The Global Politics of Domestic Labour*, Zed, London.
Anderson, B., and J. O'Connell Davidson
2003a   *Is Trafficking in Human Beings Demand Driven?: A Multi-Country Pilot Study*, IOM, Geneva.
2003b   *Demand for Trafficked Persons Labour/Services: A Multi-Country Pilot Study*, Draft Final Report.
Apap, J.
2003   *Protection Schemes for Victims of Trafficking from Selected EU Member, Candidate and Third Countries*, IOM, Geneva.
Aronowitz, A.
2001   "Smuggling and trafficking in human beings: the phenomenon, the markets that drive it and the organizations that promote it", *European Journal of Criminal Policy and Research*, 9(2): 163-195.
Bagley, B.
2001   *Globalization and Transnational Organized Crime: The Russian Mafia in Latin America and the Caribbean*, Mama Coca, www.mamacoca.org.
Bales, K.
2003   "Because she looks like a child", in B. Ehrenreich and A. Hochschild (Eds), *Global Woman: Nannies, Maids and Sex Workers in the New Economy*, Granta, London: 207-229.
Banerjee, U.
2003   "Globalization, crisis in livelihoods, migration and trafficking of women and girls: the crisis in India, Nepal and Bangladesh", unpublished paper.
Bangladesh Thematic Group on Trafficking
2004   *Revisiting the Human Trafficking Paradigm: The Bangladesh Experience (Part I: Trafficking of Adults)*, IOM, Geneva.
Bindel, J., and L. Kelly
2003   *A Critical Examination of Response to Prostitution in Four Countries: Victoria, Australia, Ireland, the Netherlands and Sweden*, Routes Out Partnership, Glasgow.
Chammartin, G.
2003   *Women Migrant Workers' Protection in Arab League States*, ILO, Geneva.
Chapkis, W.
2003   "Trafficking, migration and the law: protecting innocents, punishing immigrants", *Gender and Society*, 17(6): 923-937.
Chunjitkaruna, P.
2000   "Pitfalls and problems in the search for a better life: Thai migrant worker in Japan", in S. Chantavanich et al. (Eds), *Thai Migrant Workers in East and Southeast Asia 1996-1997*, Asian Research Center for Migration, Chulalongkorn University, Bangkok.

Corrin, C.
  2000   "Local particularities – international generalities: traffic in women in Central and South Eastern Europe", *European Consortium for Political Research*, Copenhagen, 14-19 April.
Ehrenreich, B., and A. Hochschild (Eds)
  2003   *Global Woman: Nannies, Maids and Sex Workers in the New Economy*, Granta, London.
Eltis, D.
  2002   *Coerced and Free Migration: Global Perspectives*, Stanford University Press, Stanford.
Erder, S., and S. Kaska
  2003   *Irregular Migration and Trafficking in Women: The Case of Turkey*, IOM, Geneva.
Ginzberg, O.
  2003   *Trace: Trafficking from Community to Exploitation – Project Report*, UNICEF, New York.
Goodey, J.
  2003   "Migration, crime and victimhood: responses to sex trafficking in the EU", *Punishment and Society*, 5(4): 415-431.
Hughes, D.
  2002   "The corruption of civil society: maintaining the flow of women to the sex industries", *Encunetro Internacional Sobre Trafico De Mujeres y Explotacion*, Malaga, 23 September.
  2004   "Sex slave jihad", *FrontPageMagazine.com*, 27 January, www.frontpagemag.com/Articles.
Hughes, D., and T. Denisova
  2001   "The transnational political criminal nexus of trafficking in women from Ukraine", *Trends in Organized Crime*, 6(3-4): 2-21.
Human Rights Watch
  2000   *Owed Justice: Thai Women Trafficked into Debt Bondage in Japan*, Human Rights Watch, New York.
  2002   *Hopes Betrayed: Trafficking of Women and Girls to Post-Conflict Bosnia and Herzegovina for Forced Prostitution*, Human Rights Watch, New York.
Hunzinger, L., and P. Coffey
  2003   *First Annual Report on Victims of Trafficking in South-Eastern Europe*, IOM Regional Clearing Point, Vienna.
International Labour Organization (ILO)
  2003a   *Forced Labour Outcomes of Irregular Migration and Human Trafficking in Europe*, ILO, Geneva.
  2003b   *Trafficking in Human Beings: New Approaches to Combating the Problem*, ILO-MIGRANT, Geneva.
International Labour Organization (ILO) Mekong Subregional Project
  2001   *Labour Migration and Trafficking with the Greater Mekong Subregion*, ILO, Bangkok.
International Organization for Migration (IOM)
  2004   *Trafficking in Persons: An Analysis of Afghanistan*, IOM, Geneva.

International Organization for Migration (IOM)/International Catholic Migration Commission (ICMC)
  2002   *Research Report on Third Country National Trafficking Victims in Albania*, IOM, Tirana.
Kangaspunta, K.
  2003   "Mapping the inhuman trade: preliminary findings of the database on trafficking in human beings", *Forum on Crime and Society*, 3(1-2): 81-101.
Keeler, L., and M. Jyrkinen (Eds)
  1999   *Who's Buying: The Clients of Prostitution*, Ministry of Social Affairs, Helsinki.
Kelly, L.
  1987   *Surviving Sexual Violence*, Polity Press, Cambridge.
  2002   *Journeys of Jeopardy: A Review of Research on Trafficking in Women and Children in Europe*, IOM, Geneva.
  2003   "The wrong debate: reflections on why force is not the key issue with respect to trafficking in women for sexual exploitation", *Feminist Review: Exile and Asylum – Women Seeking Refuge in "Fortress Europe"*, 73: 139-144.
  2005   *Fertile Fields: Trafficking in Persons in Central Asia,* IOM Regional Clearing Point, Vienna.
Kleveman, L.
  2003   *The New Great Game: Blood and Oil in Central Asia*, Atlantic Books, London.
Laczko, F.
  2002   "Human trafficking: the need for better data", *Migration Information Source*, November, http://www.migrationinformation.org.
Lesko, V., and E. Avdulaj
  2003   *Girls and Trafficking: Review of Trafficking in Human Beings for 2002*, Psycho-Social Centre, The Hearth, Vlore.
Levekron, N.
  2001a   *Trafficking in Women in Israel: An Updated Report – 2001*, Hotline for Migrant Workers, Tel Aviv.
  2001b   *Trafficking in Israel: The Legal and Human Dimensions*, www. protectionproject.org/vt/ns.htm.
Long, L.
  2002   "Trafficking in women as a security challenge in Southeast Europe", *Journal of Southeast Europe and Black Sea Studies*, 2(2): 53-68.
Maltzahn, K.
  2001   "Trafficking of women in prostitution", *Australian Women Speak*, www. osw.dpmc.gov.au/resources/conference/trafficking_in _women.html.
  2002   "Policing trafficking in women for prostitution", unpublished paper.
Martin, L.
  2003   "One woman is healing the scars of Albania's sex slaves", *The Herald*, 3 November, http://www.theherald.co.uk/features/3540-print.shtml.

Mattar, M.
  2001   "Commercial sexual exploitation of women: the Islamic law perspective",
          http://www.protectionproject.org/vt/mm.htm.
  2003a   "Trafficking in persons, especially women and children, in countries of
          the Middle East: the scope of the problem and the appropriate legislative
          responses", *Fordham International Law Journal*, 26: 721.
  2003b   "Monitoring the status of severe forms of trafficking in foreign countries:
          sanctions mandated under the US Trafficking Victims Protection Act",
          Brown Journal of World Affairs, X(1): 159-178.
Mikhail, S.
  2002   "Child marriage and child prostitution: two forms of sexual exploitation",
          Gender and Development: Special Issue – Trafficking and Slavery, 10(1).
Moore, C.
  2001   "Trafficking in women and children and in war and war-like conditions",
          www.protectionproject/seminar_series.
Morrison, J., and B. Crosland
  2001   "The trafficking and smuggling of refugees: the end game in European
          asylum policy?", *New Issues in Refugee Research*, Working Paper 39,
          UNHCR, Geneva.
O'Brien, M., et al.
  2004   *Joint East West Research on Trafficking in Children for Sexual Pur-
          poses in Europe: The Sending Countries*, ECPAT Europe Law Enforce-
          ment Group, Amsterdam.
O'Connell Davidson, J.
  1998   *Prostitution, Power and Freedom*, Polity Press, Cambridge.
Pearson, E.
  2003   *Study on Trafficking in Women in East Africa*, GTZ, Eschborn, www.
          gtz.de/traffickinginwomen.
Phongpaichit, P., et al.
  1998   *Guns, Girls, Gambling and Ganja: Thailand's Illegal Economy and Pub-
          lic Policy*, Silkworm Books, Chang Mai.
Poppy Project
  2004   *When Women Are Trafficked: Quantifying the Gendered Experience of
          Trafficking in the UK*, http://www.poppy.ik.com.
Poudel, M., and I. Smith
  2002   "Reducing poverty, upholding human rights: a pragmatic approach",
          Gender and Development: Special Issue – Trafficking and Slavery, 10(1).
Rathgeber, C.
  2002   "The victimization of women through human trafficking – an aftermath of
          war?", *European Journal of Crime, Criminal Law and Criminal Justice*,
          10(2-3): 152-163.
Regeringskansliet
  2003   *The Effects of Legalization of Prostitution Activities – A Critical Analysis*,
          Ministry of Justice, Stockholm.

Rousseaux, F.
2003   "The psychological impact of sexual slavery of trafficked women: paral-
        lels with torture, sexual abuse and domestic violence", *Violence Against
        Women: An Australian Feminist Journal*, July: 4-13.
SEERIGHTS
2003   "Albania: migration, prostitution and trafficking", SEERIGHTs, http://
        seerights.org/main.php?val=249.
Sen, P., and L. Kelly
2004   *Benefits, Beneficiaries and Harms: A Critical Overview of Human Traf-
        ficking and Smuggling as Lost Potentials for Poverty Alleviation and
        the Promotion of MDGs*, unpublished report to DFID.
Shelley, L.
2001   "Trafficking and smuggling in human beings", paper at *Corruption Within
        Security Forces: A Threat to National Security Conference*, Garmisch,
        14-18 May.
2002a   "Crime as the defining problem: voices of another criminology", *Inter-
        national Annals of Criminology*, 39(1-2): 73-88.
2002b   "The changing position of women: trafficking, crime and corruption",
        in D. Lane (Ed.), *The Legacy of State Socialism and the Future of Trans-
        formation*, Rowman and Littlefield: 207-222.
2003a   "Trafficking in women: the business model approach", *The Brown Jour-
        nal of World Affairs*, X(1): 119-131.
2003b   Statement to US Senate Committee on Foreign Relations, Hearing on
        Combating Transnational and Corruption in Europe, 30 October.
2003c   "The trade in people in and from the former Soviet Union", *Crime, Law
        and Social Change*, 40(2-3): 231-249.
Shelley, L., and J. Picarelli
2002   "Methods not motives: implications of the convergence of international
        organized crime and terrorism", *Police Practice and Research*, 3(4):
        305-318.
Shelley, L., et al.
2003   "Global crime inc.", in M. Love (Ed.), *Beyond Sovereignty: Issues for a
        Global Agenda*, Wadsworth, California: 143-166.
Smartt, U.
2003   "Human trafficking: simply a European problem?", *European Journal of
        Crime, Criminal Law and Criminal Justice*, 11(2): 164-177.
Stiftelsen Kvinnoforum
2003   *European Good Practice on Recovery, Return and Integration of Traf-
        ficked Persons*, Kvinnoforum, Stockholm.
Stoecker, S.
2002   "The rise in human trafficking and the role of organized crime", unpub-
        lished paper.
Tialby, R.
2001   "Organized crime and people smuggling/trafficking to Australia", *Trends
        and Issues in Crime and Criminal Justice*, 208: 1-6.

Tiefenbrun, S.
  2002   "Sex sells but drugs don't talk: trafficking of women sex workers and an
          economic solution", *Thomas Jefferson Law Review*, 24: 161-189.
United Nations (UN)
  2005   *A Comprehensive Strategy to Eliminate Future Sexual Exploitation and
          Abuse in United Nations Peacekeeping Operations*, United Nations,
          New York.
United Nations Children's Fund (UNICEF)/UNAIP
  2003   *Project TRACE: Trafficking from Community to Exploitation*, Interim
          Report.
UN Office on Drugs and Crime
  2002   *Results of a Pilot Survey on Forty Selected Organized Criminal Groups
          in Sixteen Countries*, UN, New York.
US Agency for International Development (USAID)
  2002   *Trafficking in Persons: USAID's Response*, USAID, Washington, DC.
US Department of State
  2002   *Trafficking in Persons Report*, US Department of State, Washington, DC.
  2003   *Trafficking in Persons Report*, US Department of State, Washington, DC.
  2004   *Trafficking in Persons Report*, US Department of State, Washington, DC.
Van der Kleij, A.
  2002   *Provisions for Victims of Trafficking in Bonded Labour, i.e. Prostitution
          in Six Countries*, BlinN, Amsterdam.
Zimmerman, C., et al.
  2003   *The Health Risks and Consequences of Trafficking in Women and Ado-
          lescents: Findings from a European Study*, London School of Tropical
          Hygiene and Tropical Medicine, London.

A Review of Recent Research on Human Trafficking in the Middle East[1]

Giuseppe Calandruccio*

INTRODUCTION

Migration in the Middle East is an issue that rarely receives coverage in the Western media. In the West, "Middle East" is typically associated with the Israeli-Palestinian conflict, the geopolitics of oil, or more recently with the Iraq war. Other problems that beset the region are often neglected or treated as part of a broader problem of political instability. One of these issues is migration. As this article intends to show, there is growing concern in the region about migration, especially illegal migration.

The aim of this article is threefold. First it shall provide a survey of literature and research on irregular migration, especially the trafficking of human beings. Second, by providing a literature survey, the article intends to map out some distinct characteristics of human trafficking in the Middle East. Lastly, it shall identify gaps in the literature and make some suggestions for future research on human trafficking in the Middle East.

The "Middle East" is used in this article mainly to refer to the Arab Mashreq,[2] the Arabian Peninsula,[3] and Israel. The Maghreb countries[4] are not part of this review due to their Francophone distinctiveness, different social and migratory dynamics within the Mediterranean basin, and close relation with Europe. The historic, linguistic, and cultural ties between Morocco, Algeria, and Tunisia from one side and France from the other, determined in the last decades a steady flow of economic migrants towards this European country. Moreover, northern African countries along the west Mediterranean coast have emerged in the last decade

---

* IOM Mission with Regional Functions, Cairo, Egypt.

as important transit and departure points for the movement of irregular migrants to southern Europe. Morocco, Tunisia, and Libya are the countries from where thousands of irregular migrants start their dangerous sea crossing that will take them from the African continent to Italy, Malta, and Spain.

If the migration dynamics of the Mashreq and the Arabian Peninsula are heavily geared towards Europe, the same cannot be said about the Mashreq and the Arabian Peninsula. Although there are undoubtedly cases of regular and irregular migration from Egypt to Europe, international migration predominantly follows an intra-regional pattern, with mainly Palestinian, Egyptian, Lebanese, and Jordanian workers looking at the labour markets of the Gulf Cooperation Council (GCC) countries.

This has implications for the structure of the article. Given the intra-regional nature of international migration, countries in the region are both countries of origin, of destination, and of transit for human traffickers. The phenomenon of human trafficking shall, therefore, be discussed not so much in terms of trafficking routes, although a section will be included. Rather the focus shall be on the types and practices of human trafficking, some of which may appear unique to the region. Also, it has to be noted that given the scarcity of research on human trafficking in the region, the article cannot, in its analysis, give equal weight to each country in the region.

THE MIDDLE EAST AND INTERNATIONAL MIGRATION

The Middle East accounts for more than 10 per cent of the world's total migrants and the oil-rich countries of the Arab Gulf host the highest concentration of migrant workers in the world. The presence of legal migrants, undocumented migrants, refugees, and special groups gives migration in the region a diverse face. Labour migration (or contractual labour) is typically temporary in nature, with no expectations of permanent settlement or citizenship rights for the migrant (especially in the Arab Gulf where South-East Asian migrants represent almost one-fourth of the total population). The International Organization for Migration (IOM) prudently estimates that there are currently about 14 million international migrants and 6 million refugees in the Middle East.[5]

The Kingdom of Saudi Arabia hosts the largest foreign population in the region, an estimated 6.2 million people. A large migrant presence is also found in two other countries of the GCC: the United Arab Emirates (UAE) has an estimated 1.7 million foreign nationals and Kuwait has 1.3 million foreign nationals residing within its national territory.

Indians are the largest group of international migrants found in the region (3.2 million); the group is followed by Egyptians (1.8 million mainly concentrated in Saudi Arabia and GCC countries) and Pakistanis (1.2 million). Other significant migrant groups found in the Arab Mashreq and the Arabian Peninsula are: Bangladeshis (827,000), Filipinos (849,000), Sri Lankans (582,000), Jordanians (470,000 mostly found in Saudi Arabia and other GCC countries), Yemenis (463,000, mostly in Saudi Arabia),[6] Iranians (mostly found in UAE, Kuwait, Qatar, and Bahrain) and Iraqis (393,000, mostly in Jordan and Syria).

In recent years, governments of the GCC states have begun implementing strict policies of job nationalization ("indigenization"), particularly in the private sector. Limits on the employment of non-national workers, minimum quotas for nationals, and higher costs of hiring non-nationals have been imposed. This has implications for both Arab and non-Arab migrants in the region, but whereas Arab migrants tend to have white- and blue-collar occupations, jobs that can be performed by nationals, Asian migrants fill more dangerous and difficult positions. It is, therefore, more likely that national job seekers will in the future replace Arab migrants, rather than Asian migrants, thus reducing the chances for Arab migrants to find jobs in the GCC countries.

In June 2004, the United States Department of State presented to the Congress the Fourth Annual Trafficking in Persons Report (TIP). The report consists of 140 countries believed to have a significant number of victims of severe forms of trafficking. The countries are ranked in three tiers according to the degree of the government's compliance with the minimum standards in the fight against human trafficking. Bahrain, Kuwait, Lebanon, and Saudi Arabia maintained the previous ranking on Tier 2 after being removed from the Tier 3 list in 2003,[7] due to their significant efforts exerted to comply with the minimum standards. Israel also maintained the Tier 2 ranking. The UAE promoted in 2003 from Tier 3 to Tier 1, the level of those countries that fully comply with the minimum standards established by the US Department of State, was in 2004 categorized as Tier 2 because of the lack of evidence of appreciable progress in addressing trafficking for sexual exploitation. Qatar is placed on the Tier 2 watch list "because of the lack of evidence of increasing efforts to combat severe forms of trafficking in persons". In 2003 Egypt and Iraq were considered to be special cases by the TIP report because of the lack of information or the existence of fragmentary information. In 2004, while Egypt appeared firmly in Tier 2, Iraq was still considered a special case due to its particular circumstances.

Nevertheless the promotion of some of the GCC states to Tier 2 illustrates that states in the region put more effort into combating trafficking. While the GCC states are still the prime destination, Israel is becoming an increasingly popular target for human traffickers and smugglers. It is reported that women from Moldova, Russia, Ukraine, and other countries in the former Soviet Union are trafficked to Israel for the purpose of commercial sexual exploitation. Persons in search of work are trafficked into situations of coerced labour, where they endure physical abuse or other extreme working conditions. Many low-skilled foreign workers in Israel have their passports withheld, their contracts altered, and suffer non-payment of salaries of varying degree and duration. Construction firms and other businesses have brought male labourers from China and Bulgaria into Israel to work under conditions equivalent to debt bondage or involuntary servitude (US Department of State, 2003: 83).

Even Iraq is not spared from human trafficking. The 2003 TIP report explains which form trafficking might take place in Iraq in the aftermath of the war:

> Another country in flux, Iraq is showing signs that a trafficking problem could emerge. The existence of displaced persons, widows and other vulnerable women, separated children or orphans dependent on humanitarian assistance to survive could gravitate toward peacekeepers and humanitarian workers as sources of potential income and safety only to be exploited for labor or sex. In many post-conflict situations, criminal elements have exploited the breakdown of rule of law and the desperation of vulnerable families, and abducted, forced, or tricked individuals into prostitution. Traffickers also flourish in situations with weak law enforcement. There is a lack of infrastructure for victim services and protection. This lack of medical services, counseling, and shelters are likely to discourage trafficking victims from coming forward. As we have seen elsewhere, the demand for prostitution often increases with the presence of military troops, expatriates, and international personnel who have access to disposable income (US Department of State, 2003).

Unfortunately, the widespread plague of kidnapping that surfaced in Iraq soon after the end of the major combat operations in Spring 2003 seemed to validate the concerns outlined in the 2003 TIP report and some cases of abductions for the purpose of trafficking started to be reported in Fall of the same year (Firmo-Fontan, 2004).

A great deal of media attention was recently dedicated to the many foreign workers abducted in Iraq, and the killing of some of them.[8] These abducted or murdered foreign workers had, however, willingly sought employment in the country (although some governments for security reasons discouraged or even prevented their nationals from seeking working opportunities in Iraq).

Less reported was a new pattern of migrant trafficking that emerged, apparently taking advantage of the chaos and relaxed entry requirements into Iraq during the post-conflict phase. Nationals of Bangladesh, India, Somalia, and other countries were reportedly promised work opportunities in Jordan by local and

Jordanian agents who were also charging exorbitant fees. They were instead taken across the border to the Iraqi desert and left there to fend for themselves. According to some media reports, at least 1,000 migrants had fallen victim to this scam by May 2004, and tried to cross back into Jordan after months spent in Baghdad and other parts of Iraq (sometimes exposed to situations of armed fighting) without employment, food, cash, or valid travel documents and visas (Gillespie, 2004).

RESEARCH ON TRAFFICKING IN THE COUNTRIES OF THE MIDDLE EAST

If one was to look only at the Arab Middle East, excluding the case of Israel, it can be said that no comprehensive research exists on the specific topic of human trafficking occurring in the countries of the Middle East. *Trafficking in Persons, Especially Women and Children, in Countries of the Middle East* (Mattar, 2003) is the only piece produced with the stated scope of investigating human trafficking and organically addressing the issue. However, the author, Dr. Mohamed Y. Mattar, Adjunct Professor of Law and Co-Director of the Protection Project at the Johns Hopkins University School of Advanced International Studies, focuses on making a review of international and national trafficking laws and their impact on the Middle East region. The study is not on the phenomenon of trafficking itself.

The IOM Cairo Mission with Regional Functions for the Middle East produced in June 2003 a discussion paper on migrant trafficking in the region (IOM, 2003). The paper was not intended to address a specialized audience or to be published; it was produced with the aim of increasing the awareness of national authorities and engage governments of the Middle East on the issue. The paper clarifies the distinction between smuggling and trafficking, and incorporates a description of potential counter-trafficking initiatives. The background section is not focused solely on human trafficking, but outlines the main features and trends of illegal migration and migrant smuggling in the region. The research is weighted in favour of media sources gathered from the IOM Cairo press review and from other specialized agencies. The paper acknowledges a range of legal and strategic contributions; however, no field research was conducted and IOM has not independently verified the facts and figures.

An obvious already mentioned source of valuable information about the scale and characteristics of human trafficking in the Middle East is the US Department of State's TIP report. Of the countries surveyed in this review of research produced on trafficking in the Middle East, Bahrain, Kuwait, Lebanon, Qatar,

Saudi Arabia, the UAE, and Israel are covered in the TIP report. The information contained in the report is usually gathered by the personnel of US diplomatic missions and obtained through interviews with government authorities, international organization officials, NGO workers, and consular representatives of the countries of origin of trafficked victims. The value of the information provided by the US State Department report is self-evident; however, some limitations must be noted. "The annual trafficking report [only] includes those countries determined to have a *significant* number of victims of *severe* forms of trafficking" (US Department of State, 2003: 14, emphasis added). According to US law, for trafficking in one single country to be considered significant, there must be a minimum number of 150 victims of severe forms of trafficking.[9] The US definition of severe trafficking[10] is more restrictive than that found in the UN Trafficking Protocol.[11] Therefore, it may be concluded that cases of trafficking not matching the US definition or in numbers less than 150 for one country in one year were not included in the TIP report.

In 2001, the Protection Project at the Johns Hopkins University School of Advanced International Studies started to collect and systemize information on trafficking in persons worldwide. The Protection Project takes the opposite approach of the TIP report; all countries where at least one case of trafficking has been documented are included. All the countries of the Middle East – except the Palestinian Territory – are listed in the *Human Rights Report on Trafficking of Persons, Especially Women and Children* (Protection Project, 2002). The scope of the global Protection Project report is ambitious and has the merit of providing some interesting insights about the situation of human trafficking in a number of countries for which information would otherwise not be easily available. Its major drawback is that the report depends on anecdotal information and media reporting, which is difficult to verify. There is no such thing as a structured global network of reliable first hand informants. The information provided in the Protection Project report has not been updated since March 2002.

As earlier mentioned, a noticeable amount of targeted research has been conducted on human trafficking to Israel both at the local and international level. The country has a strong tradition of protecting workers' rights and local NGOs have been active in advocating the rights of migrant workers[12] as well as now denouncing human trafficking. The Tel Aviv-based NGO *Kav La'Oved* (the Worker's Address/Hotline for Migrant Workers) has been the most active in conducting targeted research (*Kav La'Oved*, 2002, 2003a, 2003b) and networking with local institutions and international bodies (Ellman and Laacher, 2003). At least five main research papers were produced between 2000 and 2003 on human trafficking, directed specifically on the phenomenon of East European women trafficked for the purpose of sexual exploitation in the country.

The review of recent research conducted on human trafficking in the Middle East region presented so far in this paper may be considered exhaustive of what has been produced on the subject. Unfortunately – and for a set of different reasons that will be examined later in this paper – efforts to study the scale of the trafficking phenomenon in this part of the world have been very limited. In recent years, however, academic and institutional researchers have increasingly dedicated time and energy to studying issues related to different aspects of migration in the Middle East. These studies, although not directly addressing human trafficking, are important to our understanding of the socio-economic context of where and why trafficking of human beings flourishes, paying attention both to the level of the countries of origin and the countries of destination.

In the last few decades, international migration has become increasingly feminized. The Middle East region has witnessed among the highest rates of female migrant labourers joining the labour markets. It has occurred most prominently in the Arab Gulf, but also in Lebanon, Jordan, and to a lesser extent Egypt and Syria. According to a recent ILO study "the number of women migrating into GCC countries and other Arab League States is increasing rapidly in recent years. In GCC countries, for example, women migrants represented almost 30 per cent of all inflows in 2000 compared to 8 per cent in the early 1980s" (Smith and Esim, 2004). Thus, a considerable amount of recent research has been dedicated to investigating the situation of women migrant workers and especially those employed in the domestic sector. In 2002, the International Labour Organization (ILO) conducted a series of studies on the conditions of women migrant domestic workers in Lebanon (Jureidini, 2002), Bahrain (Al-Najjar, 2002), and the UAE (Sabban, 2002). Yet another ILO study on female labour migrants from Ethiopia provides revealing information about the conditions of Ethiopian female domestic workers employed in the Middle East and the Arab Gulf countries, particularly in Lebanon (Kebede, 2002).

In August 2003, IOM completed a study on the conditions of foreign domestic workers in Syria (Kahale, 2003). It is an exploratory study with the aim to address the gap in information available on the profile, legal standing, recruitment and migration trends, working and living conditions, and services available to migrant labourers in Syria.

Worth mentioning also is "Migrant workers in Lebanon" produced in 2000 by the independent researcher Michael Young for the Lebanese NGO, Forum (Young, 2000). For many years, it was the only available research on the conditions of migrant workers in an Arab country. The paper still maintains its value even after a number of additional targeted research studies have been produced.

Ray Jureidini is a specialist and prolific writer on migration in the Middle East. For the Regional Conference on Arab Migration in a Globalized World, jointly organized by IOM and the League of Arab States, he presented *Human Rights and Foreign Contract Labour: Some Implications for Management and Regulation in Arab Countries* (Jureidini, 2003b). The conference was an attempt to put into context the widespread practice of abusing migrant labourers' rights with the new realities brought about by the "spread of globalization" to the Arab world. As the author put it himself: the status and conditions of expatriates (particularly semi- and unskilled contract labour) in the Gulf States and other parts of the Arab world have attracted serious international criticism, from charges of xenophobic practices to human rights abuses. This largely theoretical paper explores these issues within the discourse of "globalism versus localism" by focusing on the universalistic principles of human rights versus cultural relativism – the human rights of migrants versus the rights of states to determine the character, privileges and size of their citizenry (Jureidini, 2003b).

Jureidini has also produced two other studies worth mentioning in this review for their ramifications into the issue of human rights of labour workers in Arab countries, and more directly for their reflections on human trafficking. "Xenophobia in Arab societies" (Jureidini, 2001) was prepared for UNESCO in 2003 as a follow-up to the "World Conference against Racism, Racial Discrimination, Xenophobia and Related Intolerance" held in Durban in September 2001. The paper looks at contemporary xenophobic elements with particular reference to foreign migrants in the Arab countries of Lebanon, Jordan, and the GCC states (Jureidini, 2001: 1).

In another recent study, the same author traces the origin of xenophobia directed against Asian migrant workers in the GCC countries. In this study, Jureidini reviews "two further disturbing components of the migrant presence; namely, the conditions akin to 'indentured labour' and processes of recruitment suggesting significant elements of 'human trafficking'". He further writes, "[c]anvassing international and regional conventions, it is concluded that existing human rights instruments are largely ineffective in the protection of vulnerable migrant workers in the GCC states" (Jureidini, 2003a).

Concluding the review is the only research effort exploring the links between forced migration and trafficking in the Middle East region. In 2002, Géraldine Chatelard wrote a paper titled "Iraqi forced migrants in Jordan: conditions, religious networks, and the smuggling process", which is yet another conference paper (Chatelard, 2002). This very detailed and documented paper may be partially outdated due to the changed situation created by the war on Iraq in March 2003 and the ensuing events, but the analysis of social networks and the smuggling process of Iraqi forced migrants in Jordan still provides invaluable insights into the illegal migration mechanisms and routes. The study also sheds light on an unknown phenomenon of human trafficking that was apparently common in the years before the 2003 war, namely the sexual exploitation of Iraqi female forced migrants transiting Jordan in their way to reach industrialized countries to seek asylum.

MAPPING ROUTES

Given the mentioned scarcity of targeted research on human trafficking occurring in the Middle East region, it is no surprise that very little has been done to investigate and map the main trafficking routes.[13] The majority of the available information is not obtained from specific field research, but rather thanks to press coverage or derived from indirect sources.

Most women trafficked for the purpose of sexual exploitation originate from Eastern Europe, Russia, and the Commonwealth of Independent States (CIS) and end up in the Arab Gulf countries and Lebanon. The same countries are the destination of some South-Eastern Asian women, often lured by promises of well-paid jobs in the domestic sector, but end up abused or sexually exploited.

There are a number of documented cases of Ethiopian women who were victims of basic human rights abuse, sexual abuse, and sexual exploitation. Ethiopian female migrants are usually brought into the countries of destination by unscrupulous illegal or semi-legal employment agents. In the case of female Ethiopian migrants, it also has been possible to detect another interesting trafficking route leading to the Middle East; "aside from leaving the country with the help of illegal agents, women also use the *Oumra* and *Hagi* (Moslem pilgrimages) as a pretext to go to Saudi Arabia and, from there, to other Arab countries" (Kebede, 2002). The pretext of the Islamic pilgrimage to gain access to Saudi Arabia is not only typical of migrants from Ethiopia, whose population is overwhelmingly Christian. It has been heard in connection to other groups of migrants as well. In particular, in connection to the trafficking of Asian and Yemeni children sent to beg in the holy Islamic places.

According to media reports, in February 2003 the Bangladeshi police discovered a smuggling/trafficking route of children and women. It started in Bangladesh, passed through India and Pakistan, and ended in the UAE. Most of the smugglers used the Calcutta-Katmandu-Dubai route because of relaxed security at border checkpoints.

Lately an increase has been noted in the number of illegal migrants using Egypt as a transit station to nearby countries such as Israel. For example, Egypt serves as transit country for Chinese job seekers and East European women entering Israel via the Sinai Desert. The migrants are aided by the same gangs that previously specialized in trafficking Egyptians abroad. In January 2003, the Egyptian Government detained several Egyptian nationals who were working in the tourism sector. They were accused of smuggling foreigners to Israel and charged with threatening the national security of Egypt.

The route through Egypt, and in particular the Sinai Peninsula, has its starting point in East Europe, Russia, and the CIS. It is perhaps the best documented route thanks to the efforts to unveil the breadth of women trafficking to Israel.[14] *Kav La'Oved* reports that "[w]omen are trafficked into Israel from Russia, Ukraine, Moldova, Uzbekistan, Lithuania, Belarus, Brazil, Colombia, Estonia, Latvia, and others. (...) The regular entries to Israel through seaports and airports are recently heavily guarded, which is why so many women are trafficked through the Egyptian border in places where there is no control" (*Kav La'Oved*, 2003a: 6).

DOCUMENTING METHODS OF RECRUITMENT

Recruitment methods in the Middle East do not differ much from the rest of the world, at least in the case of women trafficked for the purpose of sexual exploitation. The following quote refers to the situation in Israel, but there is no reason to believe that it should be different in other countries of the region:

> We estimate that 70 per cent of the cases the women are aware of the fact that they will be selling their bodies in prostitution but they are not aware of the harsh conditions that await them when they arrive to Israel. About 30 per cent are bluntly deceived and do not realize that they will end in prostitution. The traffickers promise them that they are going to work as waitresses, cooks, models, au pairs, or medical massage (*Kav La'Oved*, 2003a: 6).

As for the case of female migrants (as well as male migrants) whose rights are abused or who find themselves in a situation of physical and sexual exploitation, it has been established that the role of recruitment agencies is crucial. Recruitment agencies and middlemen serve as the link between sponsors and potential migrants. They negotiate the conditions of the contract and process travel documentation. Middlemen carefully choose the potential candidates for migration, whereof women represent the majority. Moreover, middlemen set the price of migration and explain the terms and conditions. They also determine the type of visa and the work to be done, the salary, working hours, the duration of the contract, and other important elements that will affect the migrant once arrived at destination.[15]

The nature of the agreement concluded with the migrant is informal. Even if a contract is signed in the home country of the migrant, this document won't usually bear any legal validity in the country of destination where it won't be recognized by the employer or will be simply considered as void. As a result, workers sometimes find that the conditions of their employment agreement have been modified and their passports are withheld by their sponsors. As only few examples of employment agreements/contracts are available (Kebede, 2002), it is not possible to generalize and conduct a critical analysis of what these contracts actually stipulate.

In addition, agencies and middlemen sometimes charge large recruitment fees that leave the workers or their families indebted to the agents. The recruitment agencies rarely monitor the well-being of migrants, which leaves them vulnerable to exploitation. In some cases, migrants using recruitment agencies services find that there is no promised employment when they arrive at their destination and instead they face illegal status and poverty in the destination country.

The case of Ethiopia is again illustrative of how trafficking from African and Asian countries to the Middle East takes place. Large numbers of Ethiopian women have become victims of trafficking, lured by false promises of good jobs, high salaries, and a comfortable life. Most of these women end up as modern day slaves. The process of recruitment for most victims of trafficking is similar. The women are first introduced to traffickers through friends, neighbours, and relatives or are approached by the traffickers themselves. Traffickers typically own travel agencies, import-export businesses, have contacts in the Middle East, or travel to the region regularly for various reasons. Trafficked women themselves have been instrumental in recruiting other migrants through the help of their families who act as the agents at this end (Kebede, 2002: 6).

Over the past years, a peculiar recruitment system has been discovered to be operating in Jordan. It involves Iraqi female forced migrants who are in transit in the kingdom while trying to reach industrialized countries and are exploited in the sex industry. Chatelard (2002: 27) explains:

> Bogus travel agencies offer Iraqi women who come to inquire about the costs of the trip to "employ" them as prostitutes until they have earned an amount of money considered

sufficient to pay for their (and often family members') smuggling out of Jordan. A number of work hours is determined in advance, the money earned is held in trust by the pimp who releases the women and provides them with travel documents only after they have found other women to replace them. There is no need for physical intimidation or isolation strategies as Iraqi women are already isolated, have no way to escape to, and cannot turn to the authorities. Besides they enter into these bonds "voluntarily" in the absence of other survival means. From the literature on women trafficking, there is no other evidence of this debt-bondage being exerted in the transit country and not in the destination country. Generally, traffickers are said to exploit the migrant after being transported across the border, and in the case of prostitution, it is single young women who are involved (Salt and Howarth, 2000: 62; Skeldon 2000: 7). In Jordan, on the other hand, it is mainly women with children or ageing parents, and who are single heads of households.

TYPES OF TRAFFICKING

One of the most common problems related to the trafficking of migrants in the Middle East is abuse of domestic workers and other guest workers engaged in menial work. Migrants are promised well-paid jobs, yet once in the country of destination they find themselves trapped in sub-standard living/working conditions by unfair contractual terms imposed on them by middlemen and employers.

The abuse ranges from the imposition of excessive working hours to verbal and physical abuse to sexual harassment and sexual attacks, and may extend to forcing the worker into the sex trade. Migrants residing illegally in the countries of destination are more exposed to this kind of abuses, but legal migrants are also subjected to exploitation.

Acknowledging the sponsorship system, known as *Kafala*, and its potential negative consequences is pivotal to understanding some of the roots of trafficking in the Gulf countries. In the UAE and in other Gulf countries, *Kafala* is the guarantee system for a guest worker vis-à-vis the authorities. *Kafala* is the only means through which it is possible to enter and work in the country. Through this system, the state delegates to its citizens certain functions that in the other countries usually belong to state institutions.

There are four types of visas available under the *Kafala* system: house visas, company visas, sponsorship by state institutions, and sponsorship for business partnership. Of the four, house visas and company visas are those that may hide trafficking practices (Blanchet, 2002). The house visa, issued for domestic jobs, represents the most risky option for the guest worker. The sponsor, known as the *Kafeel*, provides the guest worker with an entry visa and a job. The *Kafeel* is then responsible to the authorities if the worker changes residence or employment. More importantly, the *Kafeel* assumes control over the worker's right to act as a judicial person. In essence, the worker's freedom of movement, labour, and judicial action are handed over to the *Kafeel*.

According to experts, the sponsorship rule "entails elements of servitude, slavery, and practices similar to slavery, as defined by the UN Trafficking Protocol to Prevent, Suppress and Punish Trafficking in Persons, Especially Women and Children" (Borkholder and Mohammed, 2002). For instance, sponsors sometimes cede employees to other employers without procuring the workers' consent, and withhold their passports to prevent their escape (Borkholder and Mohammed, 2002).

It should also be noted that the recruitment agencies (whether legal or illegal) are often responsible for severe forms of abuse, particularly when female domestic workers, but also other categories of migrant workers, are returned to the agency by the sponsor. The agency will in this case try to "place" the migrant with another sponsor in order not to lose the "investment" by the recruiters in the process of bringing the migrant in the country. This practice, documented in different countries where the sponsorship system is in use, sometimes involves keeping the rejected workers in a state of detention to prevent them from running away or finding employment independently.

Trafficking of women for sexual exploitation

Trafficking for the purpose of the sex trade is a phenomenon that has grown in the last decades. Many young women are attracted to the sex industry with the promise of earning quick and easy money. However, they eventually realize they are trapped in a slave-like situation and that the money earned is taken by middlemen and agents. Physical and psychological pressure, as well as threats and fear of retaliation towards families in the countries of origin, are the most common means used by traffickers to control their victims. Withholding passports and travel tickets, as well as debt bondage are other common means of exerting control over women trafficked for the sex trade. A person enters debt bondage when his/her labour is demanded as a means of repayment of a loan or of money given in advance. Employers may pay middlemen up to US$ 5,000 in advance for a worker. These sums are then deducted by the employer from the worker's salary until the payment is reimbursed, which could take years.

Once again, Israel is the country where targeted research has allowed a clearer grasp of the conditions of women trafficked for the purpose of sexual exploitation. Reports explain the women's situation as follows:

Many of them are going through intimidation, repeated rapes, their papers are confiscated and they are sold in auctions. Often they are forced to prostitute themselves without getting any money until they reimburse their "debts" of transportation and sale. In many cases once they are done they are sold to another pimp and have to reimburse the new "debt". Many women are threatened that if they complain to the police they will be locked in jail for life as they are in Israel illegally. Since they have no knowledge of their rights and no knowledge of the language, they are afraid to do any move that might put them in a harsher situation. Some of them end in private locked up apartments with no possibility of escape, some are sold again and again from brothel to brothel until they are used up and constitute a burden for their "employers" and are handed over to the police (*Kav La'Oved*, 2003a: 6).

Child and other forms of trafficking

A significant number of children were trafficked every year from South-East Asia and Sudan to the Gulf States for employment as jockeys in the popular camel races. Due to their light weight, children as young as two years old have been used. These children were reportedly either kidnapped or sold by their families. In most cases the children were sold by their own families, sometimes for as little as US$ 75, but more commonly in exchange for monthly payments of a few hundred dollars for one or two years of service. Traffickers could get as much as US$ 5,000 for each child.

According to media reports, the children trafficked into the Gulf States for the purpose of camel jockeying were denied adequate food and rest to ensure that they did not gain too much weight. They were kept in inhumane conditions, crammed in small rooms, and often starved before a big race. Most of the children who were returned to their families failed to remember or recognize their parents since they were trafficked between the ages of two to five years. Many were unable to speak their mother tongue and did not know the ways of their cultures of origin due to their prolonged stay in the Gulf countries. The majority of trafficked camel jockeys experienced severe emotional traumas. Freed when they become older, many jockeys were cast aside and often become illegal aliens.

A second form of trafficking particular of the Middle East is customary marriage. According to media investigations, some wealthy nationals of Gulf countries (Saudi Arabia and Qatar in particular) marry young women from poorer Islamic countries like Egypt[16] or Islamic societies in Asian countries, such as India. A dowry is paid to the family, which is a form of payment for the person. It appears that this type of marriage contract can be finalized in less than one week. Allegedly, in many cases the families get a false certificate from a doctor stating that their daughter is of a legal age to marry. This certification is required either because many of these young women are underage or were not registered at birth. In either case, they are essentially invisible to society and ineligible for full protection under the law. Once abroad, the brides could find themselves quickly divorced, forced into menial unpaid jobs, or married to someone else by proxy. The young women are often unable to escape, to communicate with their families, or even to reach their diplomatic representative offices. Cases of Arab migrant workers who are pushed by their sponsors to marry off their sisters or relatives in exchange for work permits have also been reported.

POLICY APPROACHES TAKEN TO COMBAT TRAFFICKING[17]

In March 2004, Egypt ratified the Protocol to Prevent, Suppress and Punish Trafficking in Persons, Especially Women and Children. The other four countries of the Middle East signatories to the protocol are Israel, Lebanon, Saudi Arabia, and Syria (United Nations Office on Drugs and Crime, 2003).

Egypt explicitly prohibits sex trafficking and penalizes anyone facilitating the entry of another person into Egypt for the purpose of sex work. Egypt is trying to monitor the activities of recruitment agencies and a new law passed in November 2002 requires all agencies to be operated solely by Egyptians.

In Israel, a parliamentary investigation committee on trafficking in women was created in 2000. This committee included members of all the parties in the Israeli Parliament. Representatives from the two NGOs, *Machon Toda'a* and *Kav La'Oved* were invited to the meetings of this committee (*Kav La'Oved*, 2003a: 27). *Kav La'Oved* was pleased to announce:

> In December 2002, the Investigation committee issued its interim report, which grants the phenomenon of trafficking in women for prostitution purposes the utmost importance of national concern. In addition to the amendments of the existing laws some of which have already been passed a first reading, the report offers a global operative legal approach to the issue (*Kav La'Oved*, 2003a: 27).

Among the main amendments to existing Israeli laws proposed by the committee: (1) the victims will be allowed to testify without the perpetrator physically present in order to avoid the threat that might constitute the meeting with the perpetrator; and (2) the legal assistance of the Ministry of Justice will assist the victims of trafficking both in the question of their administrative detention and in their civil suites against the pimps. In January 2001, an Inter-ministerial committee to study and combat the trafficking in persons for the purpose of sexual exploitation was created. The interim report published in November 2002 recommended additional measures such as the establishment of shelter facilities, the confiscation of traffickers' earnings, reinforcing cooperation with the authorities of the countries of origin, as well as training and awareness activities both in Israel and in the countries of origin of the victims. These activities will supplement the work by the already existing eight NGOs actively involved in assisting victims of trafficking and advocating their rights.

In Lebanon, law enforcement officials are generally responsive to complaints of trafficking and the Government has taken some measures to counter traffick-ing. For example, in 2001 the Ministry of Labour shut down ten employment agencies that violated labour regulations. In addition, the *Surete Generale* (Gen-eral Security Directorate) has improved its record keeping and enforcement of regulations. The Government has given an NGO full access to the Detention Centre for Foreign Persons so that the NGO may provide legal assistance, coun-selling, and medical care to foreign workers held there. The Ministry of Labour meets regularly with embassies of countries of origin to ensure that migrant workers are aware of new employment agency regulations and of the existence of the "complaint line", a hotline for reporting violations. Moreover, Lebanon and Sri Lanka have established a training programme for Sri Lankan domestics bound for Lebanon, and the Ministry of Labour is working to develop a similar programme in Ethiopia. Finally, the Government has developed a pamphlet to raise awareness of migrant trafficking, outline the complaint process, and pro-vide contact information for government agencies, law enforcement, and NGOs.

In Saudi Arabia, slavery and the smuggling of persons into the country is pro-hibited by law. Until 2001, the Government stated that trafficking in persons did not represent a problem for the country. It primarily focused on identifying and deporting illegal workers and did not devote significant efforts or resources to counter-trafficking activity. Nevertheless, some steps have been made recently regarding the protection of victims of trafficking. These measures include a reception centre for runaway domestic servants, managed by the Ministry of Labour. Currently in Saudi Arabia there are three shelters that are operating in the largest cities. These so-called "welfare camps" host abused or trafficked female foreign workers. Women are provided with shelter, food, and medical care while law enforcement agencies investigate their cases. In August 2002, the Grand Mufti of Saudi Arabia promulgated a *fatwa* (a legal statement in Islamic law issued by a religious leader or lawyer on a specific issue) condemn-ing the exploitation of guest workers. The Saudi Arabia National Recruitment Committee instituted a unified labour contract for foreign workers, clarifying requirements and expectations of recruitment agencies and workers. The Gov-ernment is funding an awareness-training programme in Sri Lanka for women seeking domestic work in Saudi Arabia. The women receive information on their rights and useful telephone numbers.

Although the Bahraini Government does not guarantee assistance to the victims of trafficking, it encourages victims to pursue legal action in cases when their embassies are not effective. The country's penal code outlaws forced labour, forced sex work, and withholding of salary. It does not, however, specifically prohibit trafficking in persons. Amendments to the Labour Law passed in 1993 raised the penalties for abuse of the sponsorship system to include jail sentences for the sponsor of up to six months per every illegally sponsored worker. As of yet, no sponsor has received a jail sentence. On the preventive side, early in 2002, the Government formed an Inter-ministerial Anti-trafficking Task Force. The Task Force collects information from relevant ministries to document the extent and nature of trafficking and develops a National Plan of Action against Trafficking in Persons. Also in 2002, a national workshop was held on trafficking.

In Jordan, a 1926 law prohibits trafficking in children, but otherwise trafficking in persons is not specifically prohibited by law. On the preventive side, the UN Development Fund for Women (UNIFEM) initiated a study on the situation of female domestic workers in Jordan in 2000. In January 2003, Jordan and UNIFEM agreed on a model work contract that would protect the rights of foreign domestic workers in the country (UNIFEM, 2003). The contract protects workers' rights to life insurance, medical care, rest days, and repatriation. The contract will be considered as a requirement for obtaining an entry visa, without which no worker will be admitted to Jordan. The countries of origin covered by the programme are Nepal, Indonesia, Sri Lanka, India, and Pakistan.

In Kuwait, a crackdown on several sex worker rings in 2002 resulted in the arrest of approximately 100 sex workers, middlemen, and clients, most of them Asian. Fifty were young Asian women who had been traded as sex slaves between rings, run by Asians living in Kuwait. Patterns of assault, rape, and murder of Asian maids working in Kuwait has led to an outcry in the maids' home countries and may provoke a ban by some Asian governments on women taking jobs as maids abroad (Protection Project, 2002). From the side of the destination country, more than 4,000 Kuwaiti sponsors have been blacklisted from sponsoring domestic workers due to their failure to provide prescribed benefits. In order to fight the phenomenon of trafficking and exploitation of foreign (mainly Asian) children as camel jockeys, the Camel Racing Club mandates that all camel jockeys must be 18 years of age or older to minimize the chances that very young children would be involved into the trafficking rings linked to such races.

Qatari law specifically prohibits trafficking in persons. Penalties for traffickers include fines and imprisonment. However, the Government has not prosecuted any cases against traffickers. The Government strictly monitors its borders as well as its immigration and emigration flows for evidence of trafficking. The Qatari Labour Department maintains a "black list" of companies that have severely violated labour laws or abused their workers. The Government repatriates victims of trafficking upon discovering their presence, but does not provide special assistance. With respect to camel jockeying, a national campaign was undertaken in April 2001 to set the minimum age to 15 and minimum weight of 100 pounds for camel jockeys. The Supreme Council for Family Affairs states that the issue of jockeys is a top priority and it was made the subject of an ongoing media and public awareness campaign. The Government runs a 24-hour hotline staffed by the Ministry of Interior and Supreme Council for Family Affairs personnel to advise and assist abused women and children.

Although the UAE does not have a law criminalizing trafficking in persons, the country has informed IOM that they are currently studying such a law and expect to adopt it in the next few months. However, forced or compulsory labour is illegal and labour regulations prohibit the employment of persons less than 15 years old. Traffickers can be prosecuted for child smuggling. The authorities have prosecuted foreign child smugglers, but do not usually investigate citizens involved in trafficking. In July 2002, the UAE introduced a law banning the use of children as jockeys in camel races. Entering into effect on 1 September 2002, the law banned the use of children as camel jockeys who were younger than age 15 and weighed less than 45 kilograms. In May 2003, the UAE strengthened measures to curb the trade in camel jockeys and, in cooperation with the Pakistani Embassy, repatriated several children trafficked for that purpose. These children were identified as victims of trafficking when accompanied by their employers for the visa renewals at the Pakistani Embassy. A number of state bodies are involved in the issue. According to the latest press reviews, a cabinet decision based on a draft law issued by the Ministry of Justice and Islamic Affairs and Endowments decided that jockeys must enter the UAE through the proper channels, have a valid visa stamped in the passport, and be issued a card in order to be able to participate in the camel races. Those who fail to register will be disqualified from the next race season. The Ministry of Information and Culture supported a public awareness campaign in English and Arabic about the law banning the use of child camel jockeys. Furthermore, the Ministry of Health requires annual physical exams for foreign employees and medical personnel with specialized training to look for signs of abuse.

While existence of sex work is widely acknowledged to exist, the UAE Government does not address the issue publicly because of societal sensitivities. However, the Government provides assistance and protection to victims of sexual abuse; they are not detained, jailed, nor deported. The police departments provide shelter for these victims, separate from the regular jail facilities. The Government works with foreign governments and NGOs on trafficking in women when cases are brought to their attention. In September 2002, a Dubai police team from the Human Rights Department participated in a course organized by the US Department of State that took place in the United States. UAE entry policy has recently become more constrained with regards to issuing visas to single women younger than 40 years old.

RESEARCH METHODS USED

Almost all the research works reviewed in this paper draw the analysis from secondary sources. Existing literature is complemented with information derived from press articles published by national and international media, mainly newspapers and Internet periodicals.

A significant number of the authors examined provide extensive reviews of national and international legislations concerning trafficking, slavery, immigration laws, labour laws, and in some cases also law enforcement, judiciary and detention procedures and practices.[18]

The work of Dr. Mattar deserves special attention for not only being the most comprehensive review of national and international law on trafficking, but also for its attempt to understand the reflections of these relatively recent laws on the different legal systems of the countries of the Middle East. By analysing the legal frameworks on trafficking of almost all the countries of the Middle East, the paper can also be read as a comparative analysis of these different legislations. Dr. Mattar ventures into the realm of reading modern legislations in light of Quranic and Islamic Law. Given that the Quran and Islamic Law provide the sources for most legal systems of Middle Eastern countries, Mattar accounts for a facet of tremendous importance bypassed by other researchers in the field.

The interview method provided the highest quality information on trafficking. Interviews have been conducted with government officials of different ministries, police, immigration and refugee authorities, consular and diplomatic personnel of trafficked/abused victims' countries of origin, private employment agencies, key informants working on the issues of migrant women under exploitative situations, as well as representatives of civil society organizations, NGOs, and international agencies.[19]

Two reports on the situation of trafficking of women to Israel were the result of mission visits to the country by a team of delegate experts (Ellman and Laacher, 2003; Amnesty International, 2000).

Kav La'Oved makes extensive use of documents obtained from government institutions, police reports, affidavits, declarations, and letters from detained victims, as well as letters and statements from lawyers defending victims of abuse in Israel. In three instances, researchers have resorted to the analysis of questionnaires submitted to a limited number of case studies comprising both migrant women workers and visa sponsors.[20] Another researcher was able to organize focus group discussions with migrants who were planning to migrate and returned migrants (Kebede, 2002).

The research initiatives of *Kav La'Oved* in Israel are based on information collected by volunteers of the hotline on women trafficking victims imprisoned between 2000 and 2002. One hundred in-depth interviews were also conducted with women in prisons, detention facilities, and police lockups throughout the country; women waiting to provide testimony; and women who had escaped from their traffickers but feared turning to the authorities. The organization also researched police files, indictments, and a number of cases of trafficking in women and related offences that reached trial in 1998, 1999, and 2000. A 2003 International Federation for Human Rights (FIDH) (see Ellman and Laacher, 2003) report on the situation of trafficked migrants in Israel is similarly based on interviews (unspecified number) conducted with foreign workers, legal and illegal.

Two other studies, not focused but containing information on human trafficking, also relied on interviews for gathering information. The study "Iraqi forced migrants in Jordan" contains 40 informal interviews of Iraqi forced migrants in Amman and the "Exploratory study on foreign domestic work in Syria" conducted interviews with 57 workers from a variety of foreign communities.

DATA ON HUMAN TRAFFICKING: AN ASSESSMENT OF CURRENT DATA SOURCES

It will hardly surprise any practitioner in the field of counter-trafficking or any researcher of Middle Eastern affairs, that the extent of data collection on trafficking in the Middle East is severely limited. Only in the case of Israel, has an organization been able to collect some sort of hard data.[21] For all other countries, researchers concede that even government and law enforcement authorities do not have access to statistics regarding human trafficking.

The present review of recent research on human trafficking in the Middle East region did not find any reference to agencies collecting data on trafficking or to mechanisms for the sharing of data within countries and between countries in the region.

Number and profile of victims

Israel is the only country with estimates of the number of trafficked victims. The Parliamentary Investigation Committee on Trafficking in Women (December 2002) estimated the number of trafficked women each year to be 3,000 (*Kav La'Oved*, 2003a: 7). It deserves mention that this figure has been reached based on the number of prosecutions against perpetrators of human trafficking, i.e. it reflects only cases that have been investigated or persecuted by the police.

For all other countries in the region, even guesstimates are difficult to come by. Some researchers attempt a comparison between official statistics of foreign labour workers present in a given countries and the estimated numbers of illegal migrants. Others simply resort to expressions such as "some", "many", and "a number", or refer to "thousands of cases" when discussing figures of trafficking. Unfortunately, no one is able to substantiate these vague approximations with any hard evidence.

Regarding profiling, it is again thanks to the dedicated efforts of *Kav La'Oved* that we are able to know the profile of trafficked victims to Israel. The majority of women come from the former countries of the Soviet Union; mainly Moldova, Ukraine, Russia, and recently also in growing numbers the women are trafficked from Uzbekistan. "Most trafficked women are young, in their 20s", the report says (*Kav La'Oved*, 2003a: 16).

Although no hard data are available for Lebanon, in 2002, the eminent Middle East correspondent Robert Fisk, published an article on young Eastern European women looking for easy earnings in Beirut's nightclubs (Fisk, 2003). The article is partly an interview with a Russian girl. The story became legendary and from her name, Eastern European women working in the entertainment industry in Arab countries started to be called "Natashas", as it is the case in many other parts of the world.

No data are available for other groups of trafficking victims in other countries of the Middle East, particularly what regards minors and Asian women. The profile of Ethiopian trafficked women, sketched by the 2002 ILO report gives the following information:

> Various sources indicate that most women who are victims of trafficking are within the 20 to 30 age group. According to a study on 'Trafficking of women from Ethiopia', the 36 women returnees who used to work as housemaids in the Middle East interviewed for the study were between 20 and 30 years of age and have some high school education or are graduates. The focus group discussions conducted for this study with returnees, as well as women who are about to migrate to the Middle East, also confirm this fact.

Most of the girls interviewed for the earlier study mentioned above migrated from Addis Ababa, while some were from the rural parts of the country (Kebede, 2002: 6).[22]

Profile of traffickers

Data on the profile of trafficking perpetrators is even more difficult to obtain than of the victims. In the case of Israel, it appears that traffickers are overwhelmingly, but not exclusively, connected to Russian organized criminal rings. In the last few decades, the arrival of successive waves of Russian and Eastern European immigrants has facilitated the establishment of these rings and guaranteed at the same time, a certain degree of invisibility in society.

The route of human trafficking to Israel recently opened through the Sinai desert has been described by many press reports and can be summarized as follows: "The women land in Egyptian airports, mainly in Cairo, Hurghada, and Sharm-al-Sheikh, and are then taken to the Sinai by car. From there they cross the border on foot accompanied by a Bedouin escort" (*Kav La'Oved*, 2003a: 19). Bedouins on the Egyptian side exploit their knowledge of the inhospitable desert territory as well as their tribal links with other Bedouins on the Israeli side. Separated by the establishment of international borders between them in 1948, Bedouin communities have always been able to keep strong links across these borders, which have not deterred them from conducting "unofficial trade activities", mostly connected to the smuggling of goods, between the two sides.[23] It is noticeable that the "escorting" activities conducted by Bedouins in the Sinai desert are undeterred by the heavy security surveillance of this sensitive international border, which is patrolled on the Egyptian side by a multilateral military force.

Main obstacles to improving data collection on trafficking

As pointed out by different authors in different contexts, the vast majority of states worldwide are still unable to provide reliable data as to the number of cases or the characteristics of trafficking victims and perpetrators. The obstacles faced by researchers in the Middle East are basically the same as that in other regions of the world. The nature itself of the trafficking phenomenon, illegal and transactional, makes it very difficult to investigate even when law enforcement authorities fully cooperate in the data gathering and data sharing effort.

Victims themselves are often reluctant to disclose information on recruiting methods, the trafficking routes, and the profile of the perpetrators. This is not only due to the understandable fear for their personal security and potential traffickers reprisals against the trafficked person and members of his/her families. This is the case especially when in most countries, including those that have adopted advanced anti-trafficking legislations, law enforcement and judiciary authorities still do not always distinguish between the perpetrators and the victims of trafficking. Victims of trafficking are often distressed by a sense of guilt for having fallen prey to deceptive pledges and entrusted their destiny to unscrupulous people and seductive promises of easy money. In almost every society, social stigma plays an important role preventing victims of trafficking from divulging their stories.

An additional complication present in the Middle East is the fact that the issue of human trafficking has been closely associated by the majority of government officials to the monitoring of human rights violations by human rights groups. It results in situations such as when a government official discussing a potential anti-trafficking intervention with an international agency insists on calling the draft project document "the human rights report" and rejects it due to the claim that his country had a "clear bill of human rights".[24] In cases like this one, it has been found useful to share and discuss documents such as the annual TIP report which show that trafficking is not an issue necessarily linked with the violations of human rights per se and that countries that are considered fully respecting human rights are not immune from experiencing – sometimes vast – occurrences of human trafficking.

The assonance between *"human* trafficking" and *"human* rights" has further contributed to make government officials reluctant to openly discuss their national trafficking files, especially when national and international agencies tend to use terminology and language borrowed from human rights groups. Human rights groups play an invaluable role in carrying out their mandate of denouncing violations of fundamental rights, sometimes being at the forefront of very difficult and dangerous battles, and have largely contributed to unveil hidden aspects of the human trafficking phenomenon. While human rights groups should continue to play their necessary role, other national and international agencies working in the fight against human trafficking should try to make additional efforts to increase coordination with these groups, better define the respective roles, agree on a division of labour, and possibly concert common strategies.

Another serious obstacle hampering the gathering of data on human trafficking is represented by the discrepancies that have been often noticed about the definition itself of human trafficking as given by different actors and the level of awareness of human trafficking not only of government authorities, but also of international agencies officials, donor representatives, diplomatic personnel, research experts, human rights activists, and legal practitioners. The UN Trafficking Protocol definition, when known to the different interlocutors, is often narrowed or overstretched according to personal interpretation, cultural sensitivity, or simply contingent on convenience. In one instance, a representative of a donor country asked why the IOM definition of human trafficking was broader than the UN definition, implying that he had read and compared both, whereas in fact the organizations share the same definition.[25] In another case, a diplomat of a country of origin of trafficked women stated that he was happy when the "girls" were jailed for a few days because this was the only way "to teach them a lesson".[26] Effectively, the different interpretations of what is human trafficking and who is a victim – coupled with diverse personal and cultural sensitivities and sometimes also cultural and linguistic misunderstandings – are factors that thwart data gathering efforts simply because there is no agreement on what should be considered data on human trafficking.

GAPS IN KNOWLEDGE, PRIORITY AREAS FOR FURTHER ACTION TO IMPROVE RESEARCH AND DATA ON TRAFFICKING

While research on human trafficking in the Middle East region conducted so far makes it possible to depict the broad contours of the phenomenon, it is obvious that more work is needed to better investigate its multifaceted aspects and define its scale. It appears that research has been not been conducted systematically, but only responding to contingent and localized realities and incidentally touching on core issues. Issues such as the social and psychological impact on individual victims, the relations with the communities of origin and destination, as well as the gender and health dimensions, have so far not been adequately investigated.

Moreover, although specialists in human trafficking can rely on the definition provided by the UN Trafficking Protocol, many still use the term "trafficking" to describe different aspects of irregular migration. Asylum seekers, irregular migrants, and regular migrants whose labour or human rights have been violated or abused at some stage, are readily called victims of "trafficking". The general press and even specialists tend to confuse the process – which does not necessarily start as a process of trafficking at inception, but rather *turns* from other forms of irregular migration into trafficking – with those who are the victims of the process. At the same time, it must be said that there is a tendency to neglect the strong links between human trafficking and the complex dynamics of irregular migration.

It also appears that more coordination and exchange of information between researchers based in countries of origin of victims of human trafficking with those in countries of destination is needed. It is noticeable that researchers seem to rely on literature and information specific to each respective region and that only very limited cross-reference is made between countries of origin and countries of destination.

Critical assessment of counter-trafficking initiatives

Despite the many difficulties experienced by counter-trafficking practitioners, some counter-trafficking activities have been launched in recent years in a number of Middle Eastern countries mainly by IOM and local NGOs with the assistance of the donor community.

In September 2002, IOM Addis Ababa started a pre-departure counselling project – Preventing Trafficking through Counselling Services in Ethiopia. It is aimed at contributing to the Ethiopian Government's efforts to prevent trafficking in human beings, specifically to the Arab Gulf countries and Lebanon, by providing information about the realities of irregular migration, and in particular the risks for women. The project offers hotline support to give anonymous counselling services. IOM has also established an outreach network with governmental and non-governmental organizations to refer selected clients to further specialized counselling. This project, operational until 30 October 2004, complements an already existing IOM counter trafficking information campaign called "Be Informed! Countering Trafficking through Information" that began in 2002.

In June 2004, IOM launched the first phase of the three-year project "Counter-trafficking and Migrants Rights Capacity Building of Bahraini National Institutions". It aims to increase the capacity of Bahraini Government institutions and NGOs to develop national instruments to protect migrant workers from abuse, prevent the exploitation of migrant workers, and establish mechanisms to fight and prevent migrant trafficking.

A similar initiative developed for Lebanon – "Counter-trafficking: Capacity Building of National Institutions and Assisted Returns of Victims" – still awaits funding from the donor community although it has been fully endorsed by national authorities. Also in Lebanon, the Caritas Migrant Centre is helping migrants return to the country of origin. The centre also has a prison aid programme to take care of detained illegal migrants.

During 2004, IOM engaged in a "Field Assessment of Trafficking in Persons in Iraq". This initial research project aims to study and assess the current situation regarding trafficking in persons, particularly women and children to and from Iraq. The project will collect information from community groups dealing with victims and those who are vulnerable to traffickers. The study will outline the scale and trends of trafficking in persons within the Iraqi context, draw up recommendations, publish a report on trafficking to and from Iraq, and contribute towards establishing a network of governmental, NGO, and IGO partners.

Through its Global Assistance Fund or with funds managed directly by field missions, IOM is assisting trafficking victims, including minors, returning from the UAE back to the countries. These funds are allocated to the assistance of the victims, their return, and reintegration process. Discussions with the UAE and other Gulf countries are underway to propose additional IOM interventions in the field of victims' assistance. In April 2004, the Saudi Ministry of Interior sought the assistance of UNICEF and IOM to repatriate 500 Afghani and Pakistani children who were trafficked to Saudi Arabia during Hajj season to beg.

Apart from the above-mentioned counter-trafficking initiatives, the governments of the region have not been sufficiently engaged by international agencies and donor countries. Excessive emphasis has instead been placed on reporting and denouncing cases of human trafficking, without proposing practical answers and offering assistance. The donor countries – albeit concerned about human trafficking and forthcoming in allocating considerable resources to curb the flows of irregular migrants "menacing" their borders – risk losing credibility, and in turn effectiveness, if they critique and point out problem areas without being able to be pro-active when practical issues arise. Not only financial, but also technical assistance is needed to address problems that many countries where the abuse is committed will be glad to solve.

Priority areas for further research in the region

It might appear circumscribed to affirm that, given the overall situation of human trafficking research in the region, any area could be chosen as priority to improve our knowledge of this phenomenon. That is, however, the picture that emerges from this brief review of recent research on human trafficking in the Middle East. Hence, it is the conclusion of this review that the scale of the phenomenon must be measured in the different countries (Israel being the exception where the work has already begun) and in the region as a whole, in order to set detailed priorities, develop counter-trafficking interventions, and direct further targeted research.

There are a few evident areas that, although inspiring state reactions, reported by the press or otherwise known about through anecdotal evidence, have not been seriously explored by any researcher. Child trafficking is one of them.

For instance, repeated press reports denounce the use of Asian children for camel jockeying in the Arab Gulf region. A number of legal measures have also been adopted by the affected countries. The impact of these measures is, however, difficult to gauge because little is known about the situation that preceded their promulgation or the fate of those children after the changed situation.

It appears that some field research has been conducted on Yemeni children trafficked to Saudi Arabia for begging during the Hajj season. Unfortunately, it appears that the results of these research efforts are not available to the public and little is known about other children brought to Saudi Arabia for the same purpose from Afghanistan, Pakistan, and Bangladesh. It is not known whether children of yet other nationalities are involved or are brought to other countries in the region for similar purposes.

Similarly, no one has dedicated any appreciable effort to shed light on the phenomenon of underage girls from poor Islamic countries married to wealthy Arab nationals. The Government of Egypt recently launched a national campaign to ensure that birth certificates and identification papers are issued to all female newborn babies and underage girls to prevent child marriages. The subject warrants an investigation into the situation of also other countries in the region and how they have dealt with the issue, as well as underlying factors like poverty and low levels of education.

The relation of human trafficking with poverty and social conditions is an essential element to any understanding of the causes of human trafficking. It should be made a priority to identify potential remedies starting from the countries of origin. Additionally, the cultural gap between the societies from where victims of human trafficking originate and the region where they are brought – in this case mostly Islamic and in some cases conservative countries – is a factor that should not be underestimated in any research on the subject.

NOTES

1. The views expressed in this paper are personal and do not necessarily express those of the organizers and sponsors of this international expert meeting.

2. The countries include Egypt, Iraq, Jordan, Lebanon, the Palestinian Territory, and Syria.

3. The countries include Bahrain, Saudi Arabia, Kuwait, Oman, Qatar, the United Arab Emirates, and Yemen.

4. The countries include Libya, Tunisia, Algeria, Morocco, and Mauritania.

5. There are no official or reliable data on international migrants for majority of the surveyed countries. The estimate provided here is the result of a compilation and cross reference done by IOM Cairo in 2003 from a variety of different sources (using the lowest mean). Data on refugees were compiled from UNHCR, US Committee for Refugees, and UNRWA, 2003.

6. Hundreds of thousand of Yemenis left Saudi Arabia after 1991 due to the political support of their Government to Saddam Hussein.

7. According to the US Department of State definition, Tier 3 includes those countries that do not fully comply with the minimum standards and those who are not making significant efforts to bring themselves into compliance. In fact some of these governments refuse to acknowledge the trafficking problem within their territory. Others in this category are starting to make positive and concrete steps to combat trafficking.

8. See for instance "Nepalese hostages killed in Iraq", BBC News, 31 August 2004, http://news.bbc.co.uk/1/hi/world/south_asia/3614866.stm.

9. Interview with US diplomat, Cairo, March 2004.

10. The Definition set by the Trafficking Victims Protection Act of 2000 reads: (a) sex trafficking in which a commercial sex act is induced by force, fraud, or coercion, or in which the person induced to perform such an act has not attained 18 years of age; or (b) the recruitment, harbouring, transportation, provision, or obtaining of a person for labour or services, through the use of force, fraud or coercion for the purpose of subjection to involuntary servitude, peonage, debt bondage, or slavery (US Department of State, 2003: 12).

11. Also in accordance with the IOM definition, trafficking in persons shall mean, "the recruitment, transportation, transfer, harbouring or receipt of persons, by means of the threat or use offence or other forms of coercion, of abduction, of fraud, of deception, of the abuse of power or of a position of vulnerability or of the giving or receiving payments or benefits to achieve the consent of a person having control over another person, for the purpose of exploitation" (UN, 2000).

12. Starting in the 1980s, the Israeli labour market was opened to guest workers mainly from East Europe and Asia, thereby replacing thousands of Palestinian daily workers commuting from the West Bank and the Gaza Strip. The cycle of violence between Israel and the Palestinians culminated in 2000 with the eruption of the latest and fiercest uprising (*Intifadah*), which has caused an almost total stop to Palestinians working in Israel.

13. It is possible to download trafficking route maps for the Middle East as well as for some countries of the region from the Protection Project web site. As earlier

mentioned, however, the Protection Project would give account of any episode of trafficking, even if marginal. It also appears that maps have not been updated since 2002. For the Protection Project maps see: "Trafficking Routes to the Middle East", http://209.190.246.239/pdfmaps/me.pdf; "Trafficking Routes from Easter Europe to the Middle East", http://209.190.246.239/pdfmaps/ee1.pdf; "Trafficking Routes to Bahrain", http://209.190.246.239/pdfmaps/bahrain.pdf; "Trafficking Routes to Kuwait", http://209.190.246.239/pdfmaps/ku.pdf; "Trafficking Routes to Qatar", http://209.190.246.239/pdfmaps/qa.pdf; "Trafficking Routes to Saudi Arabia", http://209.190.246.239/pdfmaps/saa.pdf; and "Trafficking Routes to the United Arab Emirates", http://209.190.246.239/pdfmaps/uae.pdf.

14. The following quote was chosen as representative, but all the other studies mentioned in the present paper give account of similar dynamics.

15. One could assume that these migrant workers are mainly going to be employed as domestic helpers. However the research studies consulted for the purpose of this review do not specifically indicate this condition only.

16. According to a survey conducted by UNICEF in 1999, young girls in five very poor villages in Egypt were married off to much older men from oil-rich Middle Eastern countries via brokers; see "Early marriage in selected villages in Giza Governorate", a study carried out by the Ministry of Social Affairs, Egypt, and supported by UNICEF Egypt, 1999.

17. The information contained in this section is exclusively drawn (with the exception of the paragraph on Israel) from IOM, 2003.

18. See Al-Najjar, Mattar, Emebet, Jureidini, Young, Chaterland, Sabban, Ellman and Laacher, Amnesty International and *Kav La'Oved*/Migrant Workers Hotline.

19. See Al-Najjar, Emebet, Young, Chaterland, Sabban, *Kav La'Oved*/Migrant Workers Hotline, and IOM Damascus.

20. See al-Najjar on Bahrain, Jureidini on Lebanon, and Sabban for the UAE.

21. *Kav La'Oved* was able to access data from police files opened for trafficking in women and related offenses, number of indictments, and number of cases that reached trial between 1998 and 2000.

22. See also Tekle and Belayneh, 2000.

23. It is important to clarify here that it would be utterly unfair to criminalize Bedouins as a group for the illegal activities of some of its members. Bedouin communities on both sides of the border suffer from social exclusion and are extremely underprivileged in comparison to the rest of the societies they officially belong to.

24. Source withheld.

25. IOM has adopted the definition of the *Protocol to the Convention Against Transnational Organized Crime*.

26. Source withheld.

REFERENCES

Al-Najjar, S.
2002   "Women migrant domestic workers in Bahrain", *International Migration Papers*, 47, International Labour Office, http://www.ilo.org/public/english/protection/migrant/download/imp/imp47e.pdf.

Al-Zaidi, H.
2004   "25 children received from Saudi", *Yemen Times*, 13(721), http://www.yementimes.com/ article.shtml?i=721&p=front&a=3.

Amnesty International
2000   *Human Rights Abuses of Women Trafficked from Countries of the Former Soviet Union into Israel's Sex Industry*, Amnesty International, May, http://web.amnesty.org/aidoc/aidoc_pdf.nsf/Index/MDE150172000 ENGLISH/$File/MDE1501700.pdf.

BBC News
2004   "Nepalese hostages killed in Iraq", BBC News, 31 August, http:// news.bbc.co.uk/1/hi/world/south_asia/3614866.stm.

Blanchet, T.
2002   "Beyond boundaries: a critical look at women labor migration and the trafficking within", USAID, Dhaka.

Borkholder, J.L., and M. Mohammed
2002   "Domestic service as a form of trafficking in persons in the Middle East", First World Congress for Middle Eastern Studies, Mainz, Germany, 12 September, http://www.protectionproject.org/commentary/ele.htm.

Chatelard, G.
2002   "Iraqi forced migrants in Jordan: conditions, religious networks, and the smuggling process", paper presented at the WIDER Conference on Poverty, International Migration and Asylum, 27-28 September, Helsinki, http://www.wider.unu.edu/conference/conference-2002-3/conference% 20papers/ chatelard.pdf.

Chemali Khalaf, M.
2003   "Women's international labor migration in the Arab world: historical and socio-economic perspectives: United Nations Division for the Advancement of Women (DAW)", paper presented at the Consultative Meeting on *Migration and Mobility and How this Movement Affects Women*, Malmö, Sweden, 2-4 December, http://www.un.org/womenwatch/daw/meetings/consult/CM-Dec03-EP5.pdf.

Ellman, M., and S. Laacher
2003   *Migrant Workers in Israel A Contemporary Form on Slavery*, International Federation for Human Rights, 25 August, http://www.fidh.org/magmoyen/rapport/2003/il1806a.pdf.

Firmo-Fontan, V.
2004   "Abducted, beaten and sold into prostitution: two women's story from an Iraq in turmoil", *The Independent*, 24 July, http://news.independent.co.uk/world/middle_east/story.jsp?story=544122.

Fisk, R.
  2003   "A nation's worst kept secret: the women lured to Lebanon with a one-
          way ticket into slavery", *The Independent*, April, http://www.robert-fisk.
          com/articles93.htm.
Gillespie, K.
  2004   "1,000 'hapless foreigners' fall victim to contractors' scam", *The Daily
          Star*, 31 May, http://www.dailystar.com.lb/article.asp?edition_id=10
          &categ_id=2&article_id=469.
Harel, Z.
  2004   "Former cop jailed for four years for sex-slave trading", *Ha'aretz*,
          19 January, quoted in *Middle East Migration News*, no. 65, 13 January.
Hughes, D.M.
  2002   "Trafficking for sexual exploitation: the case of the Russian Federation",
          International Organization for Migration, no. 7, *IOM Migration Research
          Series*, IOM, Geneva, http://www.iom.int//DOCUMENTS/PUBLICATION/
          EN/mrs_7_2002.pdf.
International Organization for Migration (IOM)
  2001   "Deceived migrants from Tajikistan: a study of trafficking in women and
          children", IOM, Dushanbe, Tajikistan, http://www.iom.int//DOCUMENTS/
          PUBLICATION/EN/Tajikistan_study_august2001.pdf.
  2002   *Irregular Migration and Smuggling of Migrants from Armenia*, IOM,
          Yerevan, Armenia, http://www.iom.int//DOCUMENTS/PUBLICATION/
          EN/armenia_trafficking.pdf.
  2003   "Migrant trafficking in the Middle East and potential IOM responses",
          Discussion Paper, IOM, Egypt, June (unpublished).
  2004   *Arab Migration in a Globalized World*, IOM, Geneva.
Jureidini, R.
  2001   "Xenophobia in Arab societies", paper presented at the World Conference
          against Racism, Racial Discrimination, Xenophobia and Related
          Intolerance, Durban, 3-5 September, http://portal.unesco.org/shs/en/
          file_download.php/a77c8bf17abd8da973d0222ff6e7c067R.+Jareidini.doc.
  2002   "Women migrant domestic workers in Lebanon", International Migration
          Papers 48, International Labour Organization, http://www.ilo.org/public/
          english/protection/ migrant/download/imp/ imp48e.pdf.
  2003a   "Migrant labour: xenophobia, indenture and trafficking in the Gulf States",
          paper presented at the Fourth Mediterranean Social and Political Research
          Meeting, Florence and Montecatini Terme, 19-23 March, organized by
          the Mediterranean Programme of the Robert Schuman Centre for
          Advanced Studies at the European University Institute, http://www.iue.it/
          RSCAS/RestrictedPapers/conmed2003free/200303Jureidini05.pdf.
  2003b   "Human rights and foreign contract labour: some implications for
          management and regulation in Arab countries", paper presented at the
          Regional Conference on Arab Migration in a Globalized World, Cairo, 2-4
          September, organized by IOM and the League of Arab States.

Kahale, S.
 2003   "Exploratory study on foreign domestic work in Syria", IOM, Damascus,
         Syria, http://iom.un.org.sy/documents/Foreign_Domestic_Workers_
         Report%20.pdf.
Kav La'Oved
 2002   "Workers trafficking from Romania to Israel", *Kav La'Oved*, 22 October,
         http://www.kavlaoved.org.il/ word/251002.rtf.
 2003a   "UN Commission on Human Rights, 59th Session 17 March-24 April,
         National NGOs Report to the Annual UN Commission on Human Rights:
         Evaluation of National Authorities Activities and Actual Facts on the
         Trafficking in Persons for the Purpose of Prostitution in Israel", *Kav
         La'Oved*, 6 April, http://www.kavlaoved.org.il/word/060403.html.
 2003b   "Women as commodities: trafficking in women in Israel, 2003", *Kav
         La'Oved*, 24 August-11 September, http://www.kavlaoved.org.il/katava_
         main.asp?news_ id=620&sivug_ id=3 (Hebrew only).
Kebede, E.
 2002   "Ethiopia: an assessment of the international labour migration situation:
         the case of female labour migrants", GENPROM Working Paper No. 3,
         Series on Women and Migration, Gender Promotion Programme,
         International Labour Organization, 6 December, http://www.ilo.org/public/
         english/employment/gems/download/swmeth.pdf.
Kuwait Times
 2004   "Gulf states to halt trafficking of children as camel jockeys", *Kuwait
         Times*, 28 January, quoted in *Middle East Migration News*, no. 65,
         13 January.
Mattar, M.Y.
 2003   "Trafficking in persons, especially women and children, in the countries
         of the Middle East: scope of the problem and the appropriate legislative
         responses", *Fordham International Law Journal*, 26(3): 721, http://
         209.190.246.239/article.pdf.
Protection Project
 2002   *A Human Rights Report on Trafficking of Persons, Especially Women
         and Children*, The Protection Project, Johns Hopkins University, Paul H.
         Nitze School of Advanced International Studies, Washington, DC.
Reeves, P.
 2003   "Stolen, smuggled and sold: the frightened boys forced to become camel
         jockeys in a foreign land", *The Independent*, 29 October, http://news.
         independent.co.uk/ world/asia/story.jsp?story=458312.
Sabban, R.
 2002   "Migrant women in the United Arab Emirates: the case of female domestic
         workers", GENPROM Working Paper No. 10, Series on Women and
         Migration, International Labour Organization, http://www.ilo.org/public/
         english/employment/gems/download/swmuae.pdf.
Smith, M., and S. Esim (Eds)
 2004   "Gender and migration in Arab states: the case of domestic workers",
         International Labour Organization, Regional Office for Arab States, Beirut.

Tekle, A., and T. Belayneh
  2000   "Trafficking of women from Ethiopia", a study commissioned by the Women's Affairs sub-sector in the Prime Minister's office and the IOM in Addis Ababa, June 2000, http://www.gtz.de/violence-against-women/downloads/e-negash-presentation.pdf.
United Nations (UN)
  2000   "Protocol to the Convention Against Transnational Organized Crime, The Trafficking Protocol to Prevent, Suppress and Punish Trafficking in Persons, especially Women and Children", United Nations, General Assembly, 11th Session, adopted by Resolution 55/25, signed 12-15 December 2000, Palermo, http://www.uncjin.org/Documents/Conventions/dcatoc/final_documents_2/convention_%20traff_eng.pdf.
United Nations Children's Fund (UNICEF)
  1999   "Early marriage in selected villages in Giza Governorate", a study carried out by the Ministry of Social Affairs, Egypt, and supported by UNICEF Egypt.
United Nations Development Fund for Women (UNIFEM)
  2003   "Special working contract for non-Jordanian domestic workers: an opportunity to enhance protection for a particularly vulnerable group of women workers", press release from UNIFEM Arab States Regional Office, Amman, 2 February, http://www.unifem.org.jo/press_releases.htm.
United Nations Office on Drugs and Crime
  2003   *Protocol to Prevent, Suppress and Punish Trafficking in Persons, Especially Women and Children: Signatories and Parties*, United Nations Office on Drugs and Crime, 19 April, http://www.unods.org/unodc/en/crime_cicp_signatories_trafficking.html.
United States Department of State
  2003   *Trafficking in Persons Report*, US Department of State, Bureau of Public Affairs, 11 June, http://www.state.gov/documents/organization/21555.pdf.
Young, M.
  2000   "Migrant workers in Lebanon", Lebanese NGO Forum, September, http://www.lnf.org.lb/migrationnetwork/mig1.html.

Human Trafficking: Bibliography by Region

Romaine Farquet, Heikki Mattila, and Frank Laczko*

EUROPE

General

Berman, J.
2003   "(Un)popular strangers and crises (un)bounded: discourses of sex-trafficking, the European political community and the panicked state of the modern state", *European Journal of International Relations*, 9(1): 97-86.

Council of Europe
2002   *Trafficking in Human Beings and Corruption*, report on the regional seminar, Portoroz, Slovenia, 19-22 June, Council of Europe, Programme against Corruption and Organized Crime (PACO), Strasbourg.

Drew, S.
2002   "Human trafficking: a modern form of slavery?", *European Human Rights Law Review*, 4: 481-492.

End Child Prostitution, Child Pornography and Trafficking of Children for Sexual Purposes (ECPAT)
2004   *Joint East West Research on Trafficking in Minors for Sexual Purposes in Europe: the Sending Countries*, Programme against Trafficking in Children for Sexual Purposes in Europe, ECPAT, Amsterdam.

Freedman, J.
2003   "Selling sex: trafficking, prostitution and sex work amongst migrant women in Europe", *Gender and Insecurity: Migrant Women in Europe*, Aldershot, Ashgate: 119-136.

Gao, Y.
2004   "Chinese migrants and forced labour in Europe", ILO, Geneva.

* Research and Publications Division, International Organization for Migration (IOM) Geneva, Switzerland.

Goodey, J.
2003   "Migration, crime and victimhood: responses to sex trafficking in the EU", *Punishment and Society*, 5(4): 415-431.
Holmes, P., and K. Berta
2002   *Comparative Matrix on Legislation and Best Practices in Preventing and Combating Trafficking in Human Beings in EU Member States and Candidate Countries*, European Conference on Preventing and Combating Trafficking in Human Beings: Global Challenge for the 21st Century, http://www.belgium.iom.int/STOPConference/Conference%20Papers/Trafficking%20Legislation%20Matrix.pdf.
International Labour Organization (ILO)
2003   *Forced Labour Outcomes of Irregular Migration and Human Trafficking in Europe*, ILO, Geneva.
International Organization for Migration (IOM)
2000   *Migrant Trafficking and Human Smuggling in Europe: A Review of the Evidence with Case Studies from Hungary, Poland and Ukraine*, IOM, Geneva.
International Organization for Migration (IOM) and European Commission
2002   *Trafficking in Unaccompanied Minors in the European Union: Belgium, France, Greece, Italy, The Netherlands, Spain*, http://www.iom.int/DOCUMENTS/PUBLICATION/EN/Traff_Unac_minors_2003_En.pdf.
2004   *Action-oriented Research on Infiltration by Trafficking Networks into Organizations Working to Combat – or Working with Victims of – Trafficking in Human Beings*, report of an IOM research project carried out within the Hippokrates Programme of the European Commission, Brussels.
Kartusch, A.
2002   *Menschenhandel: eine menschenrechtliche Herausforderung an die OSZE*, OSZE, 8 Jahrbuch.
Kelly, E.
2005   "You can find anything you want: research on human trafficking in Europe in the twenty-first century, *International Migration*, 43(1/2).
Lehti, M.
2003   "Trafficking in women and children in Europe", HEUNI paper no. 18, http://www.heuni.fi/uploads/xsba5z.pdf.
Luckhoo, F., and M. Tzvetkova
2003   *Cooperation: Practices and Constraints – A Report on Inter-agency Collaboration in Combating Trafficking in the Czech Republic, Italy and Romania*, Change, London.
Meier, D.
2002   *The Future Role of Parliaments in the Prevention of Trafficking in Human Beings by Example of the European, German and Hungarian Parliaments*, Miller und Meier Consulting, Berlin.
Morrison, J., and B. Crosland
2001   "The trafficking and smuggling of refugees: the end game in European asylum policy?", *New Issues in Refugee Research*, Working Paper no. 39, UNHCR, Geneva.

Niesner, E., and C. Jones-Pauly
2001   *Trafficking in Women in Europe: Prosecution and Victim Protection in a European Context*, Kleine Verlag, Bielefeld.

Rijken, C.
2003   *Trafficking in Persons: Prosecution from a European Perspective*, Asser Press, The Hague.

Salt, J.
2000   "Trafficking and human smuggling: a European perspective", *Perspectives on Trafficking of Migrants*, IOM, Geneva.

Salt, J., and J. Hogarth
2000   "Migrant trafficking and human smuggling in Europe: a review of the evidence", in F. Laczko (Ed.), *Migrant Trafficking and Human Smuggling in Europe*, IOM, Geneva.

Save the Children Italy
2004   *A Report on Child Trafficking: Bulgaria, Denmark, Italy, Romania, Spain, United Kingdom*, Save the Children Italy, Rome.

Smartt, U.
2003   "Human trafficking: simply a European problem?", *European Journal of Crime, Criminal Law and Criminal Justice*, 11(2): 164-177.

Stiftelsen Kvinnoforum
2003   *European Good Practice on Recovery, Return and Integration of Trafficked Persons*, Kvinnoforum, Stockholm.

Transcrime
2002   *MON-EU-TRAF: A Pilot Study on Three European Union Key Immigration Points for Monitoring the Trafficking of Human Beings for the Purpose of Sexual Exploitation across the European Union*, Transcrime, University of Trento.

Tyldum. G., and A. Brunovskis
2005   "Current practices and challenges in empirical studies on trafficking: a discussion paper from a northern European perspective", *International Migration*, 43(1/2).

Uherek, Z., et al.
2001   *Women Asylum Seekers and Trafficking*, research report for UNHCR, Branch Office, Prague.

Van Liemt, G.
2003   "Human trafficking in Europe: an economic perspective", paper presented for International Labour Organization's Special Action Programme to Combat Forced Labour, August.

Wijers, M.
2000   "European union policy on trafficking in women", in M. Rossilli (Ed.), *Gender Policies in the European Union*, Peter Lang, New York.

Zimmermann, C.
2003   *The Health Risks and Consequences of Trafficking in Women and Adolescents. Findings from a European Study*, London School of Hygiene and Tropical Medicine, London.

WESTERN EUROPE

Association for Cooperation with the South (ACSUR-Las Segovias)
   2001   *Trafico e Inmigración de Mujeres en España: Colombianas y Ecuatorianas*
           en los Servicios Doméstico y Sexuales (Trafficking and Immigration of
           Women in Spain: Colombian and Ecuadorean Women's Involvement in
           Domestic and Sexual Services), ACSUR-Las Segovias, Spain.

Ayotte, W.
   2000   *Separated Children Coming to Western Europe: Why They Travel and*
           How They Arrive, Save the Children, London.

Ayotte, W., and L. Williamson
   2002   *Separated Children in the UK: An Overview of the Current Situation*,
           Refugee Council and Save the Children, London.

Bertschi, S.
   2002   "Sexarbeit tabuisiert? Zum Nachteil der Frauen: eine juristische Analyse
           von Straf- und AusländerInnenrecht zur Unterbindung von Frauen-
           handel", NFP40, *Violence in Daily Life and Organized Crime*.

Bindel, J., and L. Kelly
   2003   *A Critical Examination of Response to Prostitution in Four Countries:*
           Victoria, Australia, Ireland, the Netherlands and Sweden, Routes Out
           Partnership, Glasgow.

Campani, G.
   2004   "Trafficking for sexual exploitation and sex business in the new context
           of international migration: the case of southern Europe", paper presented
           in the international expert meeting Improving Data and Research on
           Human Trafficking, arranged by IOM and the Government of Italy in
           Rome, May.

Carchedi, F., et al.
   2002   *Il Lavoro Servile e le Nuove Schiavitù*, FrancoAngeli, Milano.

Estermann, J., and R. Zschokke
   2001   "The organizational structures of trafficking in women: the example of
           Switzerland", in J. Estermann and R. Zschokke, *Organisationsstrukturen*
           des Frauenhandels am Beispiel der Schweiz, Orlux, Luzern.

European Commission (EC)
   2001   *Preventing and Combating Trafficking in Women: A Comprehensive*
           European Strategy, EC, Brussels, http://europa.eu.int/comm/justice_
           home/news/8mars_en.htm#a2.

   2002   *Brussels Declaration on Preventing and Combating Trafficking in*
           Human Beings, http://www.coe.int/T/E/Human_Rights/Trafficking/3_
           Documents/International_legal_instruments/UE%20brudeclaration.pdf.

   2004   *Report of the Experts Group on Trafficking in Human Beings*, Directorate-
           General Justice, Freedom and Security, Brussels.

European Migration Centre (EMZ)
   2002   "Prevention and fight against trafficking: institutional developments in
           Europe", country reports on Belgium, Denmark, Finland, Ireland, Swe-
           den, Greece, Netherlands, Portugal, Spain, United Kingdom (2002-2003),
           http://www.emz-berlin.de/projekte_e/pj37_1E.htm.

EUROPOL (European Police Office)

2003 *Crime Assessment: Trafficking in Human Beings in the European Union*, EUROPOL, The Hague.

Gao, Y., and V. Poisson

"Rapport final de l'enquête de terrain sur le travail forcé et la traite en France: la situation des Chinois clandestins", ILO/SAP-FL, Geneva (forthcoming).

German Federal Criminal Police Office (BKA)

2000 *Lagebild Menschenhandel: Yearly Report on Human Trafficking 2000-2004* (separate yearly reports for years 1999 to 2003), http://www.bka.de/lageberichte (in German).

2002 *Trafficking in Human Beings: Situation Report 2002*, Bundeskriminalamt, Wiesbaden, http://www.bka.de/.

Goodey, J.

2003 "Migration, crime and victimhood: responses to sex trafficking in the EU", *Punishment and Society*, 5(4): 415-431.

Government of Belgium

n.d. *Policy and Approach Regarding Trafficking in Persons in Belgium*, Government of Belgium, http://www.belgium.iom.int/STOPConference/Conference%20Papers/03.Belgian%20paper%20-%20STOP%20Conference.%20English.pdf.

Hofmann, J.

2001 Meschenhandel: Beziehungen zur organisierten Kriminalität und Versuche der strafrechtlichen Bekämpfung, Würzburger Schriften zur Kriminalwissenschaft, Würzburg.

International Labour Organization (ILO)

n.d. *Forced Labour and Human Trafficking in Germany*, ILO/SAP-FL, Geneva.

International Organization for Migration (IOM)

1998 *Analysis of Data and Statistical Resources Available in the EU Member States on Trafficking in Humans, Particularly in Women and Children, for Purposes of Sexual Exploitation*, a report to EU's STOP Programme, unpublished.

2002 *Protection Schemes for Victims of Trafficking in Selected EU Member Countries, Candidate and Third Countries*, IOM, Geneva, http://www.iom.int/DOCUMENTS/PUBLICATION/EN/Protection_Schemes.pdf.

2002 "Journeys of jeopardy: a review of research on trafficking in women and children in Europe", by F. Kelly, *Migration Research Series*, no. 11, http://www.iom.int/DOCUMENTS/PUBLICATION/EN/mrs_11_2002.pdf, IOM, Geneva.

2003 "Is trafficking in human beings demand driven? A multi-country pilot study", by B. Anderson and J. O'Connell Davidson, *Migration Research Series*, no. 15, http://www.iom.int//DOCUMENTS/PUBLICATION/EN/mrs_15_2003.pdf, IOM, Geneva.

2004 "Trafficking in unaccompanied minors in Ireland", study carried out in EC's STOP Programme, IOM, Dublin.

Kelly, E.
2002   *From Rhetoric to Curiosity: Urgent Questions from the UK about Responses to Trafficking in Women*, Stop the Traffic Symposium, Melbourne, http://mams.rmit.edu.au/m7hzlfflbayq1.pdf.

Kelly, E., and R. Linda
2000   "Stopping traffic: exploring the extent of, and responses to, trafficking in women for sexual exploitation in the UK", Home Office UK, *Police Research Series*, no. 125, http://www.homeoffice.gov.uk/rds/prgpdfs/fprs 125.pdf.

Korvinus, A.
2002   *Trafficking in Human Beings – First Report of the Dutch National Rapporteur*, Bureau NRM, The Hague, http://www.victimology.nl/onlpub/ national/nl-nrmengels2002.pdf.
2003   *Trafficking in Human Beings*: *Additional Quantitative Data – Second Report of the Dutch National Rapporteur*, Bureau NRM, The Hague, http://www.victimology.nl/onlpub/national/NL-NRMEngels2.pdf.
2004   *Trafficking in Human Beings – Third Report of the Dutch National Rapporteur*, Bureau NRM, The Hague.

Le Breton Baumgartner, M., and U. Fiechter
2000   Gesellschatliche Determinanten des Frauenhandels aus der Perspektive betroffener Migrantinnen in der Schweiz, FIZ, Zürich.

Locher, B.
2002   "International norms and European policy making: trafficking in women in the EU", CeuS working paper no. 2002/6, http://www.monnet-centre.uni-bremen.de/pdf/wp/2002-6-Locher.pdf.

Manceau, C.
1999   *L'esclavage Domestique des Mineurs en France*, Comité Contre l'Esclavage Moderne, http://www.ccem-antislavery.org/PDF/esclavage_ mineurs.pdf.

Medved, F., and P. Cullen
2002   "Counteracting human trafficking: an analysis of European union policy", in M. Anderson and J. Apap, *Police and Justice Cooperation and the New European Borders*, Kluwer Law International, The Hague, London, New York.

Mitsilegas, V., et al.
2003   *The European Union and Internal Security: Guardian of the People?*, Palgrave Macmillan, Basingstoke, Hampshire, New York.

Morrison, J.
1998   *The Cost of Survival: The Trafficking of Refugees to the UK*, The Refugee Council, London.

Obokata, T.
2003   "EU council framework decision on combating trafficking in human trafficking: a critical appraisal", *Common Market Law Review*, 40(4).

Poppy Project
2004   *When Women Are Trafficked: Quantifying the Gendered Experience of Trafficking in the UK*, Poppy Project, http://www.poppy.ik.com.

Prina, F.
2003   *Trade and Exploitation of Minors and Young Nigerian Women for Prostitution in Italy*, Action Programme against the Traffic from Nigeria to
Italy of Minors and Young Women for Sexual Exploitation, Research Report, UNICRI, Italy.

Smith, T.
2003   *Separated Children in Europe: Policies and Practices in European
Union Member States – A Comparative Analysis*, Separated Children in
Europe Programme, Copenhagen, Save the Children, published with the
funding by the European Refugee Fund.

Swiss Federal Office of Justice
2001   *Traite des êtres humains en Suisse*, Rapport du groupe de travail inter-
départemental traite des êtres humains, au Départment fédéral de justice
et Police, Berne.

United Nations Interregional Crime and Justice Research Institute (UNICRI)
2003   *Desk Review for the Programme of Action against Trafficking in Minors
and Young Women from Nigeria into Italy for the Purpose of Sexual
Exploitation*, UNICRI/UNODC Project on Trafficking, Italy.

Vandekerckhove, W., et al.
2003   "Research based on case studies of victims of trafficking in human
beings in 3 EU member states, i.e. Belgium, Italy and the Netherlands",
Payoke, On the Road, De Rode Draad, European Commission, University
of Ghent, http://www.ircp.be/uploaded/eindrapport%20Hippokrates.pdf.

Van der Kleij, A.
2002   *Provisions for Victims of Trafficking in Bonded Sexual Labour, i.e. Prostitution in 6 European Countries*, Bonded Labour in Netherlands,
Amsterdam, http://www.humanitas.nl/project/Blinn_Final_Report.pdf.

Vaz Cabral, G.
2001   *Les formes contemporaines d'esclavage dans six pays de l'Union
Européenne*, Comité Contre l'Esclavage Moderne.

Wolthuis, A., and M. Blaak
2001   *Trafficking in Children for Sexual Purposes from Eastern Europe to
Western Europe*, ECPAT Europe Law Enforcement Group, Amsterdam.

Zschokke, R.
2002   *Frauenhandel und Rechtsprechung. Osteuropäische Sexmigration in
die Schweiz*, ELSA-Schriftenreihe.

CENTRAL AND EASTERN EUROPE

Fehér, L.
1999   *Legal Study on the Combat of Trafficking in Women for the Purpose of
Forced Prostitution in Hungary*, Ludwig Boltzmann Institute of Human
Rights, Vienna.

International Organization for Migration (IOM)
  2002   *Trafficking in Women and Prostitution in the Baltic States: Social and Legal Aspects*, IOM Regional Office for the Baltic and Nordic Countries, Helsinki.
  2003   "Irregular migration and trafficking in women: the case of Turkey", by S. Erder and S. Kaska, IOM, Geneva.
  2003   *Analysis of Institutional and Legal Frameworks and Overview of Cooperation Patterns in the Field of Counter-trafficking in Eastern Europe and Central Asia*, research report, November.
  2004   *Who is the Next Victim? Vulnerability of Young Romanian Women to Trafficking in Human Beings*, IOM, Bucharest.
  2004   *Unaccompanied Minors in Central Europe: Regional Assessment and Overview*, IOM, Budapest.
Kvinnoforum
  2003   *A Resource Book for Working against Trafficking in Women and Girls: Baltic Sea Region*, Kvinnoforum, Stockholm, http://www.qweb.kvinnoforum.se/../misc/resurs2002x.pdf.
Laczko, F., et al.
  2004   "Trafficking in women from Central and Eastern Europe: a review of statistical data", in F. Laczko et al., *New Challenges for Migration Policy in Central and Eastern Europe*, IOM and ICMPD, Geneva and Vienna.
Okólski, M.
  1999   *Migrant Trafficking in Poland: Actors, Mechanisms and Combating*, Institute for Social Studies, University of Warsaw, http://www.iss.uw.edu.pl/osrodki/cmr/wpapers/pdf/024.pdf.
Popa, M.
  2000   *Legal Study on the Combat of Trafficking in Women for the Purpose of Forced Prostitution in Romania*, Ludwig Boltzmann Intitute of Human Rights, Vienna.
Tass, T.A., and P. Futo
  2003   *2002 Year Book on Illegal Migration and Trafficking in Central and Eastern Europe*, ICMPD, Wien.

SOUTH-EAST EUROPE AND THE BALKANS

Carchedi, F.
  2003   *Il traffico internatzionale di minori. Piccoli schiave senza frontiere. Il caso dell'Albania e della Romania*, Terre des hommes Italia, Fondazione Internazionale Lelio Basso, Save the Children Italia, Associazone Parsec, Convegno Internazionale, Roma, Dicembre.
Corrin, C.
  2000   "Local particularities – international generalities: traffic in women in Central and South-Eastern Europe", *European Consortium for Political Research*, Copenhagen, 14-19 April.

Gronow, J.
2000   *Trafficking in Human Beings in South-Eastern Europe: An Inventory of the Current Situation and Responses to Trafficking in Human Beings in Albania, Bosnia and Herzegovina, Croatia, the Federal Republic of Yugoslavia, and the former Yugoslav Republic of Macedonia*, UNICEF, Area Office for the Balkans, http://www.unicef.org/evaldatabase/ CEE_CIS_2000_Trafficking.pdf.

Human Rights Watch
2002   *Hopes Betrayed: Trafficking of Women and Girls to Post-conflict Bosnia and Herzegovina for Forced Prostitution*, Human Rights Watch, New York, http://www.hrw.org/reports/2002/bosnia/.

Hunzinger, L., and P. Coffey
2003   *First Annual Report on Victims of Trafficking in South-Eastern Europe*, Regional Clearing Point, Vienna.

International Labour Organization (ILO)
2002   *Human Trafficking from Albania, Moldova, Romania and Ukraine for Labour and Sexual Exploitation: Methodology Guidelines for the Rapid Assessment Survey*, ILO/SAP-FL, Geneva (unpublished).

International Organization for Migration (IOM)
2001   *Victims of Trafficking in the Balkans*, IOM, Geneva, http://www.iom.int/ DOCUMENTS/PUBLICATION/EN/balkan_trafficking.pdf.

2001   *Return and Reintegration Project – Counter Trafficking – Situation Report in Kosovo*, IOM, http://www.iom.int//DOCUMENTS/PUBLICA-TION/EN/Kosovo_sit_report.pdf.

2002   *Report on the Nationwide Survey Conducted on Attitude of Albanian Teenagers on Migration and Trafficking in Human Beings*, IOM, Tirana.

2003   *Where in the Puzzle: Trafficking from, to and through Slovenia*, IOM, Ljubljana.

2004   *Changing Patterns and Trends of Trafficking in Persons in the Balkan Region*, IOM, http://www.iom.int/iomwebsite/Publication/Servlet SearchPublication?event=detail&id=3831.

2004   "Psychosocial support to groups of victims of human trafficking in transit situations", *Psychosocial Notebook*, 4 February.

International Organization for Migration (IOM)/International Catholic Migration Commission (ICMC)
2002   *Research Report on Third Country National Trafficking Victims in Albania*, IOM, Tirana.

Kartusch, A.
2001   *Reference Guide for Anti-trafficking Legislative Review with Particular Emphasis on South Eastern Europe*, Ludwig Boltzmann Institute of Human Rights, Vienna.

Long, L.
2002   "Trafficking in women as a security challenge in Southeast Europe", *Journal of Southeast Europe and Black Sea Studies*, 2(2): 53-68.

OSCE, UNICEF, and UNOHCHR
2002   *Trafficking in Human Beings in Southeastern Europe*, http://www.osce.
         org/odihr/documents/trafficking/trafficking-see.pdf.
2003   *Trafficking in Human Beings in Southeastern Europe: 2003 Update on
         Situation and Responses to Trafficking in Human Beings in Albania,
         Bosnia and Herzegovina, Bulgaria, Croatia, the Former Yugoslav
         Republic of Macedonia, Moldova, Serbia and Montenegro including
         the UN Administered Province of Kosovo, Romania,* http://www.osce.org/
         odihr/documents/trafficking/trafficking-see_2003update.pdf.
2005   *Trafficking in Human Beings in Southeastern Europe: 2004 – Focus in
         Prevention,* http:/www.osce.org/odihr/documents/trafficking.
Pencheva Filipova, R.
2000   *Legal Study on the Combat of Trafficking in Women for the Purpose of
         Forced Prostitution in Bulgaria,* Ludwig Boltzmann Institute of Human
         Rights, Vienna.
Radovanovic, M., and A. Kartusch
2005   *Report on the Combat of Trafficking in Women for the Purpose of Forced
         Prostitution in Bosnia and Herzegovina,* Ludwig Boltzmann Institute of
         Human Rights, Vienna.
Renton, D.
2001   *Child Trafficking in Albania,* Save the Children UK, http://www.
         globalmarch.org/child-trafficking/virtual-library/child-trafficking-in-
         albania.pdf.
Roopnaraine, T.
2002   *Child Trafficking in Kosovo,* Save the Children Kosovo, http://www.
         tdhitaly.org/ita/attivita_in_italia/schede_progetti/convegno_
         traffico_minori/pdf/SaveTheChildren2_ENG.pdf.
SEERIGHTs
2003   "Albania: migration, prostitution and trafficking", SEERIGHTs, http://
         seerights.org/main.php?val=249.
Seremet, B., and A. Zahiragic
1999   "The human being trade: Bosnian-Herzegovinian aspects", paper pre-
         sented at the International Conference on New Frontiers of Crime:
         Trafficking in Human Beings and New Forms of Slavery, Verona,
         22-23 October.
Štulhofer, A., et al.
2002   *Trafficking in Women and Children for Sexual Exploitation: An Assess-
         ment Study: The Extent of the Problem and the Need for Counter Traf-
         ficking Measures in Croatia,* IOM, Zagreb.
Terre des Hommes
2003   *The Trafficking of Albanian Children in Greece,* http://www.
         seerights.org/data/reports/Reports/Terre_des_hommes_the_
         trafficking_of_Alba.pdf.
United States Office of the Inspector General
2003   *Assessment of Department of Defense Efforts to Combat Trafficking in
         Persons, Phase II, Bosnia, Herzegovina and Kosovo,* US Department of
         Defense, http://www.dodig.osd.mil/AIM/alsd/HT-Phase_II.pdf.

EASTERN EUROPE AND CIS

Amnesty International
  2002   *Human Rights Abuses of Women Trafficked from Countries of the Former Soviet Union into Israeli's Sex Industry*, Amnesty International, http://www.web.amnesty.org/aidoc/aidoc_pdf.nsf/index/MDE150172000 ENGLISH/$File/MDE1501700.pdf.

Arnold, J., and C. Doni
  2002   *USAID/Moldova Anti-trafficking Assessment: Critical Gaps in and Recommendations for Anti-trafficking Activities*, Development Alternatives, Washington DC, http://www.widtech.org/Publications/USAID%20Moldova%20Anti-Trafficking%20Assessment.pdf.

Caldwell, G., et al.
  1999   "Capitalizing on transition economies: the role of the Russian mafia in trafficking women for forced prostitution", in P. Williams (Ed.), *Illegal Immigration and Commercial Sex: The New Slave Trade*, Frank Cass, London.

Finckenauer, J.O.
  2001   "Russian transnational organized crime and human trafficking", in D. Kyle and R. Koslowski, *Global Human Smuggling: Comparative Perspectives*, The Johns Hopkins University Press, Baltimore and London.

Hughes, D.
  2000   "The 'Natasha' trade: the transnational shadow market of trafficking in women", *Journal of International Affairs*, Spring.

Hughes, D., and T. Denisova
  2001   "The transnational political criminal nexus of trafficking in women from Ukraine", *Trends in Organized Crime*, 6(3-4): 2-21.

International Labour Organization (ILO)
  2003   *ILO Study on Forced Labour Outcomes of Human Trafficking and Irregular Migration in Russia: Main Theses of the Study, Conclusions and Recommendations*, ILO, Geneva.

International Organization for Migration (IOM)
  2001   *Trafficking of Women and Children from the Republic of Armenia: A Study*, IOM, Yerevan, http://www.iom.int/DOCUMENTS/PUBLICATION/EN/Armenia_traff_report.pdf.
  2002   "Trafficking for sexual exploitation: the case of the Russian Federation", by D. Hughes, *Migration Research Series*, no. 7, IOM, Geneva, http://www.iom.int//DOCUMENTS/PUBLICATION/EN/mrs_7_2002.pdf.
  2003   *Analysis of Institutional and Legal Framework and Overview of Cooperation Patterns in the Field of Counter-trafficking in Eastern Europe and Central Asia: Research Report*, IOM, Vienna.

Klinchenko, T.
  2000   "Migrant trafficking and human smuggling in Ukraine", *Migrant Trafficking and Human Smuggling in Europe*, IOM, Geneva.

Pyshchulina, O.
  2003   "An evaluation of Ukrainian legislation to counter and criminalize human trafficking", *Demokratizatsiya*, 11(3).

Scanlan, S.
  2002   *Report on Trafficking from Moldova: Irregular Labour Markets and
          Restrictive Migration Policies in Western Europe*, ILO, Geneva, http://
          www.antitraffic.md/files/report_scanlan_2002_05.pdf.
Zavratnik Zimic, S. et al.
  2003   *Where in the Puzzle: Trafficking from, to and through Slovenia: An Assess-
          ment Study*, Ljubljana, IOM.

AMERICAS

North America

Belleau, M-C, and L. Langevin
  2000   *Trafficking in Women in Canada: A Critical Analysis of the Legal Frame-
          work Governing Immigrant Live-In Caregivers and Mail Order Brides*,
          Status of Women Canada, http://www.swc-cfc.gc.ca/pubs/066231252X/
          index_e.html.
Blackwill, R.D.
  2003   "Dealing with trafficking in persons: another dimension of United States
          and India transformation", *DISAM Journal of International Security
          Assistance Management*, Summer 2003, 25(4).
Brennan, D.
  2005   "Methodological challenges to doing research on trafficking: tales from
          the field", *International Migration*, 43(1/2).
Cadet, J-R
  1998   *Restavec: From Haitian Slave Child to Middle-Class American*, Univer-
          sity of Texas Press, Austin.
Caliber Associates
  2001   *Needs Assessment for Service Providers and Trafficking Victims*, Caliber
          Associates, Virginia.
Canadian Council for Refugees
  2004   *Trafficking in Women and Girls*, Canadian Council for Refugees, www.web.
          net/~ccr/trafficking.htm.
Estes, R.J., and N.A. Weiner
  2002   *The Commercial Sexual Exploitation of Children in the United States,
          Canada and Mexico*, University of Pennsylvania, Philadelphia, http://
          caster.ssw.upenn.edu/~restes/CSEC_Files/Complete_CSEC_020220.pdf.
Florida State University
  2003   *Florida Responds to Human Trafficking*, Center for the Advancement of
          Human Rights, Tallahassee.
Free the Slaves and Human Rights Center
  2004   "Hidden slaves: forced labor in the United States", Free the Slaves,
          Washington, DC and Human Rights Center, University of California,
          Berkeley.

Goulet, L.
2001   *Out from the Shadows: Good Practices in Working with Sexually Exploited Youth in the Americas*, International Institute for Child Rights and Development, University of Victoria.

Gozdziak, E.M. and E.A. Collett
2005   "Not much to write home about: research on human trafficking in North America", *International Migration*, 43(1/2).

Haines, D.W.
1999   "Labor at risk: the exploitation and protection of undocumented workers", in D.W. Haines and K.E. Rosenblum, *Illegal Immigration in America: A Reference Handbook*, Greenwood Press, Westport.

Hughes, D.M.
2003   "Trafficking of women and children in East Asia and beyond: a review of US policy", *Subcommittee of East Asian and Pacific Affairs Senate Foreign Relations Committee*, Washington, DC.

2003   "The driving force of sex trafficking: the demand", *Vital Speeches of the Day*, 69(6): 182-184.

Human Rights Watch
2001   "Hidden in the home: abuse of domestic workers with special visas in the United States", *Human Rights Watch Reports*, 13(2), http://www.hrw.org/reports/2001/usadom/.

2003   *"You'll Learn Not to Cry": Child Combatants in Colombia*, Human Rights Watch, New York.

Hyland, K.E.
2001   "Protecting human victims of trafficking: an American framework", *Berkeley Women's Law Journal*, 16(29), available http://www.lexisnexis.com/universe.

Hynes, P., and J.G. Raymond.
2002   "The neglected health consequences of sex trafficking in the United States", in J. Siliman and A. Bhattacharjee, *Policing the National Body: Sex, Race and Criminalization*, South End Press, Cambridge.

IOM, OAS, and Inter-American Commission of Women
2004   *Trafficking in Persons: National Researchers*, CD-ROM.

Langevin, L., and M-C Belleau
2000   *Trafficking in Women in Canada: A Critical Analysis of the Legal Framework Governing Immigrant Live-in Caregivers and Mail-Order Brides*, Status of Women Canada, Ottawa.

MacDonald, L., et al.
1999   *Migrant Sex Workers from Eastern Europe and the Former Soviet Union: The Canadian Case*, Centre for Applied Social Research, University of Toronto, http://www.walnet.org/csis/papers/MCDONALD.pdf.

Macklin, A.
2003   "Dancing across borders: 'exotic dancers', trafficking, and Canadian immigration policy", *International Migration Review*, 37(2): 464-500.

Mattar, M.Y.
2003   "Monitoring the status of severe forms of trafficking in foreign countries: sanctions mandated under the US Trafficking Victims Protection Act",

Brown Journal of World Affairs, Summer/Fall 2003, XX(1), http://209.190.
246.239/zz.pdf.

Miko, F.T.
2000   "Trafficking in women and children: the US and international response",
        US Department of State Congressional Research Service Report, 98-649C.

Miller, J.R.
2003   *The United States' Effort to Combat Trafficking in Persons*, US Depart-
        ment of State, Washington, DC: 6-9.

O'Neill Richard, A.
2000   *International Trafficking in Women to the United States: A Contempor-
        ary Manifestation of Slavery and Organized Crime*, Center for the Study
        of Intelligence, Washington, DC, http://www.cia.gov/csi/monograph/
        women/trafficking.pdf.

Organization of American States (OAS)
2002   "Fighting the crime of trafficking in persons, especially women, adoles-
        cents and children", resolution adopted by the Assembly of Delegates of
        the Inter-American Commission of Women, OAS (CIM/RES.225(XXXI-
        O-02), 31 October, Dominican Republic.
2003   "Fighting the crime of trafficking in persons, especially women, adoles-
        cents and children", resolution adopted by the General Assembly of OAS
        (AG/RES.1948 (XXXIII-O-03), 10 June, Chile.
2004   "Fifth meeting of Ministers of Justice or Attorneys General of the Amer-
        icas: conclusions and recommendations", (OAS/Ser.K/XXXIV.5, REMJA-
        V/doc.7/04 rev.4), 30 April, Washington, DC.

Oxman-Martinez, J., et al.
2005   "Canadian policy on human trafficking: a four-year analysis", *Inter-
        national Migration*, forthcoming.

Protection Project
2002   *Trafficking in Persons, Especially Women and Children in the Coun-
        tries of the America: A Regional Report on the Scope of the Problems
        and Governmental and Non-governmental Responses*, Johns Hopkins
        University School of International Studies, Washington, http://209.
        190.246.239/iomz.pdf.

Raymond, J.G., and D.M. Hughes
2001   *Sex Trafficking of Women in the Unites States, International and Domestic
        Trends*, Coalition Against Trafficking in Women-International (CATW),
        http://action.web.ca/home/catw/attach/sex_traff_us.pdf.

Ryf, K.
2002   "The first modern anti-slavery law: the Trafficking Victims Protection Act
        of 2000", *Case Western Reserve Journal of International Law*, 34(1).

Schwartz, M.D. (Ed.)
1997   *Researching Sexual Violence Against Women: Methodological and Per-
        sonal Perspectives*, Sage Publications, California and London.

Shirk, D., and A. Webber
2004   "Slavery without borders: human trafficking in the US-Mexican context",
        Hemisphere Focus, XII(5).

Spangenburg, M.
2002   "International trafficking of children to New York City for sexual pur-
        poses", ECPAT-USA, www.ecpatusa.org/trafficking.asp.
Status of Women Canada
2000   *Canada: The New Frontier for Filipino Mail-Order Brides*, Status of
        Women Canada, Ottawa, http://www.swc-cfc.gc.ca/pubs/0662653343/
        200011_0662653343_e.pdf.
2000   *Trafficking in Women in Canada: A Critical Analysis of the Legal Frame-
        work Governing Immigrant Live-in Caregivers and Mail-order Brides*,
        Status of Women Canada, Ottawa, http://www.swc-cfc.gc.ca/pubs/
        066231252X/200010_066231252X_9_e.html.
US Department of Justice
        Anti-Trafficking News Bulletin, newsletter published by US Department
        of Justice Civil Rights Division, www.usdoj.gov/trafficking.htm.
US Office to Monitor and Combat Trafficking in Persons
2003   "The US Government's international trafficking programs fiscal year
        2002", US State Department, http://www.state.gov/g/tip/rls/rpt/17858.htm.
Zarembka, J.M.
2003   "America's dirty work: migrant maids and modern-day slavery", in
        B. Ehrenreich and A. Russell Hochschild (Eds), *Global Woman: Nannies,
        Maids, and Sex Workers in the New Economy*, Metropolitan Books, New
        York: 142-153.

LATIN AMERICA AND THE CARIBBEAN

Acharya, A.K.
2004   *Agrarian Conflict, Internal Displacement and Trafficking of Mexican
        Women: The Case of Chiapas State*, Universidad Nacional Autónoma de
        México (UNAM), 2004 Annual Meeting of Population Association of
        America.
Artigas, C.
2004   "Latin American approach to the improving of data and research on
        human trafficking", paper presented in the international expert meeting
        Improving Data and Research on Human Trafficking, arranged by IOM
        and the Government of Italy in Rome, May.
Azaola, E.
2001   *La Explotación Sexual de Niños en las Fronteras*, UNICEF, Mexico City.
Bagley, B.
2001   *Globalization and Transnational Organized Crime: The Russian Mafia
        in Latin America and the Caribbean*, Mama Coca, www.mamacoca.org.
Bibes, P.
2001   *The Status of Human Trafficking in Latin America,* Transnational Crime
        and Corruption Center, Washington DC, http://www.american.edu/traccc/
        Publications/Phibes_StatusHTinLatinA.doc.

Brennan, D.
   2004   *What's Love Got to Do With It? Transnational Desires and Sex Tourism in the Dominican Republic*, Duke University Press, Durham.
Britos, J.G.
   2002   *Explotación Sexual Comercial de Niñas e Adolescentes*, IPEC, Paraguay.
Bureau of Women's Affairs Costa Rica
   2004   Follow-up Meeting to the Second World Congress Against Commercial Sexual Exploitation of Children, 19-20 May, San Jose, Costa Rica.
Carranza, E., and R. Woodbridge
   2003   *Trata de Seres Humanos especialments Mujeres, Niñas y Niños*, ILANUD, Presentación en la XII Sesión de la Comisión de las Naciones Unidas sobre Prevención, del Delito y Justicia Penal, Vienna, 13-22 May, http://www.unicri.it/ILANUD%20(Workshop).doc.
Casa Alianza
   2001   *Regional Investigation on Trafficking, Prostitution, Child Pornography and Sex Tourism with Children in Central America and Mexico*, http://www.casa-alianza.org/EN/human-rights/sexual-exploit/regional_report_CSE.pdf.
   2003   *Trafficking in Children in Latin America and the Caribbean*, http://www.casa-alianza.org/EN/human-rights/trafic/ILANUD.pdf.
Casa Alianza/Global Rights
   2004   *Taller Regional sobre Trata de Personas y Derechos Humanos en las Americas y el Caribe*, San Jose, January.
CELADE/Comisión Económica para América Latina y el Caribe (CEPAL), OIM, UNFPA
   2003   *Derechos Humanos y Trata de Personas en las Américas: Resumen y Aspectos Destacados de la Conferencia Hemisférica sobre Migración Internacional*, Santiago de Chile, November.
Chiarotti, S.
   2003   *La trata de mujeres: sus conexiones y desconexiones con la migración y los derechos humanos*, Santiago de Chile, Centro Latinoamericano y Caribeño de Demografia (CELADE), Series CEPAL, no. 39, May, http://www.cepal.org/publicaciones/Poblacion/0/LCL1910P/lcl1910-p.pdf.
Coffey, P.S., et al.
   2004   *Literature Review of Trafficking in Persons in Latin America and the Caribbean*, carried out for USAID by Development Alternatives, Inc., Maryland.
Colazo, C.
   2002   *Prevención y Eliminación del Trabajo Infantil Comestico en Sudamerica. Estudio Tematico: Politicas Socials y Oferta Institutional Frente al Trabajo Infantile Domestico*, ILO/IPEC, updated after 2002.
ECPAT, IOM, and Casa Alianza
   2002   "Explotación sexual comercial de niñas, niños y adolescentes en Guatemala", *Cuadernos de Trabajo sobre Migración*, no. 8, OIM Guatemala.
Estes, R.J., and N.A. Weiner
   2002   *The Commercial Sexual Exploitation of Children in the US, Canada and Mexico*, University of Pennsylvania, Philadelphia, http://caster.ssw.upenn.edu/~restes/CSEC_Files/Complete_CSEC_020220.pdf.

Goolsby, C.M.
2003   *Dynamics of Prostitution and Sex Trafficking from Latin America into the United States*, http://www.libertadlatina.org/LL_LatAm_US_Slavery_Report_01_2003.htm.

Guinn, D.E., and E. Steglich
2003   *In Modern Bondage: Sex Trafficking in the Americas: National and Regional Overview of Central America and the Caribbean*, Transnational Publishers, Inc., New York.

Inter-American Commission on Human Rights (IACHR)
1999   *Report on the Situation of Human Rights in the Dominican Republic*, Inter-American Commission on Human Rights, Washington, DC.

International Human Rights Law Institute (IHRLI)
2002   "In modern bondage: sex trafficking in the Americas, Central America and the Caribbean", DePaul University College of Law, in Association with the Inter-American Commission of Women and the Inter-American Children's Institute of the Organization of American States, October.

International Organization for Migration (IOM)
2002   *Trata de Personas y Migración Internacional Feminina: Un Estudio Cualitativo en Dos Comunidades de República Dominicana*, IOM, Santo Domingo.
2003   "Migración, prostitución y trata de mujeres dominicanas en la Argentina", IOM, Buenos Aires.
2004   *Exploratory Assessment of Trafficking in Persons in the Caribbean Region*, IOM, Washington DC.

Kempadoo, K.
1999   *Sea and Gold: Tourism and Sex Work in the Caribbean*, Rowman and Littlefield, New York.

Langberg, L.
2005   "A review of recent research in human trafficking in the Latin American and Caribbean regions", *International Migration*, 43(1/2).

Leal, M.L., and M. de Fatima Leal (Eds)
2003   *Study on Trafficking in Women, Children, and Adolescents for Commercial Sexual Exploitation in Brazil*, CECRIA.

Lopes, J., and T. Stoltz
2002   *Exploracao Sexual Commercial de Criancas e Adolescents, Brasil – Foz do Igacu, Rapid Assessment*, April.

Phinney, A.
2001   "Trafficking of women and children for sexual exploitation in the Americas", Report of the Inter-American Commission of Women of the Organization of American States and the Women, Health, and Development Program of the Pan-American Health Organization, http://www.oas.org/cim/English/Proj.Traf.AlisonPaper.htm.

Red Regional de Organizaciones Civiles para las Migraciones (RROCM)
2003   *La Trata y el Trafico de Personas en los Paises Miembros de la Conferencia Regional sobre Migracion (CRM): Consideraciones Relacionadas con Iniciativas para Combatir la Trata y el Trafico*, May.

Smucker, G.R., and G.F. Murray
  2004   *The Use of Children: A Study of Trafficking in Haitian Children*, draft report, USAID/Haiti, 15 July.
Sorensen, B.
  n.d.   *Protecting Children and Adolescents Against Commercial Sexual Exploitation in Central America, Panama and the Dominican Republic*, ILO, Geneva.
Survivor Rights International
  n.d.   *Trafficking in Persons: Latin America and the Caribbean*, Survivor Rights International, Washington, DC.
Thomas-Hope, E.
  2003   "Irregular migration and asylum seekers in the Caribbean", discussion paper no. 2003/48, UN University/World Institute for Development Economics Research, Helsinki.
  2005   "Data and research on human trafficking on the Caribbean", paper presented in the international expert meeting Improving Data and Research on Human Trafficking, arranged by IOM and the Government of Italy in Rome, May.
Thompson, B.R.
  2003   "People trafficking, a national security risk in Mexico", *Mexidata*, www.mexidata.info/id93.html.

AFRICA

General

Adepoju, A.
  2005   "Review of research and data on human trafficking in sub-Saharan Africa", *International Migration*, 43(1/2).
Butegwa, F.
  1997   *Regional Report on Trafficking in Women, Forced Prostitution and Slavery-like Practices*, Associates for Change, Kampala.
Endvig, J.C., et al.
  2001   "Issues in child labour in Africa", *Africa Region Human Development Working Paper Series*, The World Bank, Washington, DC, http://www.worldbank.org/afr/hd/wps/child_labor.pdf.
Fitzgibbon, K.
  2003   "Modern-day slavery? The scope of trafficking in persons in Africa", *African Security Review*, 12(1), http://www.iss.co.za/Pubs/ASR/12No1/EFitz.html.
Martens, J.
  2003   "Assistance to victims of trafficking as an effective means of combating organized crime", paper submitted to the American Anthropological Association's Conference in Chicago, November.

Salah, R.
2004   "Child trafficking: a challenge to child protection in Africa", paper pre-
        sented at the Fourth African Regional Conference on Child Abuse and
        Neglect, Enugu, March.
Sita, N. M.
2003   *Trafficking in Women and Children: Situation and Some Trends in African
        Countries*, UNAFRI, Kampala, May.
UNICEF
2003   *Trafficking in Human Beings, Especially Women and Children in Africa*,
        UNICEF, Innocenti Research Centre, Florence.

EAST AFRICA

Anti-Slavery International
2001   "Is there slavery in Sudan?", Anti-slavery International, London, http://
        www.antislavery.org/homepage/resources/isthereslaveryinsudanreport.pdf.
Pearson, E.
2003   *Study on Trafficking in Women in East Africa*, Deutsche Gesellschaft für
        Technische Zusammenarbeit, Germany, http://www.antislavery.org/
        homepage/traffic%20news/East%20Africa.pdf.
Tekle, A., and T. Belayneh
2000   *Trafficking of Women from Ethiopia*, Women's Affairs sub-Sector in the
        Prime Minister's Office and IOM, Addis Ababa.
US Department of State
2002   "Slavery, abduction and forced servitude in Sudan", Report of the Inter-
        national Eminent Persons Group, Bureau of African Affairs, US Department
        of State, Washington, DC, http://www.state.gov/p/af/rls/rpt/10445.htm.

CENTRAL AND WEST AFRICA

Aderinto, A.A.
2003   "Socio-economic profiles, reproductive health behaviour and problems
        of street children in Ibadan, Nigeria", paper presented at The Fourth
        African Population Conference: Population and Poverty in Africa –
        Facing Up to the Challenges of the 21st Century, UAPS, Tunis, 8-12
        December.
Agbu, O.
2003   "Corruption and human trafficking: the Nigerian case", *West Africa Review*,
        4(1).
Afonja, S.
2001   "An assessment of trafficking in women and girls in Nigeria Ile Ife",
        unpublished mimeo.

Castle, S., and A. Diarra
  2003   *The International Migration of Young Malians: Tradition, Necessity or Rites of Passage?*, London School of Hygiene and Tropical Medicine, London.
Dottridge, M.
  2002   "Trafficking in children in West and Central Africa", *Gender and Development*, 10(1).
Fanou-Ako, N., and A.F. Adihou
  n.d.   *Rapport de recherche sur le trafic des enfants entre le Bénin et le Gabon*, Anti-Slavery International and ESAM, Cotonou.
Human Rights Watch
  2003   "Borderline slavery: child trafficking in Togo", *Human Rights Watch*, 15(8)A.
International Labour Organization (ILO)
  2001   *Combating Trafficking in Children for Labour Exploitation in West and Central Africa, Synthesis Report*, ILO, Geneva, http://www.ilo.org/public /english/standards/ipec/publ/field/africa/central.pdf.
Kielland, A., and I. Sanogo
  2002   "Burkina Faso: child labour migration from rural areas", Workshop of Interpretation and Validation, Ouagadougou, 16-17 July, http://home. online.no/~annekie/Africa_docs/BFEnglish.pdf.
Nagel, I.
  2000   *Le traffic d'Enfants en Afrique de l'Ouest*, Rapport d'étude, Osnabrück, Terre des hommes, janvier.
Ojomo, A.J.
  1999   "Trafficking in human beings: Nigerian law enforcement perspective", paper presented at the International Conference on New Frontiers of Crime: Trafficking in Human Beings and New Forms of Slavery, Verona, 22-23 October.
Olateru-Olagbegi, B.
  2000   *The Social and Legal Implications of Trafficking in Women and Children in Nigeria*, Women's Consortium of Nigeria (WOCON), Lagos.
Prina, F.
  2003   "Trade and exploitation of minors and young Nigerian women for prostitution in Italy", Action Programme against the Traffic from Nigeria to Italy of Minors and Young Women for Sexual Exploitation, UNICRI, Italy.
Taylor, E.
  2002   "Trafficking in women and girls, Ghana", Expert Group Meeting, 18-22 November, New York, http://www.un.org/womenwatch/daw/egm/ trafficking2002/reports/EP-Taylor.PDF.
UNICEF
  2002   "Child trafficking in West Africa: policy responses", UNICEF Innocenti Research Centre, Florence, http://www.unicef-icdc.org/publications/pdf/ insight7.pdf.

United Nations Interregional Crime and Justice Research Institute (UNICRI)

2003   *Desk Review for the Programme of Action against Trafficking in Minors and Young Women from Nigeria into Italy for the Purpose of Sexual Exploitation*, UNICRI/UNODC Project on Trafficking, Italy.

2003   *Programme of Action against Trafficking in Minors and Young Women from Nigeria into Italy for the Purpose of Sexual Exploitation: Report of Field Survey in Edo State*, UNICRI, Nigeria.

Veil, L.

1998   "The issue of child domestic labour and trafficking in West and Central Africa", report prepared for the UNICEF Subregional Workshop on Trafficking in Child Domestic Workers, Particularly Girls in Domestic Service, West and Central Africa Region, Cotonou, 6-8 July.

SOUTHERN AFRICA

International Organization for Migration (IOM)

2003   *Seduction, Sale and Slavery: Trafficking in Women and Children for Sexual Exploitation in Southern Africa*, IOM Regional Office for Southern Africa, Pretoria.

Selabe, B.

2000   "Trafficking in migration and forced labour in the southern African labour market", paper presented at The Regional Labour Migration Seminar for Southern Africa, Lusaka, 6-9 March.

MIDDLE EAST

Amnesty International

2000   "Human rights abuses of women trafficked from countries of the former Soviet Union into Israeli's sex industry", Amnesty International, New York, http://www.web.amnesty.org/aidoc/aidoc_pdf.nsf/index/MDE15017 2000ENGLISH/$File/MDE1501700.pdf.

Anti-Slavery International

2003   "Trafficking and forced labour of children in the United Arab Emirates (UAE)", United Nations Commission on Human Rights, Sub-Commission on the Promotion and Protection of Human Rights Working Group on Contemporary Forms of Slavery, 28th session, Geneva.

Borkholder, J.L., and M. Mohammed

2002   "Domestic service as a form of trafficking in persons in the Middle East", First World Congress for Middle Eastern Studies, Mainz, Germany, 12 September, http://www.protectionproject.org/commentary/ele.htm.

Calandruccio, G.

2005   "Review of recent research on human trafficking in the Middle East", *International Migration*, 43(1/2).

Chammartin, G.
2003   *Women Migrant Workers' Protection in Arab League States*, ILO, Geneva.
Chatelard, G.
2002   "Jordan as a transit country: semi-protectionist immigration policies and their effects on Iraqi forced migrants", *New Issues in Refugee Research*, Working Paper no. 61, UNHCR, Geneva.
Içduygu, A., and S. Toktas
2002   "How do smuggling and trafficking operate via irregular border crossings in the Middle East?", *International Migration*, 40(6).
International Federation for Human Rights (FIDH) and the Euro-Mediterranean Human Rights Network (MHRN)
2003   *Migrant Workers in Israel: A Contemporary From of Slavery*, FIDH and MHRN, Paris and Copenhagen.
International Organization for Migration (IOM)
2003   "Migrant trafficking in the Middle East and potential IOM responses", discussion paper, IOM, Geneva.
2003   *Trafficking in Persons: An Analysis of Afghanistan*, IOM, Kabul.
Jureidini, R., and N. Moukarbel
2000   *Brief on Foreign Female Domestic Maids in Lebanon*, Lebanese NGO Forum, Beirut.
Kahale, S.
2003   "Exploratory study on foreign domestic work in Syria", IOM, Damascus.
Kav La'Oved
2002   "Workers trafficking from Romania to Israel", *Kav La'Oved*, 22 October.
2003   "UN Commission on Human Rights, 59th Session, 17 March-24 April, National NGOs Report to the Annual UN Commission on Human Rights: Evaluation of National Authorities Activities and Actual Facts on the Trafficking in Persons for the Purpose of Prostitution in Israel", *Kav La'Oved*, 6 April, http://www.kavlaoved.org.il/word/060403.html.
2003   "Women as commodities: trafficking in women in Israel, 2003", *Kav La'Oved*, 24 August-11 September (Hebrew only).
Levenkron, N.
2001   "Trafficking in women in Israel: an updated report 2001", Hotline for Migrant Workers, Tel Aviv.
2001   "Trafficking in Israel: the legal and human dimensions", The Protection Project Seminar Series, http://www.protectionproject.org/vt/ns.htm.
Levenkron, N., and Y. Dahan
2003   "Women as commodities: trafficking in women in Israel 2003", The Hotline for Migrant Workers, Isha L.Isha – Haifa Feminist Center, and Adva Center, http://www.antislavery.org/homepage/traffic%20news/Women%2 0as%20Commodities,%20Trafficking%20in%20women%20in%20 Israel,%202003%20Eng.pdf.
Mattar, M.Y.
2003   "Trafficking in persons, especially women and children, in countries of the Middle East: the scope of the problem and the appropriate legislative responses", *Fordham International Law Journal*, March.

Mattar, M.Y., and J.L. Borkholder
2002   *Domestic Service as a Form of Trafficking in Persons in the Middle East*,
         Congress for Middle Eastern Studies, First World Congress for the Middle
         Eastern Studies, Mainz.

ASIA – PACIFIC

General

Advisory Council of Jurists: The Asia Pacific Forum of National Human Rights
Institutions
2002   "Consideration of the issue of trafficking – background paper", Asia
         Pacific Forum, New Delhi, 11-12 November, http://www.asiapacificforum.
         net/jurists/trafficking/background.pdf.
Asis, M.M.B.
2002   "Women migrants in Asia: the hands that rock the cradle", presented
         at Globalization and International Migration: Asian and European
         Experiences, 12-13 March, CERI-Science – Po, Paris.
Brown, L.
2000   *Sex Slaves: The Trafficking of Women in Asia*, Virago, London.
Caouette, T., and Y. Saito
1999   *To Japan and Back: Thai Women Recount Their Experiences*, IOM,
         Geneva.
Dargan, P.
2003   "Trafficking and human rights: the role of national human rights institu-
         tions in the Asia Pacific region", The Asia Pacific Forum of National
         Human Rights Institutions, Stop the Traffic 2 Conference, Melbourne,
         23-24 October.
Foo, L.J.
2000   "The trafficking of Asian women", *Asian American Women: Issues, Con-
         cerns, and Responsive Human and Civil Rights*, Advocacy Ford Foun-
         dation, http://www.aapip.org/pdfs/aaw_04_chapter2.pdf.
Gallagher, A.
1999   "The role of national institutions in advancing the human rights of women:
         a case study on trafficking in the Asia-Pacific region", paper presented at
         the Fourth Annual Meeting of the Asia-Pacific Forum of Human Rights
         Institutions, Philippines, 6-8 September.
International Labour Organization (ILO)
2000   *Trafficking in Children in Asia: A Regional Overview*, ILO/IOPEC,
         Bangkok.
International Organization for Migration (IOM)
1997   *Trafficking in Women to Japan for Sexual Exploitation: A Survey on the
         Case of Filipino Women*, IOM, Geneva.
Lee, J., and T. Sangrat
2002   "Background paper", Expert Group Meeting on Preventing International
         Trafficking and Promotion of Public Awareness Campaign, 22-23 Septem-
         ber, Seoul.

Lyons, H.D.
  1999   "The representation of trafficking in persons in Asia: Orientalism and other perils", *Re/Productions*, 2.
Maltzahn, K.
  2001   "Trafficking of women in prostitution", *Australian Women Speak*, www.osw.dpmc.gov.au/resources/conference/trafficking_in _women.html.
  2002   "Policing trafficking in women for prostitution", unpublished paper.
Samarasinghe, V.
  2003   "Confronting globalization in anti-trafficking strategies in Asia", *Brown Journal of World Affairs*, 10(1): 91-104.
Skeldon, R.
  2000   "Trafficking: a perspective from Asia", *International Migration*, 38(3): 7-30.
Tialby, R.
  2001   "Organized crime and people smuggling/trafficking to Australia", *Trends and Issues in Crime and Criminal Justice*, 208: 1-6.
United Nations Economic and Social Commission for Asia and the Pacific (UNESCAP) and the International Organization for Migration
  2003   *Combating Human Trafficking in Asia: A Resource Guide to International and Regional Legal Instruments, Political Commitments and Recommended Practices*, UNESCAP and IOM.
United Nations Children's Fund (UNICEF)
  2001   *Children on the Edge: Protecting Children from Sexual Exploitation and Trafficking in East Asia and the Pacific*, UNICEF, Cambodia.

NORTH-EAST ASIA

Babidor, S.L.
  2003   "Sexual abuse and human trafficking in Japan", UCLA International Institute, 17 November.
Cheng, S.
  2002   *Transnational Desires: "Trafficked" Filipinas in US Military Camp Towns in South Korea*, Ph.D. Dissertation, Department of Anthropology, Oxford University.
  2003   "'R and R' on a 'hardship tour': GIs and Filipina entertainers in South Korea", *American Sexuality Magazine*, 1(5).
Dinan, K.A.
  2002   "Trafficking in women from Thailand to Japan: the role of organized crime and governmental response", *Harvard Asia Quarterly*, 6(3).
  2002   "Migrant Thai women subjected to slavery-like abuses in Japan", *Violence Against Women*, 8(9).
Emerton, R.
  2001   "Trafficking of women into Hong Kong for the purpose of prostitution: preliminary research findings", Occasional Paper no. 3, Centre for Comparative and Public Law, University of Hong Kong, http://www.hku.hk/ccpl/pub/occasionalpapers/paper3/paper3.doc.

Emerton, R., and C. Petersen
    2003   "Migrant nightclub/escort workers in Hong Kong: an analysis of possible human rights violations", Occasional Paper, no. 8, Centre for Comparative and Public Law, University of Hong Kong.

Human Rights Watch
    2000   *Owed Justice: Thai Women Trafficked into Debt Bondage in Japan*, Human Rights Watch, New York, http://www.hrw.org/reports/2000/japan/.
    2002   "The invisible exodus: North Koreans in the People's Republic of China", *Human Rights Watch*, 14(8)C, http://www.hrw.org/reports/2002/north korea/.

International Labour Organization (ILO)
    2002   *Yunnan Province, China Situation of Trafficking in Children and Women: A Rapid Assessment*, ILO/IPEC, Bangkok.
    2004   *Human Trafficking for Sexual Exploitation in Japan*, ILO, Japan.

International Organization for Migration (IOM)
    2002   "A review of data on trafficking in the Republic of Korea", by J. Lee, *Migration Research Series*, no. 9, IOM, Geneva, http://www.iom.int/DOCUMENTS/PUBLICATION/EN/mrs_9_2002.pdf.

Lee, J.
    2005   "Human trafficking in East Asia: current trends, data collection, and knowledge gaps", *International Migration*, 43(1/2).

Molina, F.F.
    1999   "Japan, the mecca for trafficking in Colombian women", prepared by the Global Alliance Against Traffic in Women, the International Human Rights Law Group and the Foundation Against Trafficking in Women, http://www.libertadlatina.org/paper30ColombiaJapan.pdf.

Pieke, F.N., et al.
    2004   *Transnational Chinese: Fujianese Migrants in Europe*, Stanford University Press, California.

Seol, D.H.
    2003   "International sex trafficking in women in Korea: its causes, consequences, and countermeasures", Expert Group Meeting on Prevention of International Trafficking and Promotion of Promotion of Public Awareness Campaign.

Seol, D.H., et al.
    2003   *The Current Situation of Migrant Women Employed in the Sex and Entertainment Sector of Republic of Korea* (English translation of a report written in Korean, *Oeguin Yeoseong Seongmaemae Silt'aejosa*), Ministry of Gender Equality, Republic of Korea.

The Protection Project
    2002   "A human rights report on trafficking of persons, especially women and children: Japan", The Protection Project, Washington, DC.

US Office of the Inspector General.
    2003   "Assessment of Department of Defense efforts to combat trafficking in persons, phase I, United States forces in Korea", US Department of Defense, available http://www.dodig.osd.mil/AIM/alsd/H03L88433128 PhaseI.PDF.

Zhang, S., and K-L Chin
   2004   "Characteristics of Chinese human smugglers", NIJ Research Brief, Wash-
            ington, DC, August.

SOUTH-EAST ASIA

Beyrer, C., and J. Stachowiak
   2003   "Health consequences of trafficking of women and girls in Southeast
            Asia", *Brown Journal of World Affairs*, X(1): 105-117.
Caouette, T.
   2002   *Trafficking in Women and Children in the Mekong Sub-Region (UNIAP),
            Mid-term Evaluation Report*, United Nation's Inter-Agency Project,
            Bangkok.
Chantavich, S.
   2001   *The Migration of Thai Women to Germany: Causes, Living Conditions,
            and Impacts for Thailand and Germany,* Asian Research Center for Mi-
            gration, Institute of Asian Studies, Chulalongkorn University, Bangkok.
   2003   "Recent research on human trafficking in mainland Southeast Asia", *Kyoto
            Review of Southeast Asia*, October, http://kyotoreview.cseas.kyoto-u.
            ac.jp/issue/issue3/index.html.
David, F., and P. Monzini
   2000   "Human smuggling and trafficking: a desk review on the trafficking
            in women from the Philippines", paper presented at the Tenth United
            Nations Congress on the Prevention of Crime and the Treatment of
            Offenders, Vienna, 10-17 April.
Darwin, M., et al.
   2003   *Living on the Edges: Cross-Border Mobility and Sexual Exploitation in
            the Greater South-East Asia Subregion*, Centre for Population and Policy
            Studies, Gadjah Mada University, Yogyakarta.
Dixon, J., and N. Piper
   2004   "Trafficking in humans and victim support initiatives: insights from South-
            East Asia and Oceania", background paper prepared for IOM, Geneva.
Farid, M.
   1999   "Situational analysis on the sexual abuse, sexual exploitation, and the
            commercial sexual exploitation of children in Indonesia", UNICEF Indo-
            nesia and Samin Foundation, Yogyakarta.
Ford, M.
   2001   "Sex slaves and legal loopholes: exploring the legal framework and fed-
            eral responses to the trafficking of the Thai 'contract girls' for sexual
            exploitation to Melbourne Australia", Project Respect, Melbourne.
Grant, A.
   2001   "The commercial sexual exploitation of children", *Journal of the Institute
            of Criminology*, 12(3): 269-287.

Grumiau, S.
    n.d.   "Commercial sexual exploitation of children: the situation in Thailand, Cambodia and the Philippines: what can the trade union movement do to help?", International Confederation of Free Trade Unions (ICFTU), Belgium.

Hamim, A., and R. Rosenberg
    2002   "Review of existing counter trafficking legislation in Indonesia", International Catholic Migration Commission (ICMC), Jakarta.

Human Rights Watch
    1993   "A modern form of slavery: trafficking of Burmese women and girls into brothels in Thailand", Asia Watch and the Women's Rights Project, New York, http://www.hrw.org/reports/1993/thailand/.
    2000   "Owed justice: Thai women trafficked into debt bondage in Japan", Human Rights Watch, New York, http://www.hrw.org/reports/2000/japan/.

Images Asia
    1997   *Migrating With Hope: Burmese Women Working in Thailand and the Sex Industry*, Muang Chiang, Thailand.

International Labour Organization (ILO)
    2001   *A Process-Based Approach to Combat Trafficking in Children and Women: Sharing Preliminary Experiences from an ILO-Project in the Mekong Subregion*, ILO/IPEC, Geneva.
    2001   "Labour migration and trafficking within the Greater Mekong subregion: proceedings of Mekong subregional experts meeting and exploratory policy paper", ILO/IPEC, Bangkok.
    2001   *Thailand-Lao People's Democratic Republic and Thailand-Myanmar Border Areas, Trafficking in Children into the Worst Forms of Child Labour: A Rapid Assessment*, ILO/IPEC, Geneva.
    2002   *Yunnan Province, China: Situation of Trafficking in Children and Women*, ILO-IPEC, Bangkok.

International Organization for Migration (IOM)
    2000   "Combating trafficking in South-East Asia: a review of policy and programme responses", by A. Derks, *Migration Research Series*, no. 2, http://www. iom.int/documents/publication/en/mrs_2_2000.pdf, IOM, Geneva.
    2004   *Reintegration of Victims of Trafficking: Defining Success and Developing Indicators: Cambodia, Laos, Myanmar, Vietnam*, IOM, Bangkok.

Jones, S.
    2000   *Making Money off Migrants: The Indonesian Exodus to Malaysia*, Asia 2000 Ltd, Hong Kong.

Kelly, P.F., and D. Bach Le
    1999   "Trafficking in humans from and within Viet Nam: the known from a literature review, key informant interviews and analysis", IOM, Radda Barnen; Save the Children (United Kingdom); United Nations Children's Fund, Hanoi.

Leones, C., and D. Caparas
    n.d.   "Trafficking in human beings from the Philippines: a survey of government experts and law enforcement case files", United Nations Global

Programme against Trafficking in Human beings (Coalitions against Trafficking in Human Beings in the Philippines – Phase 1), National Police Commission, Republic of the Philippines.

Lim, L.L.
1998   "The sex sector – the economic and social bases of prostitution in Southeast Asia", ILO, Geneva.

Marshall, P.
2001   "Globalization, migration and trafficking: some thoughts from the South-East Asian region", paper for the Globalization Workshop, Kuala Lumpur, 8-10 May, http://www.un.or.th/TraffickingProject/Publications/globalisation_paper.pdf.

Parliamentary Joint Committee on the Australian Crime Commission
2004   "Inquiry into the trafficking of women for sexual servitude", Commonwealth of Australia, Canberra, http://www.aph.gov.au/Senate/committee/acc_ctte/sexual_servitude/index.htm.

Pasuk, P., et al.
1998   *Guns Girls Gambling Ganja: Thailand's Illegal Economy and Public Policy,* Silkworm Books, Chiang Mai.

Piper, N.
2005   "A problem by a different name? A review of research on trafficking in South-East Asia and Oceania", *International Migration*, 43(1/2).

Piper, N., and A. Uhlin
2002   "Transnational advocacy networks, female labour migration and trafficking in East and Southeast Asia: a gendered analysis of opportunities and obstacles", *Asian and Pacific Migration Journal*, 11(2): 171-195.

Rosenborg, R. (Ed.)
2003   *Trafficking of Women and Children in Indonesia*, Solidarity Center, Jakarta.

Satterthwaite, M.
2005   "Crossing borders, claiming rights: using human rights law to empower women migrant workers", *Yale Human Rights and Development Law Journal*, 8, forthcoming.

Smith, S.
2001   "The role of employers and workers' organizations in action against the worst forms of child labour, including the trafficking of children into labour and sexual exploitation", Background Paper for ILO-Japan Meeting on Trafficking of Children for Labour and Sexual Exploitation, Manila, Philippines, 10-12 October.

Southeast Asia Watch
1998   *Roadmap on Migration of Women and Trafficking in Women in Southeast Asia*, SEAwatch, Quezon City.

Surtees, R.
2003   *Female Migration and Trafficking in Women: The Indonesian Context*, Sage, London: 99-106.

Tailby, R.
n.d.   "A cross-analysis report into smuggling and trafficking between the Philippines and Australia", United Nations Global Programme against

Trafficking in Human Beings (Coalitions against Trafficking in Human Beings in the Philippines-Phase 1), National Police Commission, Republic of the Philippines.

Tigno, J.
n.d.   "Trafficking in human beings from the Philippines: examining the experiences and perspectives of victims and non-governmental organisations", United Nations Global Programme against Trafficking in Human Beings (Coalitions against Trafficking in Human Beings in the Philippines-Phase 1), National Police Commission, Republic of the Philippines.

TRACE
2003   "Trafficking – from community to exploitation: Baan Mae Kaew Pattana village, mae or sub-district, Paan district, Chiang Rai", Thailand Research Report, TRACE, Baan Mae, Kaew Village.

United Nations Interregional Crime and Justice Research Institute (UNICRI) and the Australian Institute of Criminology (AIC)
2000   "Human smuggling and trafficking: a desk review on the trafficking in women from the Philippines", Tenth United Nations Congress on the Prevention of Crime and the Treatment of Offenders, Vienna, 10-17 April.

United Nations Office on Drugs and Crime (UNODC)
2003   "Coalitions against trafficking in human beings in the Philippines: research and action final report", http://www.unodc.org/pdf/crime/human_trafficking/coalitions_trafficking.pdf.

SOUTH ASIA

Ahmad, N.
2001   *In Search of Dreams: Study on the Situation of the Trafficked Women and Children from Bangladesh and Nepal to India*, IOM, Dhaka.

Anwar, M.
2004   *Child Trafficking for Camel Races: A Perspective from Pakistan*, Centre for Research and Social Development (CRSD), Pakistan.

Asian Development Bank (ADB)
2003   *Combating Trafficking of Women and Children in South Asia: Guide for Integrating Trafficking Concerns into ADB Operations*, ADB, Manila.

Banerjee, U.
2003   "Globalization, crisis in livelihoods, migration and trafficking of women and girls: the crisis in India, Nepal and Bangladesh", unpublished paper.

Bangladesh Counter Trafficking Thematic Group
2003   *Revisiting the Human Trafficking Paradigm: The Bangladesh Experience*, IOM-CIDA, Dhaka.

Blanchet, T.
2002   *Beyond Boundaries: A Critical Look at Women Labour Migration and the Trafficking Within*, USAID, Dhaka.

Blackwill, R.D.
  2003   "Dealing with trafficking in persons: another dimension of United States and India transformation", *DISAM Journal of International Security Assistance Management*, 25(4).

Community Action Centre
  2001   *Stock-taking of Existing Research and Data on Trafficking of Women and Girls*, Community Action Centre, Kathmandu.

Gupta, R.S.
  2001   "Prevention, care and support, and reintegration: programme models in Bangladesh", paper presented in technical consultative meeting on anti-trafficking programmes in South Asia, Nepal.

Huntington, D.
  2002   "Anti-trafficking programs in South Asia: appropriate activities, indicators and evaluation methodologies", Population Council, New Delhi.

INCIDIN Bangladesh
  2000   *Socio-Economic and Cultural Dimensions of Trafficking in Girl Children*, SCF-UK, Dhaka.

International Labour Organization (ILO)
  2002   *Rapid Assessment on Trafficking in Children for Exploitative Employment in Bangladesh*, ILO/IPEC, Dhaka.
  2002   *Trafficking and Sexual Abuse among Street Children in Kathmandu*, ILO/IPEC, Kathmandu.

Masud Ali, A.K.M
  2005   "Treading along a treacherous trail: research on trafficking in persons in South Asia", *International Migration*, 43(1/2).

Paktar, P., and P. Paktar
  2000   "Consolidating protection against ever-escalating violation: case of Prerana's intervention for protection of rights of victims of commercial sexual exploitation in India", paper presented at the Tenth United Nations Congress on the Prevention of Crime and the Treatment of Offenders, Vienna, 10-17 April.

Shamim, I.
  2001   *Mapping of Missing, Kidnapped and Trafficked Children and Women: Bangladesh Perspective*, IOM, Dhaka.

CENTRAL ASIA

International Organization for Migration (IOM)
  2001   *Deceived Migrants from Tajikistan: A Study on Trafficking in Women and Children*, IOM, Dushanbe, http://www.iom.int/DOCUMENTS/ PUBLICATION/EN/Tajikistan_study_august2001.pdf.
  2002   *Shattered Dreams: Report on Trafficking of Persons in Azerbaijan*, IOM, Baku, http://www.iom.int//DOCUMENTS/PUBLICATION/EN/ Azerbaijan_Report.pdf.
  2003   *Trafficking in Persons: An Analysis of Afghanistan*, IOM, Kabul.

2003 "Analysis of institutional and legal frameworks and overview of cooperation patterns in the field of counter-trafficking in Eastern Europe and Central Asia", Research Report, November.

2005 *Fertile Fields: Trafficking in Persons in Central Asia: Compilation of Country Reports*, by E. Kelly, IOM Technical Cooperation Centre, Vienna.

PACIFIC

Carrington, K., and J. Hearn
2003 "Trafficking and the sex industry: from impunity to protection", *Current Issues Brief*, no. 28, Information and Research Services, Australia, http://www.aph.gov.au/library/pubs/CIB/2002-03/03cib28.pdf.

David, F.
2000 "Human smuggling and trafficking: an overview of the response at the federal level", Australian Institute of Criminology, Canberra, http://www.aic.gov.au/publications/rpp/24/.

Ford, M.
2001 "Sex slaves and legal loopholes: exploring the legal framework and federal responses to the trafficking of the Thai 'contract girls' for sexual exploitation to Melbourne Australia", Project Respect, Melbourne.

Pacific Immigration Director's Conference
2003 "Pacific's regional perspective on people smuggling, people trafficking and illegal migration survey", Pacific Immigration Director's Conference, Suva.

Project Respect
2004 "'One victim of trafficking is one too many': counting the human cost of trafficking", Project Respect, Victoria.

Talcott, G.
2000 "The context and risk of organised illegal immigration to New Zealand", Working Paper no. 15/00, Centre for Strategic Studies, Victoria University of Wellington, New Zealand.

GENERAL TRAFFICKING LITERATURE

Abramson, K.
2003 "Beyond consent, toward safeguarding human rights: implementing the United Nations Trafficking Protocol", *Harvard International Law Journal*, 44(2).

Agustin, L.
2003 "Forget victimization: granting agency to migrants", *Development*, 46(3): 30-36.

Alfredson, L.
2002 "Sexual exploitation of child soldiers: an exploitation and analysis of global dimensions and trends", Coalition to Stop the Use of Child Soldiers, London.

Andrees, B., and M.N.J. van der Linden
  2005   "Designing trafficking research from a labour market perspective: the ILO experience", *International Migration*, 43(1/2).
Angathangelou, A.M., and L.H.M. Ling
  2003   "Desire industries: sex trafficking, UN peacekeeping, and the neo-liberal world order", *The Brown Journal of World Affairs*, X(1): 133-148.
Anti-Slavery International
  2003   *The Migration-Trafficking Nexus: Combating Trafficking through the Protection of Migrants' Human Rights*, Anti-slavery International, London.
Aronowitz, A.
  2001   "Smuggling and trafficking in human beings: the phenomenon, the markets that drive it and the organizations that promote it", *European Journal of Criminal Policy and Research*, 9(2): 163-195.
Bales, K.
  1999   *Disposable People: New Slavery in the Global Economy*, University of California Press, Berkeley and Los Angeles.
  2003   "Because she looks like a child", in B. Ehrenreich and A. Hochschild (Eds), *Global Woman: Nannies, Maids and Sex Workers in the New Economy*, Granta, London: 207-229.
Blanchet, T.
  2002   "Beyond boundaries: a critical look at women labour migration and trafficking within", USAID, Dhaka.
Brennan, D.
  2005   "Methodological challenges to doing research on trafficking: tales from the field", *International Migration*, 43(1/2).
Bruckert, C., and C. Parent
  2002   "Trafficking in human beings and organized crime: a literature review", Research and Evaluation Branch, Community, Contract and Aboriginal Policing Services Directorate, Royal Canadian Mounted Police, Ottawa, http://www.rcmp.ca/pdfs/traffick_e.pdf.
Brunovskis, A., and G. Tyldum
  2004   "Crossing borders: an empirical study of transnational prostitution and trafficking in human beings", Fafo, Oslo.
Bump, M.N., and J. Duncan
  2003   "Conference on identifying and serving child victims of trafficking", *International Migration*, 41(5): 201-218.
Caliber Associates.
  2003   *Needs Assessment for Service Providers and Trafficking Victims*, prepared for the US Department of Justice, National Institute of Justice, http://www.calib.com/home/practice_areas/cfcs/pdf/traffick.pdf.
Carchedi F., et al.
  2000   *I colori della notte. Migrazioni, sfruttamento sessuale, esperienze di intervento sociale*, Franco Angeli, Milan.
Carrington, K., and J. Hearn
  2003   "Trafficking and the sex industry: from impunity to protection", *Current Issues Brief*, no. 28, Information and Research Services, Australia, http://www.aph.gov.au/library/pubs/CIB/2002-03/03cib28.pdf.

Chang, G.
2000   *Disposable Domestics: Immigrant Women Workers in the Global Economy*, South End Press, Cambridge.

Chapkis, W.
2003   "Trafficking, migration and the law", *Gender and Society*, 17(6): 926.

Chiarotti, S.
2002   Trata de mujeres: Conexiones y desconexiones entre género, migración y derechos humanos, Conferencia Hemisférica sobre Migración Internacional, Derechos Humanos Trata de Personas en las Américas, Santiago de Chile, 20-22 November.

Chuang, J.
1998   "Redirecting the debate over trafficking in women: definitions, paradigms, and contexts", *Harvard Human Rights Journal*, 11(Spring): 65-107.

Clark, C.
2002   *Juvenile Justice and Child Soldiering: Trends, Challenges, Dilemmas*, Coalition to Stop the Use of Child Soldiers, London.

Cockburn, A.
2003   "21st century slaves", *National Geographic*, 204(3): 2-26.

Consulting and Audit Canada
2000   "Trafficking in women: inventory of information needs and available information", Strategic Policy, Planning and Research, http://www.cic.gc.ca/english/research/papers/trafficking/trafficking-toc.html.

Coomaraswamy, R.
2003   "Report of the Special Rapporteur on violence against women: trafficking in women and forced prostitution", UNHCR, Geneva.

Derks, A.
2000   "From white slaves to trafficking survivors: notes on the trafficking debate", Working Paper 00-02m, The Center for Migration and Development, Princeton University, Princeton.

Doezema, J.
1999   "Loose women or lost women? The re-emergence of the myth of white slavery in contemporary discourses of trafficking in women", presented at the International Studies Association Convention, Washington, DC, 17-21 February.
2002   "Who gets to choose? Coercion, consent and the UN Trafficking Protocol", *Gender and Development*, 10(1).

Dottridge, M.
2004   "Kids as commodities? Child trafficking and what to do about it", International Federation, Terre des Hommes, May, http://tdh.ch/cms/fileadmin/site_uploads/e/pdf/projekte/schwerpunktthemen/DottridgeStudy_en.pdf.

Ehrenreich, B., and A. Hochschild (Eds)
2003   *Global Woman: Nannies, Maids and Sex Workers in the New Economy*, Granta, London.

Eltis, D.
2002   *Coerced and Free Migration: Global Perspectives*, Stanford University Press, Stanford.

Enloe, C.
  2000   *Maneuvers: The International Politics of Militarizing Women's Lives*,
           University of California Press, Berkeley.
Firmo-Montan, V.
  2004   "Responses to sexual slavery: from the Balkans to Afghanistan", in
           C. van den Ankier (Ed.), *The Political Economy of New Slavery*, Palgrave
           MacMillan, New York .
Fitzpatrick, J.
  2003   "Trafficking as a human rights violation: the complex intersection of legal
           frameworks for conceptualizing and combating trafficking", *Michigan
           Journal of International Law*, 24: 1143.
Gallagher, A
  2002   "Human rights and the new UN protocols on trafficking and migrant
           smuggling: a preliminary analysis", *Human Rights Quarterly*, 23: 975-1004.
  2002   "Trafficking, smuggling and human rights: tricks and treaties", *Forced
           Migration Review*, 12, January.
Ginzberg, O.
  2003   *Trace: Trafficking from Community to Exploitation – Project Report*,
           UNICEF, New York.
Global Alliance Against Trafficking in Women (GAATW)
  2001   *Human Rights and Trafficking in Persons: A Handbook*, GAATW,
           Bangkok.
Gurgel, R.Q., et al.
  2004   "Capture-recapture to estimate the number of street children in a city in
           Brazil", *Archives of Disease in Childhood*, 89: 222-224.
Gushulak, B., and D. MacPherson
  2000   "Health issues associated with the smuggling and trafficking of migrants",
           Journal of Immigrant Health, 2(2): 67-78.
Haan, H.C.
  2002   "Non-formal education and rural skills training: tools to combat the worst
           form of child labour including trafficking", ILO, Geneva.
Hagan, F.E.
  1997   *Research Methods in Criminal Justice and Criminology*, Fourth Edition,
           Allyn and Bacon, Boston.
Haque, Md. S.
  2004   *Migration-Trafficking Nexus*, IOM, Dhaka.
Hughes, D.
  2002   "The corruption of civil society: maintaining the flow of women to the sex
           industries", *Encunetro Internacional sobre Trafico de Mujures y
           Explotacion*, Malaga, 23 September.
  2004   "Sex slave jihad", *FrontPageMagazine.com*, 27 January, www.front
           pagemag.com/Articles.
Human Rights Watch
  2004   "Child soldier use in 2003: a briefing for the 4th UN Security Council
           Open Debate on Children and Armed Conflict", Human Rights Watch,
           New York.

2004 "Child domestics: the world's invisible workers", *Human Rights Watch Backgrounder*, Human Rights Watch, New York.

Hyland, K.F.
2001 "The impact of the Protocol to Prevent Suppress and Punish Trafficking in Persons, especially Women and Children", *Human Rights Brief*, www.wcl.american.edu/pub/humanright/brief/index.htm.

International Labour Organization (ILO)
2002 "Unbearable to the human heart: child trafficking and action to eliminate it", ILO/IPEC, Geneva.
2002 "Every child counts: new global estimates on child labour", ILO/IPEC, Geneva, http://www.ilo.org/public/english/standards/ipec/simpoc/others/globalest.pdf.
2003 "Trafficking in human beings: new approaches to combating the problem: special action programme to combat forced labour", ILO, Geneva.
2003 "Fundamental rights and work and international labour standards", ILO, Geneva.
2004 "Helping hands or shackled lives: understanding child domestic labour and responses to it", ILO/IPEC, Geneva.
2005 "Human trafficking and forced labour exploitation: guidance for legislation and law enforcement", ILO, Geneva.
"Trafficking for forced labour: how to monitor the recruitment of migrant workers", ILO/SAP-FL, Geneva (forthcoming).

International Organization for Migration (IOM)
2000 "Trafficking of migrants: hidden health consequences", *Migration and Health*, 2.
2004 "Psychosocial support to groups of victims of human trafficking in transit situations", *Psychosocial Notebook*, 4.
2004 "The mental health aspects of trafficking in human beings: training manual", IOM, Budapest.

Jordan, A.
2001 "Trafficking in human beings: the slavery that surrounds us", *Global Issues*, 6(2), August, http://www.usinfo.state.gov/journals/itgic/0801/ijge/ijge0801.htm.

Kangaspunta, K.
2003 "Mapping the inhuman trade: preliminary findings of the human trafficking database", *Forum on Crime and Society*, 3(1/2).

Kapstein, E.B.
2003 "The baby trade", *Foreign Affairs*, November/December.

Kartusch, A.
2001 "Reference guide for anti-trafficking legislative review", OSCE, Warsaw.

Kasper, J.C.
2002 "Cross-national variation in sex trafficking legal activity: prohibitive legislation, regulations, and bureaucratic actions", M.A. thesis, University of Wyoming.

Kaye, M.
2003 "The migration-trafficking nexus: combating trafficking through the protection of migrants' human rights", Anti-Slavery International, London.

Keairns, Y.E.
  2002   *The Voices of Girl Child Soldiers*, Quaker United Nations Office, New
           York.
Keeler, L., and M. Jyrkinen (Eds)
  1999   *Who's Buying: The Clients of Prostitution*, Ministry of Social Affairs,
           Helsinki.
Kelly, L.
  2001   *Conducting Research on Trafficking: Guidelines and Suggestions for
           Further Research*, IOM, Geneva.
  2003   "The wrong debate: reflections on why force is not the key issue with
           respect to trafficking in women for sexual exploitation", *Feminist Review:
           Exile and Asylum – Women Seeking Refuge in "Fortress Europe"*,
           73: 139-144.
Kempadoo, K.
  1998   "Introduction: globalising sex workers' rights", in K. Kempadoo and
           J. Doezema (Eds), *Global Sex Workers: Rights, Resistance, and Re-
           definition*, Routledge, New York.
Kleemans, E., and H. van de Bunt
  2003   "The social organization of human trafficking", in D. Siegel, et al. (Eds),
           Global Organized Crime: Trends and Developments, Kluwer Academic
           Publishers, Dordrecht.
Kyle, D., and R. Koslowski (Eds)
  2001   *Global Human Smuggling: Comparative Perspectives*, Johns Hopkins
           University Press, Baltimore.
Laczko, F.
  2002   "Human trafficking: the need for better data", *Migration Information
           Source*, http://www.migrationinformation.org/Feature/display.cfm?ID=66.
Laczko, F., and M.A. Gramegna
  2002   "Developing better indicators of human trafficking", *Brown Journal of
           World Affairs*, X(1).
Lesko, V., and E. Avdulaj
  2003   "Girls and trafficking: review of trafficking in human beings for 2002",
           Psycho-Social Centre, The Hearth, Vlore.
Long, L.D.
  2003   "Anthropological perspectives on the trafficking of women for sexual
           exploitation", *International Migration*, 42(1).
Louie, M.C.Y.
  2001   *Sweatshop Warriors: Immigrant Women Workers Take On the Global
           Factory*, South End Press, Cambridge.
Luckhoo, F.
  2003   *Trafficking in the World Today: A Briefing – A Gender Lens on the Causes
           and Consequences of Trafficking in Women Around the World*, Change,
           London.
Lynggard, T.
  2001   "The silent victim, the happy hooker, and the invisible sex buyer: how to
           avoid the pitfalls, suggested journalistic guidelines", paper for The First

Seminar of the Nordic and Baltic Countries against Trafficking in Women, Tallin, 29-31 May, http://www.nikk.uio.no/publikasjoner/andre/artiklar_utlatanden/tl_trafficking.html.

Makkai, T.
2003 "Thematic discussion on trafficking in human beings", Workshop on Trafficking in Human Beings, especially Women and Children, 12th Session of the Commission on Crime Prevention and Criminal Justice, Vienna, 15 May.

Mattar, M.
2001 "Commercial sexual exploitation of women: the Islamic law perspective", The Protection Project, http://www.protectionproject.org/vt/mm.htm.
2003 "Monitoring the status of severe forms of trafficking in foreign countries: sanctions mandated under the US Trafficking Victims Protection Act", *Brown Journal of World Affairs*, X(1): 159-178.

Mattila, H. et al.
2004 "Human trafficking: a global review of literature", paper presented in the international expert meeting Improving Data and Research on Human Trafficking, arranged by IOM and the Government of Italy in Rome, May.

Mikhail, S.
2002 "Child marriage and child prostitution: two forms of sexual exploitation", *Gender and Development: Special Issue – Trafficking and Slavery*, 10(1).

Miller, A.
1999 "Human rights and sexuality: first steps toward articulating a rights framework for claims to sexual rights and freedoms", *American Society of International Law*, 1999 Proceedings.

Moore, C.
2001 "Trafficking in women and children and in war and war-like conditions", The Protection Project, www.protectionproject/seminar_series.

Muntarbhorn, V.
2004 "Combating migrant smuggling and trafficking in persons, especially women: the normative framework re-appraised", in T.A. Aleinikoff and V. Chetail (Eds), *Migration and International Legal Norms*, Asser Press, The Hague, in cooperation with IOM, Migration Policy Institute (MPI) and Graduate Institute of International Studies, Geneva.

Murphy, E., and K. Ringheim
2001 "Interview with Jo Doezema of the Network of Sex Work Projects: does attention to trafficking adversely affect sex workers' rights?", *Reproductive Health and Rights: Reaching the Hardly Reached*, PATH, Washington, DC.

Nelson, S., et al.
2004 "Literature review and analysis related to human trafficking in post-conflict situations", Development Alternatives, Inc. (DAI), June.

O'Connell Davidson, J., and B. Anderson
2002 "Trafficking: a demand led problem?", Save the Children, Sweden.

Organization for Security and Cooperation in Europe (OSCE)/Office for Democratic Institutions and Human Rights (ODIHR)

2004   *National Referral Mechanisms – Joining Efforts to Protect the Rights of Trafficked Persons: A Practical Handbook*, OSCE and ODIHR, Warsaw.

Ould, D.

2004   "Trafficking and international law", in C. van den Ankier (Ed.), *The Political Economy of New Slavery*, Palgrave MacMillan, New York.

Pearson, E.

2001   "Slavery/trafficking", *New Internationalist*, August.

2002   "Human traffic, human rights: redefining victim protection", Anti-Slavery International, London, http://www.antislavery.org/homepage/resources/humantraffichumanrights.htm.

Poudel, M., and I. Smith

2002   "Reducing poverty, upholding human rights: a pragmatic approach", *Gender and Development: Special Issue – Trafficking and Slavery*, 10(1).

Rathgeber, C.

2002   "The victimization of women through human trafficking – an aftermath of war?", *European Journal of Crime, Criminal Law and Criminal Justice*, 10(2-3): 152-163.

Raymond, J.

1999   "Health effects of prostitution", in D. Hughes and C. Roche (Eds) *Making the Harm Visible: Global Sexual Exploitation of Women and Girls*, CATW, Rhode Island.

2003   "10 reasons for not legalizing prostitution", CATW, Rhode Island.

Raymond, J., et al.

2002   "A comparative study of women trafficked in the migration process", CATW, Rhode Island.

Regeringskansliet

2003   *The Effects of Legalisation of Prostitution Activities – A Critical Analysis*, Regeringskansliet, Stockholm.

Rousseaux, F.

2003   "The psychological impact of sexual slavery of trafficked women: parallels with torture, sexual abuse and domestic violence", *Violence Against Women: An Australian Feminist Journal*, July: 4-13.

Sanglan, D.

2000   "SOS trafficking: on the tracks of stolen childhoods", *Social Alert, Research on Economic, Social and Cultural Rights*, 2.

Save the Children

2004   *Responding to Child Trafficking: An Introductory Handbook to Child Rights-based Interventions Drawn from Save the Children's Experience in Southeast Europe*, Save the Children, http://www.childcentre.info/projects/traffickin/dbaFile11301.pdf.

Sen, P., and L. Kelly

2004   "Benefits, beneficiaries and harms: a critical overview of human trafficking and smuggling as lost potentials for poverty alleviation and the promotion of MDGs", unpublished report to DFID.

Shamim, I., and F. Kabir
   1998   *Child Trafficking: The Underlying Dynamics*, Centre for Women and Children Studies, Dhaka.
Shannon, S.
   1999   "Prostitution and the mafia: the involvement of organized crime in the global economy", in P. Williams, *Illegal immigration and Commercial Sex*, Frank Cass, London.
Shearer Demir, J.
   2004   "The trafficking in women for sexual exploitation: a gender-based and well-founded fear for persecution?", *New Issues in Refugee Research*, Working paper no. 80, UNHCR, Geneva.
Shelley, L.
   2001   "Trafficking and smuggling in human beings", paper at Corruption Within Security Forces: A Threat to National Security Conference, Garmisch, 14-18 May.
   2002   "Crime as the defining problem: voices of another criminology", *International Annals of Criminology*, 39(1-2): 73-88.
   2002   "The changing position of women: trafficking, crime and corruption", in D. Lane (Ed.), *The Legacy of State Socialism and the Future of Transformation*, Rowman and Littlefield: 207-222.
   2003   "Trafficking in women: the business model approach", *The Brown Journal of World Affairs*, X(1): 119-131.
   2003   Statement to US Senate Committee on Foreign Relations, Hearing on Combating Transnational and Corruption in Europe, 30 October.
   2003   "The trade in people in and from the former Soviet Union", *Crime, Law and Social Change*, 40(2-3): 231-249.
Shelley, L., and J. Picarelli
   2002   "Methods not motives: implications of the convergence of international organized crime and terrorism", *Police Practice and Research*, 3(4): 305-318.
Shelley, L., et al.
   2002   "Global crime inc.", in M. Love (Ed.), *Beyond Sovereignty: Issues for a Global Agenda*, Wadsworth, California: 143-166.
Taran, P., and E. Geronimi
   2002   "Globalization, labour and migration: protection is paramount", *MIGRANT* (ILO), Geneva.
Taran, P., and G. Moreno-Fontes Chammartin
   2003   "Stopping exploitation of migrant workers by organised crime", *MIGRANT* (ILO), Geneva.
Taylor, E.
   2002   "Trafficking in women and girls", paper prepared for Expert Group Meeting on Trafficking in Women and Girls, Glen Cove, New York, 18-22 November.
Tiefenbrun, S.
   2002   "Sex sells but drugs don't talk: trafficking of women sex workers and an economic solution", *Thomas Jefferson Law Review*, 24: 161-189.
Tyldum, G., et al.
         "Taking stock: a review of the current research on trafficking in women for sexual exploitation", Fafo report, Oslo (forthcoming).

US Agency for International Development (USAID), Office of Women in Development
  2004   *Trafficking in Persons: USAID's Response*, March.
US Department of Justice
  2004   *2004 Assessment of US Government Activities to Combat Trafficking in Persons*, US Department of Justice, Washington, DC, http://www. usdoj.gov/crt/crim/wetf/us_assessment_2004.pdf.
US Department of Labor
  2003   *Findings on the Worst Forms of Child Labor*, US Department of Labor, Washington, DC.
US Department of State
  2004   *Trafficking in Persons Report*, US Department of State, Washington DC, June.
UNICEF
  2003   *End Child Exploitation: Stop the Traffic!*, UNICEF, London.
United Nations (UN)
  2005   *A Comprehensive Strategy to Eliminate Future Sexual Exploitation and Abuse in United Nations Peacekeeping Operations*, United Nations, New York.
United Nations Children's Fund (UNICEF)/UNAIP
  2003   "Project TRACE: trafficking from community to exploitation", Interim Report, UNICEF/UNAIP.
United Nations Office on Drugs and Crime (UNODC)
  2004   *Legislative Guide for the Implementation of the United Nations Convention against Transnational Organized Crime and the Protocols Thereto*, United Nations, New York
  2002   *Results of a Pilot Survey on Forty Selected Organized Criminal Groups in Sixteen Countries*, United Nations, New York.
Van der Kleij, A.
  2002   *Provisions for Victims of Trafficking in Bonded Labour, i.e. Prostitution in Six Countries*, BlinN, Amsterdam.
Van den Anker, C. (Ed.)
  2003   *Political Economy of New Slavery*, Palgrave MacMillan, New York.
Van Impe, K.
  2000   "People for sale: the need for a multidisciplinary approach towards human trafficking", *International Migration*, Special Issue 2000/1, 38(3): 113-130.
Väyrynen, R.
  2003   "Illegal immigration, human trafficking, and organized crime", UNU/WIDER Discussion Paper, 2003/72, UNU/WIDER Development Conference on Poverty, International Migration and Asylum, Helsinki.
Vaz-Cabral, G.
  2002   *Perspective on Trafficking in Human Beings: Phenomenon, Legislation, Assistance*, CCEM, Paris.
Wong, D.
        "The rumour of trafficking: border controls, illegal immigration and the sovereignty of the nation-state", in W. van Schenden and I. Abraham (Eds), *The Criminal Life of Things*, University of Illinois Press (forthcoming).

World Health Organization (WHO)
2003   *WHO Ethical and Safety Recommendations for Interviewing Trafficked Women*, Health Policy Unit, London School of Hygiene and Tropical Medicine.

COUNTRY REPORTS ON THE INTERNET

- Coalition Against Trafficking in Women, http://www.catwinternational. org/fb/
- Globalmarch, Stop Child Trafficking, Child Trafficking Statistics (by country), http://www.globalmarch.org/child-trafficking/statistics.html
- HumanTrafficking.org, http://www.humantrafficking.org/countries/
- Protection Project, SAIS, Johns Hopkins University, http://www. protection project.org/human_rights/country_reports.htm
- US Department of State, Office to Monitor and Combat Trafficking in Persons (2003), Victims of Trafficking and Violence Protection Act of 2000: *Trafficking in Persons Report*, US Department of State: Washington, http://www.state.gov/g/tip/rls/tiprpt/2003/

LIST OF BIBLIOGRAPHIES
AND RESOURCES ON HUMAN TRAFFICKING

- Canadian Council for Refugees, *Trafficking in Women and Girls Bibliography*, http://www.web.ca/~ccr/trafbiblio.html
- International Women's Rights Project, *Trafficking Directory: Annotated Guide to Internet Resources on Trafficking in Women*, http://www.lib.msu.edu/harris23/crimjust/human.htm
- Michigan State University, Criminal Justice Resources, Human Trafficking, http://www.lib.msu.edu/harris23/crimjust/human.htm
- Office for Victims of Crime (OVC), "Putting victims first", *Abstracts Database on the Topic of Human Trafficking*, 15 April 2003, http://www.ojp.usdoj.gov/ovc/ovcres/human_trafficking.doc
- Protection Project, Johns Hopkins University, School of Advanced International Studies, Washington, DC, http://www.protectionproject.org
- Regional Clearing Point Program, Belgrade, Serbia and Montenegro, *Annotated Guide to Internet-based Counter Trafficking Resources* by R. Surtees and S. Stojkovic, 2004, http://www.antislavery.org/homepage/traffic%20news/RCP%20-%20Annotated%20Guide%20to%20Counter-Trafficking%20Internet%20Resources.pdf
- The Initiative Against Trafficking in Persons and The International Human Rights Law Group, *Resources and Contacts on Human Trafficking*, last updated 22 August 2003, http://www.hrlawgroup.org/resources/content/Traffick_ResourcesContacts.doc

- UNESCO, *Trafficking Statistics Project*, http://www.unescobkk.org/culture/trafficking/matrix/matrix.asp
- United Nations Educational, Scientific and Cultural Organization (UNESCO), *Trafficking Project Bibliography*, http://www.unescobkk.org/culture/trafficking/publication.htm
- United Nations Interregional Crime and Justice Research Institute (UNICRI), *Selected Bibliography on Trafficking in Human Beings* (March 1998-May 2001), http://www.imadr.org/project/petw/biblioTHB.pdf
- University of Pennsylvania, School of Social Work, *The Sexual Exploitation of Children: A Working Guide to the Empirical Literature*, August 2001, http://caster.ssw.upenn.edu/~restes/CSEC_Files/CSEC_Bib_August_2001.pdf
- University of Washington, Women's Center, Program for Women and Human Rights, *Trafficking and Human Rights Resources*, http://depts.washington.edu/womenctr/violenceprevention/vpphr.htm
- US Department of State, International Information Programs, *Responses to Human Trafficking: Books and Documents*, http://usinfo.state.gov/journals/itgic/0603/ijge/gj10.htm
- Violence Against Women Online Resources, *Bibliography of Trafficking*, October 2002, http://www.vaw.umn.edu/documents/traffickbib/traffickbib.html